QUANTIFICATION OF OPERATIONAL RISK UNDER BASEL II

Also by the Author

Moosa, I.A, and Bhatti, R.H. (1997) *International Parity Conditions: Theory, Econometric Testing and Empirical Evidence*, London: Macmillan.

Moosa, I.A. (1998) (first edition) and (2004) (second edition) *International Finance: An Analytical Approach*, Sydney: McGraw Hill.

Taylor, J.B., Moosa, I.A. and Cowling, B. (2000) *Microeconomics*, Brisbane: Wiley.

Taylor, J.B. and Moosa, I.A. (2000) (first edition) and (2002) (second edition) *Macroeconomics*, Brisbane: Wiley.

Moosa, I.A. (2000) *Exchange Rate Forecasting: Techniques and Applications*, London: Macmillan.

Moosa, I.A. (2002) *Foreign Direct Investment: Theory, Evidence and Practice*, London: Palgrave Macmillan.

Moosa, I.A. (2003) *International Financial Operations: Arbitrage, Hedging, Speculation, Financing and Investment*, London: Palgrave Macmillan.

Moosa, I.A. (2005) *Exchange Rate Regimes: Fixed, Flexible or Something in Between?* London: Palgrave Macmillan.

Moosa, I.A. (2006) *Structural Time Series Modelling: Applications in Economics and Finance*, Hyderabad: ICFAI University Press.

Moosa, I.A. (2007) *Operational Risk Management*, London: Palgrave Macmillan.

Quantification of Operational Risk under Basel II: the Good, Bad and Ugly

IMAD A. MOOSA

*Professor of Finance,
Monash University,
Australia*

palgrave
macmillan

First published 2008 by
PALGRAVE MACMILLAN

Palgrave Macmillan in the UK is an imprint of Macmillan Publishers Limited, registered in England, company number 785998, of Houndmills, Basingstoke, Hampshire RG21 6XS.

Palgrave Macmillan in the US is a division of St Martin's Press LLC, 175 Fifth Avenue, New York, NY 10010.

Palgrave Macmillan is the global academic imprint of the above companies and has companies and representatives throughout the world.

Palgrave® and Macmillan® are registered trademarks in the United States, the United Kingdom, Europe and other countries.

ISBN-13: 978–0–230–22266–3 hardback
ISBN-10: 0–230–22266–8 hardback

This book is printed on paper suitable for recycling and made from fully managed and sustained forest sources. Logging, pulping and manufacturing processes are expected to conform to the environmental regulations of the country of origin.

A catalogue record for this book is available from the British Library.

Library of Congress Cataloging-in-Publication Data

Moosa, Imad A.
Quantification of operational risk under Basel II : the good, bad and ugly / Imad A. Moosa.
p. cm.—(Finance and capital markets series)
Includes index.
ISBN 978–0–230–22266–3
1. Financial risk management – Mathematical models. 2. Bank capital – Mathematical models. 3. Banks and banking, International – Risk management. I. Title.

HD61.M6144 2009
332.1′50681—dc22 2008037609

10 9 8 7 6 5 4 3 2 1
17 16 15 14 13 12 11 10 09 08

Printed and bound in Great Britain by
CPI Antony Rowe, Chippenham and Eastbourne

To Nisreen and Danny

Contents

Figures

Tables

Preface

When I first got interested in operational risk, I used to hold mainstream views. I was enthusiastic about, and fascinated by, the application of "scientific" methods to measure operational risk because, so it went, "accurate" measurement is a prerequisite for "sound" management. Subsequently, I started to question the established views on the characteristics of operational risk by identifying flaws in the underlying arguments. Eventually, I realised that there are some misconceptions about operational risk: that it is one-sided, idiosyncratic, unrecognisable and transferable by insurance. I challenged these propositions in a paper that I managed to get published in the *Journal of Operational Risk* (Moosa, 2007a).

Subsequently, my inquisition led me to question the purely quantitative approach to operational risk and the costs and benefits of the advanced measurement approach (AMA) of the Basel II Accord. There were two reasons for this change of heart, apart from my reflection on my "previous life" as an investment banker. The first was the views expressed by Rebonato (2007) in an excellent book that I enjoyed reading and learned a lot from. Rebonato is sceptical about the validity of the proposition that the quantification of risk (whatever that means) is conducive to sound risk management. In his book, Rebonato casts doubt on the ability of the quants (the "fortune tellers", as he calls them) to measure risk and to embody these measures in the decision-making process. The second reason was the observation that operational losses have been materialising irrespective of the sophistication of the methods used to measure risk. Societe Generale uses (or used) models of the highest degree of sophistication, yet a junior trader managed, single-handedly, to inflict a massive $7.2 billion loss without anyone catching him, until it was too late. It seems that while decision-makers at Societe Generale were marvelling the beauty of their models, they overlooked the simple fact that easy-to-implement risk controls could have prevented the disaster. The onslaught of the subprime crisis, which I view as an operational loss event, strengthened my belief in my views, as the crisis emerged because of malpractices that no model could have picked, and no model could have saved the institutions that have gone down (Bear Stearns and others). Then I recalled the LTCM fiasco, where highly respectable quants believed a model telling them that nothing like what happened would happen. But it did happen, and the hedge fund ended up losing $4.4 billion, nearly causing a systemic failure of the financial system. Thanks only to taxpayers' money that the systemic failure did not occur.

I then started to evaluate the advanced measurement approach of Basel II, which calls for the use of sophisticated internal models to measure operational risk and the capital charge against it. Following a thorough investigation, I reached the conclusion that the AMA was not feasible in terms of costs and benefits and that it does more bad than good. As a result, I wrote my paper "A Critique of the Advanced Measurement Approach to Regulatory Capital against Operational Risk", motivated by the often-made claim that the AMA had done a lot of good, for example, by providing the incentive for banks to invest in operational risk management. What the proponents of this view fail to (or chose not to) see is the fact that banks indulge in AMA-related activities because they want to look good, to make regulators happy. They indulge in these activities for compliance, not for risk management.

This is my second book on operational risk, which I never thought I would write. My first book (Moosa, 2007b) was mostly expository, although I expressed the view that Basel II in general was not viable in terms of costs and benefits. I was, however, either neutral or slightly supportive of the purely quantitative approach to operational risk management, because I was thinking like the mainstream at that time. But in the process of keeping abreast with the literature, I accumulated so much information that I thought a second book on the subject (by the same author) would be viable, particularly with the change of heart I went through. I thought, however, that it would be difficult for me to convince Palgrave to invest in another book on operational risk by the same author. Fortunately, I was wrong as my proposal was accepted without delay. For this reason I would like to thank the commissioning editor, Lisa von Fricks. Lisa was waiting for me to submit a proposal for a book on behavioural finance, but instead she got a proposal for a book on operational risk. I did tell Lisa then that this book would be significantly different from the first one, and it certainly is.

This book is highly (but fairly) critical of several ideas and practices pertaining to the measurement and management of operational risk. Following an expository first chapter, Chapter 2 presents a critique of the Basel Committee and its Accords (Basel I and Basel II), reaching the conclusion that Basel II is not a great leap forward as compared with Basel I. In

Chapter 3 a detailed account is presented of the definition and classification of operational risk, reaching the conclusion that finding an exact definition of operational risk is not a prerequisite for sound risk management. Chapter 4 is devoted to the description and criticism of the advanced measurement approach prescribed by Basel II. Chapter 5 presents a survey of the theoretical and empirical studies of operational risk, reaching the conclusion that model manipulation is the only reason why the advanced measurement approach may produce lower capital charges than those produced by the "less sophisticated approaches". This point is demonstrated, by using Monte Carlo simulation, in Chapter 6. Finally, Chapter 7 presents a variety of topics, including a discussion of the subprime crisis as an operational loss event.

Writing this book would not have been possible if it was not for the help and encouragement I received from family, friends and colleagues. My utmost gratitude must go to my wife and children who had to bear the opportunity cost of writing this book. My wife, Afaf, did not only bear most of the opportunity cost of writing the book, but proved once again to be my best research assistant, as she produced the diagrams shown in various chapters. I would also like to thank my colleagues, friends and students at Monash, starting with Andrew Sanford, who has been educating me on Bayesian networks. I have encouraged Andrew to utilise his knowledge of Bayesian networks in the field of operational risk, and I am confident that this endeavour will produce a successful research partnership (with me). I would also thank John Vaz, Michael Dempsey, Keryn Chalmers, Madhu Veerarghavan, Petko Kalev, Michael Skully, Kathy Avram, Param Silvapulle, Mervyn Silvapulle, Lisa Jones, Theo Gazos and Yusuf Hamza. I should not forget the friends and former colleagues I socialise with at the Eagle, including Liam Lenten, Larry Li and Tony Naughton. In preparing the manuscript, I benefited from discussions with members of Table 14 at the John Scott Meeting House, and for this reason I would like to thank Bob Parsons, Greg O'Brein, Bill Horrigan, Bill Breen, Donald MacPhee, Rodney Adams, Paul Rule and Greg Bailey. Muhareem Karamujic provided a lot of information that helped me write the book, and for this reason I am grateful to him.

Work on this book was financed by a generous grant from the Australian Research Council (ARC Discovery Grant, No DP0878954), and for this I would like to thank the ARC. My thanks also go to friends and former colleagues who live far away but provide help via means of telecommunication, including Kevin Dowd (to whom I owe intellectual debt, not in the least because he brought my attention to Rebonato's book), Razzaque Bhatti, Ron Ripple, Bob Sedgwick, Sean Holly, Dave Chappell, Dan Hemmings, Ian Baxter, Nabeel Al-Loughani, Khalid Al-Saad and Talla

Al-Deehani. Last, but not least, I would like to thank the crew at Palgrave, my favourite publisher.

Naturally, I am the only one responsible for any errors and omissions in this book. It is dedicated to my beloved children, Nisreen and Danny, who are always exposed to the operational risk of eating junk food.

Acronyms

ABS	Asset-backed securities
AC	Agency and custody
A–D	Anderson–Darling (test)
AIG	Accord Implementation Group
AM	Asset management
AMA	Advanced measurement approach
ANZ	Australia New Zealand (Bank)
APRA	Australian Prudential Regulatory Authority
APT	Arbitrage pricing theory
ARC	Australian Research Council
ATM	Automatic Telling Machine
BBA	British Bankers' Association
BCBS	Basel Committee on Banking Supervision
BCCI	Bank for Credit and Commerce International
BDSF	Business disruption and system failure
BIA	Basic indicators approach
BIS	Bank for International Settlements
CAPM	Capital asset pricing model
CB	Commercial banking
CBI	Central Bank of Iraq
CCB	China Construction Bank
CDF	Cumulative probability distribution
CDO	Collateralised debt obligation
CEO	Chief executive officer
CF	Corporate finance
CFO	Chief financial officer
CLS	Continuous line settlement
CoCoCo	Coverage, completeness and correctness
CPBP	Clients, products and business practices
CRD	Capital requirements directive

DPA	Damage to physical assets
DSV	Downside semi variance
EAD	Exposure at default
EDAM	Execution, delivery and asset management
EF	External fraud
EL	Expected loss
EPWS	Employment practices and workplace safety
ETL	Expected tail loss
EU	European Union
EVT	Extreme value theory
FDIC	Federal Deposit Insurance Corporation
FSA	Financial Services Authority
G10	Group of Ten
GB2	Generalised beta distribution of the second kind
GDP	Gross domestic product
GOLD	Global operational loss database
HR	Human resources
IF	Internal fraud
IIF	Institute of International Finance
ILG	International Liaison Group
IMA	Internal measurement approach
IOSCO	International Organisation of Securities Commissions
IRBA	Internal ratings-based approach
ISDA	International Swaps and Derivatives Association
IT	Information technology
KCI	Key cost indicator
KRD	Key risk driver
KRI	Key risk indicator
K–S	Kolmogorov–Smirnov (test)
KTI	Key trouble indicator
LDA	Loss distribution approach
LDCE	Loss data collection exercise
LGD	Loss given default
LTCM	Long-Term Capital Management
MBS	Mortgage backed securities
MIS	Management information system
MLE	Maximum likelihood estimator
MPL	Maximum possible loss
NAB	National Australia Bank
NBFI	Non-bank financial intermediaries
NGO	Non-government organisation
OLS	Ordinary least squares
ORX	Operational Riskdata eXchange

PD	Probability of default
PML	Probable maximum loss
POT	Peaks over threshold
P-P	Probability-probability (plot)
PS	Payment and settlements
QIS	Quantitative impact study
Q-Q	Quantile-quantile (plot)
RAROC	Risk-adjusted return on capital
RB	Retail banking
RCSA	Risk and controls self assessment
RDCA	Risk drivers and controls approach
RG	Retail brokerage
RMA	Risk management association
SBA	Scenario-based approach
SCA	Scorecard approach
SEC	Securities and Exchange Commission
SIV	Structured investment vehicle
SME	Subject matter expert
SP	Stabilised probability
STA	Standardised approach
STP	Straight through processing
TS	Trading and sales
UL	Unexpected loss
VAR	Value at risk

CHAPTER 1

Preliminary Concepts and Issues

1.1 DEFINITION AND MEASUREMENT OF RISK

Although distinction is typically made between risk and uncertainty, Doerig (2003) defines risk as "uncertainty about a future outcome." The distinction between risk and uncertainty, which is due to Knight (1921), is straightforward. Under conditions of risk, no-one knows for sure what outcome will materialise, but a probability distribution for the possible outcomes is available. The probability distribution may be subjective, typically based on historical experience and/or judgment about what is likely and less likely to happen in the future given the *status quo* and possible changes to the *status quo*. Alternatively, it could be objective like the probability distribution of the outcome of tossing a (fair) coin. Under uncertainty, by contrast, probability distributions are unavailable. It is possible, however, that Doerig (2003) did not use the word "uncertainty" in this strict statistical sense but rather in a non-technical sense that implies lack of knowledge about possible future outcomes. Irrespective of the definition, Doerig (2003) correctly argues that "risk is part of corporate life" and that "it is the essence of financial institutions' activities." He describes risk as being "highly multifaceted, complex and often interlinked." Eliminating risk entirely means closing down the business.

It is useful at this early stage to distinguish between the two closely related concepts of "risk" and "loss," as they are often used interchangeably. Risk is an *ex ante* concept in the sense that it is a source of potential loss. This implies that exposure to risk may or may not produce losses. Loss, on the other hand, is an *ex post* concept, in the sense that it may materialise as a result of exposure to risk. The meaning of a "loss event" will be discussed in Chapter 3.

Diversity of Definitions and Measures

Because it is multifaceted and complex, there is no general agreement on the most suitable definition of risk, and this is why definitions differ from one discipline to another. In the insurance business, for example, risk may mean either a peril insured against or a person or property protected by insurance (e.g., a young driver is not a good risk). Other definitions of risk that are typically found in the literature are as follows:

- The chance of loss.
- The possibility of loss.
- The deviation of actual outcome from expected outcome.
- The dispersion of actual results around the expected result.
- The probability of any outcome being different from the one expected.
- The significance of the hazard in terms of the likelihood and severity of any possible adversity.

All of these definitions share two common elements: indeterminacy (the possibility of more than one outcome) and loss (at least one of the possible outcomes is undesirable). In general, risk may be viewed as the mean outcome (which is the actuarial view of risk), as the variance of the outcome (typically used in finance), as a catastrophic downside outcome (focusing on the worst-case scenario), and as an upside opportunity (focusing on the favourable outcome).

Since risk is defined in a variety of ways, it follows that it can also be measured in a variety of ways, which may depend on the kind of risk under consideration (e.g., financial versus non-financial risk). If, for example, risk is defined in terms of the deviation from a desired outcome, then it should be measured in terms of the variance or the standard deviation of the underlying probability distribution. If, on the other hand, risk is defined as the potential impact of an event, then the relevant measure is the probabilistic loss amount. Table 1.1 provides a summary of the measures of risk, but it must be emphasised here that the list is representative rather than exhaustive. The formulae are written for a random variable, X, such that X_i is a value assumed by the random variable with a probability p_i, $\overline{X}$ is the mean value of X and X_t is the value of X at time t.

Measures of dispersion (variance and standard deviation) have been criticised for treating positive and negative deviations from the expected or

Table 1.1 Selected Measures of Risk

Measure	*Type*	*Formula*
Variance (Probability Distribution)	Dispersion	$\sigma^2(X) = \sum_{i=1}^{n} p_i [X_i - E(X)]^2$
Standard Deviation (Probability Distribution)	Dispersion	$\sigma(X) = \sqrt{\sum_{i=1}^{n} p_i [X_i - E(X)]^2}$
Variance (Historical Data)	Dispersion	$\sigma^2(X) = \frac{1}{n-1}\sum_{t=1}^{n}(X_t - \bar{X})^2$
Standard Deviation (Historical Data)	Dispersion	$\sigma(X) = \sqrt{\frac{1}{n-1}\sum_{t=1}^{n}(X_t - \bar{X})^2}$
Mean Absolute Deviation (MAD)	Dispersion	$MAD(X) = \frac{1}{n}\sum_{t=1}^{n}\lvert X_t - \bar{X}\rvert$
Downside Semi-Variance (DSV)	Downside Risk	$DSV(X) = \frac{1}{n-1}\sum_{t=1}^{n} Y_t^2$ where $Y_t = X_t - \bar{X}$ if $X_t < \bar{X}$ and $Y_t =$ 0 otherwise
Value at Risk (VAR)	Downside Risk	Percentile of a Loss Distribution
Expected Tail Loss (ETL)	Downside Risk	$ETL = E(L \mid L > VAR)$

desired outcome in a similar manner, although negative deviations are naturally more detrimental to the underlying business. This is why behavioural finance and behavioural economics emphasise "loss aversion" as opposed "risk aversion," implying that the disutility derived from a loss is greater than the utility derived from an equivalent gain.

Dissatisfaction with the dispersion measures of risk has led to the development of the downside risk measures, which are defined by Dhane et al (2003) as "measures of the distance between a risky situation and the corresponding risk-free situation when only unfavourable discrepancies contribute to the risk." Danielsson et al (2005) trace the downside risk measures back to the safety first rule of Roy (1952), which has led to the definition of risk as "the probability weighted function of the deviation below a target return" (Bawa, 1975; Fishburn, 1977).

VAR, ETL, MPL and PML

The measurement of operational risk, which is what this book is all about, is based on value at risk (VAR), a concept that lies at the core of the advanced measurement approach(AMA) proposed by the Basel II Accord to measure regulatory capital against operational risk. As The Economist (2008g) puts it, "VAR is a staple of the risk management toolkit and is embedded in the new Basel 2 regime on capital adequacy." The concept of VAR is used to answer the question "over a given period of time with a given probability, how much money might be lost?" The VAR (therefore) is the maximum expected loss (EL) over a given holding period at a given confidence level (i.e. with a given probability). Essentially, it is a certain percentile of the loss distribution. Picoult (2006) defines VAR as a "statistical estimate, at a specified confidence level, of the potential loss in the economic value of a portfolio of contracts over a specified time horizon." Alternatively, Shaw (2006) defines VAR as "the z in the following proposition: given a holding period of x days and a confidence level of $y\%$, find the VAR z which satisfies the following: with our current portfolio, over the next x trading days with probability at least $y\%$ we will lose no more than $\$z$, assuming no change in portfolio composition during that period." Certainly reading this unnecessarily awkward definition requires a high level of physical fitness! This is "verbal gymnastics" at its worst.

A related measure of risk is the expected tail loss (ETL), which is also known as the expected shortfall, conditional VAR, tail conditional expectation and worst conditional expectation. The concept is very simple: ETL is the expected value of a loss that is in excess of VAR. Figure 1.1 shows the VAR and ETL for a certain loss distribution, as well as the expected loss (defined as the mean of the distribution) and the unexpected loss, which is the difference between the VAR (the percentile) and the mean of the distribution. Navarrete (2006) defines expected loss as the "usual or average loss incurred by a firm in its natural course of business," whereas his definition of unexpected loss is that it is the "deviation from the average that may put a firm's stability at risk." Catastrophic loss is any loss over and above the unexpected loss.

VAR has become a widely-used method for measuring risk. Initially, it was used to measure market risk, but the use of VAR has been extended to the measurement of credit risk and operational risk. The attractiveness of the concept lies in its simplicity: in the case of market risk (and even credit risk) it represents the risk of an entire portfolio by one number (monetary

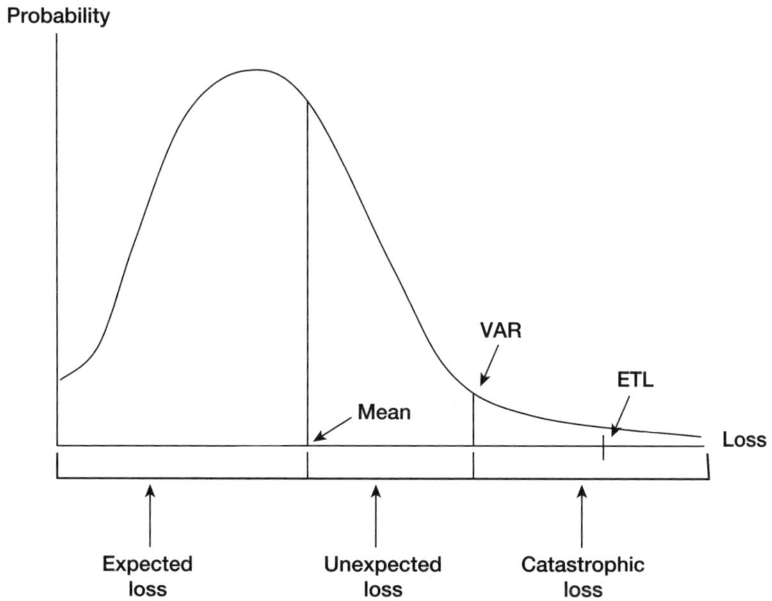

Figure 1.1 VAR, ETL, Expected Loss and Unexpected Loss

units) that is easy to comprehend by anyone. There are, however, several shortcomings associated with the VAR methodology. First, it can be misleading to the extent of giving rise to unwarranted complacency. Moreover, VAR is highly sensitive to the assumptions used to calculate it. It neglects the possibility of large and discrete jumps in financial prices, which occur quite often. In particular, the parametric approach to VAR is based on the assumption that losses follow a normal distribution, which means that losses resulting from catastrophic occurrences are overlooked, let alone the fact that losses (like financial returns) are unlikely to be normally distributed. This view is expressed by Shaw (2006) who points out that "it is well known that changes in financial time series have fatter tails than would be the case if they were normally distributed." However, VAR can be calculated from any distribution when the historical and simulation approaches are used (in Chapter 6, it will be demonstrated how VAR can be calculated from distributions generated from Monte Carlo simulations). Shaw (2006) highlights another weakness of VAR, which is that "the effects of changes in the risk factors are linear in each variable and orthogonal."

The Economist (2008g) describes VAR as "well-nigh unless at predicting catastrophe." One problem with VAR is that it is at odds with common sense because it suggests that the risk of blow-up increases (rather than diminishes) the further away we are from the last one. Since VAR is estimated from historical data, it would tell us that there is nothing to worry about the longer we go without a crisis, which means that VAR can be a source of complacency. On the downside, VAR acts as an "amplifier," creating even more volatility. Another problem with VAR, according to The Economist (2008g) is that "[it] captures how bad things can get 99% of the time, but the real trouble is caused by the outlying 1%."

In general, risk is measured in terms of two parameters: the probability of making loss and the potential amount lost if a loss event occurs. Thus, total risk may be measured as the product of the loss amount and the probability that the loss will occur. In operational risk measurement, the terms severity (amount) and frequency (probability) are used to measure risk. Both these terms are described by using separate probability distributions, which are combined (via Monte Carlo simulations) to arrive at a probability distribution of total loss. Bonafede et al (2007) point out that measuring risk in terms of these two parameters is inadequate for the purpose of guaranteeing the continuity of operations and activities, because two factors of critical importance are the management of the risk of interruption of services and recovery to a particular level of efficiency within a reasonable time frame. They provide some examples of how statistical models can be used to define the time frame for recovery and to analyse interruptions in the context of business continuity management.

Other risk measures are the maximum possible loss (MPL) and the probable maximum loss (PML). The MPL is the worst loss that could occur, given the worst possible combination of circumstances. The PML, on the other hand, is the likely loss, given the most likely combination of circumstances.

Related Concepts

Some concepts appear frequently in the literature on risk management. These include risk capacity, risk appetite and risk budget. Risk capacity is the amount of risk a firm (or an individual) is able to take, which is constrained by how much capital the firm holds. Risk appetite, on the other hand, is the level of risk capacity a firm is willing to assume. Searing (2008) defines risk appetite as a "statement or measurement of an organisation's desired level of risk," arguing that risk appetite is different from risk tolerance. However, the distinction between how much risk a firm wishes to bear and how much risk it tolerates sounds rather superficial. A firm's appetite for risk is determined by the internal culture (e.g., attitude towards risk) and external factors (e.g., rating targets). Searing (2008) suggests a procedure for the determination of a firm's risk appetite.

Risk budget, the third of the three related concepts, is a limit on risk that is determined by both risk capacity and risk appetite. It is, therefore, a constraint on business activity. Risk budget is derived from the firm's strategic objectives as well as its desired risk-return profile. In this sense, risk budget is more specific than risk appetite (Kilavuka, 2008).

1.2 CLASSIFICATION OF RISK

Risks can be classified under several schemes. For example, it is plausible to arrange risk types along a spectrum, depending on how quantifiable they are. At one extreme lie the types of risk arising from changes in the values of liquid assets. In this case, data on past history are available, which makes risk (however defined) fully quantifiable. At the other extreme lie the risks arising from infrequent events (such as a contagious financial crisis) with potentially massive consequences, in which case risk is rather difficult to quantify. The simplest and most common classification scheme is based on the distinction between financial and non-financial risk.

Financial vs Non-Financial Risk

Figure 1.2 shows that risk can be classified into two broad categories: financial risk and non-financial risk. Financial risk is the risk of losses inherent in financial transactions, hence it is classified into credit risk (the risk arising

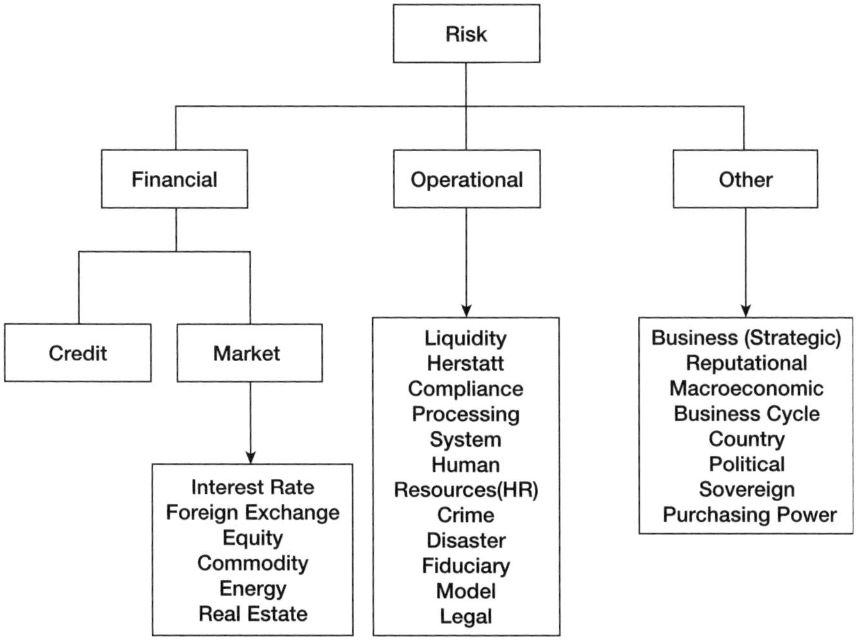

Figure 1.2 Classification of Risk

from the possibility of default on part of the borrowers) and market risk (the risk arising from fluctuations in financial prices). Depending on the underlying financial price, market risk can be classified into interest rate risk, foreign exchange risk, equity price risk, commodity price risk, energy price risk and real estate risk. But while bonds, foreign exchange and equity are financial assets, commodities, energy and real estate are not, which begs the question as to why fluctuations in energy and real estate prices are sources of financial risk. The answer to this question is that commodities, energy and real estate can be the underlying assets for derivatives (e.g., options and futures contracts). Changes in the prices of the underlying assets lead to changes in the prices of the derivatives based upon them, the latter being financial prices.

Non-financial risk may be classified into operational risk and other kinds of risk. Operational risk is the risk of loss resulting from the failure of people, processes, systems or from external events. It is more diverse than either credit risk or market risk, encompassing, among others, the following risk types:

- Liquidity risk, which is the type of settlement risk that results from the inability of a counterparty to settle a transaction because of the lack of liquidity.

- Hersttat risk, which is the type of settlement risk that results from the insolvency of a counterparty.

- Compliance risk, which is the operational risk of regulatory sanctions or financial losses resulting from failure to comply with laws and regulations.

- Processing risk, which is the risk of failed processing due to mistakes, negligence, accidents or fraud.

- System risk, which is the risk of losses due to system and telecommunication failures.

- Human resources (HR) risk, which is the risk of loss of key personnel or failure to maintain staff morale.

- Crime risk, which is the risk of losses arising from crimes such as theft, fraud, hacking and money laundering.

- Disaster risk, which is the risk of losses arising from disasters such as fire and flood.

- Fiduciary risk, which is the risk of losses arising from the possibility of product implementation differing from how it was presented to the client.

- Model risk, which is the risk of losses incurred by making a wrong decision on the basis of a faulty or inadequate model (e.g., the case of Long-Term Capital Management (LTCM)).

- Legal risk, which is the risk that a transaction proves unenforeceable in law or that it has been inadequately documented.

Other non-financial risks include the following risk types:

- Business risk (also called strategic risk), which is the risk of loss resulting from inappropriate strategic business decisions (e.g., plant location and product mix).

- Reputational risk, which is the risk of incurring losses because of the loss or downgrading of the reputation of firms and individuals.

- Macroeconomic risk, which is the risk of incurring losses because of adverse macroeconomic developments (e.g., acceleration of monetary growth, causing a hike in the inflation rate).

- Business cycle risk, which is the macroeconomic risk arising from fluctuations in economic activity.

- Country risk, which is the risk arising from unanticipated changes in the economic or political environment prevailing in a particular country.

- Political risk, which is the type of country risk arising from the possibility of incurring losses due to changes in rules and regulations or adverse political developments in a particular country.

- Sovereign risk, which is the type of country risk arising from the possibility of incurring losses on claims on foreign governments and government agencies.

- Purchasing power risk, which is the risk arising from the adverse effect of inflation on the real value of the rate of return on investment.

These lists are, however, not exhaustive. Doerig (2003) identifies 100 types of risk facing financial institutions, arguing that all of them "have at least a touch of operational risk." His list includes timing risk, social unrest risk, outsourcing risk, project risk, custody risk, globalisation risk, brand risk and so on. Globalisation risk was manifested in the subprime crisis that surfaced in 2007, as financial institutions were adversely affected across the Atlantic and Pacific. Still, Doreig correctly argues that the greatest risk is "not to take one," since it effectively means going out of business.

Several controversial issues arise as a result of categorising risk on the lines described so far. To start with, there is disagreement about whether or not legal risk, business (strategic) risk and reputational risk should be classified under operational risk. It is also arguable that macroeconomic risk and business risk are types of operational risk resulting from external factors. It is typically difficult to distinguish between operational risk and strategic risk to the extent that some risk management specialists argue that strategic risk is one form of operational risk. However, the following distinction can be made: while operational risk pertains to potential losses that could result from actions (where either the action itself or its consequences depart from the plan), strategic risk pertains to potential losses that could result from choosing the wrong plan under the current and expected market conditions. In other words, while strategic risk is the risk of losses arising from not doing the right thing, operational risk is the risk of losses resulting from not doing things right. This view is not accepted widely, however, as some risk classifications place strategic risk under operational risk. Sometimes distinction is made between strategic risk and business risk on the basis that the latter is the risk of losses resulting from business volume changes. One possible argument is that business risk is the risk of losses resulting from faulty strategic or tactical decisions.

In general, Miller (1992) considers the classification of uncertainties facing a firm as encompassing the general environment, industry and those that are firm-specific. Miller's classification is displayed in Figure 1.3. However, the classification of risk varies from one sector to another. For example, the UK's Financial Services Authority (FSA) classifies the risk insurance companies face into insurance risk, asset risk and operational risk, as shown in Figure 1.4. Unlike the classification shown in Figure 1.2, strategic risk is placed under operational risk.

The Impact of Risk Types

Risks of different kinds differ in the degree of seriousness and importance for banks. In its "Banana Skin" survey of seventy bankers worldwide, the Centre for the Study of Financial Innovation (2002) identifies the risks shown in Figure 1.5 as the kinds of risk banks face. While credit risk appears at the top, most of the risk types appearing in the diagram are forms of operational risk. It is for this reason that operational risk is regarded as being more important (in terms of potential impact) than either market

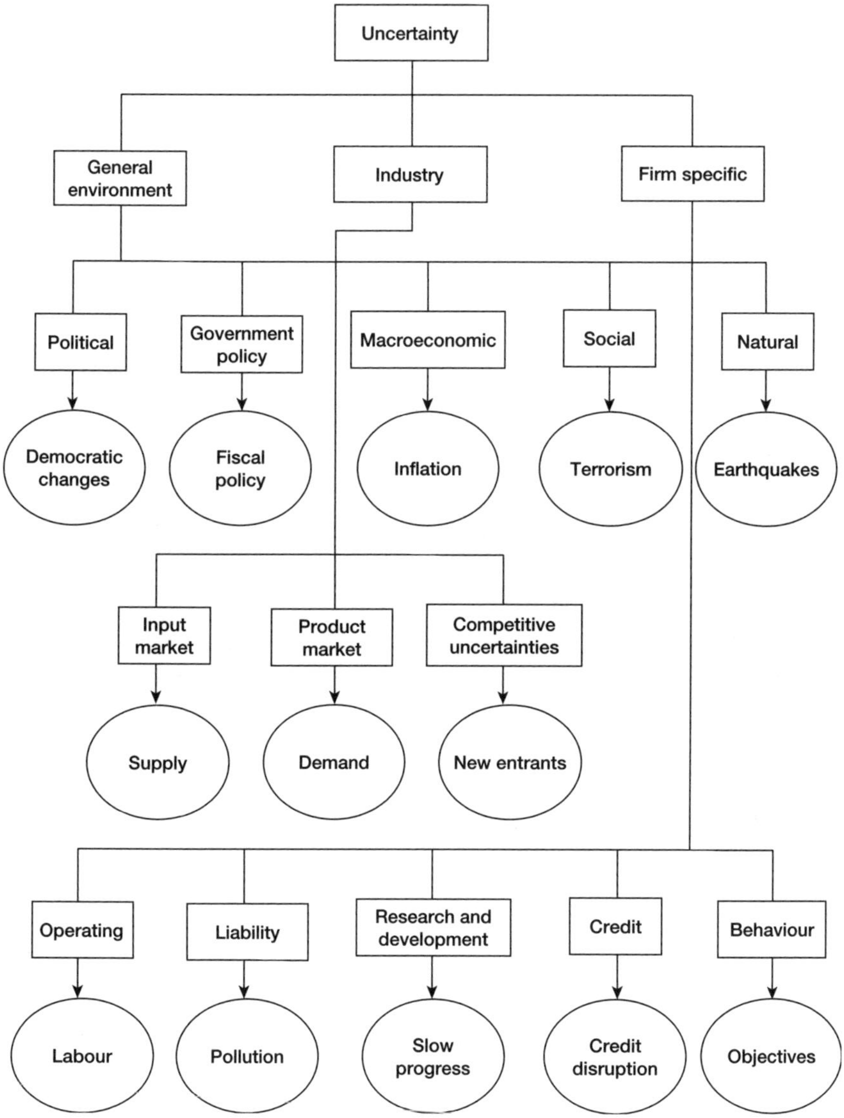

Figure 1.3 Classification of Uncertainties

risk or credit risk. Doerig (2003) argues that the priority risk categories for financial institutions include strategy (presumably meaning strategic) risk, reputational risk, market risk, credit risk, insurance underwriting risk and commission and income fee risk.

In a more recent survey, Servaes and Tufano (2006) asked the CFOs of major companies to rank the ten most important risks facing their companies.

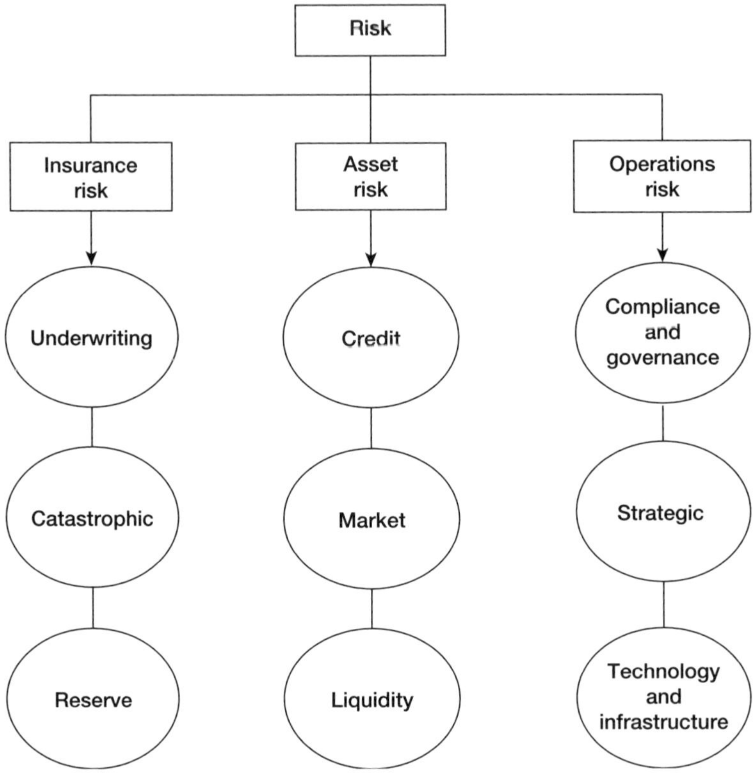

Figure 1.4 The FSA's Classification of Risk Faced by Insurance Companies

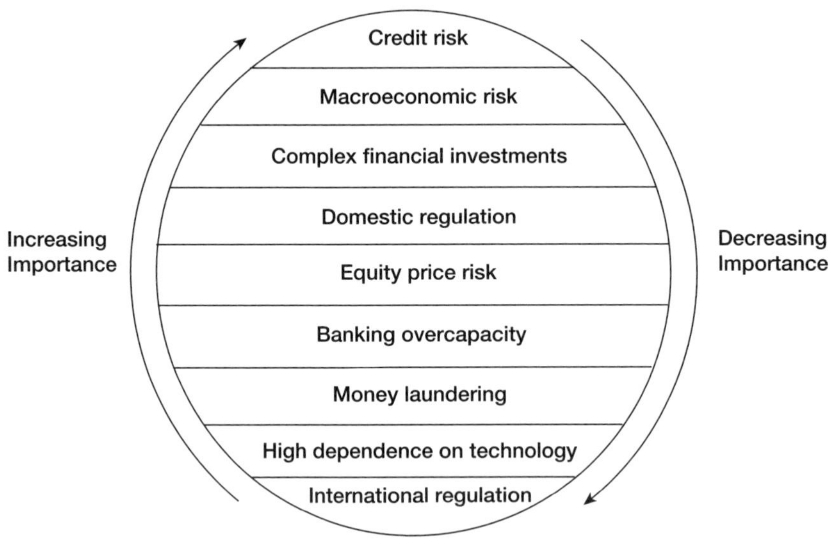

Figure 1.5 Risks Facing a Bank ("Banana Skin" Survey)

The results of the survey revealed that of the top ten risks, four were financial risks and six were broader business risks. The financial risks and their rankings are: foreign exchange risk (1), financing risk (3), commodity price risk (8) and interest rate risk (10). Foreign exchange risk assumes the top rank because of the global operations of the participating companies, whereas the low rank of interest rate risk is due to the exclusion of financial institutions from the survey.

In a survey of financial institutions conducted by PricewaterhouseCoopers in collaboration with the Economist Intelligence Unit (2004), more respondents cited reputational risk than any other risk type as the greatest potential threat to their firm's market value. A regulatory definition of reputational risk is that it is "the potential that negative publicity regarding an institution's business practices, whether true or not, will cause a decline in the customer base, costly litigation, or revenue reductions" (Federal Reserve System, 2004). But in general, "reputational risk is any risk that can potentially damage the standing or estimate of an organisation in the eyes of third-parties" (Perry and de Fontnouvelle, 2005). Reputational risk can reduce the market value of a firm through several channels including (i) loss of current or future customers; (ii) loss of employees; (iii) loss of current or future business partners; (iv) increased costs of financial funding via credit or stock markets; and (v) increased costs due to government regulations and penalties. Firms may lose reputation with respect to employees or external parties such as customers, trading partners, regulators, government departments, investors, rating agencies, vendors and suppliers, trade unions and the community at large. Because of the role they played in the subprime crisis, the rating agencies have lost reputation with respect to firms.

The Dynamics and Interdependence of Risk Types

Risk exposure is a dynamic process in the sense that the risk profile facing any firm evolves over time. Some of the risks facing business these days were not known a generation ago, including potential liability for environmental damage, discrimination in employment, sexual harassment and violence in the workplace. Other risks are linked directly to information technology (IT), such as the interruptions of business resulting from computer failure, privacy issues and computer fraud. Computer hackers have replaced bandits and pirates.

Moreover, there is interdependence and overlapping among credit risk, market risk, operational risk and business risk, as shown in Figure 1.6. For example, an unexpected decline in real estate prices could bring with it both market and credit losses. Market losses result from the decline in the value of assets (real estate), whereas credit losses would result from the inability of borrowers to repay their debt because of the decline in the value of their

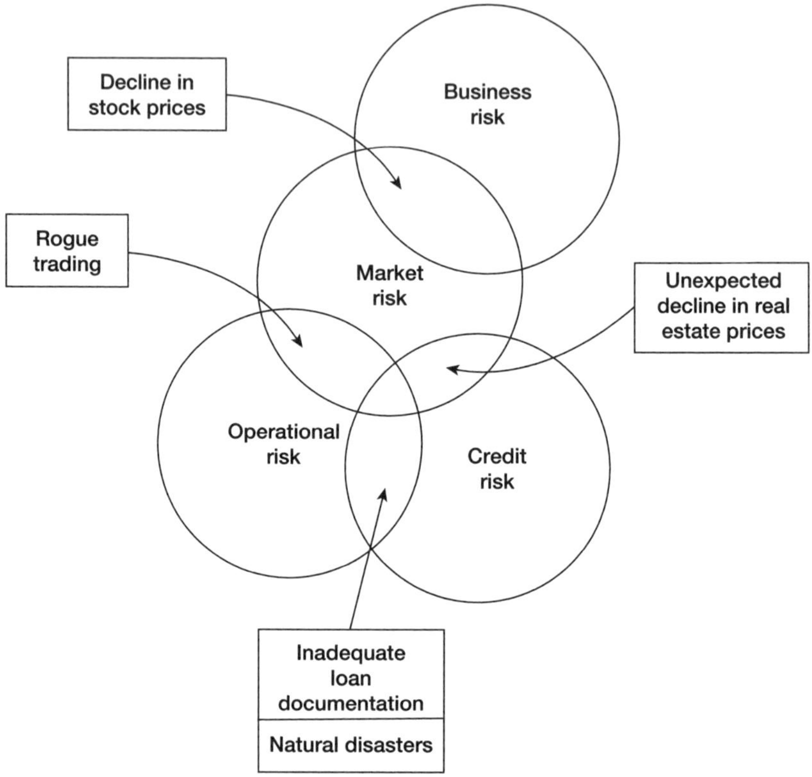

Figure 1.6 Overlapping of Risk Types

assets. The subprime crisis of 2007/2008 provides the perfect example of this overlap between credit risk and market risk. As US house prices fell, lending institutions incurred losses both because of the default of borrowers and the decline in the market value of the collateral (houses). Still, the argument that the subprime crisis constitutes an operational loss event will be put forward in Chapter 7. In Chapter 3, it will be argued that loss events of different types can be distinguished from each other on the basis of the cause or source of the loss. The overlapping portrayed in Figure 1.6 may not be as serious as it looks.

Another related issue here is that of risk transformation from one kind to another. Consider one cause of the subprime crisis, the "originate to distribute" strategy adopted by US mortgage granting institutions to remove loans from their books through securitisation. By selling mortgage-backed securities (or asset-backed securities (ABS) in general), those institutions eliminated or reduced exposure to credit risk, but at the expense of being exposed to more operational risk (e.g., the legal risk associated with securitisation). If, in addition, they retained some of the securities, exposure to market risk would also rise. The process, therefore, transforms credit risk into operational risk and market risk.

1.3 ANALYSIS OF RISK

The most common techniques for analysing risk are three: (i) best-case/worst-case analysis; (ii) what-if analysis; and (iii) simulation. We will deal with simulation in detail in Chapter 6, but we will undertake a brief comparison and some examples in this section. The special importance attached to simulation is that it is the most powerful of the three techniques, providing much more information than the information provided by the other two techniques. It is also more important for the purpose of this book, since the technique is commonly used to quantify operational risk.

Best-Case/Worst-Case Analysis

In best-case/worst-case analysis the lowest and highest possible values of the variable of interest (profit, revenue, cost, rate of return, etc.) are calculated. It is assumed that the variable of interest is determined by several other variables according to the function $y = f(x_1, x_2, \ldots x_n)$. In essence, therefore, the technique involves the formulation of two scenarios only by choosing the values of $x_1, x_2, \ldots x_n$ that give the maximum and minimum values of y.

The problem with this technique is that it does not provide information about how far away the actual outcome might be from the best and worst outcomes; neither does it produce probabilities for the best and worst cases. Figure 1.7 displays probability distributions that exhibit similar best and worst cases, but they represent different risks to the decision maker. In short, while the best-case/worst-case technique is easy to implement, it tells us nothing about the shape of the distribution that describes the variable of interest.

What-If Analysis

In what-if analysis (also called scenario analysis), several scenarios are used by assigning different values to the explanatory variables to produce a number of the values assumed by the variable of interest. While this technique provides more information about risk, it has three major flaws. First, the values assigned to the explanatory variables are typically chosen in a subjective manner, which means that the resulting values of the variable of interest will be biased. Second, it is rather tedious to perform a very large number of scenarios even with the availability of spreadsheet programs such as Excel. Third, coming up with a number of scenarios (and hence values

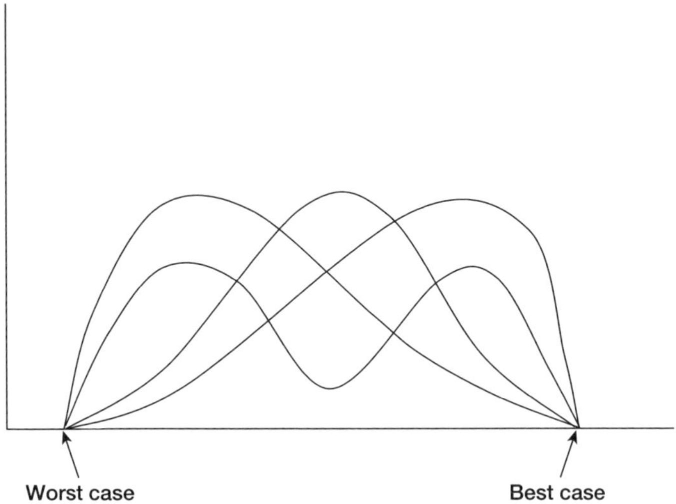

Figure 1.7 Probability Distributions with Similar Best and Worst Cases

for y) is not that useful when it comes to making a decision. Like the best-case/worst-case approach, no probability distribution is provided by this technique of risk analysis.

What-if or scenario analysis is still used widely. For example, KPMG (2005) argues that scenario analysis can help firms in attempting to find the optimal balance between risk appetite and cost reduction. It is also suggested that scenario analysis can be used in conjunction with an estimate of the influence of VAR to judge risk-adjusted profitability. With respect to operational risk, the KPMG report suggests that scenario analysis can be used to forecast the effect of strategic decisions on the operational risk profile. Indeed scenario analysis is an integral part of the AMA designed to measure operational risk under Basel II. However, its usefulness lies in its use to calibrate loss distributions that are subsequently used in Monte Carlo simulations. More will be said about scenario analysis in Chapter 4.

Simulation Analysis

Unlike the best-case/worst-case analysis, simulation is used to describe the distribution of the variable of interest, given the possible values of the explanatory variables that determine it. The process of assigning values to the explanatory variables is automated so that the results would not be biased and so that the risk analyst is relieved of the burden of coming up with these values. They are instead generated randomly from prespecified distributions, and each set of values is used to calculate the corresponding value of the variable of interest. The values generated are subsequently used to construct a statistical distribution for the variable of interest, which can be used to calculate a range of useful statistics.

Risk Analysis of Carry Trade: An Example

The three techniques of risk analysis can be demonstrated by using carry trade as an example. Carry trade is a financial operation that consists of taking a short position on a low-interest currency and a long position on a high-interest currency (see, e.g., Burnside et al (2006); Gatali et al (2007); Gynelberg and Remolona (2007) and Hottori and Shin (2007)). This operation will be profitable as long as the high-interest currency does not depreciate against the low-interest currency by a percentage that exceeds the interest rate differential. If the low-interest currency is the yen and the high-interest currency is the pound, the rate of return on this operation is

$$\pi = (i^{*} - i) + \hat{S} \tag{1.1}$$

where $i^{*} - i$ is the interest rate differential, defined as the difference between the interest rates on the pound (i^{*}) and yen (i) and $\hat{S}$ is the percentage change in the exchange rate measured as the yen price of one pound. Since the interest rates are known in advance (when the operation is implemented), the only source of risk is exchange rate variation.

At the end of 2006, the three-month interest rates on the yen and pound were 0.474% and 5.25% respectively, while the exchange rate was 230.32 (yen per pound). Carry trade would be profitable in this case, provided the exchange rate does not fall by more than 1.194% (the interest rate differential deannaulaised) between December 2006 and March 2007. The carry trader believes that the foreign exchange market is so volatile that the exchange rate at the end of March 2007 could be anywhere between 180 and 260, the two values associated with the best case and the worst case respectively. Under the two cases, the worst-case and best-case annualised rates of return are 12.9% and -13.2% respectively, as shown in Figure 1.8.

The chart also shows the outcome of what-if analysis by contemplating ten scenarios whereby the exchange rate at the end of the period assumes ten values falling between 220 and 238 at an interval of 2. We can see from Figure 1.8 that four of the scenarios produce negative rates of return ranging between -13.2% and -2.7%, whereas the remaining six scenarios produce positive rates of return ranging between 0.75% and 18.1%. It is noteworthy that the first six scenarios produce negative rates of change in the exchange rate but the rates of return under scenarios 5 and 6 are positive because the (positive) interest rate differential is higher than the absolute value of the percentage change in the exchange rate.

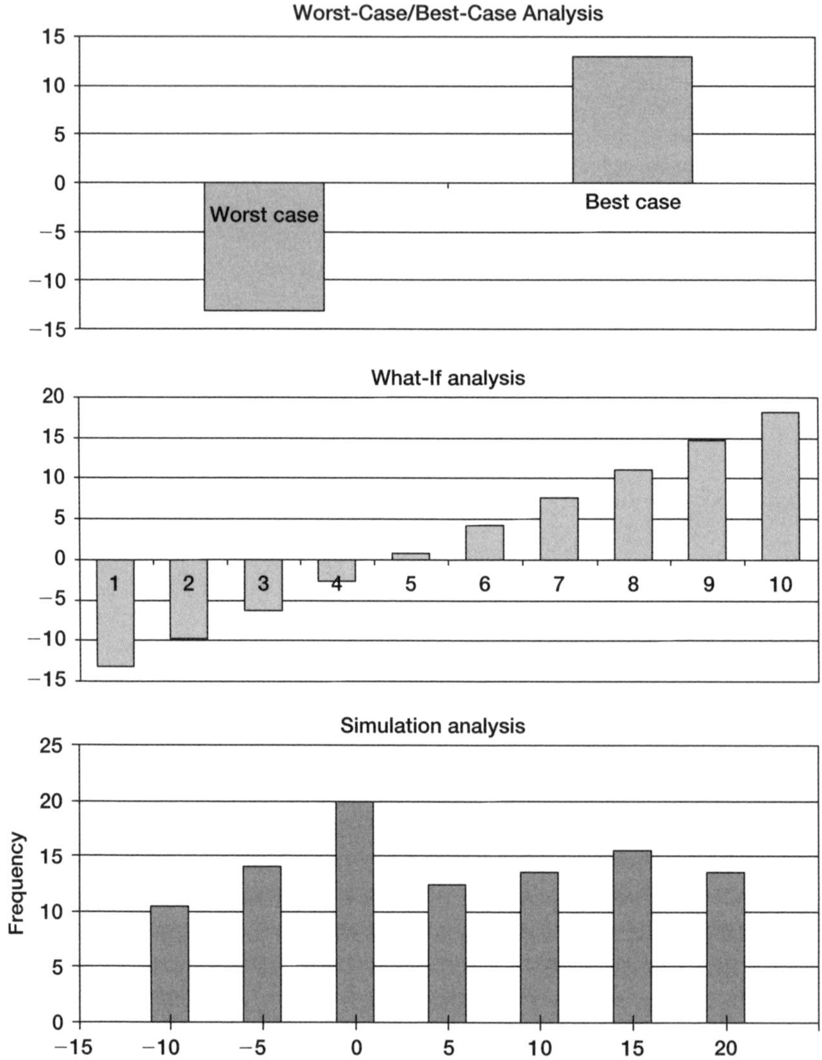

Figure 1.8 Risk Analysis of Carry Trade

The results of simulation analysis are represented by the histogram appearing at the bottom of Figure 1.8, which is constructed from 200 simulated values for the rate of return. The results show that the rate of return has a mean of 2.8% and a standard deviation of 9.4%, which makes the operation quite risky. The results also show that the probability of obtaining a positive rate of return is 0.53, or $p(\pi > 0) = 0.53$, which reduces the attractiveness of the operation in terms of the risk-return trade-off. This is not the view held by the carry trade enthusiasts.

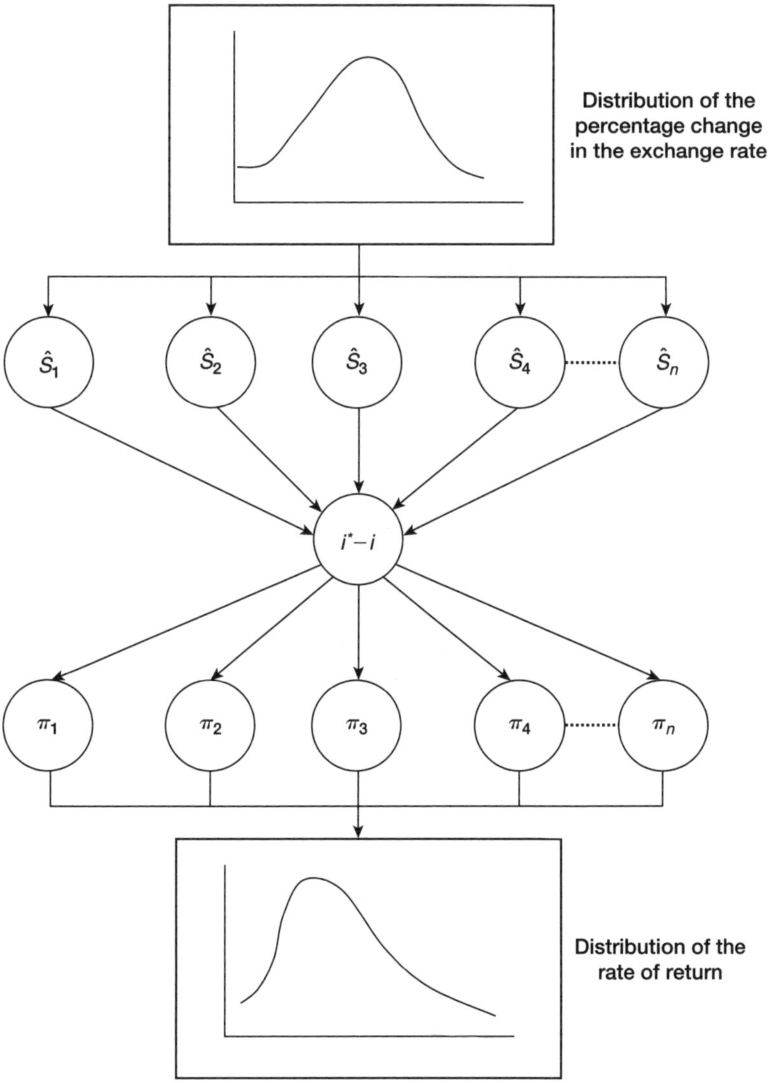

Figure 1.9 A Schematic Representation of the Simulation Exercise (1)

Figure 1.9 shows a schematic representation of the simulation exercise as applied to carry trade. The distribution of the percentage change in the exchange rate, which can be estimated from actual data, is used to generate n values of this variable ($n = 200$ in the example). Each one of these values is added to the interest rate differential, which is known in advance to generate n values of the rate of return ($\pi_1, \pi_2, \ldots, \pi_n$). The generated values are subsequently used to construct a distribution, which can be used to calculate the mean, standard deviation and the certainty level of the rate of return.

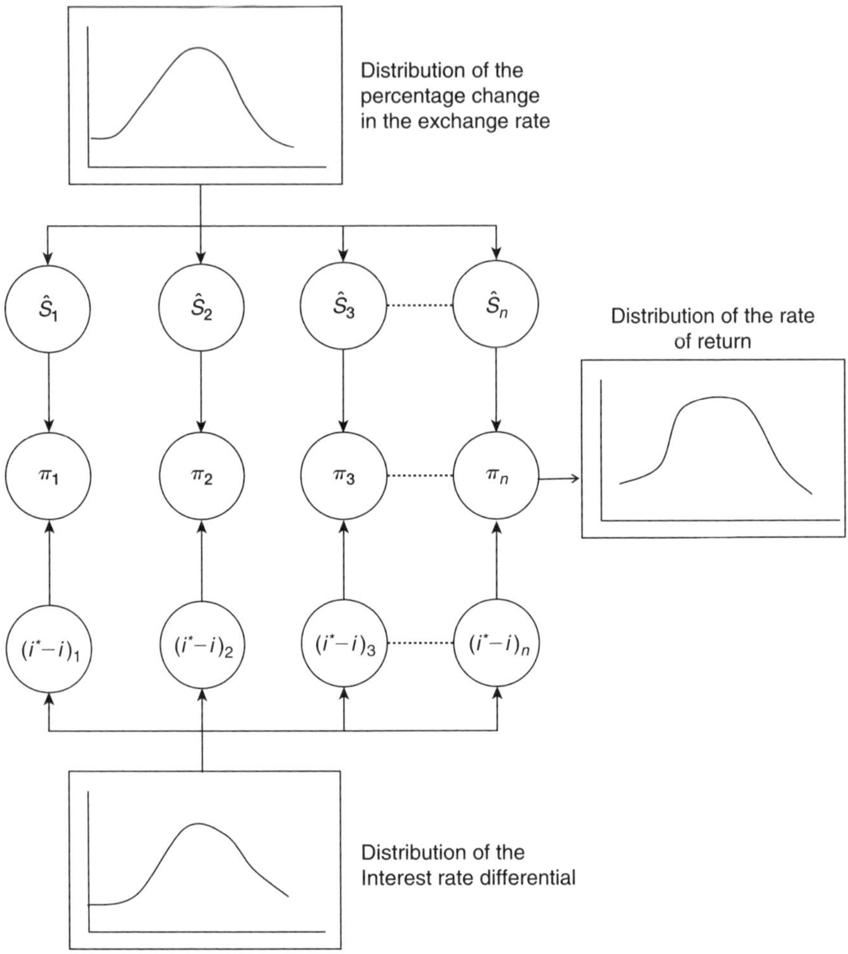

Figure 1.10 A Schematic Representation of the Simulation Exercise (2)

If the carry trader contemplates doing this operation several periods in the future, the interest rate differential will not be known in advance, which means that it has to be simulated. In this case the schematic representation of the simulation exercise appears as in Figure 1.10.

1.4 THE RISING IMPORTANCE OF OPERATIONAL RISK

The particular importance assigned to operational risk is probably motivated by the spectacular corporate collapses and headline-grabbing loss events that come to our attention quite regularly. Barings Banks, LTCM and Enron are only few examples of corporate failures resulting from the materialisation of operational loss events. But these loss events occur more frequently than corporate collapses. A number of highly-publicised operational loss events materialised in 2007 and 2008, involving British Airways, MacDonald's, Northern Rock, Societe Generale, Microsoft and MF Global.

A relatively small, but interesting, loss event was experienced by MacDonald's in October 2007 when the firm was forced to pay a former female employee \$6 million as a compensation for enduring a strip search by the restaurant manager on instructions from a fake policeman. It is either that the manger was stupid enough to believe the fake policeman and execute his orders or that he wanted to do the strip search for his own enjoyment. After all, operational losses arising from the failure of people are due to either stupidity and incompetence or malice. Other, more recent, examples of operational loss events include the following. Northern Rock was the victim of the US subprime crisis, which can be viewed as an operational rather than market or credit loss event (see Chapter 7). In January 2008, Societe Generale incurred a massive loss of \$7.2 billion due to unauthorised activities of a rogue trader. A month later, another rogue trader cost MF Global \$141.5 million in losses as a result of unauthorised trading in wheat futures contracts.

In general, operational losses involve several components including: (i) direct operational losses; (ii) indirect operational losses; (iii) opportunity losses; (vi) direct compliance costs; and (v) assurance costs. Direct operational losses include, among other things, fines and damage to physical assets (DPA). An example of indirect operational losses is the cost of employees made idle by computer downtime. Opportunity losses occur, for example, when an investment opportunity is lost due to faulty analysis. Direct regulation costs are attributable to regulatory intervention in response to operational failure. Assurance costs are associated with internal assurance resources such as internal and external audit.

The Rise and Rise of Operational Risk

It was not until the early 1990s (and possibly the mid-1990s, following the collapse of Barings Bank) that the term "operational risk" was born. Power (2005) attributes the birth of the term "operational risk" to the publication of the Basel II proposals, but he suggests that Nick Leeson, the rogue trader who brought down Barings is "the true author and unwitting inventor of operational risk, since most discussions of the topic refer to this case as a defining moment." It is not that operational risk did not exist before Leeson, because it is much older than the human race. The dinosaurs suffered a catastrophic loss event 65 million years ago resulting from an external factor: a very big rock that hit the Planet at a tremendously high speed (Moosa, 2007c). This is an example of a loss event caused by an external factor, but operational risk may also arise from internal sources. With respect to the banking industry, Buchelt and Unteregger (2004) argue that the risk of fraud and external events (such as natural disasters) have been around ever since the beginning of banking but it is technological progress that has boosted the potential of operational risk. It is not that operational risk is a new risk; it is rather that operational risk management is a new distinct and independent discipline.

However, it is not only technological progress that has led to the intensification of operational risk. Other contributory factors include more intensive competition, globalisation, e-commerce, mergers and consolidation, the growing use of outsourcing arrangements and the increasing complexity of financial assets (a major factor in the subprime crisis). Jobst (2007b) argues that the increased size and complexity of the banking industry has made operational risk amplify system-wide risk levels with a greater potential to transpire in more harmful ways than many other sources of risk. He also argues that attempts to transfer risk (of any kind) via derivatives involve exposure to operational risk. But it is not only banks that are exposed to operational risk. For example, Pennington (2008a) points out that “hedge funds face many of the same operational risks as more traditional asset managers.” Specifically, “smaller hedge funds are more prone to mis-valuations and fraud-related problems, or problems in their service provider network; while the larger funds have more complex problems such as difficulties valuing illiquid instruments, selling processes, or more general problems relating to transparency or illiquidity in their portfolios.” Doerig (2003) identifies a larger set of factors that have led to increase in the operational risk exposure of financial institutions, as shown in Figure 1.11.

Over time, operational risk attracted increasing interest from the general public, firms that are exposed to it and of course the regulators. This does not mean that only firms are exposed to operational risk, because the general public and regulators are exposed as well. Apart from exposure, Ong (2002) suggests ten reasons “why so many people are interested in operational risk.” The top three reasons of the list are: (i) it is sexy, hot and completely nebulous; (ii) people think they have already conquered both market risk and credit risk; and (iii) operational risk is a convenient catch-all “garbage dump” for all kinds of possible risks.

Firms are interested in operational risk because exposure can be fatal. Blunden (2003) argues that operational risk is as likely to bring a company to its knees as a market collapse, although it is within management control in many cases (definitely so in the cases of Barings and Societe Generale). Studies have shown that a firm can suffer a market value decline in the days surrounding the announcement of a large loss that is significantly larger than the loss itself (see Chapter 5). This is attributed by Perry and de Fontnouvelle (2005) to the indirect impact of reputational risk, because

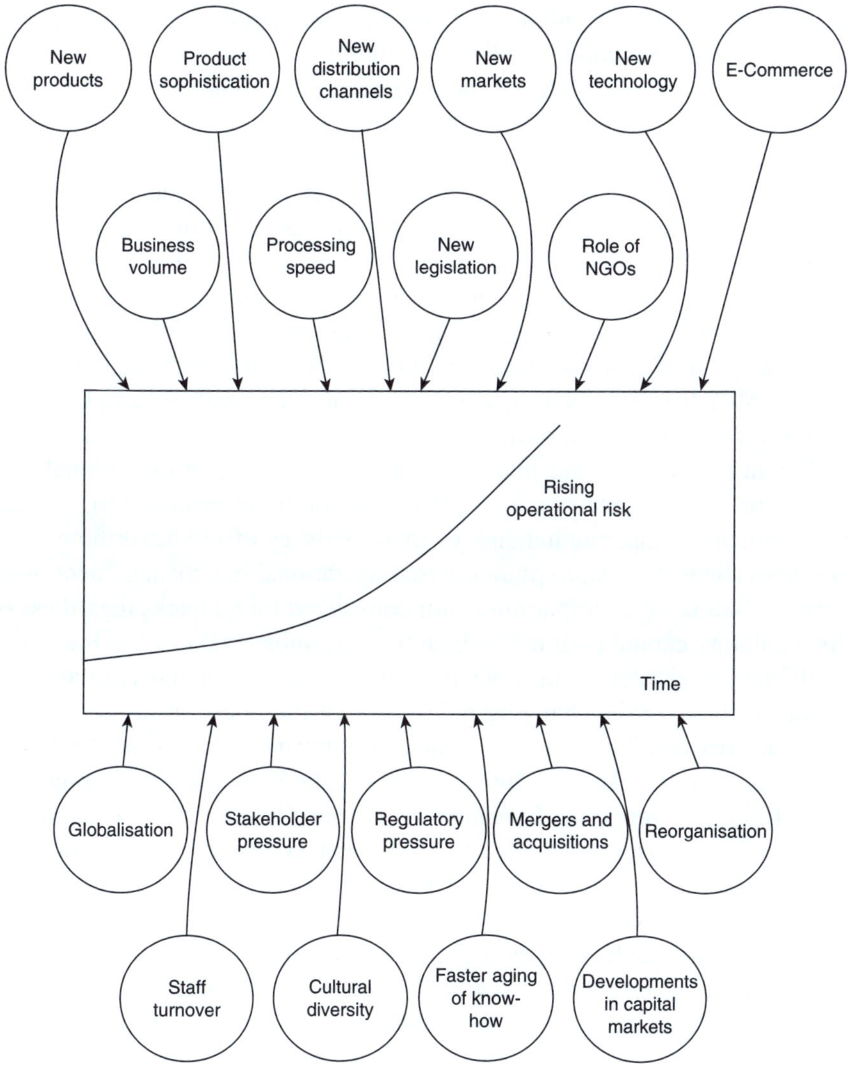

Figure 1.11 Factors Leading to Rising Exposure to Operational Risk

disclosure of fraudulent activity or improper business practices at a firm may damage the firm's reputation. In its issue of 1 March 2008, the *Wall Street Journal* reported that "after getting rid of the trader who lost $141.5 million on wheat futures ... brokerage firm MF Global Ltd is finding out how hard it will be to clean up the mess he left behind" (Lucchetti, 2008). In the two days following the discovery of the trading loss, the stock price of MF Global plunged 40%. The *Wall Street Journal* argues that "many investors are worried that plugging holes in MF Global's risk management procedures won't be enough to restore customer confidence." The reputational factor is mentioned explicitly as the newspaper stated that "clients who make trades through MF Global because of its long-time reputation as a savvy player in the topsy-turvy futures industry might take that business elsewhere."

Kilavuka (2008) points out that "the impact of operational failure can be far reaching" and that "a firm's long-term viability can be impaired by operational failures regardless of whether the immediate losses are sustainable in the short term." He further argues that the impact of operational failure may be augmented by (i) the disruption of services, which could lead to severe erosion of customer loyalty; and (ii) litigation, which could damage irrevocably a firm's reputation and brand even if the legal cost can be easily supported by the firm's resources.

Another reason for the interest of firms in general in operational risk is that the rating agencies have started to incorporate exposure to, and the management of, operational risk in their analyses of creditworthiness. de Fontnouvelle et al (2005b) point out that operational risk management practices are becoming an important factor considered for all banks regardless of the regulatory capital regime to which they are subject (Basel I or Basel II).

Hubner et al (2003) attribute the greater interest of the regulators in operational risk to the changing risk profile of the financial services sector for many reasons including the growth in e-business activity and reliance on technology. The BCBS (1999) expressed the view that operational risk is "sufficiently important for banks to devote the necessary resources to quantify." The Basel Committee initially dealt exclusively with credit risk; market risk was introduced in the 1996 amendment to Basel I. Most of the emphasis in the Basel II Accord seems to be placed on operational risk. In the UK, the Bank for Credit and Commerce International (BCCI) and Barings cases generated the political impetus for the transfer of banking supervision from the Bank of England to the newly-created regulator, the FSA. Operational risk has struck a fundamental part of doing business, and as such it cannot be eliminated completely. For this reason, financial institutions and supervisors have a common interest in identifying, monitoring and controlling operational risk.

Operational Risk in the Foreign Exchange Market

Operational risk has grown in importance with respect to the foreign exchange market, as this market has become more diverse and much larger (it is actually the largest financial market, pulling a daily turnover of over $2 trillion). One reason for the increasing level of operational risk encountered in executing foreign exchange transactions is the increasing diversity of the foreign exchange market, which is no longer dominated by commercial banks. Rather, market participants now include investment banks, brokerage companies, multinational firms, money managers, commodity trading advisors, insurance companies, governments, central banks, pension funds, hedge funds and investment companies. The proposition that the diversity of market participants leads to more operational risk is reflected in the fact that the first of the Foreign Exchange Committee's (2003) best practices to combat operational risk in the foreign exchange market is "know your customer," which means that a bank should know the identity of its counterparties, the activities they intend to undertake with the bank and why they are undertaking these activities. Naturally, increasing diversity of market participants makes this task more difficult.

Operational risk has risen in the foreign exchange market also because the increasing complexity and size of the market have made it necessary to introduce regular changes in trading procedures, trade capture systems, operational procedures and risk management tools. The Foreign Exchange Committee (2003) lists a number of changes that pertain to the increased level of operational risk in the foreign exchange market, including: (i) introduction of the euro; (ii) consolidation of foreign exchange dealers; (iii) consolidation of foreign exchange processing in global or regional processing centres; (iv) outsourcing of back office functions; (v) introduction of continuous line settlement (CLS) to reduce settlement risk; (vi) increased use of web portals to execute foreign exchange transactions; and (vii) expansion of prime brokerage.

In general, operational risk in foreign exchange arises from problems with processing, product pricing and valuation. These problems result from several factors such as natural disasters, changes in the financial details of a trade or settlement instructions on a transaction, poor planning and procedures, inadequate systems, inadequate supervision of staff, defective controls and human errors. Operational losses resulting from incorrect settlement of foreign exchange transactions can have direct costs in improper payments and receipts. Trade processing and settlement errors can lead to indirect costs, such as compensation payments to counterparties for failed settlements or the development of large losses in the underlying portfolio as a result of managing the wrong position. Furthermore, investigating problems and negotiating a resolution with a counterparty may carry additional costs.

It is also important to note that the foreign exchange business is constantly evolving, causing changes in the operational risk profile. The Foreign Exchange Committee (2003) lists the major trends that will continue to affect operational risk in the foreign exchange market, including the following: (i) advances in technology, which makes it possible to execute many more transactions during periods of market volatility; (ii) growing trading volume in emerging market currencies; (iii) the emergence of exotic types of transactions, particularly foreign exchange derivatives; and (iv) the emergence of new types of customers.

1.5 BANKS AND BANKING REGULATION

The current discussion of the regulation of operational risk (as enshrined in the Basel II Accord) centres on the objective of minimising the possibility of bank failure. Although operational risk is not restricted to banks, these institutions command more importance than other financial and non-financial firms. The failure of banks creates more turmoil in the economy than perhaps any other kind of firm. The most recent reminder of the validity of this proposition is the failure of Northern Rock in September 2007, which has created a lot of problems for the British government and cost the tax payers billions of pounds. The collapse of the banking system in Argentina earlier this century resulted not only in economic collapse but also in civil unrest. Three issues are discussed in this section: (i) why banks are important; (ii) the justification for banking regulation; and (iii) regulatory functions.

Why Do Banks Command Special Importance?

Before discussing the issue of why banks command special importance, we have to ask the question as to what is meant by a "bank." What distinguishes banks from other financial institutions and what distinguishes commercial banks from investment banks? In the US, the Glass-Steagall Act was enacted in 1933 to distinguish between commercial banks and other financial institutions (particularly investment banks). According to this distinction, (commercial) banks are deposit taking and lending institutions. Japan also adopted a legal distinction similar to the US system in the post-World War II period. In the UK, distinction between banks and securities firms has been more a matter of custom than law. By contrast, continental European countries have always had the tradition of universal banking, which is now prevailing. In November 1999, the Glass-Steagall Act was replaced by the Gramm-Leach-Biley Act, perhaps to acknowledge the emergence of broad banking (see e.g., Barth et al, 2000).

Banks are special, and this is why the banking industry is the most regulated industry. Santos (2001) highlights "the central role that banks play in financial intermediation" Palia and Porter (2003) describe banks as "unique economic entities primarily due to their ability to create money, and the impact that bank information production and liquidity services have on the real economy." White (2004) suggests that banks are important for two reasons: (i) the difference between the degrees of liquidity of their assets and liabilities, which makes them highly vulnerable to depositor withdrawal and bank runs in extreme cases; and (ii) banks are at the centre of the payment system (they are the creators of money, the medium of exchange). Benink et al (2008) suggest that banks are special because they face an asymmetric loss function, which is a consequence of handling other people's money. An asymmetric loss function means that banks reap the financial gains from taking risk but only assume a fraction of the ensuing losses. At the 2008 *International Financing Review* conference in London, a joke went that bankers had lost a lot of money but "the good news was that it was other people's money" (The Economist, 2008h). Banks are important because of their sheer size. Also, a big difference between banks (as financial firms) and non-financial firms is that banks deal in a valuable commodity, money, which makes the temptation for criminal activity (and hence exposure to operational risk) greater in the case of banks as compared with other firms (e.g., dairy factories).

The Economist (2008f) expresses similar views, suggesting that there are three reasons why banks are special. The first of these reasons is the "inherent fragility of their business model." In this respect, the argument goes, "even the strongest bank cannot survive a severe loss of confidence, because the money it owes can usually be called more quickly than the money it is owed." The second reason why banks are special is the sheer size of the interbank market, resulting from the fact that banks deal with each other on a massive scale. Hence, banking is different from other industries where the demise of one firm is typically welcomed by its competitors, which is not the case in banking. The third reason for the special importance of banks, according to The Economist (2008f), is the role they play in allocating financial resource among various sectors in the economy. The failure of banks leads to a reduction in credit flows to the rest of the economy, and hence adverse economic consequences. The Economist (2008f) expresses this point succinctly as follows: "if banks suffer, we all suffer." The Economist (2008i) also argues that banks are "particularly susceptible to failure of governance," because "they are opaque and their business is to take risk." Yet another problematic feature of banks is that the levels of turnover and product innovation are high, making it unlikely that employees would experience full business and product cycles (which weakens the institutional memory of the last crisis). Finally, The Economist makes the interesting observation that banks "seem to be poor at nurturing talented managers" (recall the drama of appointing successors to the departing CEOs at Merrill Lynch and Citi Group in the midst of the subprime crisis).

Banking Regulation: The Justification

The special importance of banks, relative to non-financial firms and non-bank financial intermediaries, provides justification for the proposition that these institutions should be regulated and closely supervised. Santos (2001) justifies bank regulation on the basis of market failure such as externalities, market power and asymmetry of information between buyers and sellers. A primary objective of bank regulation is to curtail the negative externalities arising from bank failure that could result in a systemic crisis. In the absence of regulation, banks could create violent swings in the amount of money and have real effects on business activity and prices. Banks' provision of liquidity services leaves them exposed to runs and, therefore, failure (Diamond and Dybvig, 1983), which is what happened to Northern Rock in 2007. This is because banks operate with a balance sheet that combines a large portion of liabilities in the form of demand deposits and a large portion of assets in the form of long-term illiquid loans. Deposit insurance may be the solution but it creates moral hazard and adverse selection.

The second justification for bank supervision is inability of depositors to monitor banks. Dewatripont and Tirole (1993, 1994) have put forward the "representation hypothesis" to justify banking regulation on the basis of the governance problems created by the separation of ownership from management and the inability of depositors to monitor banks. While it is important for investors to monitor banks because they are exposed to adverse selection and moral hazard, the task is costly and requires access to information. The process is further complicated by the fact that this activity will be wasteful when duplicated by several parties and the fact that deposits are held by unsophisticated depositors who may not have the incentive to monitor their banks because they hold insignificant deposits. Hence there is a need for a monitoring representative of depositors, which can be provided by regulation.

This, however, is not the consensus view, as disagreement is widespread on whether banks should be regulated and, if so, how they should be regulated. This disagreement reflects the lack of consensus on the nature of market failure that makes free banking sub-optimal. For example, Dowd (1996b) and Benston and Kaufman (1996) dispute the arguments typically presented in favour of bank regulation. There is also significant scepticism about the role of regulation as a means of achieving financial stability. For example, Kaufman and Scott (2000) argue that regulatory actions have been double-edged, if not counterproductive. Koehn and Santomero (1980) suggest that regulation does not necessarily accomplish the declared objective of reducing the probability of bank failure and that a case could be argued that the opposite result can be expected. Benston and Kaufman (1996) assert that most of the arguments that are used frequently to support special regulation for banks are not supported by either theory or empirical evidence. They also share the view that an unregulated system of enterprise tends to achieve an optimal allocation of resources. They go as far as arguing that one reason for bank regulation is the provision of revenue and power for government officials. Indeed, there is a significant volume of literature on free banking, which is the ultra-extreme view of banking regulation sceptics (see e.g., Dowd (1993, 1996a, 1996b); Glasner (1989); Horwitz (1992); Rockoff (1975); Sechrest (1993)). For some classic work on free baking and related issues, see Friedman (1960), Hayek (1976) and Meulen (1934).

Doerig (2003) argues that regulators do not take into account the fact that risk creates value and that profits come from taking risk. By attempting to avoid systemic risk (which arises from the effect of the failure of a single bank on the whole banking sector, the financial sector and the economy at large) in the name of creditors and investors, they end up making the financial system more unstable. Lack of profitability, he argues, represents a supervisory problem even if the underlying bank is compliant with the capital adequacy requirements and has the most sophisticated risk measurement models. Indeed he argues that "sustained, sound and diversified profitability is THE precondition for protecting creditors and avoiding systemic risks" Survival, the argument goes, is not only about capital, compliance and controls, it is also about performance.

Regulatory Functions

Bank regulators are preoccupied with systemic risk. The problem, as Caprio and Klingebiel (1996) argue, is that "there is no objective, generally accepted definition of when a problem in the banking sector becomes systemic" and that "central bank governors tend to behave as though they know a systemic problem when they see one." However, a widely accepted definition of systemic financial risk is that suggested by the Group of Ten (G10) (2001), which is "the risk that an event will trigger a loss of economic value or confidence in, and attendant increases in uncertainty about, a substantial portion of financial system that is serious enough to quite probably have significant adverse effects on the real economy."

Financial supervision includes three functions: (i) macroprudential supervision; (ii) microprudential supervision; and (iii) conduct-of-business regulation. Macroprudential supervision is intended to limit financial system distress that might damage the economy. Microprudential supervision focuses on the solvency of individual institutions rather than the whole system. The objective is to protect consumers from loss by monitoring the compliance of individual institutions with prudential regulations, bringing enforcement action when compliance falls short. The function of conduct-of-business regulation is also consumer protection, emphasising the safeguard of customers from unfair practices, including the monitoring of potential conflict of interest. It may also include disclosure requirements, competition issues and anti-money laundering measures.

The segregation of regulatory functions is a controversial issue on which there is no consensus. Herring and Carmassi (2008) point out that one lesson learned from the subprime crisis pertains to the segregation of supervisory roles, particularly between the central banks and other supervisors. In the case of Northern Rock, for example, it was felt that the Bank of England could not perform the function of lender of last resort when the FSA was in charge of regulating the Rock. Close co-operation with the central bank is essential because microprudential supervision requires understanding of the macroeconomic context, whereas macroprudential supervision (monetary policy) benefits from understanding financial markets and institutions. The Federal Reserve System insists that without direct involvement in microprudential supervision, its monetary policy would suffer and that it would be less able to manage the full range of crises. The Fed Chairman has reiterated this view by arguing that "the information, expertise, and powers that the Fed derives from its supervisory authority enhance its ability to contribute to efforts to prevent financial crises;" and that "when financial stresses emerge and public action is warranted, the Fed is able to respond more quickly, more effectively, and in a more informed way than would otherwise be possible" (Bernanke, 2007).

If segregation is bad and co-operation is good, why not concentrate supervisory powers in the central bank? Goodhart and Shoemaker (1995) note that macroeconomic objectives may be in conflict with microprudential objectives (e.g., monetary restraint may be bad for the solvency of banks). Masciandaro (2004, 2005, 2006) finds that the probability that a country adopts a unified regulator is higher the smaller the financial system, the more equity dominated the private governance model and the higher the standards of public governance. Goodhart (2000) puts forward another point. If the central bank is responsible for both monetary policy and microprudential supervision, it is possible that a highly visible failure in the latter may undermine confidence in the former. Padoa-Schioppa (2003) makes the observation that giving the central bank exclusive supervisory powers raises concerns about the concentration of power and conflict of interest. Herring and Carmassi (2008) argue that the main concern about establishing the microprudential supervisor outside the central bank is whether it can co-operate effectively with the central bank during a crisis. In several cases, the removal of microprudential powers from the central bank came after one or more lapses in supervision or in the wake of a financial disaster (also because of the independence of central banks).

1.6 CAPITAL, CAPITAL ADEQUACY AND RELATED CONCEPTS

Bank regulators have been preoccupied with capital adequacy as the vehicle to control the underlying levels of risk. Palia and Porter (2003) argue that equating bank viability with capital adequacy seems to be axiomatic because capital is the cushion that protects liability holders from declining asset values, which means that the deposit insurer will also be protected. To understand the concept of capital adequacy, we need to understand the concept of capital first.

What is Capital?

Capital is often described as one of the most fundamental and elusive concepts. It is simply the arithmetic difference between assets and liabilities, which is also known as net worth or shareholders' equity. Thus, a bank is solvent if the difference between assets and liabilities is positive and vice versa. Benink and Wihlborg (2002) point out that capital serves three functions: (i) it is a buffer against unexpected losses causing bankruptcy; (ii) equity capital creates incentives for managing risk appropriately from the perspective of the shareholders; and (iii) equity capital of sufficient magnitude signals that lenders to the firm will not be taken advantage of.

Mainelli (2004) emphasises the importance of capital by arguing that "capital is pivotal to everything that a bank does, and changing it... has wide-ranging implications for bank management and bank investors." Specifically, he suggests that changing capital requirements has the effect of changing banks' behaviour towards risk because capital levels (i) constrain a key performance measure (return on equity); (ii) influence a bank's ability to lend and spend; and (iii) limit dividends and capital repatriation. Capital, therefore, is the cushion that protects banks from insolvency. But bank failure may occur because of illiquidity even if a bank is solvent. Is not this exactly what happened to Northern Rock, which endured a bank run on its deposits in September 2007? Then what is so good for the bank itself about being solvent if, as a result of a loss event, it is not in a position to resume business as usual. Solvent or insolvent, Northern Rock could not resume business as usual, creating significant problems for the British government and forcing the nationalisation of the bank in February 2008. We will return to the issue of capital-based regulation at a later stage.

The accounting definition of capital is that it is the difference between the book values of assets and liabilities, which may be adjusted for off-balance sheet items. The problem with the accounting definition is that assets may include undepreciated investment in obsolete technology or goodwill. In this case the liquidation value of capital will be smaller than its accounting value. This is why an alternative measure of capital is the market value of equity, which is reasonable because it is a reflection of the market's valuation of the underlying firm. The problem with this measure of capital is that the market value of a firm may not be an accurate representation of its fundamental value, particularly if the market is experiencing a crash or a bubble. In general, capital can be thought of as the financial resources available to absorb unanticipated losses, thus providing protection for parties having claims on the firm's assets.

There are several capital concepts. Distinction is typically made between economic capital and regulatory capital. Economic capital is the capital that a firm must hold to protect itself against insolvency with a chosen level of certainty over a given period of time. The Economist (2003) defines economic capital as "the theoretically ideal cushion against unexpected losses." de Fontnouvelle et al (2005b) define economic capital as "the amount that bank management believes it should hold to reflect the risks arising from the bank's various positions and activities." And Kilavuka (2008) defines it as "an estimate of the amount of capital that is required to cover and protect the shareholders from potential (unexpected) economic losses at a selected confidence level, over a given time horizon." Economic capital may be assigned to a certain kind of risk or to individual business lines or activities.

While economic capital is calculated by the firm according to its internal models, regulatory capital (also called regulatory capital requirements or the regulatory capital charge) is determined by regulators, for example as a given percentage of the risk-weighted value of assets. It is, therefore, defined as the minimum amount of capital that regulators require a bank to hold. Under Basel I and Basel II, banks are required to maintain a minimum capital ratio of 8% of risk-weighted assets. de Fontnouvelle et al (2005b) point out that while Basel II retains the minimum regulatory capital concept of Basel I, the former employs principles of economic capital to make the minimum regulatory capital measure more risk-sensitive. Economic capital and regulatory capital are bound to differ, perhaps significantly, unless the regulator agrees to make regulatory capital equal to economic capital as determined by internal models. This is one of the stated objectives of Basel II, but whether or not this is a good idea remains a debateable topic. Again, this is an issue that will be revisited later on in this book.

There are other capital concepts, including market-determined capital and buffer capital. Market-determined capital (or market capital) is the amount of capital that market participants require an institution to hold. Berger et al (1995) define market capital as the capital that maximises the value of the firm in the absence of regulatory capital requirements. While in principle market-determined capital and economic capital should be identical, they differ in practice because of a lack of transparency or investor uncertainty (de Fontnouvelle et al, 2005b). Rating agencies play a key role in determining market capital as rating is a function of, among other variables, the capital required to maintain a target risk profile. Banks typically hold more capital than the regulatory minimum to meet economic and/or market-determined capital requirements. Excess regulatory capital is called "buffer capital," which is deemed necessary to absorb unexpected shocks to the balance sheet and earnings. de Fontnouvelle et al (2005b) note that regulatory minimum capital and the total amount of capital held are the only capital concepts that can be readily observed by the public.

The concept of capital adequacy refers to the requirement that banks hold adequate capital to protect themselves against insolvency. It is typically measured in terms of the capital ratio, k, which is calculated as

$$k = \frac{K}{A} \tag{1.2}$$

where K is capital and A is the value of assets. To account for risk, the risk-adjusted capital ratio is calculated as

$$k' = \frac{K}{A'} \tag{1.3}$$

where $A' = \Sigma\, w_i A_i$ is a weighted sum of assets where the weights reflect the degree of risk embodied in the assets, such that $0 \leq w_i \leq 1$.

Several criteria can in theory be used to determine capital adequacy. A general theme is that capital must be sufficient to sustain current operations, provide for adverse reserve changes or decline in the value of assets and support growth. Another approach to setting capital requirements is based on the objective of avoiding total (or significant) loss of capital. Yet another criterion is the maximisation of value, which includes things such as customer base, reputation, expertise etc. Capital in this case should be adequate for maximising value. Two more criteria that are particularly applicable to banks involve setting aside sufficient capital to (i) meet customers' withdrawal, and (ii) not only survive a major catastrophe but thrive in the aftermath. As we are going to see later, the Basel II Accord requires banks to hold capital to protect it from insolvency, which is equal to unexpected losses at a certain (high) confidence level. For regulatory purposes, capital consists of equity and retained earnings (tier 1 or core capital) and supplementary capital (tier 2 capital). Figure 1.12 shows the components of tier 1 and tier 2 capital. Sometimes, short-term subordinated debt is classified as tier 3 capital.

The Risk-Adjusted Rate of Return on Capital

The concept of risk-adjusted rate of return on capital (RAROC) is based on the idea that the profit generated by a particular business unit should be calculated after a charge for capital at risk (Jorion, 2000). The usefulness of this concept as a measure of performance is that it allows the comparison of the performance of different units. This measure of the rate of return requires the quantification of the capital at risk. Kilavuka (2008) describes RAROC as a "common metric used to compare activities against each other or against a target."

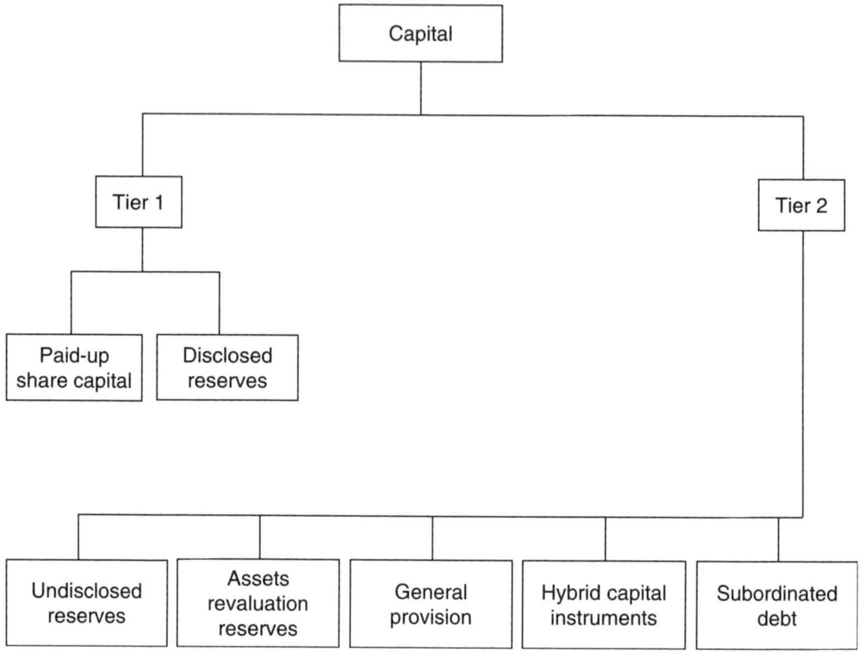

Figure 1.12 Components of Tier 1 and Tier 2 Capital

RAROC, which is related to the concept of economic capital, is calculated as

$$RAROC = \frac{\pi}{K} \tag{1.4}$$

where π is economic profit and K is economic capital. Economic profit is calculated as the difference between net income and the cost of capital.

The banking industry has become increasingly interested in the concept of RAROC because of dissatisfaction with the regulatory capital ratios as defined above. In the early 1990s, banks became interested in searching for measures of "true economic risk" or at least a better representation of risk than the arbitrary (and perhaps biased) regulatory ratios. This desire led to the adoption of internal models to calculate market risk in 1996 (see Chapter 2). Power (2005) argues that the RAROC "is more than a technical device" and that "it represents a programme which potentially aligns regulatory objectives for safety via a capital cushion, with managerial objectives for efficient allocation of resources and performance appraisal."

The problem with the RAROC, however, is that if line managers cannot understand the approach, it cannot gain acceptance across a bank

(Jameson, 2001). Furthermore, it will be argued strongly that aligning regulatory requirements with the managerial objectives of running a business is not a good idea. Power (2005) also argues that "while RAROC provides an ideal for decision-making and a language for risk management, there is also looseness of fit with the way RAROC calculations are used" and that "behavioural issues are as critical as technical ones." He also points out that "despite a clear theoretical specification, RAROC is operationally indeterminate, not least because of the data collection ironies." A detailed discussion of the data collection ironies (problems) will be presented in coming chapters. Kilavuka (2008) identifies the problem of using RAROC in conjunction with a specific kind of risk (such as operational risk) arising from the need to distinguish between the returns and costs associated with the kind of risk under consideration and those associated with other kinds of risk.

Regulatory Capital Arbitrage

Regulatory capital arbitrage is a process whereby banks exploit differences between a portfolio's true economic risk and regulatory risk by, for example, shifting the portfolio's composition towards high-yield, low-quality assets. For example, in order to boost its return on equity, a bank may replace high-quality loans with low-quality ones. If high-quality and low-quality loans receive the same regulatory risk weight, the replacement would lead to an increase in the bank's overall risk without changing the regulatory capital ratio (the ratio of capital to risk-weighted assets).

Jones (2000) presents a detailed description of the practices in the presence of regulatory capital arbitrage. Some common techniques include the use of securitisation to concentrate and transfer credit, the creation of special-purpose vehicles to transfer ownership, and the use of indirect credit enhancements. Jackson et al (1999) provide a series of examples to illustrate the use of securitisation in regulatory capital arbitrage, arguing that the securitisation of revolving credits is one of the fastest forms of regulatory capital arbitrage.

Consider Figure 1.13, which shows a bank that holds five types of assets (loans) in equal amounts ($X_1 = X_2 = X_3 = X_4 = X_5 = X$). Assume that the regulator classifies these assets as having the same risk, assigning a weight of 100% to each of them. If the capital ratio is k, the bank has to hold at least $K = 5kX$. The economic risk of these assets are, however, different because the probability of default (PD) associated with asset i is p_i, such that $p_i = p_{i-1} + \varepsilon$, where $\varepsilon > 0$. Assuming that default events are independent of each other, the *MPL* on this portfolio will materialise when default occurs on the five assets at the maximum exposure (X_i). Hence

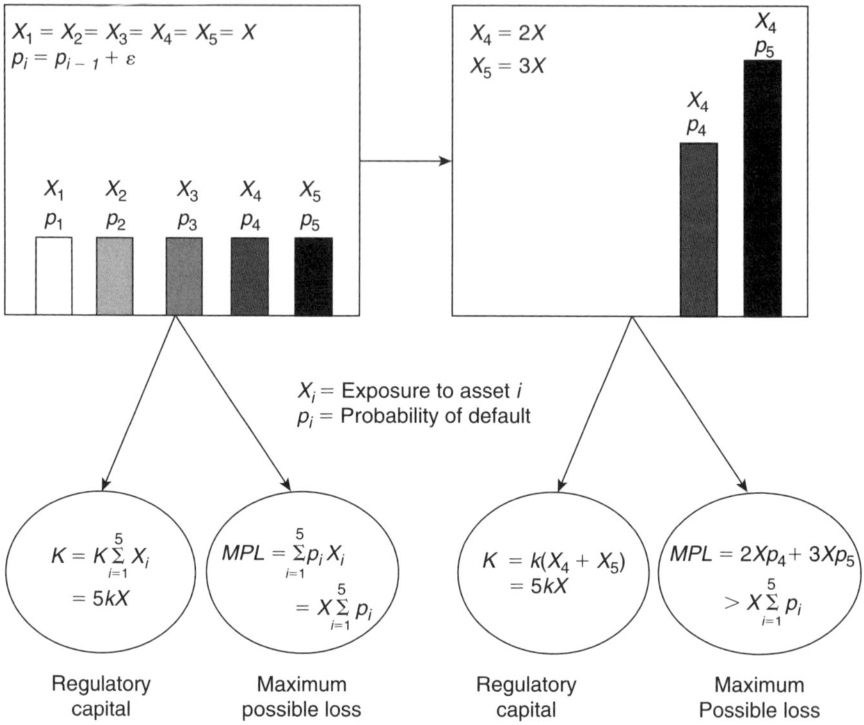

Figure 1.13 An Illustration of Regulatory Capital Arbitrage

$$MPL = \sum_{i=1}^{5} p_i X_i = X\sum_{i=1}^{5} p_i = X(5p_1 + 10\varepsilon) \tag{1.5}$$

Assuming now that there is positive risk-return trade off, which means that the bank can boost its return by moving to the more risky assets 4 and 5. By choosing a portfolio consisting of $2X$ of asset 4 and $3X$ of asset 5, the bank can obtain higher potential return at the expense of being exposed to more risk. This move, however, does not affect the size of regulatory capital because the capital charge following the restructuring of the asset portfolio is

$$K = 2kX_4 + 3kX_5 = 5kX \tag{1.6}$$

However, the bank will be exposed to more risk, because the MPL now is

$$\begin{aligned} MPL &= 2p_4X + 3p_5X = 2X(p_1 + 3\varepsilon) + 3X(p_1 + 4\varepsilon) \\ &= X(5p_1 + 18\varepsilon) > X\sum_{i=1}^{5} p_i \end{aligned} \tag{1.7}$$

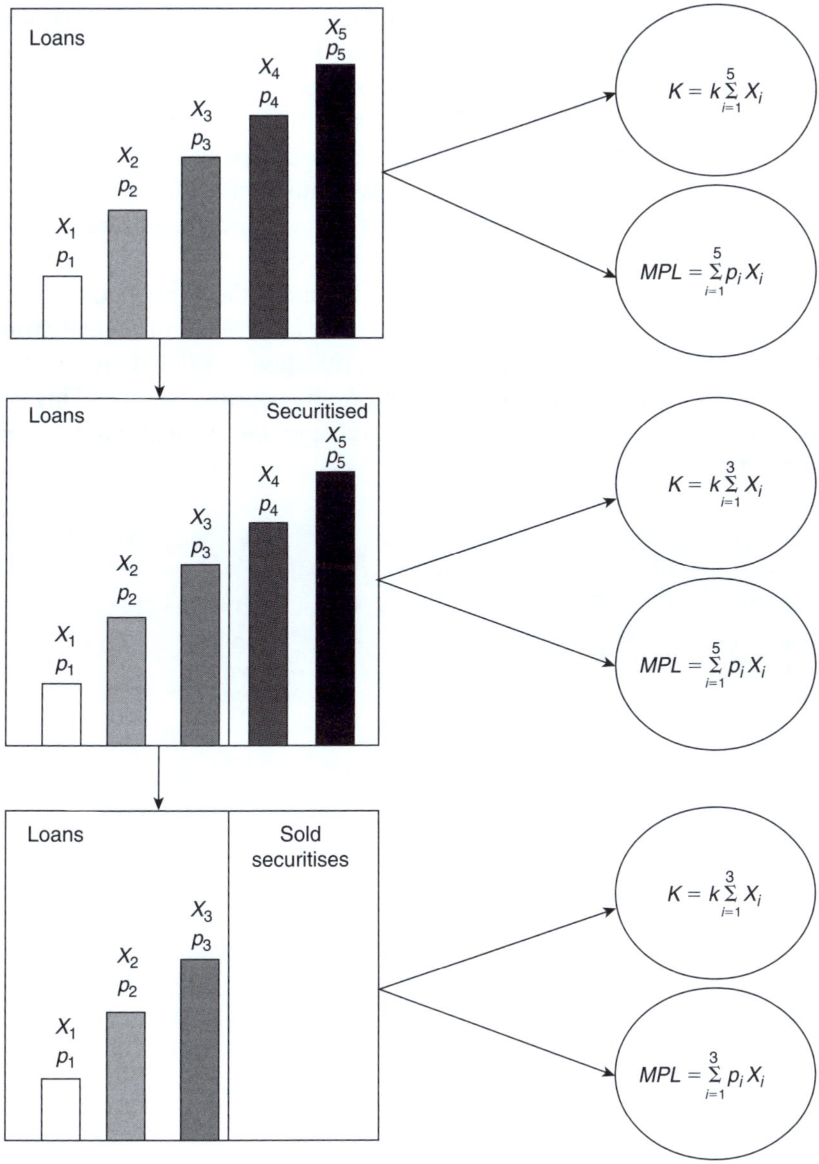

Figure 1.14 The Effect of Securitisation

By restructuring the loan portfolio in such a way as to hold more low-quality, high-yield assets, the bank in question is exposed to more risk, without having to hold more regulatory capital.

Consider now Figure 1.14, which shows the effect of securitisation. The bank starts with an asset portfolio as in the previous example. The bank then decides to securitise the cash flows resulting from assets 4 and 5. If securities, as opposed to loans, are not subject to regulatory capital requirements, the capital charge is reduced without there being any change in risk exposure if the assets are held by the bank. This is how banks managed to circumvent the Basel I regulation through securitisation. If the bank decides to sell these securities, it will reduce its exposure as well. As long as the bank does not provide loans to finance the acquisition of these securities by customers, the bank will have neither direct nor indirect exposure to these securities.

The ability of banks to securitise loans has made them more complacent about granting subprime loans, leading to the emergence of the subprime crisis. As a matter of fact, (excessive) securitisation is a failed process that has led to the operational losses resulting from subprime lending. This is a rather sombre, but valid, note to close this chapter on. We will return to this issue in Chapter 7.

CHAPTER 2

From Basel I to Basel II: A Great Leap Forward?

2.1 THE BASEL COMMITTEE

On 26 June 1974, Bankhaus Herstatt, a German bank, executed foreign exchange transactions with some New York based banks whereby Herstatt received payments in German mark but it was forced into liquidation by the German authorities before the delivery of the US dollar funds it owed to the counterparties. This happened because the exchange of cash flows to settle a foreign exchange transaction is not simultaneous (that is, one counterparty receives payment before paying the other counterparty). It was as if Herstatt had received a collateral-free loan that it subsequently defaulted on. As a result, the counterparties incurred operational losses because of exposure to a particular kind of operational risk, what has come to be known as Herstatt risk, which is one of two types of settlement risk (the other being liquidity risk).

Irrespective of whether the closure of Bankhaus Herstatt led to operational or credit losses, this event raised concern about the possibility of systemic failure caused by the failure of one bank. This is because the failure of Herstatt brought with it significant adverse implications for the foreign exchange market and banks in other countries. As a result, the Basel Committee on Banking Supervision (BCBS or the Committee) was established by the central bank governors of the Group of Ten (G10) countries to co-ordinate and strengthen banking supervision practices worldwide.

The Role and Structure of the BCBS

The Basel Committee does not have any supranational authority with respect to banking supervision, and this is why its recommendations and set standards do not have legal force, in the sense that it is up to the national authorities to implement them. Over time, the BCBS became concerned with the following: (i) defining the role of regulators in cross-jurisdictional situations; (ii) ensuring that international banks do not escape comprehensive supervision by the domestic regulatory authority; and (iii) promoting uniform capital requirements so that banks from different countries may compete with each other on a "level playing field."

As the losses incurred by some large international banks from third-world loans mounted in the late 1970s, the Committee became increasingly concerned about the potential failure of one or more of these banks and the serious adverse effects such failure could have on the international financial system in general. Fear of cross-border contagion mounted, and so did concern about the inadequate capital held by large banks in relation to the risks they were assuming, as indicated by the deteriorating capital ratios. In the 1980s, concern about capital inadequacy was particularly directed at Japanese banks, which were expanding at a rapid pace, buoyed by valuations of capital that included large amounts of unrealised capital gains on Japanese stock holdings. As a result, the BCBS began to focus on the development of international regulation with the objective of establishing and implementing higher and more uniform capital standards for banks across countries. These capital standards were introduced in 1988 as the Basel I Accord.

The BCBS met for the first time in February 1975, and since then has been meeting regularly, three or four times a year. The Committee has 12 member countries: Belgium, Canada, Germany, Italy, Japan, Luxembourg, the Netherlands, Spain, Sweden, Switzerland, the UK and the US.

The member countries are represented by their central banks as well as other banking supervision authorities (such as the Financial Services Authority (FSA) of the UK). The name "Basel Committee" comes from the fact that the Committee's secretariat is provided by the Bank for International Settlements (BIS), which is based in Basel, Switzerland, where the meetings of the Committee take place. The Committee has constituent components in the form of units that carry out various tasks, as indicated by the names of the units shown in Figure 2.1. This structure, however, was abandoned in October 2006 in favour of the present structure, which is shown in Figure 2.2.

The move to the present structure was motivated by the Committee's desire to reflect in a better way its strategic objectives, including the following: (i) promoting a strong capital foundation at banks; (ii) strengthening supervision and risk management practices in the face of rapid financial innovation; (iii) promoting understanding of the links between risk management, disclosure and accounting practices; and (iv) strengthening outreach to non-member

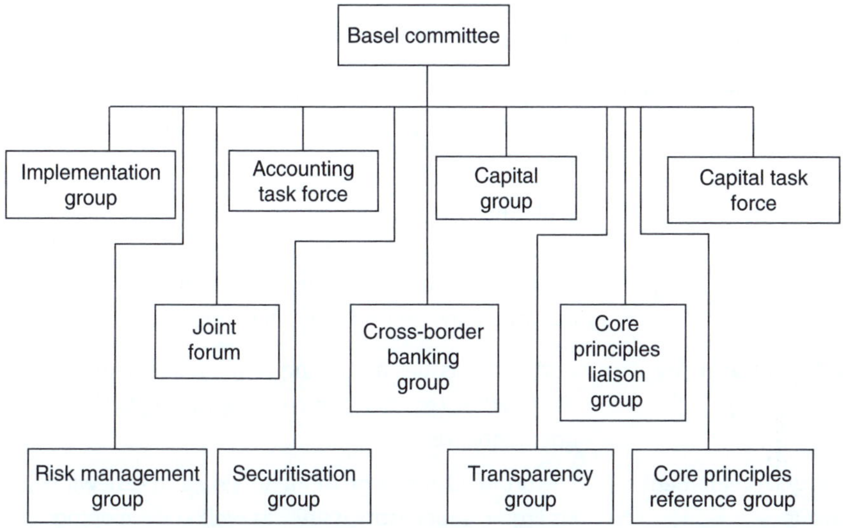

Figure 2.1 The Basel Committee's Structure (up to October 2006)

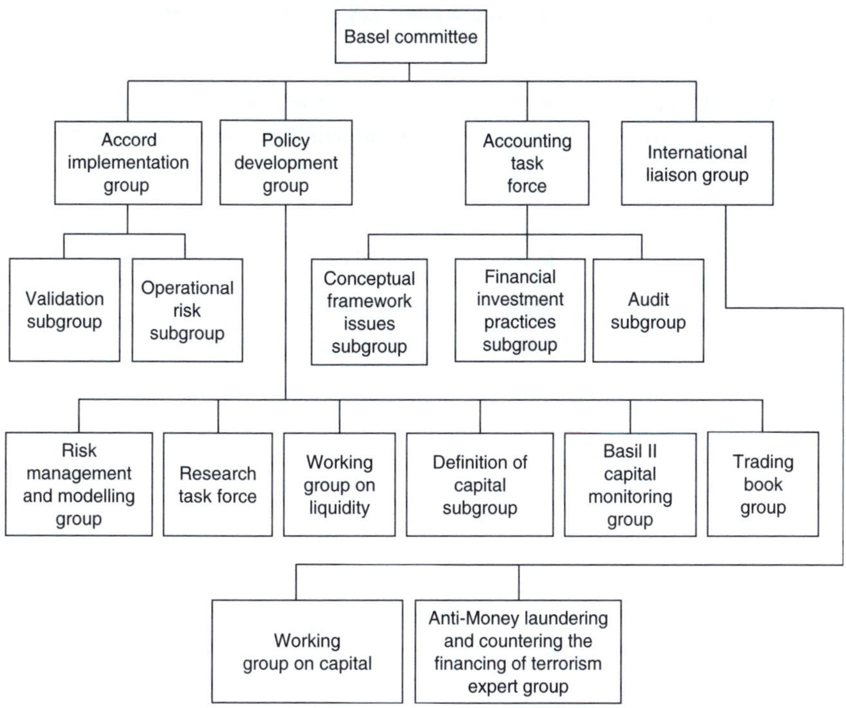

Figure 2.2 The Basel Committee's Present Structure

Table 2.1 Description of the Components of the BCBS's Present Structure

Group/Subgroup	*Description*
Accord Implementation Group (AIG)	The group is in charge of sharing information and promoting consistency in the implementation of the Basel II Accord.
■ Validation Subgroup	Exploring issues pertaining to the validation of the systems used for generating the ratings and parameters required for the implementation of the internal ratings-based approach (IRBA) to credit risk.
■ Operational Risk Subgroup	Addressing issues pertaining to the implementation of the advanced measurement approach (AMA) to operational risk.
Policy Development Group	The group is in charge of identifying and reviewing emerging supervisory issues, as well as developing policies to promote sound banking and high supervisory standards.
■ Risk Management and Modelling Group	The Committee's point of contact with the industry on the latest advances in risk measurement and management.
■ Research Task Force	A forum for research economists from member institutions to exchange information and engage in research projects.
■ Working Group on Liquidity	A forum for the exchange of information on national approaches to liquidity risk regulation and supervision.
■ Definition of Capital Subgroup	Exploring emerging trends in eligible capital instruments in member jurisdictions
■ Basel II Capital Monitoring Group	Sharing national experiences in monitoring capital requirements.
■ Trading Book Group	Addressing issues pertaining to the application of Basel II to trading activities and the treatment of double default effects.
Accounting Task Force	The task force works to ensure that international accounting and auditing standards and practices promote sound risk management in financial institutions.

Continued

Table 2.1 Continued

Conceptual Framework Issues Subgroup	Monitoring and responding to the conceptual accounting framework project of the International Accounting Standards Board.
▪ Financial Instruments Practices Subgroup	Examining the implementation of international accounting standards with respect to financial instruments and the link between accounting practices in this area and prudential supervision.
▪ Audit Subgroup	Promoting reliable financial information by exploring audit issues from a banking supervision perspective.
International Liaison Group(ILG)	The group provides a forum for deepening the Committee's engagement with supervisors around the world on a broad range of issues.
▪ ILG Working Group on Capital	Working with the AIG on the implementation of Basel II.
▪ Anti-Money Laundering and Countering the Financing of Terrorism Expert Group	Monitoring money laundering and terrorism financing issues that have a bearing on banking supervision.

countries, industry participants and other constituents. Table 2.1 provides a brief description of the components of the BCBS's present structure.

Activities of the BCBS

The BCBS has been engaged in activities that fall mainly in the areas of banking supervision and capital standards, disseminating information and research findings via its publications, which are available on the website of the Bank for International Settlements (BIS)(www.bis.org). The Committee has addressed particular issues, including supervision of banks' foreign exchange positions, management of international lending, management of off-balance sheet exposures, customer due diligence, supervision of large exposures, risk management guidelines for derivatives, loan accounting and disclosure, corporate governance, credit risk management and electronic banking. Some new work streams, which are described in Table 2.2, were initiated in the first half of 2007.

Recent work of the BCBS has been dominated by issues pertaining to the Basel II Accord. In October 2006, the BCBS released the results of a study on the range of practices dealing with the progress (or otherwise) made by

Table 2.2 New Work Streams of the BCBS

Work Stream	*Description*
Liquidity Risk	The BCBS initiated a review of jurisdictions' approaches to supervising and regulating liquidity risk. The working group on liquidity started to conduct a survey of regulatory and supervisory practices.
Definition of Capital Initiative	The BCBS has launched an initiative to review the definition of regulatory capital across jurisdictions. In its March 2007 meeting, the Committee gave its Risk Management and Modelling Group the mandate to assess the range of practices of banks' approaches to economic capital measurement and management.
Accounting and Auditing Work	The Accounting Task Force is engaged in several areas of work related to accounting and audit standards that have a potentially large impact on financial institutions.
Outreach to Non-member Countries	The BCBS continues to expand co-operation with the broader supervisory community and the industry. This has been made necessary by the rapid globalisation of banks, the pace of financial innovation and changes in risk management practices. The ILG has initiated work on the following: (i) a project to assess the range of practices and approaches to risk-based supervision; (ii) information exchange on jurisdictions' approaches to risk-based supervision; and (iii) assessing how the rapidly growing area of microfinance fits into existing supervisory frameworks.

the world's largest banks towards the development of the advanced measurement approach (AMA) to operational risk (BCBS, 2006b). While the study reported progress in adopting consistent approaches to the achievement of qualitative standards, there is much less consistency in the field of developing methods for the calculation of operational risk capital. The study found a "wide range" of practices for operational risk modelling across the industry, warning that this situation "raises the possibility that banks with similar risk profiles could hold different levels of capital under the AMA if they rely on substantially different modelling approaches and assumptions." On 7 February 2007, the BCBS released a consultative paper on the principles governing home–host supervisory co-operation and allocation mechanisms with respect to the AMA (BCBS, 2007a). And in November 2007, the BCBS (2007b) published the final paper on these principles. These papers will be discussed later on, as recent developments pertaining to the implementation of Basel II.

The failure of Northern Rock in September 2007 was triggered not by insolvency but by the lack of liquidity. This is why Moosa (2008a) argues that the subprime crisis, the root cause of the failure of Northern Rock, provides a lesson for regulators emphasising capital adequacy as enshrined in the Basel Accords. Northern Rock experienced a run on its deposits not because it was insolvent but because it was illiquid, having for a long time operated with a significant gap between loans and deposits (the so-called funding gap). Allen (2008) argues that banks should take liquidity risk into account in their economic capital calculations, which is contrary to the recommendation of the Institute of International Finance (IIF) (2007) that "regulatory and economic capital should not be directly tied to funding liquidity risk." This had probably initiated the publication in February 2008 of a report on liquidity risk (BCBS, 2008). The report was admittedly initiated by "the market turmoil that began in mid-2007" (meaning the subprime crisis), which "has highlighted the crucial importance of market liquidity to the banking sector." The report highlights financial market developments that affect liquidity risk management, discusses national supervisory regimes and outlines the initial observations on the stress caused by the subprime crisis.

Criticism of the BCBS

The Basel Committee, its structure and its work have not escaped criticism from academics, practitioners and even politicians from various countries. Most of the criticism is directed at the Committee's "products," the Basel Accords, which we will deal with later in this chapter. Here, we discuss on the criticisms directed at the Committee itself.

Howard Davies (2005), the former chief of the UK's Financial services authority (FSA), criticises several aspects of the composition and working of the Basel Committee, which he describes as "a self appointed group of supervisors and central bankers from industrialized countries, with heavy domination from Europe, at least numerically." He finds it rather difficult to justify this representation, particularly the exclusion of Australia, which has internationally active banks, presumably the main target of the Basel II Accord. Therefore, he suggests a reconsideration of the composition of the Committee. Citing Leyshon (1994) and Underhill (1991), Power (2005) sounds as if he believes that there is some sort of Anglo-American bias in the Committee when he argues that setting the capital adequacy ratio at 8% initially favoured the interest of the Anglo-American banks at the expense of German and Japanese banks.

But it is not only the membership of the Committee that Howard Davies (2005) criticises, as he also casts doubt on the accountability of the Committee, which he describes as being "anachronistic." The Committee reports to the governors of the central banks of the G10 countries, but some of these central banks do not act as bank supervisors in their own countries. For example, the supervisor in the UK is the FSA, not the Bank of England, whereas other central banks share the responsibility with other supervisors (e.g., the Federal Reserve System is one of the four banking supervisors in the US).

Pezier (2003a) wonders why it is that the BCBS is in a privileged position to carry out the task of promoting knowledge about risk management when banks and other institutions (such as universities and professional bodies) strive to carry out research aiming at promoting knowledge in this field. This is the same line of reasoning put forward by the critics of the International Monetary Fund (including the present author). In effect, therefore, Pezier casts doubt on the very viability (in terms of costs and benefits) of the BCBS. Some bankers having to implement the Basel II Accord often complain by saying "who are they [the BCBS] to tell us what to do?"

2.2 THE BASEL I ACCORD

In 1988, the BCBS established a global standard for measuring capital adequacy for banks, which has come to be known as the Basel I Accord (also known as the 1988 Accord). According to Santos (2001), Basel I has made an important contribution to the prominence of bank regulation. The objectives of Basel I were the following: (i) to establish a more "level playing field" for international competition among banks; and (ii) to reduce the probability that such competition would lead to bidding down of capital ratios to excessively low levels.

Allen (2004) describes the Basel I Accord as being "revolutionary in that it sought to develop a single risk-adjusted capital standard that would be applied throughout the major banking countries of the world." She describes the "level playing field" as a conduit to the "best practices to be adopted by banks throughout the world, thereby enhancing efficiency, productivity, safety and soundness of the global financial system." Keeton (1989) attributes the adoption of Basel I by a large number of countries over a relatively short period of time to the desire to enhance the safety and soundness of the banking system by encouraging safe banks to grow faster and risky banks to grow more slowly.

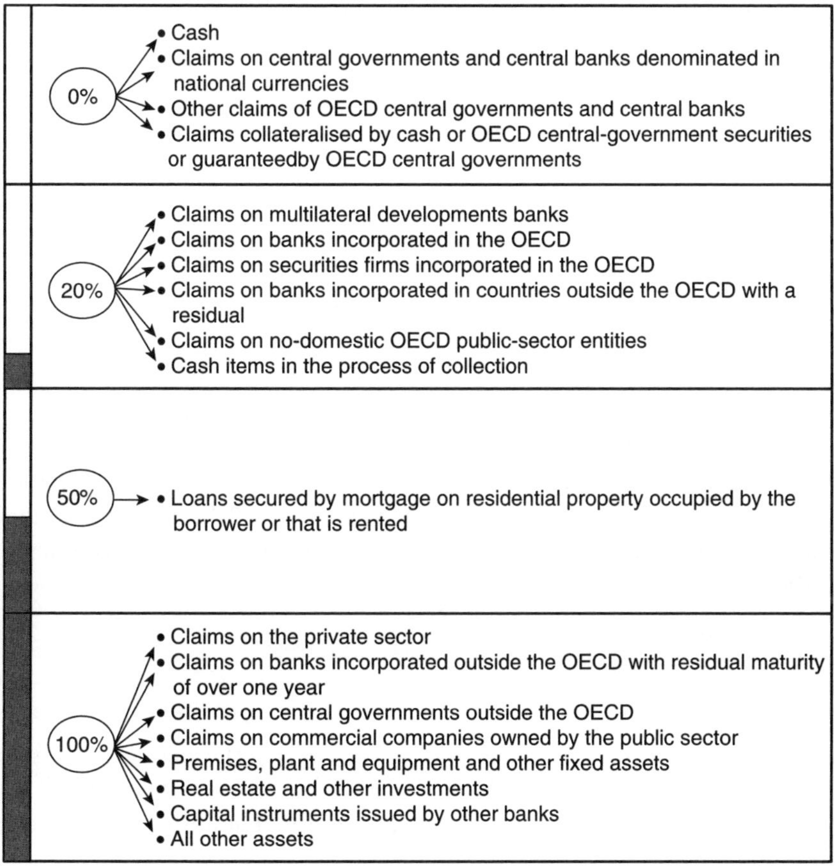

Figure 2.3 Risk-Based Weights under Basel I

The Capital Ratio under Basel I

The most important feature of Basel I is the provision that a bank must hold capital that varies according to the perceived credit risk of the bank's loan portfolio. Before that, regulators had focused on simple leverage ratios calculated by using total assets as the base (that is, the assets are not adjusted for risk). Under Basel I, individual assets are divided into four basic credit risk categories, according to the creditworthiness of the counterparty, and each category is assigned a weight ranging from 0 (risk-free assets) to 100% (most risky assets). Banks are required to hold as capital an amount of no less than 8% of their risk-weighted assets. Figure 2.3 shows the risk-based weights assigned to assets under Basel I. The capital ratio, k, can be calculated as

$$k = \frac{K}{CR} \geq 0.08 \tag{2.1}$$

where K is the amount of capital held and CR is a measure of credit risk proxied by the weighted value of assets (loans). CR is calculated as

$$CR = \sum_{i}^{n} w_i A_i \tag{2.2}$$

where w_i is the weight assigned to asset i and A_i the value of asset (or asset class) i, such that $0 \leq w_i \leq 1$.

While the Basel I Accord was primarily concerned with credit risk, the BCBS amended the Accord in 1996 to incorporate the market risk arising from open foreign exchange positions, traded debt securities, equities, commodities and options. That was in effect the introduction of regulatory capital against market risk. One important implication of this amendment was that banks were allowed to use internal value at risk (VAR) models to measure the required capital as an alternative to a standardised measurement method. As a result, the capital ratio was amended to the following:

$$k = \frac{K}{CR + MR} \geq 0.08 \tag{2.3}$$

where MR is market risk measured as VAR at a certain confidence interval and time period. Basel I, therefore, did not recognise operational risk, as there is no measure of operational risk in the denominator of the capital ratio.

The 1996 amendment, which went into effect in 1998, allowed banks to use either a regulatory building block VAR measure or their own internal VAR measures to calculate regulatory capital. The use of own models was subject to the approval of the regulators, which would be granted only if the regulators were satisfied that the underlying bank had a sound risk management system. An acceptable VAR model should allow the calculation of a 10-day, 99% VAR and should be able to handle the non-linear exposure resulting from positions on options. Diversification effects would only be recognised within broad asset categories but not across the categories.

A Critique of Basel I

The Basel I Accord has been criticised as having significant shortcomings. The following is a summary of the criticisms that can be found in the literature and the media, and which this author may or may not agree with. The stance taken by this author will become clear later on in this book. Irrespective of the details, this author is not enthusiastic about capital-based regulation.

To start with, Basel I is typically criticized as having very limited sensitivity to risk, giving rise to a gap between regulatory capital, as assigned by the regulators, and economic capital as required by market forces. Moreover, lack of risk sensitivity results from the classification of assets with diverse credit risk under the same asset class, which is conducive to regulatory capital arbitrage as we saw from the example presented at the end of Chapter 1. Failure to differentiate between high-quality and low-quality credits within a particular asset class (such as commercial and industrial credit) contributed to a steady increase in the credit risk of bank loan portfolios. The formula that is used to calculate regulatory capital against credit risk is relatively simple, treating all banks in the same manner.

Another adverse feature of the Basel I Accord is the arbitrary way whereby risk classes and weights (shown in Figure 2.3) are determined, which means that the resulting risk-based capital requirements are neither realistic nor useful. Furthermore, adding up the credit risks of individual assets ignores the gains from diversification across less-than-perfectly correlated assets. As a result, the calculated regulatory capital turns out to be higher than what it would be if correlation is taken into account. In the example on regulatory capital arbitrage presented in Chapter 1, the correlation factor was not considered only for the sake of simplicity, and this is why the maximum possible loss (MPL) was calculated. While this assumption would not make a difference for the conclusion derived from the example, it would lead to overestimation of the capital charge against credit risk. This is because the MPL is calculated on the basis of unconditional probabilities when correlations are not taken into account; otherwise conditional probabilities are used instead.

Allen (2004) argues that while the Basel I Accord produced many successes it also revealed several important failures and unintended consequences. Apart from regulatory capital arbitrage, which she describes as the product of loopholes in regulation, she suggests that the initial exclusion of market risk from capital requirements and high regulatory costs induced banks to shift their risk exposure (via securitisation) from priced credit risk to unpriced market risk. This practice led to the elimination of high-quality loans from the balance sheets and left banks with low-quality loans on their books (which is a major reason for the materialisation of the subprime crisis in 2007). This, however, can be the case only if high-quality loans, rather than low-quality loans, are securitised. Remember that prior to the implementation of the 1996 amendment in 1998, Basel I did not have provisions for market risk (hence, it was "unpriced").

Another shortcoming of Basel I is that it completely ignores operational risk. This sounds odd when it has become a consensus view that operational risk can be more detrimental to the wellbeing of a bank or any business firm for that matter. Moreover, the Accord gives very limited attention to credit risk mitigation despite the remarkable growth in credit derivatives as a risk management tool. This means that two banks with loan portfolios of similar risk characteristics are required to hold the same regulatory capital although one of them has a lower risk exposure resulting from the use of credit derivatives for hedging purposes. Furthermore, Allen (2004) argues that Basel I did not have the provisions to measure credit risk in the mortgage market adequately, creating disincentives for banks to purchase mortgage insurance and encouraging the issuance of uninsured mortgages. In general, Basel I ignores the risk management process and risk mitigation tools.

The introduction of Basel I has led to the emergence of a strand of research dealing with the controversial issue of the effect of introducing regulatory capital requirements on the risk and profitability of banks (hence evaluating Basel I as a form of banking regulation). While these issues are equally relevant (and the arguments are equally valid) for the Basel II Accord, the discussion here is presented in relation to Basel I only.

Avery and Berger (1991) concluded that the introduction of risk-based capital requirements would set higher capital standards for large banks than for small banks. While Avery and Berger find an inverse relation between risk-based capital requirements and bank risk taking, Furlong and Keeley (1989), Gennotte and Pyle (1991), Keeley (1980) and Keeley and Furlong (1990) show that capital regulations may boost risk by encouraging banks to seek out more risky activities. Rochet (1992) found that capital regulations can limit bank risk taking for risk averse (as opposed to risk neutral) banks only. Thakor (1996) found that higher capital requirements raise the risk exposure of the banking sector, but Flannery (1989) used an option–theoretic model to show that risk-based capital requirements (such as those prescribed by Basel I) encourage a bank to invest in less risky individual assets but more risky portfolios. Allen (2004) explains this apparent contradiction in that capital regulations do not incorporate correlations adequately, which means that banks can reduce their capital requirements if they invest in highly correlated, relatively low-risk individual assets.

Further studies of the effect of capital regulation on bank profitability have been carried out by Allen and Jagtiani (1997), Allen et al (1996), Bikker and Hu (2002), Blum (1999), Greenspan (1998), Hovakimian and Kane (2000), Rime (2000) and Wall and Peterson (1995). Blum (1999) used a dynamic model to demonstrate that capital regulation like Basel I may reduce bank profitability, which induces banks to take on more risk to boost profitability. Bikker and Hu (2002) used an international sample of banks in 26 developing and developed countries to find that the profit margin on high risk loans is relatively small, suggesting that the additional costs and losses of these risky loans are not covered sufficiently by higher credit spreads.

Allen and Jagtiani (1997) found that the introduction of Basel I led to higher exposure to the systematic market risk of US banks, which at the same time limited their interest rate exposure. Wall and Peterson (1995) tested banks' responses to the introduction of Basel I, concluding that banks considered themselves well capitalised in 1989 and that Basel I meant increasing capital levels over and above their private targets. Rime (2000) found that Basel I induced Swiss banks to boost their capital levels but not to reduce risk exposure. Hovakimian and Kane (2000) found evidence supporting the proposition that capital regulation over the period 1985–1994 did not deter banks from shifting risk onto the public safety net by exploiting the deposit insurance scheme.

Allen et al (1996) supported the proposition that Basel I has perverse risk-taking incentives by showing that the implementation of the Accord encouraged banks to switch from priced credit risk exposure to unpriced interest rate risk exposure, concluding that it was unclear whether Basel I led to a higher or lower level of overall risk exposure of US banks. A more precise proposition had been put forward by Calem and Rob (1996) who found that the relation between risk and capital requirements is a U-shaped function of the initial capital position. Greenspan (1998) notes that Basel I has been successful in raising bank capital levels but not necessarily in controlling bank insolvency risk.

Acharya (2000) casts doubt on the usefulness of the international harmonisation of capital adequacy regulation as enshrined in the Basel I Accord. By using a model of "optimal regulation," he shows that when capital standards are harmonised across countries that have different rescue policies, the presence of international banks leads to a spill over effect from the country with a more forbearing policy to the other country. This, he argues, would boost the vulnerability of banks in the latter, forcing the authorities in that country to adopt a more forbearing policy. The outcome is a "regression to the worst regulation."

A good summary of the problems of Basel I is presented by Palia and Porter (2003) under what they call the "seven sins," which are the following (some of them have been mentioned in the discussion so far):

- The categories of bank assets (loans) are so broadly defined that they are not suitable for micromanaging credit risk and provide incentives for regulatory arbitrage.
- Inconsistency with respect to the definition of capital from one country to another.
- No justification is provided for the 8% capital ratio (why not 7% or 9%?). As stated earlier in this chapter, Leyshon (1994) and Underhill (1991) believe that the 8% capital adequacy ratio favoured Anglo-American banks at the expense of German banks (which typically operated with much higher ratios) and Japanese banks (which were required to reduce assets to comply).

- The assumption that equity is better capital than debt.
- No capital accord by itself can achieve the objective of levelling the playing field for international competition.
- The Accord does not consider the potential of risk reduction through diversification.
- The underlying rules are too simplistic and rigid to govern the complex world of banking, particularly off-balance sheet activity (the Accord focused on the traditional lending activity).

Apart from the criticism directed at Basel I, the principal motivation for the desire to upgrade the Accord was that it had become outdated as the banking system was becoming increasingly more complex with the emergence of new risks and opportunities. Furthermore, some banks have learned how to "play" the system, particularly in international banking. However, Benink and Wihlborg (2002) argue that there is no way to design any set of regulation in such a way as to eliminate all possibilities to "game the system."

In general, changes in the banking environment were the driving force behind the need for a new accord on capital adequacy. Many aspects of the banking environment are relevant here, including greater use of automated technology, emergence of e-commerce, tendency of banks to act as large-volume service providers, use of market and credit risk mitigation techniques (which may produce other kinds of risk), outsourcing arrangements and participation in clearing and settlement systems. As a result of these developments, a new Accord was born following a process that started in the late 1990s. Allen (2004) attributes the move to Basel II to "compromises in Basel I," as the new Accord is designed to "address the original regulations' unintended consequences." Whether or not Basel II has the provisions to plug the loopholes in Basel I is a debatable topic.

2.3 THE BASEL II ACCORD

In response to the criticism of the Basel I Accord and to address changes in the banking environment that the 1988 Accord could not deal with effectively, the BCBS decided to create a new capital Accord, Basel II. The new Accord was intended to deal with market innovations and a fundamental shift towards more complexity in the banking industry and to narrow the gap between regulatory capital and economic capital. In this section, the pluses of the Basel II Accord are discussed, leaving the minuses to a subsequent section in which a detailed critique of the Accord is presented.

Progress Towards Basel II

Following the publication of the first round of proposals for revising the capital adequacy framework in November 1999 (BCBS, 1999), the BCBS subsequently released additional proposals in January 2001 and April 2003 (Consultative Papers 2 and 3; BCBS, 2001a, 2003c) and conducted quantitative impact studies (QISs) pertaining to these proposals. This consultation process has resulted in the revised framework that was published in June 2004 (BCBS, 2004). Revised frameworks appeared in November 2005 and June 2006 (BCBS, 2005; 2006a).

On 7 February 2007, the BCBS released a consultative document on the principles for home–host supervisory co-operation and allocation mechanisms in the context of the AMA (BCBS, 2007a). The paper was open for comments until 18 April 2007. In November 2007, the Committee released the final paper (BCBS, 2007b) that discusses home-host supervisory co-operation (particularly the general principles for information sharing) as well as the hybrid AMA allocation mechanism. This issue is important because internationally active banks with cross-border presence should be supervised on a consolidated basis. While supervisors are responsible for the supervision of banking operations in their respective jurisdictions, the assessment and approval of the AMA in internationally active banks require an enhanced level of information sharing between the home and host supervisors. The document asserts that irrespective of the operational risk approach adopted by a subsidiary, it is essential that the local management and board of directors of the subsidiary understand and manage the subsidiary's operational risk and ensure that it is capitalised adequately.

In May 2007, the Basel Committee announced that "the implementation of the Basel II Accord continues to move forward around the globe" and that "a significant number of countries and banks already implemented the standardised and foundation approaches as of the beginning of this year." Furthermore, the Committee announced that the necessary infrastructure (legislation, regulation, supervisory guidance, etc.) to implement Basel II is "either in place or in process," which would "allow a growing number of countries to proceed with the implementation of Basel II's advanced approaches in 2008 and 2009" (BCBS, 2007c).

Presumably, Basel II "went live" in 2007 when the simpler approaches became available for banks. In 2008 the advanced approaches became available to qualifying banks. From 2007 to 2009 banks would be expected to make parallel calculations using both the Basel I and Basel II Accords to ensure that regulatory capital requirements do not decline too steeply. This would be a rather confusing and time-consuming endeavour that may prove to be of little value in practice. There is no doubt, however, that the banking industry has been changing as a result of Basel II. Krall (2008) presents the findings of a survey conducted in 2004/2005 on the operational and strategic implications of Basel II. For example, the survey revealed that Basel II has triggered a substantial wave of investment in risk management systems. The problem is that this means nothing if it is done only for the purpose of regulatory compliance.

What is New about Basel II?

Comparing Basel II with Basel I, Howard Davies (2005) points out that "the contrast between the two accords is indeed marked." Caruana (2005) argues that "Basel II represents a significant step towards achieving more comprehensive and risk-sensitive approach to banking supervision." He also argues that while much of the public attention that has been focused on Basel II pertains to the actual calculations of capital, it is important to understand that the Accord is about more than quantitative minimum capital requirements. He further points out that Basel II represents "an unparalleled opportunity for banks to improve their capital strategies and risk management systems," and that "it also provides supervisors with an opportunity to improve their ability to identify banking risk and to enhance the dialogue with the industry and with each other." Duebel (2002) views favourably the Basel II proposals regarding market discipline, enhanced transparency of financial reporting, and the flexible wielding of regulatory oversight. Le Pan (2008) suggests that "a few years from now, we will be able to conclude that Basel II contributed to internationally active banks." It is not clear at all what this means, but it may be taken to mean that Basel II discriminates against internationally inactive banks, which is nothing to be proud of.

While retaining the key elements of the Basel I Accord, including the general requirement that banks ought to hold total capital equivalent to at least 8% of their risk-weighted assets, Basel II provides a range of options for determining the capital requirements, allowing banks to use approaches that are most appropriate for their operations. Because Basel II considers operational risk as well as credit risk and market risk, the capital ratio formula becomes:

$$k = \frac{K}{CR + MR + OR} \geq 0.08 \tag{2.4}$$

where *OR* is operational risk measured as (the operational) VAR with a 99.9% confidence level.

Arguably, the Basel II Accord includes a more sophisticated measurement framework for evaluating capital adequacy in banks. Furthermore, it is not only about capital adequacy, because it is designed to improve risk management in the finance industry by providing the correct incentives for better corporate governance and fostering transparency. Unlike Basel I, Basel II assigns explicit weights to operational risk and is more risk-sensitive. Finally, a proclaimed significant innovation of the Basel II Accord is the greater use of internal models for risk assessment and the calculation of regulatory capital. The Accord provides a range of options for determining the capital requirements for credit risk and operational risk. It has also been suggested that Basel II would lead to lower capital requirements across all institutions. For example, Carpenter et al (2001) used Moody's data on US firms to demonstrate that capital requirements would be lower under Basel II. If this is the case, then banks should hold less capital against credit risk and market risk than under Basel I. It is not clear how this would be accomplished, except perhaps by manipulating the internal models used to calculate capital charges. This view will be put more forcefully in Chapter 4.

Allen (2004) points out that Basel II proposes fairly strict tests to ascertain whether a "clean break" has been made before the assets can be removed from the originating bank's balance sheet for the sake of capital regulation, which is an anti-regulatory arbitrage measure. A clean break requires the following: (i) the transferred assets have been legally separated from the originating banks so that they are beyond the reach of the bank's creditors in the event of bankruptcy; (ii) the assets underlying asset-backed securities (ABS) are placed into a special-purpose vehicle; and (iii) the originating bank has neither direct nor indirect control over the assets transferred into the special-purpose vehicle.

Despite all of these proclaimed benefits of Basel II, the Accord has been subject to a barrage of criticism from academics, practitioners and even regulators, some of whom have said that the Accord might blow up two European banking systems (The Economist, 2006), whereas some bankers think that it is complex and dangerous (Centre for the Study of Financial Innovation, 2002). Before embarking on a critique of Basel II, we present a description of the three pillars of the Accord.

2.4 THE PILLARS OF BASEL II

The Basel II Accord has been introduced to circumvent the shortcomings of Basel I and accomplish the following objectives: (i) promoting the safety and soundness of the financial system; (ii) enhancing competitive equality; (iii) establishing a more comprehensive approach to risk; and (iv) equating economic capital and regulatory capital (by allowing banks to use their internal models), which would eliminate incentives for regulatory capital arbitrage. Unlike the Basel I Accord, which had one pillar (minimum capital requirements or capital adequacy), the Basel II Accord has three pillars: (i) minimum regulatory capital requirements; (ii) the supervisory review process; and (iii) market discipline through disclosure requirements. Pillar 1 deals with the calculation of regulatory capital against credit risk, market risk and operational risk. The three pillars are designed to achieve the objectives of the Accord, as shown in Figure 2.4. These pillars will be discussed in turn.

Pillar 1: Credit Risk

Calculating capital requirements for credit risk can be based on the standardised approach (STA) and the internal ratings-based approach (IRBA). The latter may be one of two versions: the foundation IRBA and the advanced IRBA. The STA is structurally similar to what is found in the 1988 Accord. Banks

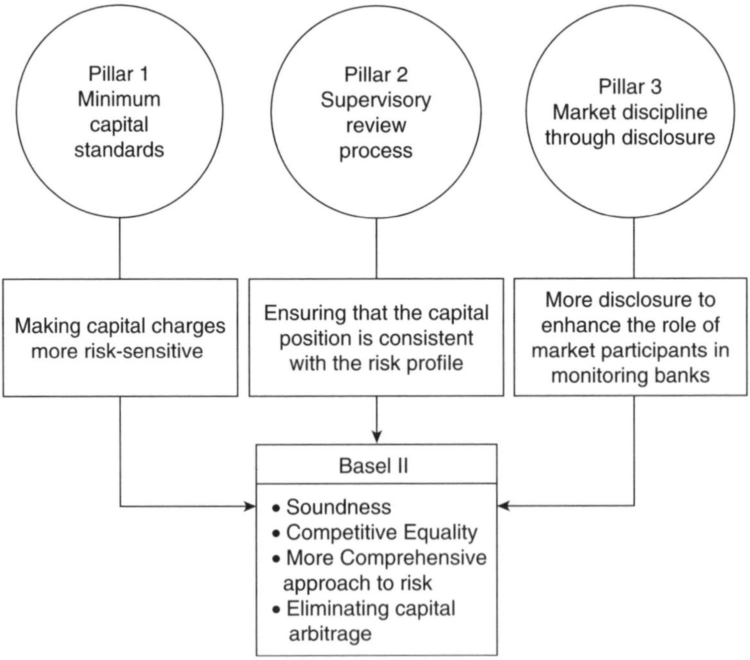

Figure 2.4 The Three Pillars and Objectives of Basel II

are required to classify their exposures into broad categories, such as the loans they have extended to corporate and sovereign borrowers and other banks. An (alleged) improvement over the 1988 Accord is aligning risk weights with a borrower's creditworthiness as indicated by external rating, provided that rating is determined by a rating agency. The use of the word "alleged" here is motivated by doubt about the ability of the rating agencies to rate assets correctly. In 2007 there was an outcry that the rating agencies are in part responsible for the subprime crisis (see e.g., Moosa, 2008a).

The IRBA goes further than the STA. Subject to certain minimum conditions and disclosure requirements, banks that have received supervisory approval to use the IRBA may rely on their own internal estimates of credit risk to determine the capital requirement for a given exposure. The internal models are designed to estimate or predict the constituent components of credit risk: probability of default (*PD*), loss given default (*LGD*) and exposure at default (*EAD*). The product of these components is the expected loss (*EL*), as shown in Figure 2.5. *PD*, *LGD* and *EAD* are alternatively known as expected default frequency, loss severity and usage given default, respectively.

The difference between the foundation IRBA and the advanced IRBA is straightforward. In the foundation approach, banks compute their own *PD* for individual loans but use the values for *LGD* provided by regulators. In the advanced IRBA, on the other hand, banks are permitted to determine own values for both *PD* and *LGD*. The BCBS (2006c) describes the so-called "use test," which pertains to the internal employment by a bank of the estimates of *PD*, *LGD* and *EAD*. An objective of the use test is to ensure that these estimates are used in the risk management process and not only for calculating regulatory capital.

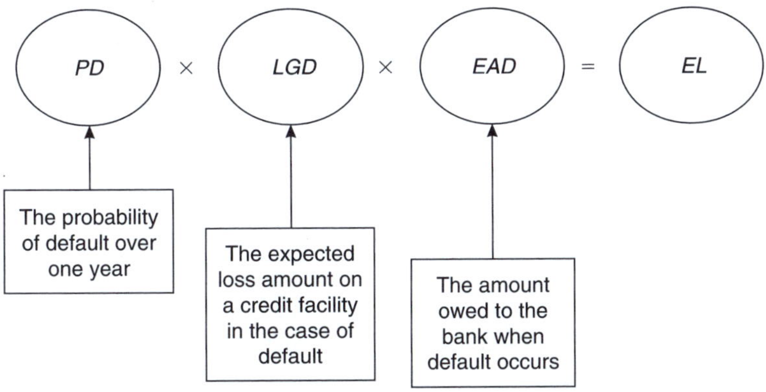

Figure 2.5 Components of Credit Risk

Pillar 1: Market Risk

Two approaches are used to measure market risk: the STA and the internal models approach. To be eligible for the use of internal models, a bank must satisfy certain conditions pertaining to the adequacy of the risk management system, as well as guidelines and rules for specifying an appropriate set of risk factors, stress testing and external oversight of the use of models.

In the STA, regulatory capital is measured as a fixed percentage of the value of a position, depending on certain rules for the classification and calculation of gross and net positions. The incentive for banks to use the internal models approach, which relies on the (VAR) models developed by the banks themselves, is that it produces lower capital charges. A bank can only use internal models after the supervisory authority has approved it. However, it is not clear at all why a VAR model would produce a capital charge that is lower than that produced by a formula relating the capital charge to the value of a position. The only possible explanation is that the underlying VAR model can be manipulated in various ways to produce a lower capital charge than what is produced by a rigid formula. The implied subjectivity of the internal models methodology can hardly be a reason for celebrating this aspect of Basel II.

Pillar 1: Operational Risk

The BCBS initiated work on operational risk for the first time in September 1998 when it published the results of an informal survey on the operational risk exposure in various types of banking activities (BCBS, 1998). The Basel II Accord suggests three methods for calculating operational risk capital charges: (i) the basic indicators approach (BIA); (ii) the STA; and (iii) the AMA. As banks become more "sophisticated," they are encouraged to move along the spectrum of available approaches. The underlying hypothesis here is that the use of "sophisticated" approaches to the calculation of regulatory capital should result in lower operational risk minimum regulatory capital. It is also suggested that, by providing a range of approaches, the Basel Committee sought to allow a bank to select the most appropriate procedure for its size, the complexity of its operations and the nature of the risk the bank is exposed to.

Again, it is not clear why the regulatory capital charge will decline as banks move along the "spectrum of sophistication." In Appendix 2.1, we demonstrate the conditions under which the STA produces lower capital charges than the BIA. The proposition that the AMA leads to lower capital charges than the other two approaches will be examined in Chapter 4. Suggesting different approaches for banks of different sizes is a troublesome feature of Basel II, which may be taken by small banks to imply favouritism for large banks and vice versa.

The BIA is designed for small domestic banks. According to Basel II, banks must hold capital for operational risk that is equal to the average of the previous three years of a fixed percentage (α) of positive annual gross income. This means that regulatory capital, *K*, is calculated by using the formula

$$K = \frac{\alpha \sum_{i=1}^{n} y_i}{n} \tag{2.5}$$

where *y* is positive gross income over the previous three years and *n* is the number of the previous three years for which gross income is positive. The fraction α is set by the Basel Committee at 15%. For the purpose of estimating *K*, the Committee defines gross income as net interest income plus net non-interest income as determined by the national supervisors and/or national accounting standards.

Accepting the proposition that some activities are more exposed than others to operational risk, the BCBS divides banks' activities into eight business lines. The gross income generated from a particular business line is taken to be a proxy for the scale of the business operation and hence a likely measure of the extent of operational risk (as in the BIA). The capital charge for each business line is calculated by multiplying the gross income of the business line by a factor (β) that is assigned (by the BCBS) to each business line. The total capital charge is calculated as a three-year average of the simple sum of capital charges of individual business lines in each year. Hence

$$K = \frac{\sum_{t=1}^{3} \max[\sum_{j=1}^{8} \beta_j y_j, 0]}{3} \tag{2.6}$$

Figure 2.6 displays the betas assigned to the eight business lines, whereas Figure 2.7 shows examples of the activities involved in each business line. The eight business lines may be classified under three business units: (i) investment banking, which encompasses corporate finance (CF) and trading and sales (TS); (ii) banking, which covers retail banking, commercial banking, and payment and settlement; and (iii) others, including retail brokerage (RB) and asset management (AM). The term "banking" covers the commercial banking functions, whereas the other functions are traditionally performed by non-bank financial intermediaries. It seems, therefore, that this classification of business lines is designed for "total" or "broad" or "universal" banking.

Figure 2.6 The Betas Assigned to Business Lines

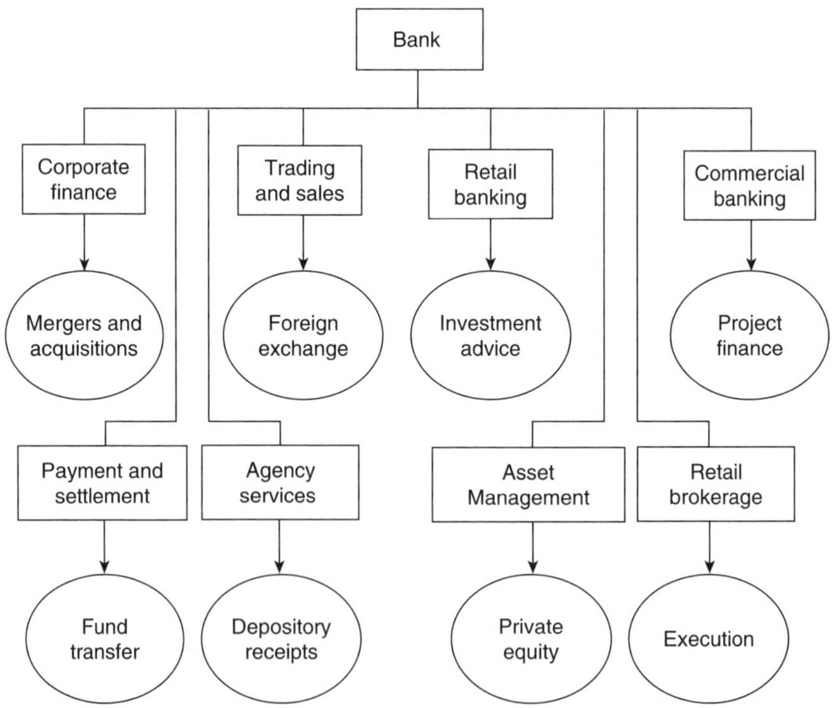

Figure 2.7 The BCBS Business Lines with Examples

One problem with the BCBS's classification of business lines is that it is too rigid and standardised, creating problems in practice. For example, one of the main problems encountered in the US 2004 loss data selection exercise (Federal Reserve System et al, 2005) is the problem of mapping actual loss events to those categories. In that study, mappings were completed using public information, such as business line descriptions in annual reports and guidance provided by those who are familiar with the structure of participating institutions. Even with this information, loss data did not necessarily map on a one-to-one basis to the BCBS's business lines, either because institutions did not apportion losses across business lines or because information was not sufficient to complete the mapping. Indicative of the severity of this problem is that 70.8% of the total loss amount was placed under "unclassified," and only 29.2% was mapped to the Basel business lines (see Federal Reserve System et al, 2005, Table 4).

A slight modification of the STA produces what is known as the alternative STA, which is similar to the STA except that the capital charges for retail banking and commercial banking are calculated in different ways. Instead of using gross income as the exposure indicator, the value of loans and advances is used for this purpose. Thus, gross income is replaced by a figure that amounts to 0.035 times the value of loans and advances, which gives

$$K_{RB} = 0.035\beta_{RB}L_{RB} \tag{2.7}$$

where K_{RB} is the capital charge against retail banking, β_{RB} is the beta assigned to retail banking (0.12) and L_{RB} is the total outstanding loans and advances averaged over the previous three years. Likewise, the capital charge for commercial banking is calculated as

$$K_{CB} = 0.035\beta_{CB}L_{CB} \tag{2.8}$$

where the subscript CB refers to commercial banking. Supervisors may allow the use of the alternative STA if it provides an improved basis for the calculation of the capital charge. Laker (2008) puts forward an Australian point of view with respect to the use of the alternative STA in preference to the STA, arguing that the use of gross income as a risk indicator "would produce wide variations in outcomes that cannot be tied readily to differences in operational risk." In general, alternative measures of exposure to operational risk have been suggested as shown in Figure 2.8 (see, e.g., Tinca, 2007).

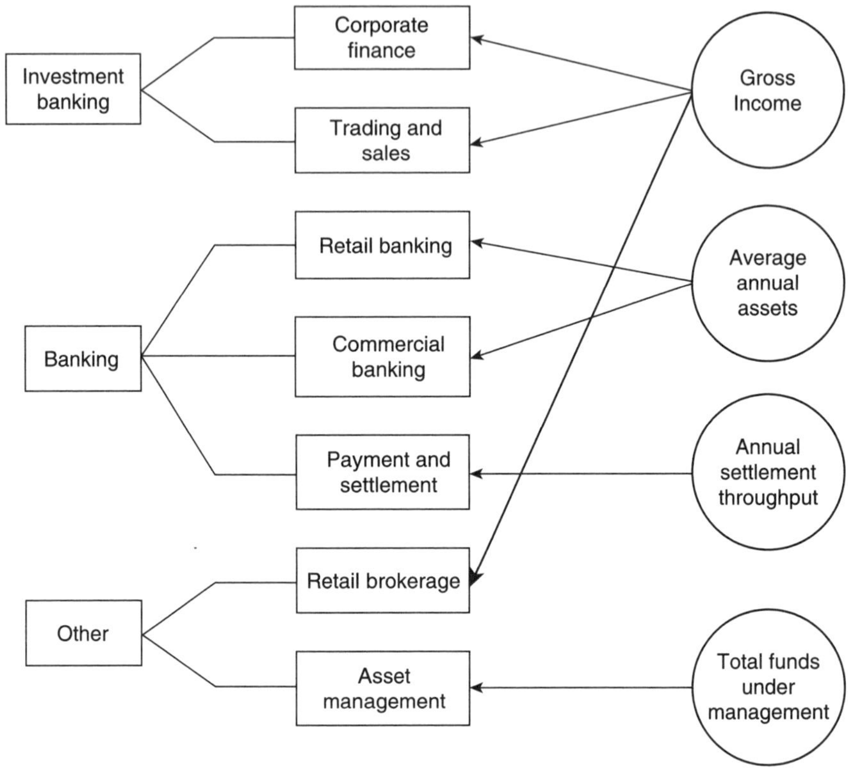

Figure 2.8 Alternative Measures of Exposure to Operational Risk by Business Line

According to the AMA, regulatory capital is calculated by using the bank's internal operational risk models. The Basel II Accord allows three alternative approaches under the AMA: (i) the loss distribution approach (LDA); (ii) the scenario-based approach (SBA); and (iii) the scorecard approach (SCA), which is also called the risk drivers and controls approach (RDCA). An alternative version of the LDA is the internal measurement approach (IMA), which is equivalent to the IRBA used to evaluate credit risk.

For some reason, the IMA has disappeared from the BCBS publications. For example, the BCBS (2001a, p. 94) outlines three methods for calculating operational risk capital charge: (i) the BIA; (ii) the STA; and (iii) the IMA. However, it is also stated that "in future, a Loss Distribution Approach, in which the bank specifies its own loss distributions, business lines and risk types may be available." In BCBS (2006a), however, there is no mention of the IMA. The AMA is described briefly on page 147 in terms of the use of "the bank's internal operational risk management system using the quantitative and qualitative criteria for the AMA." The criteria pertain to the use of internal loss data, relevant external data, scenario analysis and business environment and internal control factors. Hence, the AMA will be taken to encompass the LDA, SBA and SCA. We will return to this point in Chapter 4, where it is argued that one of the problems of the AMA is that no-one knows what it encompasses.

The three approaches differ only in the emphasis on the information used to calculate regulatory capital. While the LDA depends on historical data, the SBA uses forward-looking "what-if" scenarios, but both of them utilise Monte Carlo simulations to estimate the capital charge. The SCA is based on a series of weighted questions whose answers yield scores for the allocation of the overall capital charge to individual business units. Unlike the other two approaches, the SCA reflects improvement in the control environment that reduces both the frequency and severity of operational losses. Banks are allowed to adjust their capital charges for operational risk under the AMA by (i) the amount of expected losses; (ii) diversification benefits from loss correlation among event types and business lines; and (iii) the risk mitigating impact of insurance. Capital adjustment is limited to 20% of the total operational risk capital charge calculated under the AMA.

To qualify for the AMA, banks must satisfy the following criteria:

- Be able to demonstrate that its approach captures potentially severe tail loss events.
- Track internal loss data based on a minimum five-year observation period.
- Use relevant external data, particularly when there is a reason to believe that the bank is exposed to infrequent, yet potentially severe losses.
- Use scenario analysis of expert opinion in conjunction with external data to evaluate its exposure to high-severity events.

These points are related to the concepts of "model validation" and "use test." One reason for conducting model validation is that "there is no operational risk model" because "different firms in different countries operating in different business environments face different exposures, which may culminate in one form of operational risk or another." Hence, the validation approach cannot be "one size fits all" (Khoo, 2008). Back testing and stress testing may be used to ensure that the underlying model is valid and that it measures risk exposure appropriately. Validation, therefore, is fundamentally about assessing the predictive ability of a bank's risk estimates (e.g., Blochwitz, 2008; de la Pena and Rivera, 2008). Blochwitz

(2008) argues that "Basel II documents .... do not explicitly specify what constitutes validation." In the case of operational risk, the "use test" is used to ascertain that the operational risk assessment system is closely integrated into the risk management process. The objective is to ensure that the internal methodology is used for risk management purposes and not only for calculating regulatory capital (see e.g., Financial Services Authority, 2005).

Pillars 2 and 3

Pillar 2 of the Basel II Accord, which pertains to the supervisory review process, is designed to ensure that an operational risk framework has been developed within the firm and that the process is adequately audited and supervised. Basel II, therefore, is concerned not only with capital adequacy but also with the risk management process. In other words the idea is that banks are encouraged to take preventative measures against the possibility of incurring operational losses, but at the same time they should hold adequate capital to protect themselves from insolvency should a loss event materialise. Wihlborg (2005) argues that supervision under Pillar 2 is designed to counteract incentives for banks to assign risk weights that do not properly reflect the economic risk of loans by equating regulatory capital and economic capital. Herring and Carmassi (2008) point out that Pillar 2 is related to macroprudential supervision, as it requires supervisors to impose capital charges above the minimum regulatory requirement (or demand a reduction of risk exposure) if they believe that exposure to the risk of insolvency is not adequately captured by Pillar 1. A legitimate question, therefore, is the following: why bother about Pillar 1?

Pillar 2 is based on the following principles:

- A strong national supervisory and regulatory process ensures the maintenance of adequate capital, hence supporting (or perhaps undermining) Pillar 1.
- Supervisors expect, and have the authority to require, banks to hold more than the minimum regulatory capital requirements.
- Banks must have internal procedures, tools and strategy to determine and maintain an adequate capital level.
- Supervisors are authorised to examine the internal capital measurements, strategies of the banks and compliance with regulatory capital requirements.

- Supervisors should intervene early in the case of a threat of capital inadequacy and when the underlying bank requires prompt remedial action.

Pillar 3 is designed to complement the minimum capital requirements (Pillar 1) and the supervisory review process (Pillar 2). The Committee notes that the disclosure provided under Pillar 3 is essential to ensure that market discipline is an effective complement to the other two pillars. The objective is to encourage market discipline by developing a set of disclosure requirements that allow market participants to assess key pieces of information on the scope of capital, risk exposure, risk assessment processes and the capital adequacy of the institution. Benink and Wihlborg (2002) emphasise the importance of Pillar 3 as an element of Basel II.

2.5 A CRITIQUE OF BASEL II

While Basel II goes a long way towards addressing some of the main defects of Basel I, it still has several loopholes. Indeed, some observers believe that the new Accord is not that superior to its predecessor. In this section we present the main arguments against Basel II. Before we do that, we have to point out that some of the criticism directed at Basel I as a form of banking regulation (which was discussed earlier) is equally applicable to Basel II. Banking regulation in general, and capital-based regulation in particular, have been severely criticised (as we have seen) and this criticism spills over to Basel II.

Criticism of the Basel II Accord can be general or specific, the latter pertaining to a particular pillar or element of the Accord. One element of the Accord, which is the advanced measurement approach to operational risk, will be evaluated in detail in Chapter 4, providing further criticism of Basel II for this particular aspect. Here we start with the general criticism of Basel II, then move on to the specific criticism of pillars 1, 2 and 3. We then address the question of whether or not Basel II is superior to Basel I as it is typically portrayed. The general criticism pertains to the Accord as a form of banking regulation not discussed under Basel I, the implementation-related problems, the cyclical effect of the Accord, reliance on rating agencies as well as some other general aspects of the Accord.

Basel II as a Form of Banking Regulation

In the light of the subprime crisis, Moosa (2008a) argues that Basel II may be suggesting inappropriate or inadequate financial supervision. While capital adequacy requirements are designed to protect banks from insolvency, the problem faced by banks during the onslaught of the crisis was illiquidity. The British bank, Northern Rock, suffered a run on its deposits in September 2007 not because it was insolvent but because it was illiquid. Basel II has no provisions for illiquidity and therefore no provisions for monitoring the funding gap (the gap between deposits and loans).

Another facet of the claim that Basel II may be suggesting inappropriate supervision can be found in the point raised by Rebonato (2007), who argues that banks should not be regulated in the same way as they are managed. The underlying idea is that while regulators are concerned about the systemic effect of a catastrophic loss event hitting one bank, bank managers are more concerned about the risk-return trade off associated with the day-to-day running of the business. This means that the objective of aligning regulatory capital with economic capital (which implies managing the bank the same way as regulating it) is way off the mark. McConnell (2006) also makes a distinction between regulators and shareholders. The role of the regulators is to protect the soundness of the financial system, which makes holding excess capital desirable. From the managers' (shareholders') perspective, excess capital is not available for income generation, which reduces return on equity. Doerig (2003) argues that, unlike managers, regulators do not take into account the fact that risk creates value and that by attempting to avoid systemic risk in the name of the general public they end up making the financial system more unstable. This is why he suggests that sustained and diversified profitability is a "precondition" for the protection of customers. He also argues that this proposition should be introduced formally as Pillar 4 of Basel II. Jobst (2007b) argues that because of the fat-tailed behaviour of operational losses, the concept of capital adequacy is insufficient to guide the allocation of economic capital with a view to curb risk exposure while allowing banks to operate profitably. Then, there is the problem of implementing the "use test" as a source of conflict between regulators and banks. Regulators may impose the use test requirement that banks should assign the same importance to internal data, external data and other components of the AMA in the calculation of regulatory capital as in risk management. Banks may justifiably complain that this is not the way they manage their business.

The European Shadow Financial Regulatory Committee (2003) points out that the supervisors' important role in validating risk models is conducive to "regulatory capture," as well as the possibility that supervisors will be held politically responsible for bank failure. This is probably a reason why it is felt that the BIA and STA factors (alphas and betas) are too high. Regulatory capture, according to Wihlborg (2005), implies that "the regulator fails to keep an arm's length relation with the industry but tends to incorporate the interests and objectives of the regulated firms in its own objectives." Wihlborg also argues that "the implementation of Basel II seems to create an almost perfect setting for 'regulatory capture' and that "the deep involvement of supervisors in critical areas of bank management implies that the failure of a bank may be interpreted as a supervisory failure in the eyes of the public and policy makers. On the basis of these political economy arguments, he reaches the conclusion that "Basel II can increase forbearance with respect to risk-taking" These arguments, however, would not be present if banks' depositors and other creditors were in a position to penalise banks with higher funding costs.

Kaufman (2005) compares Basel II with alternative systems of structured early intervention, including prompt corrective action and a legal closure rule at positive capital, which was introduced in the US in 1991 to enhance bank stability. He concludes that with respect to achieving public policy objectives Basel II compares poorly in terms of maintaining a safe and sound banking system. He also argues that Basel II may do damage by encouraging some large banks to put pressure on their regulators to lower the capital ratio.

The Implementation Problems

The BCBS gives so much latitude to individual countries that de Fontnouvelle et al (2005b) argue that "the [capital] charge will depend as much on supervisory implementation in each jurisdiction as it does on actual regulations." The Accord will differ from one country to another in a way that has led Imeson (2006) to conclude that "it [Basel II] looks as though it will become another example of disunity among nations and a monument to discord." Consider, for example, the difference between implementation in the US, and the European Union (EU). In the US, Basel II will be mandatory only for the largest US banks (those with more than $250 billion in total assets or $10 billion in international exposure). Other banks will be allowed to opt in, provided that their risk management infrastructure meets the same standards required for mandatory banks. The rest of the banks will remain on Basel I. The EU, on the other hand, will implement Basel II via the new Capital Adequacy Directive, CAD3, which will be applied to all credit institutions and investment firms.

In March 2008, Davis (2008b) reported that the progress towards the implementation of Basel II in the Asia-Pacific region, particularly the AMA, is rather slow. Apart from Australia and South Korea, countries in the region have either delayed the implementation to 2010 or beyond. For example, Zhiling (2008) announced that the China Construction Bank (CCB) is making progress towards adopting the foundation IRBA in 2010. One of the problems facing these firms is that it is becoming difficult to hire and retain risk management talent, in part because of the economic boom in the region. Regulatory bodies are in an even worse shape, as they find it difficult to compete with the private sector to attract these talents. One can justifiably ask the following question: how can regulators without talented risk management personnel approve or not approve internal models?

The implementation of the Accord will be extremely difficult in certain countries, requiring, according to Howard Davies (2005), “massive re-engineering of the regulating body and huge increases of staff.” In other words, he argues, “the Capital Accord will involve a major cultural shift in regulation.” This pertains in particular to emerging economies, an issue that Fischer (2002) deals with in detail. Fischer argues that certain elements of Basel II will pose difficulties for banks and supervisors in emerging market economies because the Accord will likely affect the banks operating in emerging markets (local banks and internationally active banks) differently. Furthermore, Fischer seems to be concerned about the ability of supervisory authorities in many emerging and developing countries to meet the standards set by Basel II. Howard Davies (2005) raises a similar point, advocating a role for emerging economies at an earlier stage. He actually warns of the risk of adopting advanced approaches in emerging countries because of the belief that this is the global standard, although it is not appropriate for their banks at the current stage of development. Currie (2006) seems to share this point of view, arguing that “many smaller banks and emerging nations may not be able to use the sophisticated approaches and hence will suffer a competitive disadvantage.”

The implementation problem is that without flexibility, the Accord would not have been signed, but this flexibility means it will be applied around the world inconsistently, which makes the Accord a “sad case of banking discord,” as Imeson (2006) puts it. Furthermore, Imeson identifies five areas of inconsistencies: (i) each country can implement a different version of Basel II; (ii) each country has a different time table for implementation; (iii) each country is likely to have different home-host methods of banking supervision; (iv) emerging countries are not bound by any time table and might not implement Basel II; and (v) in the EU, which has transposed Basel II into law through the Capital Requirements Directive (CRD), each country can implement a different version of the directive.

Procyclicality of Basel II

The Basel II Accord has been criticised severely because it is believed that the resulting risk-sensitive capital requirements enhance the procyclicality of the banking system. The underlying idea is that banking is a procyclical business, in the sense that banks tend to contract their lending activity in downturns and expand it in booms. As The Economist (2008c) puts it, “banks are notorious for lending people umbrellas when the sun is shining and asking for them back when the rain starts to fall.” This tends to boost the amplitude of the business cycle, making recessions more severe and booms more inflationary. Allen (2004) argues that increased risk sensitivity of bank capital requirements may exacerbate the procyclical tendencies of the banking industry. Being constrained by risk-sensitive capital requirements, banks will be more unable to lend in recessions and more willing to do so in booms, because risk-sensitive capital requirements increase when the estimates of default risk are higher, and vice versa.

In an empirical study, Bikker and Hu (2002) found strong evidence of procyclcality in bank profitability and provisions for loan losses for an international sample of banks in 26 countries over the period 1979–1999. Monfort and Mulder (2000) revealed strong evidence for procyclicality of credit ratings for 20 emerging market economies. Their simulations show that capital requirements under the Basel II STA increases dramatically during times of economic or financial crises. Likewise, Purhonen (2002) found evidence indicating considerable procyclicality in the foundation IRBA. Kashyap and Stein (2004) concluded, on the basis of their simulation results, that "the new Basel II capital requirements have the potential to create an amount of additional cyclicality in capital charges." Altman and Saunders (2001) believe that the use of agency ratings under the STA could produce cyclically lagging rather than leading capital requirements. However, Jordan et al (2002) express the view that concern about procyclicality in Basel II is misplaced, in the sense that other regulations, including Basel I, are also procyclical. This argument, however, implies that capital-based regulation in general is procyclical, which does not exonerate Basel II.

While Caruana (2005), who is a Basel II enthusiast, believes that some of the arguments about procyclicality in Basel II have merit, the Accord on the whole has positive macroeconomic implications. Caruana puts forward some arguments to cast doubt on the seriousness of the procyclicality problem. He argues that the extent to which capital requirements swing in response to economic conditions depends largely on the dynamic features of specific banks' rating systems and the specific characteristics of bank estimates of the probability of default. He also argues that a number of factors that are built into the framework are designed to ease some of the procyclicality effects, particularly under pillars 2 and 3. For example, banks are required under Pillar 2 to hold capital in excess of the minimum, which puts them in a position to wither a downturn without having to cut lending dramatically. The most important offset against the procyclical effects of Basel II, he argues, is the increased emphasis on effective risk management in the form of better control structures, sound corporate governance, and investment in technology, information systems and human capital.

The counterargument to the last point put forward by Caruana is that that banks will endeavour for better risk management practices to boost their profitability, with or without Basel II. One point remains valid, however: banking is a risk-sensitive business, which brings about a natural tendency towards procyclicality even in the absence of regulation. It is difficult to argue against the proposition that Basel II, as a form of capital-based regulation, boosts the procyclical tendencies of the banking business.

Over-Reliance on Rating Agencies

Over-reliance on the ratings of the rating agencies to determine the riskiness of assets sounds ludicrous in the post-subprime crisis era. Even without the subprime crisis, reliance on the STA to credit risk on credit rating agencies is misguided because these agencies do not provide consistent estimates of creditworthiness.

There is a widespread belief that through malpractice, the rating agencies played a major role in the materialisation of the subprime crisis in 2007. This is because these agencies have been too generous in giving out top AAA ratings to securities backed by subprime loans to please paying clients (issuers of the securities). This is why Moosa (2008c) finds it "ironic" that regulators, who are in charge of implementing Basel II, depend extensively on the ratings of the rating agencies, describing them as comprising "an oligopolistic unregulated industry." In the May 2008 issue of *OpRisk & Compliance* (p. 10), it is reported that "industry bodies such as the European Savings Banks Group, British Bankers' association (BBA), and the European Banking Federation agree the ratings agencies have failed to deliver sufficient transparency regarding their ratings methodologies or to demonstrate enough independence." Moosa (2008b) suggests that the interest of the rating agencies should be aligned with the interest of investors rather than that of the issuers of securities. One way to do that, he argues, is to put in place an arrangement whereby rating agencies are paid by the investors (e.g., as a subscription).

Howard Davies (2005) finds it rather strange that Basel II relies heavily on the work of the rating agencies when discussion is under way on the question of regulating these agencies and keeping them on leash. Yet, there has been little interaction between the Basel Committee and those bodies taking part in discussions on how to regulate the rating agencies (such as the European Commission and the Securities and Exchange Commission (SEC)). Howard Davies (2005) also believes that Basel II will deliver a significantly lower capital charge than what the rating agencies look for, at a time when banks are more influenced by the rating agencies than by Basel II.

Other General Criticism

Kupiec (2001) argues that the three-part evolutionary structure of Basel II can create perverse incentives. For example, capital requirements for low-quality, high-risk instruments are significantly lower under the STA than under the foundation IRBA, which means that banks using the STA have an incentive to specialise in high risk credits, therefore increasing the overall risk of the banking system. Kaufman (2003) criticises Basel II on the grounds that pillars 2 and 3 have major design flaws that make the achievement of the capital requirements determined by Pillar 1 questionable.

What is more fundamental, as far as Herring (2002) is concerned, is that it is not clear why the Basel Committee insists on dealing with operational risk under Pillar 1, which means that it is an issue of capital adequacy. He insists that Pillar 2 is the most efficient way of dealing with internal events and that insurance is the most effective way of dealing with external events. He believes that dealing with operational risk under Pillar 1 may end up distorting competition even further. A related view is expressed by McConnell (2006) who argues that "the problem with using operational risk capital to act as a deterrent.... is that it creates a form of moral hazard." Sheedy (1999) points out that the process of quantifying risk can create a "false sense of precision and a false impression that measurement has by necessity resulted in management." He further argues that managers may wrongly think that operational risk has been addressed, in which case they may reduce their vigilance, creating an environment where losses are more likely to occur. Calomiris and Herring (2002) point out that Basel II overstates the applicability of the "capital cushion philosophy" when insurance and internal process controls should do the job of risk management as well. They also argue that insurance is part of the risk management process and that the focus of capital adequacy should be on residual risk after insurance.

Pezier (2003a) argues that business and reputational risks, which are not recognised by Basel II (as they are excluded from the BCBS's definition of operational risk), may be more significant than the direct operational losses that the banking industry has been asked to monitor. These risks are left out not because they are small but because they are difficult to assess. Another facet of the Basel II exclusionary design is that the Accord covers banks only, which is a point raised by Briault (2002). He cites the German draft legislation to establish BaFin as an integrated supervisor, arguing that "banks, insurance companies and securities firms are now competing in the same markets for the same customers, with similar and often identical products and with the same distribution channels." Doerig (2003) criticises Basel II because it is concerned with banks only, arguing that non-bank financial intermediaries (NBFIs) are exposed to the same operational risk as banks and both represent similar systemic risk. A series of questions can be raised in relation to this issue. What are the measures designed to avoid potential systemic risk from NBFIs? Why care about systemic risk by banks while ignoring NBFIs? Why should banks be subject to a special operational risk capital charge? Does not this make banks less competitive?

KPMG (2005) argues that "although Basel II was developed to help banks improve risk management, the Accord is perceived as being yet another regulatory compliance obligation," which brings with it the risk of non-compliance and the potential losses associated with it. As a result, the focus (as far as banks are concerned) has become meeting the requirements rather than driving business value from the effort, given time and resource constrains. Wihlborg (2005) criticises the complexity of Basel II, arguing that although the intention of its designers has been to create a capital standard that can be implemented across jurisdictions in such a way that banks compete on a "level playing field," the many dimensions of bank risk make national and bank-specific discretion inevitable. Kaufman (2005) also argues that "by increasing its complexity, Pillar I does not necessarily make the regulation more accurate." Increased complexity, however, raises compliance costs and reduces banks' and supervisors' understanding of the underlying concepts and issues. If the weights are incorrectly selected, they would increase the potential for "gaming" the system.

Klopfer (2002) criticises the Basel II proposals for mortgages, arguing that the STA is insufficiently risk sensitive. He also argues that the IRBA is not well suited to mortgage credit assessment (in particular because the one year time horizon is not relevant for long-term mortgage loans), demonstrating that expected losses on mortgages peak 3–7 years after origination. Limiting the time horizon to one year understates the expected losses on a mortgage portfolio, not to mention that one year is insufficient to capture economic fluctuations and the other factors contributing to the mortgage portfolio's long-term performance. Duebel (2002) criticises the potential impact of Basel II on the mortgage market as potentially reducing capital too much by noting that capital is endogenous.

Another awkward issue, identified by Howard Davies (2005), is the interface between the Basel rules and domestic legislation. The question that arises in this respect pertains to the legitimacy of the Basel II Accord, in the sense that it is not clear if the Basel rules should be subject to domestic procedures of legislative review. More specifically, the following question may arise: does the implementation of the Accord and subsequent amendments (which are inevitable) require parliamentary approval in the countries where it is implemented? Some national authorities are already making noise, demanding more scrutiny of the provisions of Basel II. Pickworth (2008) refers to the "regulatory minefield" resulting from the introduction of Basel II when there are other domestic and international regulatory provisions such as the FSA regulation, Sarbanes-Oxley, Money Laundering Regulations 2007, Data Protection Act 1988 and the Companies Act 2006.

Criticism of Pillar 1

Basel II involves some dilemmas, which may be relevant to the perception of the Accord by the financial community. To start with, both small and large banks may claim that Basel II favours the others over them. Small banks may (and do) complain that Basel II favours large banks because the use of the BIA and STA produces greater capital charges than those of large banks produced by the AMA (which is what the BCBS claims). Small banks may, therefore, feel that Basel II puts them at a competitive disadvantage vis-à-vis large banks, which makes them attractive potential takeover targets. Conversely, large banks may (and do) complain that unlike small banks they have to spend a fortune on the development of internal models to measure regulatory capital under the AMA. Small banks may (and do) claim that the 15% capital charge against operational risk under the BIA is too high, but the BCBS cannot reduce this number without enraging the large banks adopting the AMA.

Wihlborg (2005) identifies another dilemma facing the BCBS, which is the assignment of risk weights for different kinds of loans to calculate regulatory capital against credit risk. This is a dilemma because assigning the same risk weight to a wide variety of loans with different risks invites regulatory arbitrage, as we have seen. However, detailed specification of risk weights renders banks' expertise in risk evaluation irrelevant for the funding costs in different loans. This is inconsistent with the valid proposition that risk evaluation is the basis for banks' competitive advantage in the loan markets of different kinds. Wihlborg argues that the current Basel proposals with respect to supervision and market discipline (pillars 2 and 3) seem to defeat the whole purpose of using banks' internal ratings to determine risk weights. Indeed, he argues that the more specific the Basel Committee has become, the stronger are the reasons to doubt that Basel II will achieve its objectives. The same point is made by Benink et al (2008).

Some authors and observers criticise Pillar 1 in particular, sometimes with respect to its treatment of one of the three categories of risk. Bugie et al (2003) express concern about the omission from Pillar 1 of any treatment of interest rate risk in the banking book, business and reputational risk and concentration risk. Given the complexity of the Pillar 1 rules, Bugie et al (2003) believe that banks will be preoccupied with the assessment of the covered risk while neglecting omitted risks.

There seems to be some disagreement about the appropriateness of the IRBA risk weights, but both views can be taken as a criticism of Basel II in the sense that the Accord does not pinpoint the appropriate level of capital. Dietsch and Petey (2002) used a portfolio of 22,000 French small and medium-sized enterprises loans to show that the IRBA risk weights are set too high for all risk levels. Conversely, Frerichs and Wahrenberg (2003) use data from Deutsche

Bundesbank to show that capital requirements are set too low when they are based on historical rating class default rates as in the STA of Basel II.

As far as operational risk is concerned, Pillar 1 is criticised on the grounds that operational risk modelling is not possible in the absence of comprehensive databases, even if a meaningful and satisfactory definition of operational risk does exist (which is not the case anyway). Any estimation of operational risk is bound to be hampered by the absence of data and a proper definition. The data problem is particularly acute in the estimation of the probability of extreme loss events. We will come back to the problems of defining and measuring operational risk (including the data problem) at a later stage.

Like others, Herring (2002) casts doubt on the usefulness of the BIA for the calculation of the capital charge as a percentage of gross income. Herring argues that it is doubtful if this indicator captures even the scale of an institution's operations adequately and that it has no tenuous link to the risk of an expected loss due to internal or external events. Pezier (2003a) suggests that the connection between gross income and operational risk is loose: gross income is about the past whereas operational risk is about the future. de Fontnouvelle et al (2005b) describe measurement based on a volume indicator as measurement in "an *ad hoc* manner." Jobst (2007b) argues that relating operational risk exposure to business volume amounts to an incomplete regulatory measure that engenders misleading conclusions about operational risk exposure and the associated capital charges. The problem with using size to measure operational risk is that the results of empirical research show that firm size only explains 5% of reported losses.

McConnell (2008) casts doubt on the relation between operational losses and gross income by using two operational loss events: the terrorist attack on the World Trade Center in 2001 and the foreign exchange losses at the National Australia Bank (NAB) in January 2004. The severity of the losses incurred as a result of the attack on the World Trade Center were less than 5% of the average gross income for the largest 15 US banks. The reported losses incurred by the NAB are only 3.8% of the gross income of the big four Australian banks according to their 2005 reports. He argues that "there would have to be something in the order of one NAB-size event each and every quarter to consume the BIA-calculated capital for each major bank." Herring (2002) argues that the losses revealed by the quantitative impact study (QIS) of the Basel Committee (referring to QIS2) do not necessarily reflect differences in risk. And Sundmacher (2007a) believes that gross income would not have reflected the actual risk taken in situations resulting in high-profile operational losses, such as Barings and the Allied Irish Bank. He actually suggests that trading volume may be a better indicator of operational risk than gross income.

Herring's (2002) criticism of the AMA is based on the argument that the approach "requires multiple pages of preconditions that most institutions could not be expected to meet for years." He also points out that neither the BIA nor the STA provides a persuasive way of relating capital charges to actual differences in operational risk across firms, whereas the AMA remains to be fully specified. Pezier (2003a) raises the question whether or not the AMA leads to better operational risk management. If so, then all banks should put into place some sort of advanced methodology.

One aspect of Basel II that has been criticised by McConnell (2006) is the role of insurance. Although the Accord recognises the mitigating impact of insurance on operational risk, this recognition is limited to 20% of the total operational risk charge calculated by the AMA. McConnell argues that this "one size fits all" approach to the use of insurance may result in more (not less) risk, because at a certain point in time the acquisition of insurance would be discouraged. McConnell suggests the removal of insurable loss events (such as damage to physical assets (DPA)) from the calculation of the capital charge, resorting instead to the discipline of Pillar 3, augmented by audit scrutiny, to make sure that insurable risks are properly covered.

Kaufman (2005) describes Pillar 1 as no more than a "best practices guide for bank management." Thomas and Wang (2005) argue that the internal ratings model underlying the regulation is outdated even as it is being proposed. While there is substantial empirical evidence of a negative relation between leverage ratios and bank insolvency, there is no such evidence on the relation between risk-based capital ratios and bank insolvency (Evanoff and Wall, 2001). Kaufman (2005) further argues that risk-weighted assets are an inferior scalar to total assets to gauge how much capital is available to a bank before insolvency. For most countries, the adoption of Basel II by itself could undermine the adoption of better public policy structures, thus increasing both the likelihood and cost of financial instability.

Doerig (2003) puts forward the following arguments against the operational risk provisions of Pillar 1.

- A minimum charge may provide a false sense of security instead of fostering adequate controls.
- One-size fits all is an unsatisfactory approach.
- Any unreasonable charge makes banks uncompetitive.
- Operational risk management is much more than a capital charge. It is about good management.
- In the case of a loss event, the shareholders will suffer first. The real issue is liquidity and funding, as argued earlier with respect to Northern Rock.

- An operational risk charge under Pillar 1 means that supervisors are not convinced about their successful implementation of Pillar 2. This is an excellent point that raises a legitimate question that will be repeated here because it is crucial. If, in accordance with Pillar 2, regulators are in a position to tell banks that the capital charge calculated according to Pillar 1 is inadequate, why bother about Pillar 1 at all?

As a result, Doreig argues that there should be no charge under pillar 1 until certain conditions have been satisfied. These include (among others): (i) agreed-upon definition of operational risk; and (ii) a credible attempt made to create a level playing field with non-banks. The second condition seems to make more sense as the convergence on a common definition may not be achieved. In any case, the definition may not be as crucial as pinpointing the set of losses that constitute operational loss events.

Criticism of Pillars 2 and 3

Kaufman (2005) suggests that Pillar 2 contains very few specifics, focusing primarily on general principles and does not consider the wide variation in supervisory competence across countries. If Pillar 2 is designed in part to allow supervisors to impose capital charges above the minimum required by Pillar 1, this boils down to admitting the inadequacy of Pillar 1 (as argued earlier). Then it is not clear how supervisors determine the required capital over and above the Pillar 1 minimum (perhaps by a more "advanced" approach than the AMA, if at all they are capable of hiring the talent to do that). Most likely, they tend to impose capital charges above the minimum as they are caught in regulatory capture.

Kaufman (2005) also argues that Pillar 3 is not really about market discipline but about creating transparency and disclosure. A particular criticism is directed at Pillar 3 by Lopez (2003) who argues that the requirements for effective market discipline are not discussed in as much detail as what information on a bank's financial and risk positions need to be disclosed to the public. Kaufman (2003), on the other hand, argues that disclosure and transparency constitute a necessary but not sufficient condition for effective market discipline. In any case, Sundmacher and Ford (2007) found a lot of variability in the quality and quantity of disclosure on operational risk. By examining the 2004 annual reports of fifty seven financial institutions, they reached the conclusion that there is a lack of consistency in the way financial institutions report operational risk information, which casts doubt over its usefulness for external parties.

Wihlborg (2005) casts doubt on the effectiveness of Pillar 3, arguing that "market discipline is not likely to boost the sensitivity of banks' funding costs to changes in bank risk-taking," because "the proposal is limited to information disclosure." In this respect, the Basel Committee seems to overlook the proposition that the amount and truthfulness of information available in the market depend on both the demand for and supply of information. Without increased market discipline, he argues, "Basel II is not likely to resolve the regulatory problem caused by explicit and implicit guarantees of depositors and other creditors of banks."

Basel II: Final Thoughts

Pezier (2003a) concludes that it is doubtful if Basel II is going to be feasible in terms of costs and benefits. Herring (2005) shares this view, arguing that "Basel II will be very costly for banks, home and host country supervisors, and, to the extent that it exacerbates macroeconomic cycles, to the broader economy as well." Moosa (2007b) advocates this view by raising the question whether or not Basel II is worthwhile in terms of costs and benefits. His argument is that Basel II should not be seen as providing better ways for measuring regulatory capital and incentives for better risk management practices without taking into account the costs of implementing the Accord. In particular, he believes that spending millions of dollars to develop internal models for regulatory purposes is not worthwhile.

Wihlborg (2005) argues that Basel II is likely to achieve its objectives partially by inducing banks to develop state-of-the-art risk evaluation systems, but this success will be short lived because Basel II contains the seeds of its own failure in the long run. This results from the need for supervisory discretion to implement the complex rules for using the banks' internal risk scoring models and the deep involvement of supervisors in the process of validation and implementation of the models. This would make supervisors less tolerant of underestimating capital charges.

Practitioners subscribe to most of the views criticising Basel II. It has been said that Basel II could, at worst, blow up one or two European banking systems (The Economist, 2003). In a survey of seventy bankers worldwide conducted by the Centre for the Study of Financial Innovation (2002), the participants expressed the view that Basel II is "dangerous and complex." Howard Davies (2005) argues that practitioners have some sort of an ambivalent view of Basel II as "some are very nervous about the new Accord" while "others are more positive because they are true believers, or perhaps because they follow the advice of a Chinese proverb: 'If a thing is inevitable, welcome it'."

The title of this chapter invokes the question as to whether or not Basel II represents a "great leap forward" in comparison with Basel I. Kaufman (2005) seems to imply that the answer to this question is "no," as he argues that Basel II provides only partial and flawed improvements over Basel I as a tool for public policy to achieve the goal of enhanced financial stability. Palia and Porter

(2003) argue on similar lines, suggesting that the seven sins of Basel I are also the seven sins of Basel II, and that Basel II is no more than a "superficial change." As far as the seven sins are concerned, Palia and Porter put forward the following points:

- The new risk weights under the STA and IRBA still allow limited categories, such that there is only insignificant reduction in the propensity for regulatory arbitrage (sin 1). Benink et al (2008) argue that the potential for arbitrage will remain under Basel II for at least two reasons: (i) not all banks will qualify for using the internal ratings based approach either because they do not have the required expertise or because they must have five years of history of estimating probabilities of default; and (ii) internal ratings need to be continuous, but loans may still be placed in relatively broad risk buckets. Sundmacher (2007b) identifies one form of regulatory arbitrage under the STA, which is shifting gross income from high-beta to low-beta business lines.

- Basel II does not address the question of a standard definition of capital (sin 2).

- There is no explanation for why the 8% ratio is chosen (sin 3).

- The superiority of equity over debt capital is addressed to some extent by the Committee's acknowledgement of market discipline (sin 4).

- The Basel II Accord makes things worse than better with respect to levelling the international playing field, because sophisticated methodologies are only available for sophisticated banks (sin 5).

- Basel II gives only limited acknowledgement to diversification (sin 6).

- No significant changes in the assessment of derivatives and other off-balance sheet items are suggested (sin 7).

Basel II, it seems, is a very expensive exercise that adds nothing significant and worthy over and above Basel I. But then Basel I has not contributed much to financial stability. A natural question arises here: why bother at all?

APPENDIX 2.1: CAPITAL CHARGES UNDER THE BIA AND STA

In this appendix we explore the conditions under which the BIA produces higher capital charges than the STA. Let K_{BIA} and K_{STA} be the capital charges under the BIA and STA, respectively. These capital charges are calculated as

$$K_{BIA} = \alpha \sum_{i=1}^{8} y_i \tag{2A1.1}$$

$$K_{STA} = \sum_{i=1}^{8} \beta_i y_i \tag{2A1.2}$$

where $\alpha = 0.15$, β_i is the beta assigned to business line i and y_i is the gross income attributable to business line i such that $i = 1, 2, \ldots, 8$. The BIA produces a higher capital charge than the STA when

$$\alpha \sum_{i=1}^{8} y_i > \sum_{i=1}^{8} \beta_i y_i \tag{2A1.3}$$

or when

$$\alpha > \frac{\sum_{i=1}^{8} \beta_i y_i}{\sum_{i=1}^{8} y_i} \tag{2A1.4}$$

Therefore, the condition under which the BIA produces a higher capital charge than the STA is that the alpha factor under the BIA is greater than the weighted average of the individual betas under the STA. Whether or not this condition is satisfied depends on the distribution of gross income across business lines. What is important is that there is no guarantee that the condition will be satisfied, which means that moving from the BIA to the STA may or may not produce a lower capital charge.

A simulation exercise can be used to illustrate this point. Assume first that all eight business lines generate any level of income between 0 and 100. A random number generator is used to simulate 100 observations on the gross incomes of the eight business lines, and these are subsequently used to calculate capital charges under the BIA and STA. The difference between the two capital charges ($K_{BIA} - K_{STA}$) is plotted in Figure 2A1.1, showing that the difference can be positive or negative, which means that the capital charge under the BIA may be higher or lower than the capital charge under the STA. Figure 2A1.2 shows the weighted average of the beta plotted against alpha, again showing that the condition required for the BIA to produce a higher capital charge than the STA may or may not be satisfied. We call this Case 1.

In Case 2 the incomes are generated randomly but scaled by the percentage of the contribution of the underlying business line measured as the

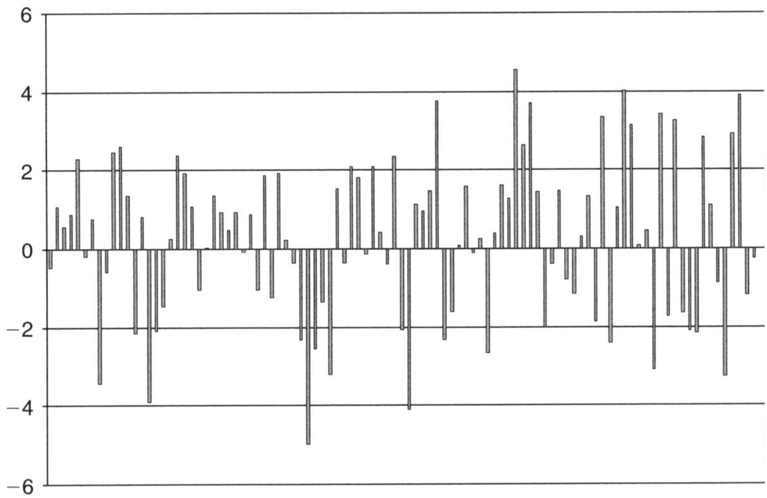

Figure 2A1.1 Difference between Capital Charges under the BIA and STA Case (1)

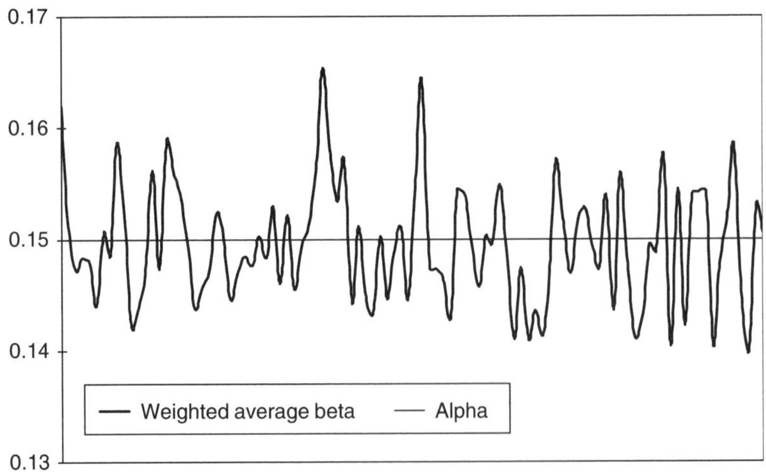

Figure 2A1.2 The Weighted Average of Business Line Betas (Case 1)

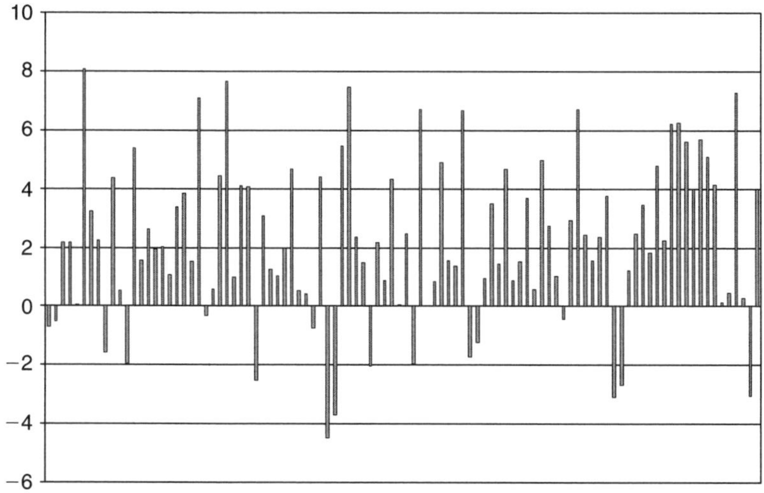

Figure 2A1.3 Difference between Capital Charges under the BIA and STA (Case 2)

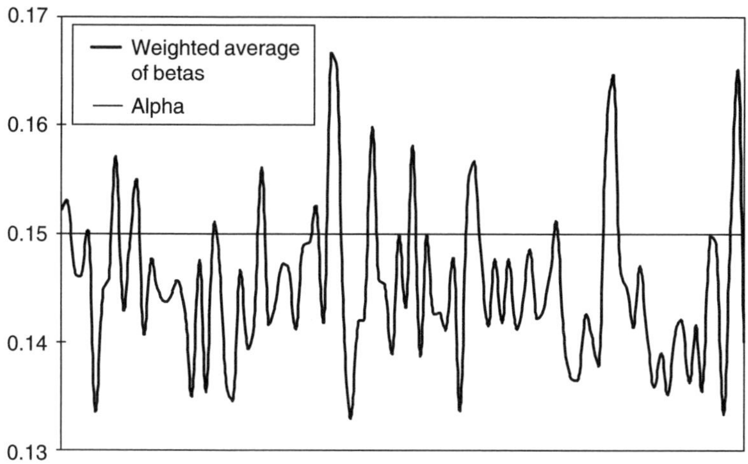

Figure 2A1.4 The Weighted Average of Business Line Betas (Case 2)

average of the observations recorded in the three loss data collection exercises (LDCEs) of the BCBS, the US and Japan. Figures 2A1.3 and 2A1.4 respectively show the difference between the capital charges under the BIA and STA, and the weighted average of betas plotted against the fixed alpha. Again, the BIA may or may not produce a higher capital charge than the STA. In both cases, the null hypothesis of the equality of the means of the capital charges under the BIA and STA ($H_0: K_{BIA} = K_{STA}$) cannot be rejected with t statistics of 0.95 and 0.72, respectively.

Sundmacher (2007c) demonstrates, using hypothetical data, the conditions under which the BIA produces a lower capital charge than the STA, in which case it would be advantageous for the underlying bank to remain on the BIA. This would be the case if the bank generates the bulk of its gross income in high-beta business lines and only a small portion in low-beta business lines. Sundmacher concludes that "the institution would face little incentive to invest in the infrastructure necessary to gradate to the STA given the costs of such an investment would provide little return in terms of capital relief."

CHAPTER 3

Operational Risk: Definition, Features and Classification

3.1 DEFINITION OF OPERATIONAL RISK

Defining operational risk is typically portrayed as a prerequisite for a range of tasks, including raising awareness (of operational risk) at the management level and the calculation of regulatory (and economic) capital. Power (2005) argues that definitions of key concepts are "an intimate and central part of the logic of any practice." He describes definitions as "attention-directing devices and strategies which determine objects of management and regulatory interest." He even argues that "the process of defining operational risk has been a major regulatory and managerial innovation, creating the conceptual condition of possibility for an emerging discipline." This may sound somewhat like exaggeration, not to mention that obsession with finding an exact definition of operational risk may be a distraction from a more important task, which is risk management.

Because of its diversity, defining operational risk is not an easy task, and this is why Allen and Bali (2004) note that defining operational risk is easier said than done. For the same reason, operational risk is dubbed "Risk X" by Metcalfe (2003). Crouchy (2001) suggests that operational risk is a "fuzzy concept" because "it is hard to make a clear-cut distinction between operational risk and the normal uncertainties faced by the organisation in its daily operations." This is why Doerig (2003) sums up the *status quo* by suggesting that "a common practical definition of OpRisk does not exist in the literature nor in the industry." But does the absence of a common practical definition bring a halt to attempts to manage operational risk? The answer to this question is bound to be "no."

The Negative Definition of Operational Risk

For a long time it was rather tempting to define operational risk negatively (or in an exclusionary way) as any risk that is not related to market risk and credit risk. With respect to banking, Power (2005) argues that operational risk "started life as a residual category, something left over from market and credit risk management practices, a fear category with a problematic reality and status." This is why, he argues, "it has proved problematic to define, although such difficulties in fixing meaning have advanced, rather than detracted from its importance." However, defining operational risk as any risk simply by excluding market and credit risk is difficult to work with and cannot be the basis of operational risk measurement. This is why Buchelt and Unteregger (2004) argue that "the negative definition of operational risk is hardly suitable for recognising its scope precisely." Doerig (2003) holds a similar view as he argues that defining operational risk in this way is not conducive to identifying a structured way of managing it.

Despite these (plausible) arguments, Medova and Kyriacou (2001) are convinced that the negative definition of operational risk remains the one most often used by practitioners. This view is also held by Jameson (1998) who indicated that the negative definition was most frequently given in telephone interviews. Indeed, Tinca (2007) still defines operational risk as the risk that "covers all non-market or credit risk, therefore including management risk." It is not clear though what is meant by "management risk" but it could be business or strategic risk, which is typically distinguished from operational risk although this distinction is not accepted universally.

Like Tinca, Valle et al (2007) define operational risk as "all financial risks that are not classified as market or credit risks." The use of the word "financial" is rather unfortunate because operational risk is not a financial risk in the sense that it is not caused by fluctuations in market prices. It seems, however, that the word "financial" is used (wrongly) to imply "monetary" losses resulting from exposure to operational risk. Lack of authorisation (which they list as an example of operational risk) is by no means a type of financial risk. It is also not clear why Valle et al use the expression "financial risk management of operational risk"!

Early and Inadequate Definitions

Early definitions of operational risk appeared in the published literature of major international banks and other bodies in the 1990s before the Basel Committee adopted its official definition. For example, the Group of Thirty (1993) defined operational risk as "uncertainty related to losses resulting from inadequate systems or controls, human error or management." An early definition of operational risk came up in a seminar at the Federal Reserve

Bank of New York when Shepheard-Walwyn and Litterman (1998) defined operational risk by saying that "operational risk can be seen as a general term that applies to all the risk failures that influence the volatility of the firm's cost structure as opposed to its revenue structure." The implication of this definition is that operational risk is one-sided, which is a controversial point that will be discussed later when we consider the characteristics of operational risk.

Tripe (2000) defines operational risk as "the risk of operational loss," which in essence means nothing, as the definition does not imply anything at all about the difference between operational and non-operational losses. Other inadequate definitions of operational risk have been suggested. Lopez (2002) believes that operational risk is "every type of unquantifiable risk faced by a bank," which is the antithesis of the Basel II Accord, particularly the advanced measurement approach (AMA) that encompasses several techniques designed to quantify operational risk (whether or not these techniques do a good job in this respect is a different matter). Another inadequate definition has been put forward by Crouchy (2001) who describes operational risk as "the risk associated with operating a business" (no comment here)! More specific than Tripe, Lopez and Crouchy is Halperin (2001) who defines operational risk as a "loose-limbed concept that includes potential losses from business interruptions, technological failures, natural disasters, errors, lawsuits, trade fixing, faulty compliance, fraud and damage to reputation, often intangible fallout from these events." This is not as much a definition as it is a listing of some loss event types, but it may be that listing of loss events is the best way to "define" operational risk.

The BCBS Definition

The most common definition of operational risk first appeared in Robert Morris Associates et al (1999), which is as follows: "operational risk is the direct or indirect loss resulting from inadequate or failed internal processes, people and systems, or from external events." The Basel Committee adopted this definition, as it was initially, but subsequently eliminated the reference to indirect losses. More specifically, the BCBS (2004) defines operational risk as "the risk arising from inadequate or failed internal processes, people and systems or from external events." This modification eliminates a flaw in the Robert Morris Associates et al definition, the failure to distinguish between "risk" and "loss," as pointed out in Chapter 1. The BCBS definition, which is based on the underlying causes of operational risk, includes legal risk but excludes business and reputational risk.

Some modified versions of the BCBS definition have appeared. For example, Jobst (2007a) defines operational risk as "the risk of loss arising from adverse outcome resulting from acts undertaken (or neglected) in carrying out business activities, such as inadequate or failed internal processes and information systems, from misconduct by people or from external events." Another example is the definition suggested by Doerig (2003) who defines operational risk as "the risk of adverse impact to business as a consequence of conducting it in an improper or inadequate manner and may result from external factors." One may justifiably wonder if there is any value or practical significance in these modified definitions over and above what is in the original definition. However, expressions like "the risk of loss" and "the risk of adverse impact" add more precision to the definition relative to the original Robert Morris Associates et al definition.

Mestchian (2003) suggests a decomposition of the definition of the BCBS into four components, as shown in Figure 3.1. The sinking of the Titanic in 1912 is the best example of an operational loss event that took place because of the failure of people (the crew, passengers and the boss), systems (the ship and its equipment, particularly the inadequate number of life boats), processes (emergency plans and procedures and the decision-making process pertaining to the choice of speed and course) and (of course) the iceberg, which was the external factor. The same can be said about the "mother of all operational failures," the US-led invasion and occupation of Iraq.

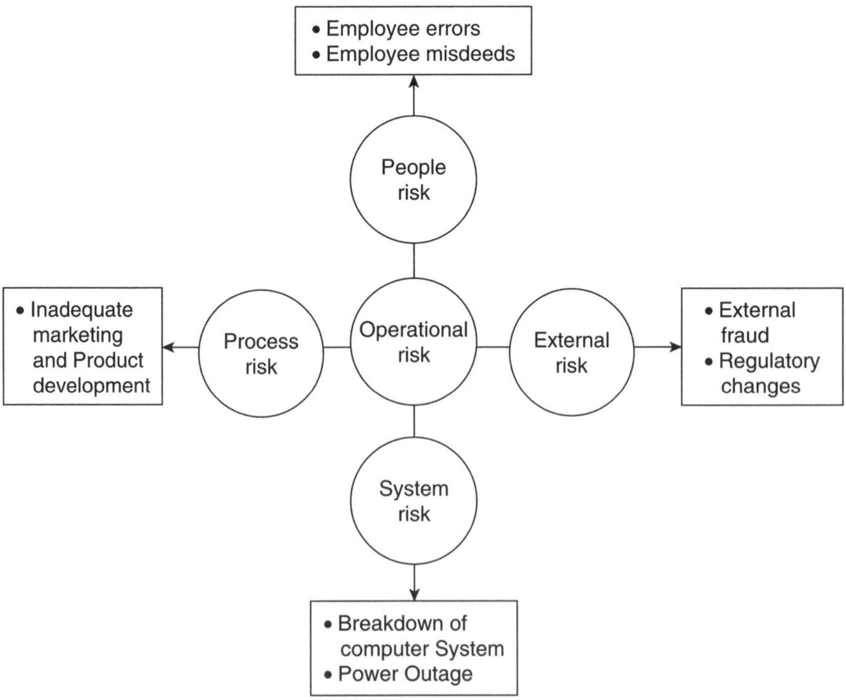

Figure 3.1 Decomposition of the BCBS Definition of Operational Risk

The BCBS's definition of operational risk has been challenged by academics and practitioners. Turing (2003) describes the definition as "so broad as to be totally unhelpful," whereas Herring (2002) criticises the definition on the grounds that it omits altogether basic business risk and that it ignores the Committee's earlier attempt to include indirect costs and reputational risk. The exclusion of reputational risk is particularly troublesome, as it is sometimes portrayed to encompass (or overlap with) both strategic risk and operational risk. Doerig (2003) describes reputational risk as "the aggregation of the outcome of all risks plus other internal and external factors." He describes reputation as "the outcome of the mix of doing the right thing and doing things right over an extended period," and that it is "a reflection of facts, perceptions and expectations and a key factor for the share price." Recalling the difference between operational risk and business risk as "doing things the wrong way" and "doing the wrong things" respectively, one may be tempted to think that reputational risk is a mixture of operational and strategic risk. It is the mix of "doing the right thing" and "doing things right" that calls into question the exclusion of reputational risk from the definition of operational risk.

Hadjiemmanuil (2003) describes the BCBS's definition as being "opaque" and "open-ended" because it fails to specify the component factors of operational risk or its relation to other forms of risk. Mango and Venter (2007) argue that the BCBS's definition is "deceptively short for such a broad area [of risk]," arguing that inadequacy of the definition is the reason why the Committee complemented the definition by a description of seven types of loss events (e.g., BCBS, 2004). This cause and effect line of thinking may reinforce the proposition that the best way to define operational risk is to list operational loss events. There is only so much that can be said in a definition, but not in a detailed description. Despite their negative view of the BCBS's definition, they point out that while the definition is banking focused, it has gained substantial visibility and acceptance.

Other Definitions

Doerig (2003) points out that there are as many definitions as there are financial institutions. He refers to the results of a survey conducted by the British Bankers' Association et al (1999) on the definition of operational risk in the finance industry, showing that 49% of the participants have single positive definitions, 15% have exclusive definitions, 31% have no formal definitions and 5% have multiple definitions. The following is a sample of the definitions obtained from the survey:

- The risk of everything other than credit and market risk (15% of the participants adopted this negative definition).

- The risk associated with the operations department. This definition is wrong because every department and business line is exposed to operational risk (e.g., the risk of fire).

- The risk that deficiencies in information systems or internal controls will result in unexpected loss. This definition wrongly excludes external sources of operational risk.

Other definitions of operational risk have been suggested in the academic and professional literature, including the following:

- The risk that a firm will suffer loss as a result of human error or deficiencies in systems or controls.

- The risk run by a firm that its internal practices, policies and systems are not rigorous or sophisticated enough to cope with untoward market conditions or human or technological errors.

- The risk of loss resulting from errors in the processing of transactions/breakdown in controls/errors or failures in system support.

Convergence of Definitions?

As we can see, a wide variety of definitions are used to describe operational risk, ranging from the useless to the less-useless and from the narrow to the wide definition. While this may be an unsatisfactory state of affairs, the following question may be raised: is the definition of operational risk such a critical issue that it triggers so much disagreement?

A typical answer to this question is the following: to measure something, we must first define it. But Lam (2003) seems to believe that being "fussy" about the definition of operational risk does not serve any meaningful purpose with respect to operational risk management, which is presumably the ultimate objective of research on operational risk. This is why the first step in his "ten steps to operational risk management" is "define it and move on." Lam's underlying argument is that "many institutions do not get off the ground because too much time is spent trying to come up with the perfect definition of operational risk," an objective that will probably never be achieved. And while Doerig (2003) expects a convergence on a common definition, he argues that this "does not mean that a unique, industry wide definition of OpRisk will emerge." One cannot help wondering about the apparent contradiction between "convergence on a common definition" and the unlikely event of a "unique, industry wide definition" appearing. In another prediction pertaining to the definition of operational risk,

Pennington (2008b) cites Philippa Girling, the director of operational risk management at Nomura Holdings America, as saying that "the definition of operational risk could become broader and spill outside of that determined by Basel II."

One could safely argue that a precise definition of operational risk is not as important (for risk management purposes) as pinpointing the categories of risk that fall under operational risk. A more important issue than defining operational risk is to resolve the controversy on whether business (strategic) and reputational risks are operational risk types. Identification and classification are more useful for practical purposes than coming up with an abstract definition of something that is not easy to define because of its diversity and multi-dimensionality.

3.2 THE DISTINGUISHING FEATURES OF OPERATIONAL RISK

Doerig (2003) summarises what he believes to be the distinguishing features of operational risk as opposed to market risk and credit risk by stating that "OpRisks are primarily institutional, bank made, internal, context dependent, incredibly multifaceted, often judgmental, interdependent, often not clearly discernable vis a vis e.g. market and credit risks and not diversifiable." It is debatable if operational risk is bank made or internal, because external factors can be the culprit, but it is definitely "incredibly multifaceted." This is why we start with a discussion of this feature of operational risk.

The Diversity of Operational Risk

The diversity of operational risk is definitely a feature that distinguishes it from the relatively narrowly defined market risk and credit risk, which are more widely understood and appreciated (by firms and regulators). This feature of operational risk makes it difficult to limit the number of dimensions required to describe it (and naturally hampers attempts to define it). Operational risk encompasses the types of risk emanating from all areas of the firm, which makes it more difficult to identify (and define) than market risk and credit risk.

The Economist (2003) describes operational risk as "the risk of all manner of mishaps and foul-ups, from a lost document to a bomb blast." McCuaig (2005) describes operational risk as being associated with losses that "range from uncollectible receivables from unhappy customers, lost sales due to call centre failures and unproductive employee downtime when computer systems are unavailable." It is suggested that although some of these losses are large, very few are "measured in any accounting system and rarely are the loss incidents tracked and analyzed." The diversity exhibited by the description of The Economist may be a reason why operational risk is not as well understood as market risk and credit risk, with consequences for risk management. Power (2005) suggests that operational risk is "no simple or self-evident [risk] category" and that "it is a label for adverse range of practices, a vision of control and regulation in an elusive field."

Difficulty of Measurement, Management and Regulation

Because of its diversity and other factors, operational risk is more difficult to measure and manage than either market risk or credit risk. KPMG (2003) describes operational risk as "often difficult to perceive, quantify and manage." On the difficulty of modelling, Samad-Khan et al (2006) argue that "modeling operational risk is very different from modeling other types of risk because operational risk modeling is fundamentally about addressing the data issue." Unlike credit and market risks, the modelling of operational risk starts with an objective assessment of the data, particularly biases in the data. Jobst (2007a) argues that the diversity of operational risk makes it even more difficult to regulate. Jobst (2007b) explains why the regulation of operational risk is quite distinct from the regulation of other types of risk by saying that it requires risk management techniques that deal mainly with tail events rather than central projections.

Several consistent views about the difficulty of managing operational risk have been put forward. Doerig (2003) describes the confusion about operational risk and its management as "quite impressive," encompassing the following facets: (i) not-yet settled definitions; (ii) different frameworks; (iii) hazy data; (iv) complex and/or not yet credible models; (v) impractical academics; (vi) consultants who lack track record; and (vii) quants who are hungry for fresh challenges.

On the difficulty of managing operational risk because of its diversity, Mainelli (2004) describes the day-to-day management of operational risk as involving "decisions about opening times, cleaning standards, rodent control in dealing rooms, secure electricity supply, security controls and other management decisions not suitable to real-time spreadsheet analysis." KPMG (2005) suggests that credit risk management is a "more mature process" than operational risk management because the latter has suffered from either an inaccurate perception about its nature or the lack of appropriate understanding by senior management, as there seems to be a tendency to believe that operational risk is already being managed.

It is also suggested that operational risk management has been affected by lack of resources, little regulatory guidance on specific but important issues and by few proven methodologies, processes and tools. KPMG (2003) differentiates between the management of operational risk, on the one hand, and the management of credit risk and market risk, on the other, because "operational risk affects every activity and process in a financial institution." This is why "the responsibility for the management of operational risk cannot be fully centralized but must take place both at the group/corporate level and within the business line." KPMG (2003) identifies structural differences among operational risk, market risk and credit risk at the inspection level, risk categories, portfolio elements, maximum total loss and maximum number of losses. For example, the maximum number of losses caused by market risk, credit risk and operational risk are, respectively, the market value of the portfolio, credit volume and the bank's liquidation value.

Adusei-Poku (2005) argues that unlike market and credit risk management, operational risk management faces many challenges, including the relatively short time span of historical loss data, the role of internal control, environment and its changing nature and the important role of infrequent but large losses. One reason for the relative difficulty of managing operational risk is the cultural barrier that prevents people and institutions from disclosing minimum information about loss events. This is what Doerig (2003) describes as the tendency to avoid "twisting the knife in the wound," because of the view that mistakes as shameful.

Indicative of the difficulty of managing operational risk is that the Foreign Exchange Committee (2003) lists 60 best practices for dealing with operational risk in the foreign exchange business (see Appendix 3.1). Best practice 50 is stated as "understand operational risk," which involves the assessment on a regular basis of "current as well as potential operational risk associated with new industry process changes (for example, the CLS Bank, web portals, and so on)." The Basel Committee has issued a frequently cited document that sets ten principles of sound practices (BCBS, 2002, 2003a). Commenting on these practices, Philippa Girling of Nomura is cited by Pennington (2008b) as saying that "from an op risk point of view, we believe in the 10 sound practices," and that "we should have all of them in place in the operational risk management framework." These best practices are listed in Appendix 3.2.

The Risk-Return Trade-off

Some would argue that another distinguishing feature of operational risk is that it is "one-sided" in the sense that it is driven solely by its role as an undesired by-product of increasingly complex business operations. In this sense, the risk-return trade-off associated with market risk has no equivalence in the case of operational risk, meaning that exposure to operational risk can cause losses without boosting the potential rate of return on capital and assets. It is however wrong to believe that operational risk is one-sided in the sense that it is a source of losses only, because firms take it deliberately for the sake of realising potential return. By taking on operational risk, firms earn income while exposing themselves to the risk of incurring operational losses if and when a loss event materialises. Does not this sound like risk-return trade-off? It is risk-return trade-off as argued by Kilavuka (2008) who agrees strongly with Moosa (2007a) on this issue. Kilavuka gives a rather good example to support this point of view, that of a bank with Automatic Telling Machines (ATMs) that are subject to fees when used and also susceptible to fraud. He suggests that "doubling the number of ATMs should increase fee income, but it also increases exposure to fraudulent loss." What matters, he adds, is that "the return justifies the risk."

Doerig (2003, p. 8) disputes the view that operational risk is one-sided by arguing that "OpRisk and OpRisk management are not only about risks and threats" and that "both are chances and opportunities as well." This is why it is rather strange that Doerig subsequently argues that "market and credit risks are revenue driven, OpRisks are not" (p. 11). Another contradictory statement made by Doerig is that "contrary to market and credit risks, OpRisks are usually not willingly incurred" (p. 11). Why is it then that financial institutions expose themselves to the risk of rogue trading when they can avoid it completely by not trading? This is exactly what Doerig implies by stating that "OpRisks are only eliminated if a bank ceases to be." But then he argues that "risk creates value, profits come from risk" (p. 16). There is certainly significant contradiction and inconsistency in these statements, but one tends to think that statements such as that describing operational risk as providing threats and opportunities to be more plausible than those indicating otherwise.

The Idiosyncratic Nature of Operational Risk?

A view that has been put forward repeatedly is that unlike market risk and credit risk, operational risk is idiosyncratic in the sense that when it hits one firm, it does not spread to other firms, implying the absence of contagion and system-wide effects (that is, it is firm-specific, not systemic). For example, Ford and Sundmacher (2007) argue that "operational risk is idiosyncratic because it depends on "the financial institution's particular risk culture and vulnerability." Again, this argument is questionable, because if Bank A suffers losses because of the activities of a rogue trader, and if Banks B and C deal with Bank A, then it is likely (depending on the size of loss) that Bank A will fail to meet its obligations towards them. Hence, contagion and systemic effects would arise, in the sense that Banks B and C will incur losses as a consequence of the rogue trading losses incurred by Bank A.

In a recent editorial of *OpRisk & Compliance*, Davis (2008a) declares: "It's official. Operational risk has just as much potential to be systemic as credit risk and market risk." Operational risk is systemic, not idiosyncratic, because operational losses (at least some event types) are correlated with macroeconomic factors. The risk of credit card fraud increases when the economy is booming and the risk of lawsuits pertaining to employment termination is higher when the economy is in recession. In banking, the profitability associated with certain products depends on the health of the economy, particularly consumer confidence and household income. Then think about the very reason for the establishment of the Basel Committee: the (operational) failure of Bankhaus Herstatt that was liquidated by the German authorities before it had met its obligations to transaction counterparties. The operational failure of one bank affected other banks, and hence the loss event was not idiosyncratic. The same reasoning is valid for the subprime crisis of 2007/2008, which can be thought of as a series of operational failures. If this is the case, and given that the crisis has caused systemic, cross-border losses, it can be safely concluded that operational risk is not idiosyncratic but rather systemic.

Other Distinguishing Features of Operational Risk

Anders (2003) distinguishes operational risk from credit risk and market risks (what he calls external risks) on the grounds that it is the risk inherent in the firm (i.e. within the operational processes and projects). This distinction was actually accepted for some time before the advent of the BCBS's definition of operational risk, which stipulates that operational risk can also result from external factors.

One major difference between operational risk, on the one hand, and market and credit risk, on the other, is the difficulty of defining a suitable "unit" of risk in the case of operational risk (McConnell, 2003). In the case of credit risk, the unit of risk is the entity or individual who could default. In the case of market risk, the unit of risk is an asset (bond, equity, currency, etc.) whose adverse market price movements cause losses. But in the case of operational risk, the unit of risk is an "operational process" whose failure causes a loss.

Buchelt and Unteregger (2004) distinguish operational risk from credit risk and market risk in the banking industry on the grounds that credit risk and market risk are business risks specific to the banking industry, whereas operational risk is a general business risk that has particular features in the banking industry. What is important to bear in mind is that operational risk is not limited to the operations function (the settling of transactions) because it is found across the entire firm. This is the reason for distinguishing between "operational risk" and "operations risk," the latter being a subset of the former.

Another difference between operational risk and other kinds of risk is that the concept of exposure is not clear in the case of operational risk. In the case of credit risk, for example, exposure is the amount lent to a customer, but in the case of operational risk there is no clear-cut equivalent measure of exposure. Jobst (2007a) suggests another distinguishing feature of operational risk by arguing that "operational risk deals mainly with tail events rather than the central projections or tendencies, reflecting the aberrant rather than the normal behavior and situations." This makes it rather difficult to model and predict exposure to operational risk. He adds that "a typical loss profile from operational risk contains occasional extreme losses among frequent events of low loss severity."

Distinguishing Operational Loss Events

Despite the distinction between operational risk on the one hand and market risk and credit risk on the other, it may sometimes appear to be difficult to distinguish among loss events attributed to the three kinds of risk. For example, KPMG (2005) argues that "operational risk losses cannot often be separated clearly from those resulting from credit, market, or other risk types." However, KPMG (2003) considers a view that objects to the treatment of operational risk as a distinct risk type because major consequences will ultimately show up in the credit or market risk "buckets."

KPMG (2003) lists a number of examples of operational loss events that manifest themselves as market risk, including (i) market losses resulting from trading products for which the dealer has no authorization; and (ii) unwanted positions resulting from inappropriate entry and acceptance of orders into electronic trading systems. Likewise, a large number of losses associated with the credit business result from operational risk. One example is a defaulted credit in the wake of mismanaged loan-granting procedure that results in the assignment of an incorrect rating. Another example is losses resulting from the mismanagement of collaterals. The subprime crisis of 2007/2008 provides good examples of operational losses that appear to be market or credit losses.

As an illustrative example, consider the $7.2 billion loss incurred by Societe Generale in early 2008. That was an operational loss event caused by unauthorised trading (failure of people) although the severity of the loss was driven by adverse market movements (the market went down on long positions). It is the cause of the loss that determines whether a loss event is operational or otherwise. It may be tempting to think that the cause of the loss in the case of Societe Generale was adverse market movement and that the severity of the loss was caused by the divergence between what the trader was supposed to do and what he actually did (the extent of the violation of position limits, which was huge). This line of reasoning is not plausible, however, because the cause must precede the consequence (event). Adverse market movements took place after the trader had taken his positions, which means that unauthorised trading was the cause of the loss. Hence, the Societe Generale case represents an operational loss event.

Consider another example that pertains to the foreign exchange market. The risk of losses resulting from an adverse market movement is market risk. In this case, losses could result when the currency denominating a long position depreciates or when the currency denominating a short position appreciates. If that happens, the trader will incur market losses. Operational risk, on the other hand, is the risk of losses arising from failure in the execution of the underlying foreign exchange transaction, particularly in the absence (or lack) of procedures, processes and systems that ensure that proper controls are in place. In January 2004, the National Australia Bank (NAB) incurred significant foreign exchange losses because four traders (three in Melbourne and one in London) had mistakenly forecast depreciation of the Australian and New Zealand currencies against the US dollar. On the surface these are market losses, but they are in fact operational losses because the four traders exploited the weakness in NAB's internal procedures and breached trading limits. Had they not done that, the losses would have been purely market losses. Ford and Sundmacher (2007) argue that "although these losses occurred in daily operations, and this appears more attuned to market risk than operational risk, the fact that these losses arose from inadequate and failed internal processes, systems and people classifies them as operational risk-related from the perspective of bank regulators."

3.3 CLASSIFICATION OF OPERATIONAL RISK

The heterogeneity of operational risk makes it necessary to come up with a system for classifying it and identifying its components. However, this is not an easy task as admitted by the BCBS (2001b), stating that "there is often a high degree of ambiguity inherent in the process of categorizing losses and costs." The classification of operational losses (resulting from exposure to operational risk) can be approached from three alternative angles: the causes of operational failure, the resulting loss events, and the legal and accounting forms of consequential losses. It is possible, however, to link the three criteria of classification as in Figure 3.2. We will concentrate on the second criterion, the loss event, but we start with a description of classification by cause and loss form.

Classification by Cause and Loss Form

The BCBS's definition seems to be more consistent with the first alternative, the causes of operational failure, as the definition encompasses the four broad categories of causes (people, processes, systems and external events) as shown in Figure 3.1. Mainelli (2004) refers the classification of operational

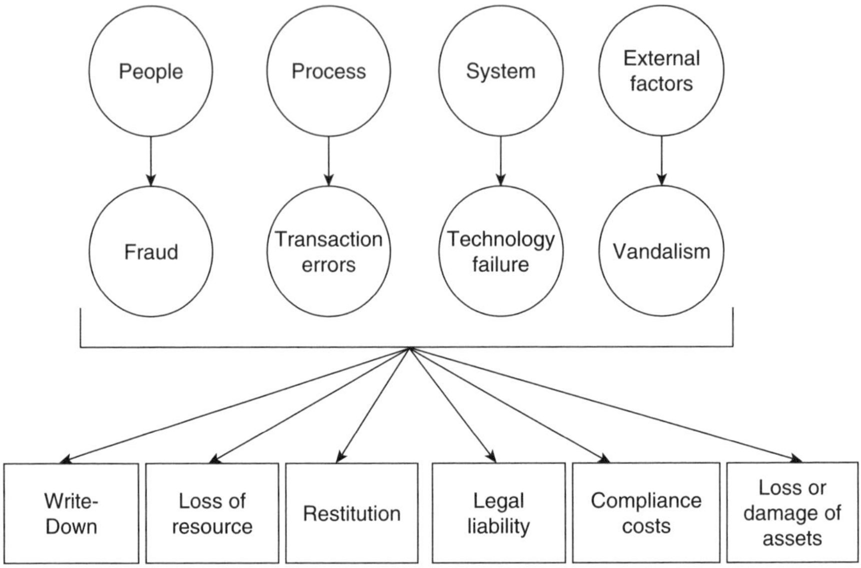

Figure 3.2 Operational Risk: Causes, Events and Forms of Loss

risk by decomposing the BCBS definition by stating that "operational risk has many pseudo-standard sub-taxonomies," arguing that risk classification is more empirical than analytical. He warns of the possibility that operational risk categories may appear to be arbitrary, overlapping or in contradiction with each other. For instance, external risk includes external fraud (EF) (such as external money laundering), natural disasters (such as floods) and non-natural disasters (such as arson), as shown in Figure 3.3, which exhibits a limited set of examples of the risk categories. A more expanded list can be found in Table 3.1.

Doerig (2003) suggests a slightly different classification, which is adopted by Credit Suisse, by adding "organisations" as a source of risk. In this case, operational risk arises from such issues as changes in management, project management, corporate culture and communication, responsibilities and business continuity planning. He calls the process category "policy/process" and the systems category "technology." He further divides these categories into twenty subcategories as shown in Figure 3.4, but he warns of the hazard of considering the twenty subcategories as a complete list, arguing that they would be refined with the passage of time. Doerig emphasises the classification of risk by cause, arguing that "by linking causation to relevant business activities, it is intended to use this structure as a tool with which to act upon OpRisk, thereby providing management with an OpRisk framework."

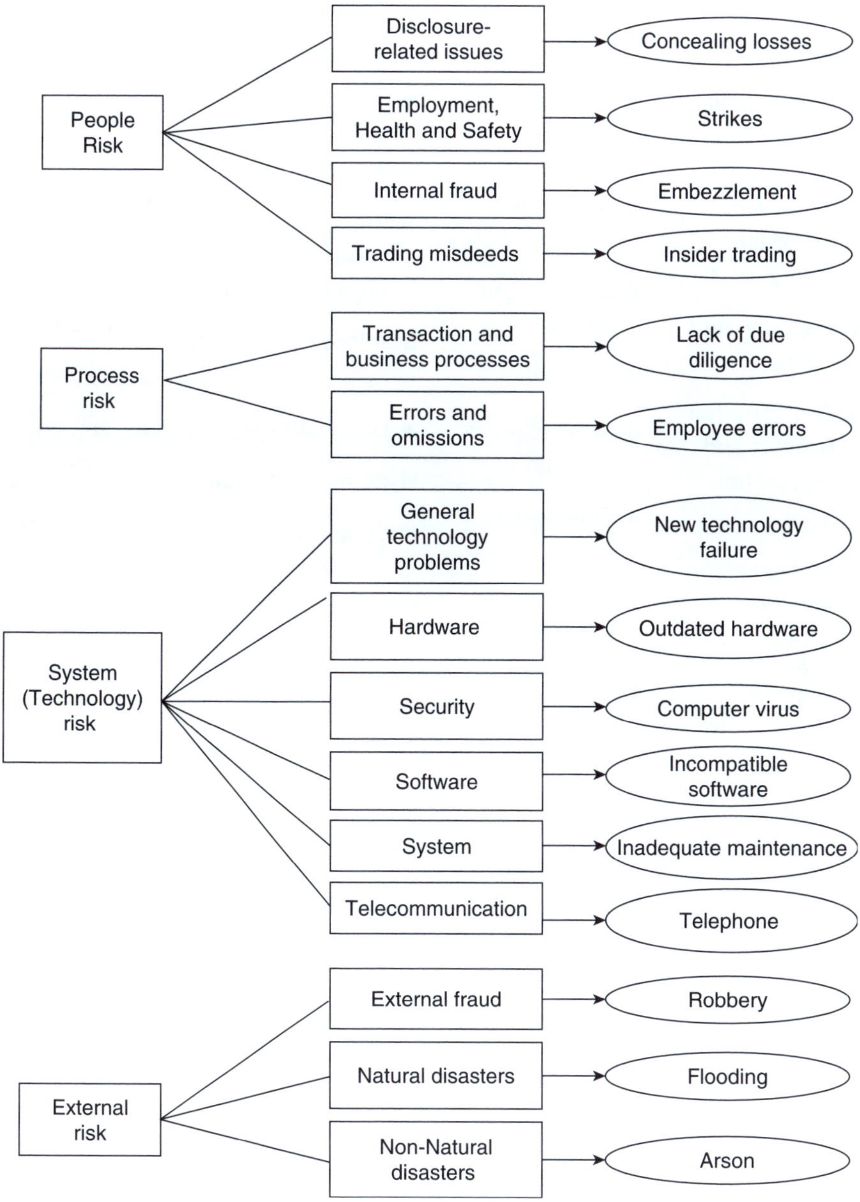

Figure 3.3 Operational Risk by Cause

Table 3.1 Examples of Operational Risk by Cause

People	*Processes*	*Systems*	*External*
■ Unauthorised trading ■ Insider dealing ■ Fraud ■ Employee illness and injury ■ Discrimination claims ■ Compensation benefits and termination issues ■ Problems recruiting or retaining staff ■ Organised labour activity ■ Other legal issues	■ Breach of mandate ■ Incorrect/ untimely transaction execution and settlement ■ Loss of client assets ■ Mispricing ■ Incorrect asset allocation ■ Compliance issues ■ Corporate action errors ■ Stock lending errors ■ Accounting and taxation errors ■ Inadequate record-keeping ■ Subscription and redemption errors	■ Hardware/software failure ■ Unavailability and questionable integrity of data ■ Unauthorised access to information and systems security ■ Telecommunication failure ■ Utility outage ■ Computer hacking ■ Computer viruses	■ Operational failure at suppliers or outsourced operations ■ Fire and natural disasters ■ Terrorism ■ Vandalism ■ Theft and robbery

Source: KPMG (2003).

Classification of operational losses can be based on the criterion of the form of losses. Materialised losses can take several forms, including asset write-down, loss of recourse, restitution, legal liability, regulation and compliance cost, and the loss or damage of assets. This classification scheme is arguably not useful for any meaningful purpose. Restitution refers to payments to third parties resulting from operational losses for which the firm is legally responsible. Loss of recourse refers to losses experienced when a

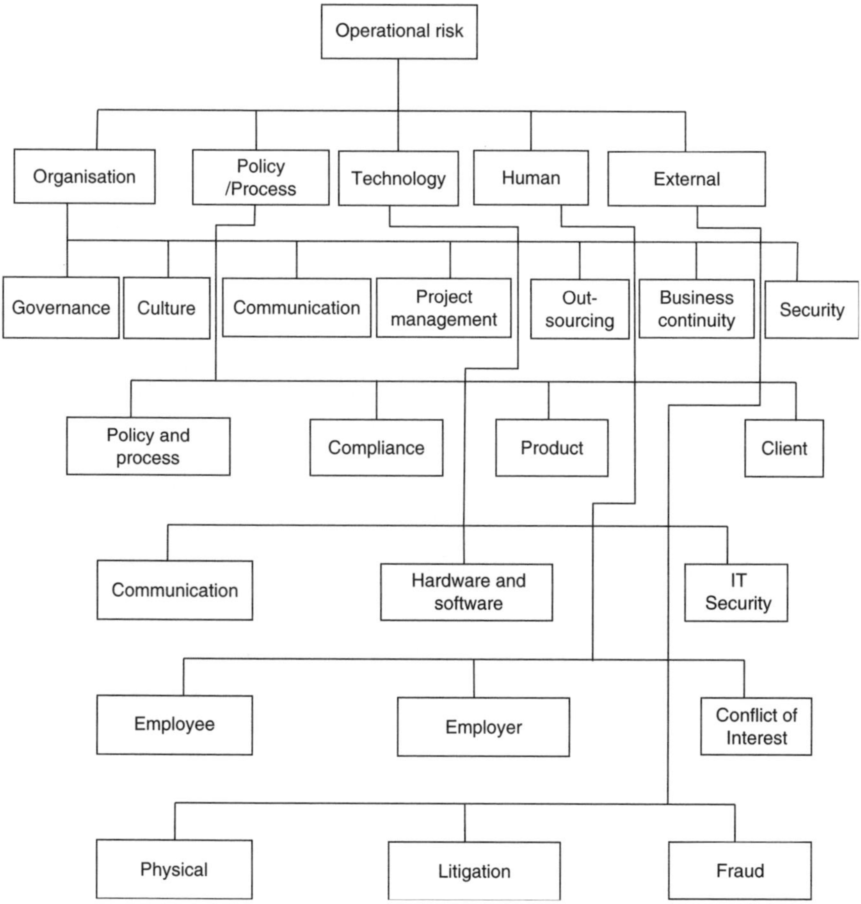

Figure 3.4 The Credit Suisse Classification of Operational Risk by Cause

third party does not meet its obligations to the firm, provided the outcome is attributable to an operational loss event.

The BCBS's Classification of Loss Events

The BCBS has come up with a classification of operational loss events into seven categories, as shown in Figure 3.5. These categories are (i) internal fraud (IF); (ii) external fraud (EF); (iii) employment practices and workplace safety (EPWS); (iv) clients, products and business practices (CPBP); (v) damage to physical assets (DPA); (vi) business disruption and system failure (BDSF); and (vii) execution, delivery and process management (EDPM).

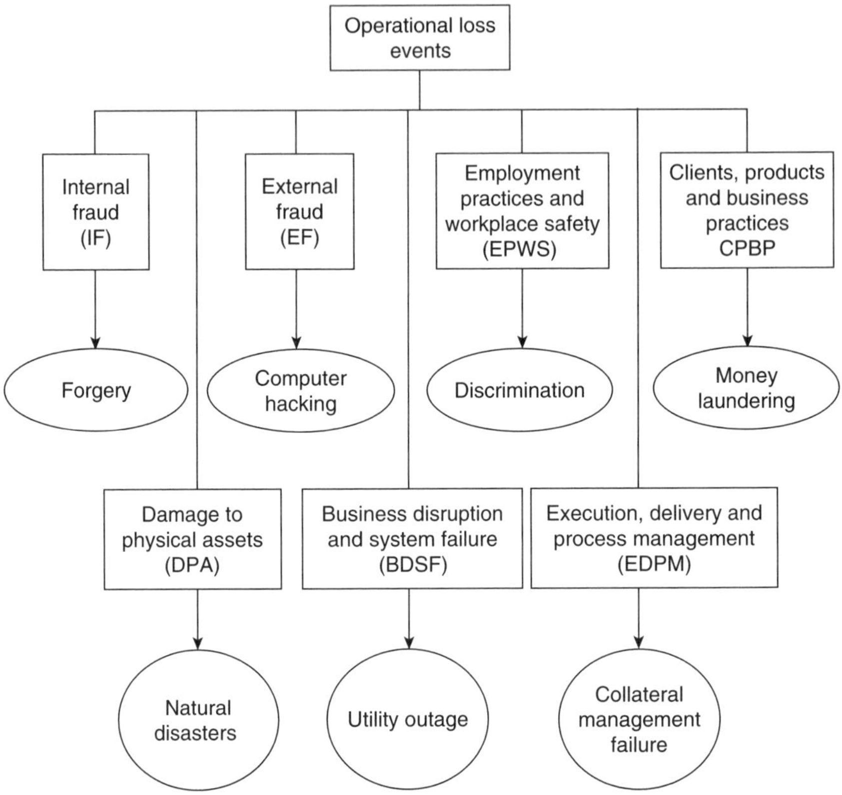

Figure 3.5 The BCBS Classification of Operational Losses by Event Type

One problem with the BCBS classification is that some of the subcategories, such as fraud, do not have an exact legal or regulatory meaning. The term is used in a generic way to designate a variety of forms of (mostly non-violent) economic wrongdoing, whose commission constitutes a criminal offence and/or civil wrong. Examples of fraud are theft, unauthorised withdrawal of money from ATMs, forgery and unauthorised trading. In relation to loss events involving rogue trading as fraud, Adusei-Poku (2005) makes the following two observations on the basis of a report by the Committee for Professionalism of the International Financial Market Association: (i) fraud is usually perpetrated through a simple exploitation of lax controls through the transaction flow process, such as poor confirmation details checking and poor oversight by a firm's managers; and (ii) the ultimate responsibility for fraud must rest with senior management who should ensure that the systems and controls in place within their organisations are robust enough to identify erroneous trades and employee wrongdoing.

It may also be the case that some important subcategories are missing from this classification scheme. In an article in *Financial Times*, Sanghera (2005) concluded that "dealing with smelly employees in these days of windowless workplaces and cubicles may be one of the biggest management challenges of our time." Therefore, should employment practices and workplace safety have a category called "employee offensive odour"? Also, McConnell (2006) argues that many large operational loss events do not "fit easily into very broad one size fits all Basel II event type classification" and that they "cut across many of the mandated categories."

In a paper on the classification of operational loss events, OpRisk Analytics (2002) describe the BCBS classification by saying that "categorizing in this manner is like categorizing by shape – using squares, circles, triangles and rectangles – while simultaneously categorizing by color – identifying some objects as red, others as blue and then making an exception, for example, by moving all rectangles of perimeter 16 in the square category, since 16 is equal to four squares." In a more serious and less sarcastic statement, OpRisk Analytics describes the BCBS classification as "logically inconsistent and contains overlapping identifications, and hence is conceptually flawed." For example, the argument goes, the category of consumers, products and business practices is defined in terms of cause, which makes it span multiple events and potentially correlated with other categories, such as internal fraud and execution, delivery and process management. Given this potential for overlaps, it is suggested that the need arises for rules to determine how to draw lines between two risk categories. The OpRisk Analytics report suggests classification criteria that take into account the following considerations: (i) management information (so that the information would be useful for management purposes); (ii) logical consistency (between categories and subcategories); and (iii) statistical purity (the underlying data should not be correlated, and at the lowest level should represent homogenous distributions).

Cech (2007) agrees with the view that the Basel event types are not perfect but he suggests that arguments against the classification have subsided because "the Basel Committee issued a series of interpretive papers without reopening the hierarchy for discussion or clarifying its ambiguities." He further contends that "event types remain something of an uneasy fixture on the landscape, neither actively vetted and embraced by the community, nor likely to disappear any time soon." Cech attributes the difficulty of classifying risk events to the imprecise concept of event type. He starts his re-examination of the classification by defining a loss event as "something that happens (or fails to happen) in executing an operational process, and which causes the final results of the process to differ from our original desires or expectations." Subsequently, he suggests a number of criteria for defining categories of operational loss events. These criteria include the following: (i) the hierarchy should be of manageable size and scope; (ii) labels should be as intuitive as possible; (iii) each event should fall (ideally) into only one category; (iv) category "buckets" should reflect differences in the way risk managers react to particular breakouts; (v) category boundaries should be defined clearly and used consistently; (vi) category definitions should be based on event characteristics, not impact types, causes or controls; and (vii) high-level categories generally should not be defined in terms of specific business lines or products.

Classification by Frequency and Severity

Operational loss events differ in terms of frequency (probability) and severity (size, impact or intensity). Loss events can be divided into high-frequency, low-severity events (which occur regularly) and low-frequency, high-severity events (which are rare but produce huge losses if they occur). The low-frequency, high-severity risks (such as internal fraud, which could jeopardise the whole future of the firm) are risks associated with loss events that lie in the right tail of the total loss distribution. High-frequency, low-severity risks (such as credit card fraud and some human risks) have high expected loss but relatively low unexpected loss.

Frequency and severity are determined by different factors. In the case of a financial institution encountering contractual problems in selling its services, the frequency of loss events is determined by the number of different products on offer, whereas severity is determined by the number of customers and the balance sheet of the institution. Another example is the frequency and severity of robberies in retail banking: frequency is determined by the number of branches, whereas severity is determined by the amount of cash in a particular branch. Frequency and severity, therefore, are independent of each other.

Figures 3.6–3.9 illustrate the BCBS's classification of loss events by frequency and severity, using the low-medium-high (L-M-H) scale. In Figure 3.6, internal fraud is classified as a low-frequency, high-severity event, whereas external fraud can be in any one of four cells. Also, nothing appears in the high-frequency, high-severity cell, which is logical (e.g., rogue traders *a la* Societe Generale et al appear once in a life time, if ever). In Figure 3.7, the loss events are classified by frequency and severity across business lines. For example, internal fraud is a low-frequency, high-severity event in commercial banking (CB) but a low-frequency, medium-severity event in retail banking. External fraud is a high-frequency, low-severity event in retail banking and a low-frequency, low-severity event in payment and settlement. Figures 3.8 and 3.9 show the frequency and severity of loss events across business lines. In Figure 3.8, internal fraud is a low-frequency event across all business lines. In Figure 3.9, external fraud is a medium-severity

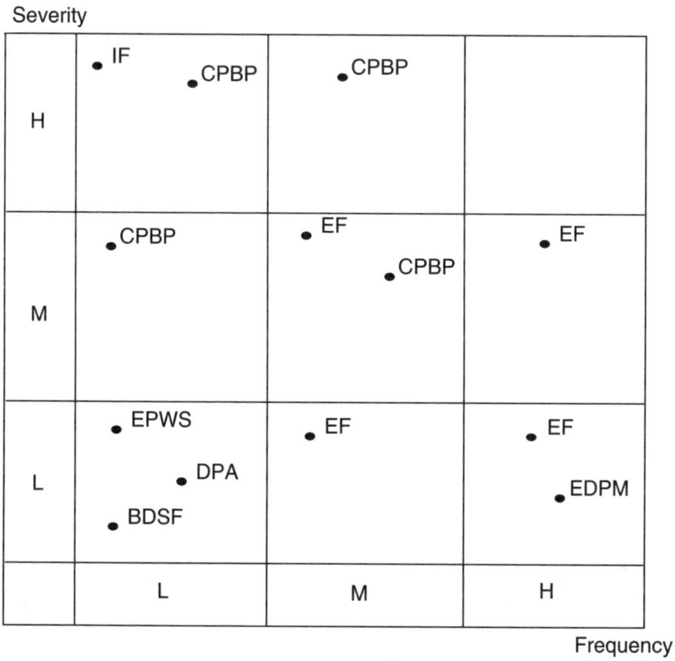

Figure 3.6 Classification of Loss Events by Frequency and Severity

event in CF and a low-severity event in AM. These classifications are, however, theoretical and may differ from the classification of actual loss data, as we are going to see later when we examine three sets of loss data.

Based on the frequency and severity of events, Doerig (2003) refers to the classification of the system used by the US Air Force modified to be applicable to banking. According to frequency, loss events are classified into unlikely, seldom, occasional, likely and frequent. According to severity, losses are classified under negligible, moderate, critical and catastrophic. The combinations of these categories of frequency and severity produce low risk, medium risk, high risk and extremely high risk. This framework is shown in Figure 3.10.

Apart from frequency and severity, another two facets of operational risk events are context dependency and interaction (contagion/correlation) with other events. Context dependency refers to variation of loss events across different situations and whether or not operational risk events are unique or show regularity in occurrence. Because the major drivers of operational risk are people and firms, context dependency is high for operational risk compared with credit risk and market risk. Interaction describes the interlinkages between events and how they are correlated.

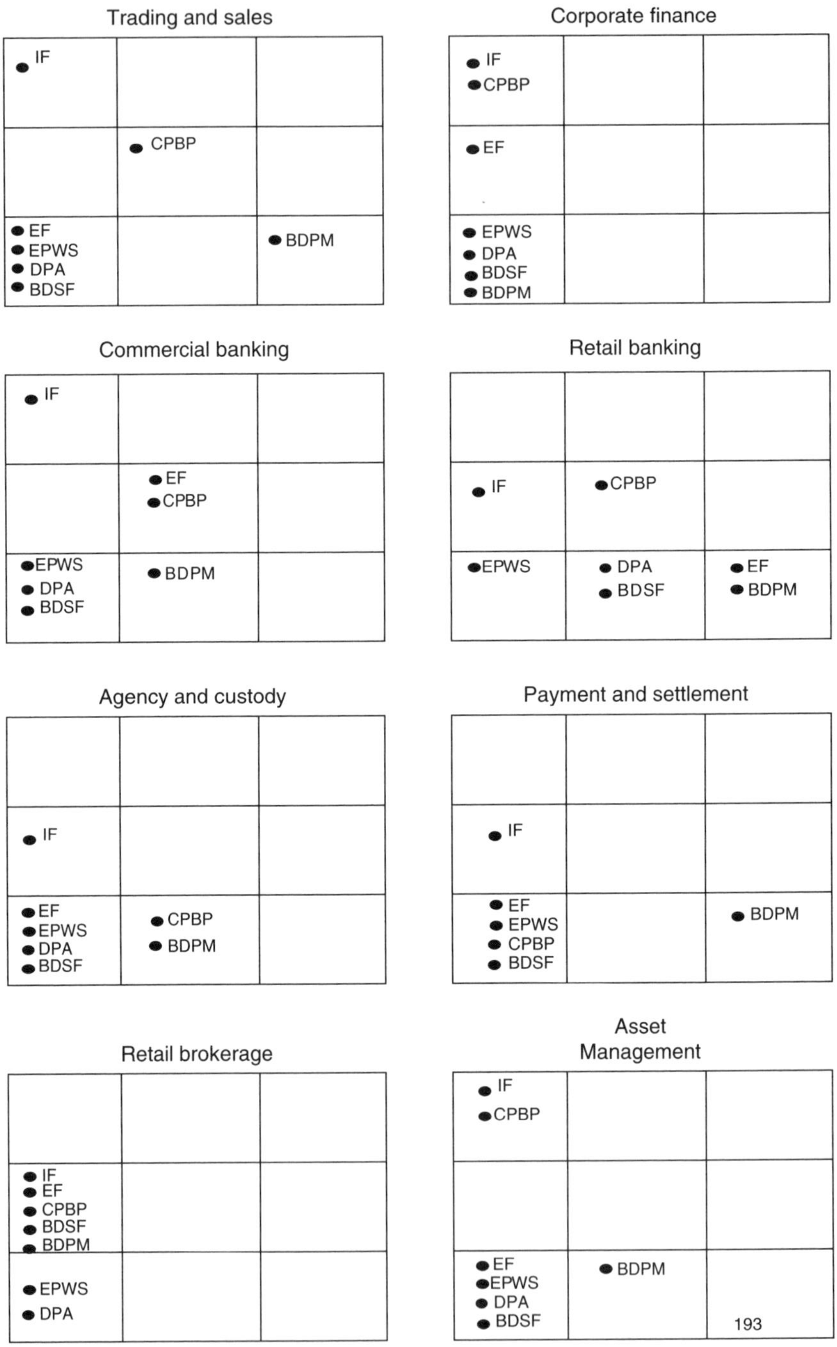

Figure 3.7 Classification of Loss Events by Frequency, Severity and Business Line

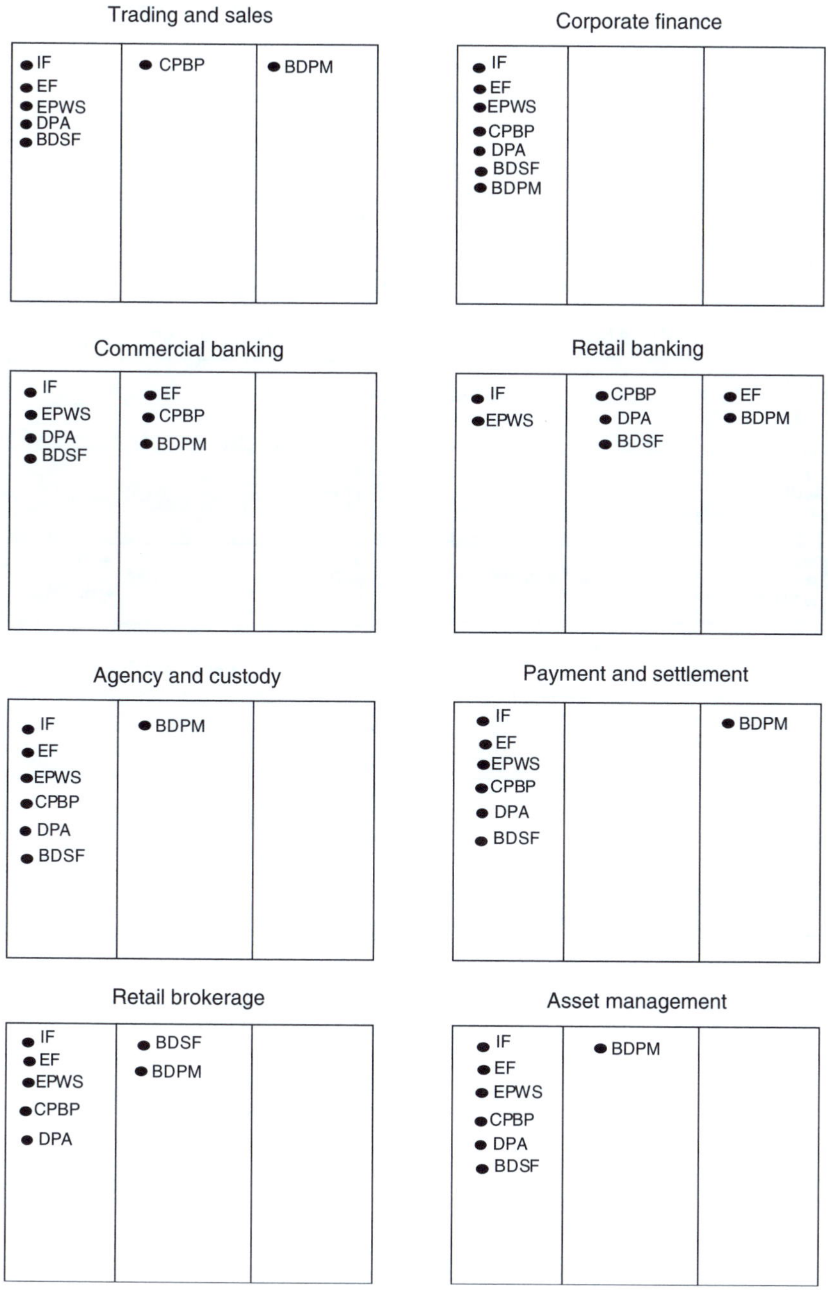

Figure 3.8 Frequency of Loss Events by Business Line

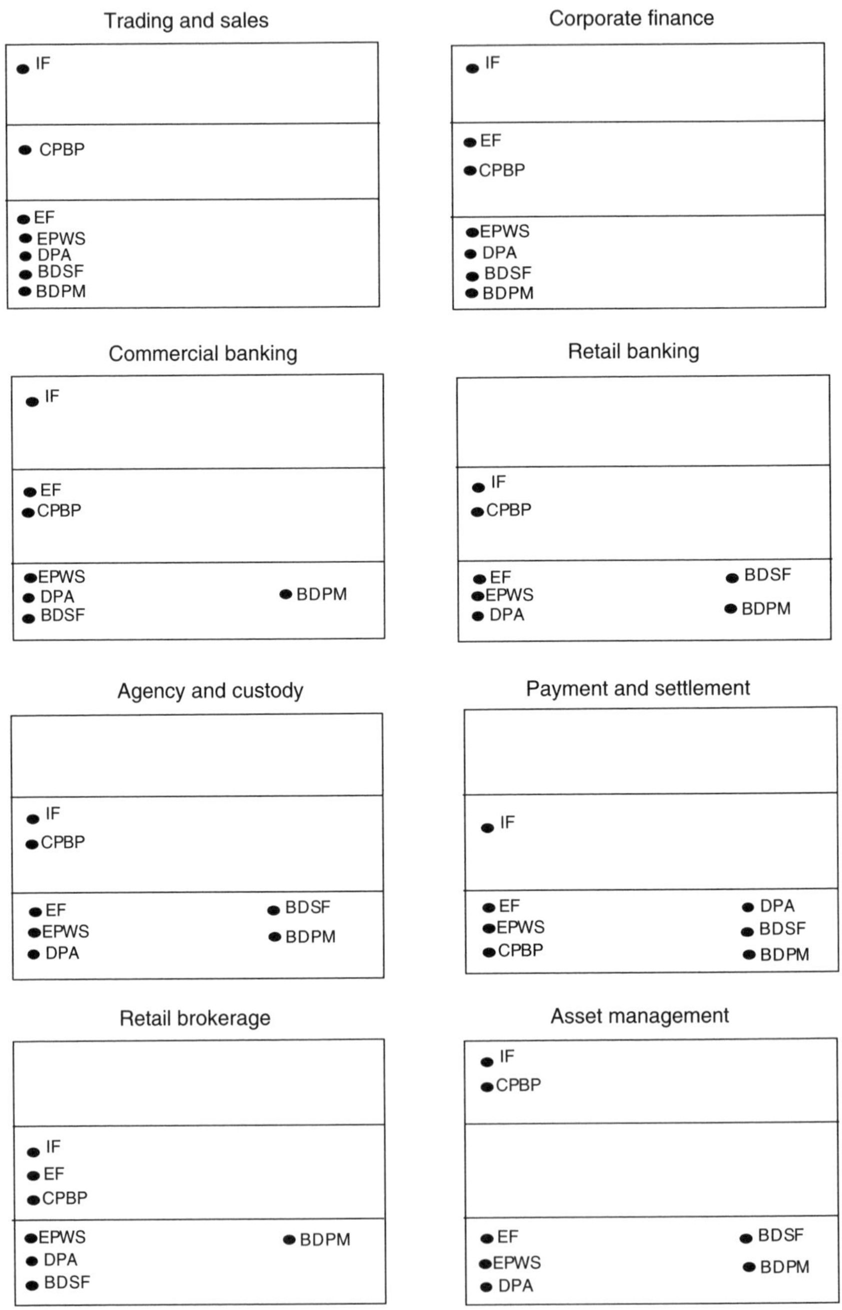

Figure 3.9 Severity of Loss Events by Business Line

Severity					
Catastrophic	Medium	High	Extremely high	Extremely High	Extremely high
Critical	Low	Medium	High	High	Extremely High
Moderate	Low	Low	Medium	Medium	High
Negligible	Low	Low	Low	Low	Medium
	Unlikely	Seldom	Occasional	Likely	Frequent
					Frequency

Figure 3.10 A Modified US Air Force Risk Classification System

Nominal, Ordinary and Exceptional Risk

Based on the frequency of loss events, Pezier (2003b) classifies operational risk into nominal, ordinary and exceptional, as shown in Figure 3.11. Nominal operational risk is the risk of repetitive losses (say, losses that may occur on average once a week or more frequently) associated with an ongoing activity such as settlement, minor external fraud (credit cards), or human error in transaction processing. Ordinary operational risk is the risk of less frequent (say, between once a week and once every generation) but larger losses, yet not life-threatening for the firm.

Exceptional operational risk produces losses that have no more than a few per cent chance of occurrence over a year, but those losses may be life-threatening. Examples of exceptional loss events include the losses experienced by the Bank of Commerce and Credit International (1993), Barings Bank (1995), Diawa Securities (1995), Long-Term Capital Management (LTCM) (1998), Allied Irish Bank (2002), CBI (2003), Yukos Oil Company (2004), Central Bank of Brazil (2005) and Societe Generale (2008). These exceptional losses resulted from illegal activities, rogue trading, management incompetence, conflict of interest, model bias, internal fraud and external fraud (including robbery). A brief description of these loss events, as well as some other highly publicised events that have been mentioned earlier, can be found in Appendix 3.1.

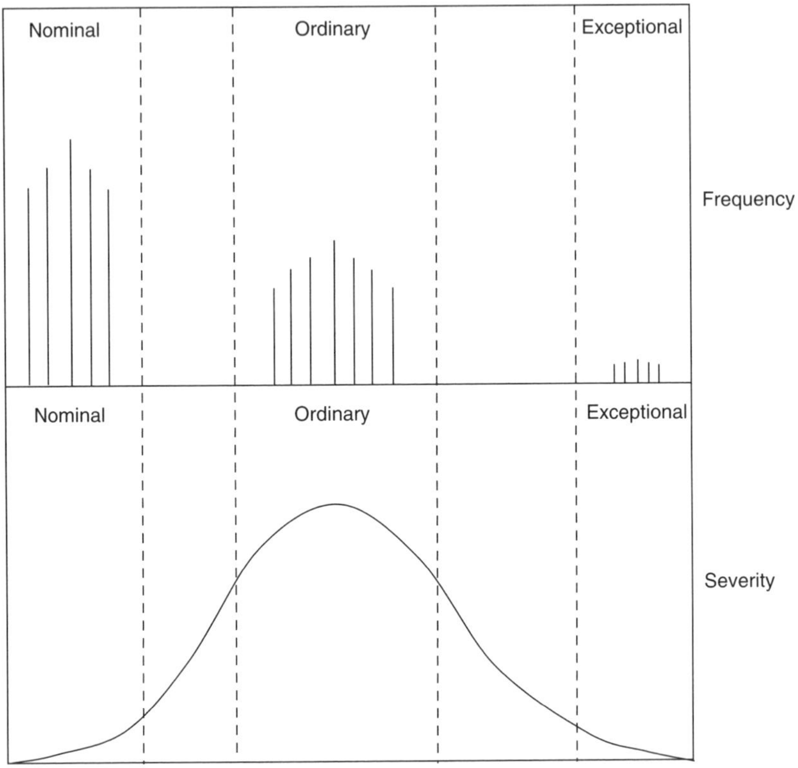

Figure 3.11 Nominal, Ordinary and Exceptional Operational Risk

Classification of Extreme Loss Events

McConnell (2006) suggests a classification of extreme operational loss events into (i) perfect storm; (ii) ethical meltdown; (iii) infrastructure disasters; and (iv) learning curve. A perfect storm means "the confluence of a number of different seemingly innocuous factors to create a once-in-a-life-time catastrophic event." McConnell attributes perfect storms (such as the one that hit Societe Generale) to a combination of risk drivers, including (i) fraudulent activity on the part of one person or a group (primarily to protect and boost bonuses); (ii) trading in derivatives; (iii) a major market movement precipitating losses; (iv) no adherence to policies and procedures; and (v) aberrant corporate culture that does not encourage open questioning about risk.

An ethical meltdown refers to scandals involving improper activities such as inappropriate use of investment research, preferential allocation of shares in new initial public offerings, and inappropriate pricing of mutual funds (this malpractice is called spinning). Infrastructure disasters may result from terrorist attacks. Finally, a learning curve refers to the losses that may result in the process of adopting new technology. The learning curve is a representation of reliability theory, designed to determine the likelihood of a component failure at a particular point in time. McConnell (2003) demonstrates how reliability theory is applied to operational risk.

Inherent versus Residual Risk

Operational risk may be classified, by taking into account the effect of risk controls, into inherent (or gross) risk and residual (or net) risk. Inherent risk in a business unit, which is the present level of risk without the effect of risk controls, depends on the level of activity relative to the firm's resources, number of transactions, complexity of the activity and the potential loss to the firm. Residual risk, on the other hand, is the risk remaining after accounting for risk controls. A simple example on the distinction between inherent risk and residual risk is that placing limits on the value of the credit lines that can be approved by a loan officer would reduce the potential loss if this loan officer approves a loan to a less-than-creditworthy customer.

Risk mitigation (such as insurance) has the same effect. Insurance reduces the potential loss, in which case the level of risk without taking insurance into account is inherent risk, whereas the risk net of the expected insurance compensation is residual risk. The difference between the effects of risk controls and mitigation is that, controls can be used to reduce the probability of loss, whereas risk mitigation cannot be used for the same purpose. Figure 3.12 shows how the application of risk controls and mitigation changes the loss distribution, effectively creating separate distributions for inherent and residual risks. Two distributions are associated with residual risk: one exhibits a reduction in potential loss without any change in probability whereas the other shows reduction in both the size of potential loss and the probability of incurring losses.

Classification Based on Quantifiability

A classification scheme may be based on risk quantification. Under this scheme, operational risk can be classified into quantifiable risk, transferable/insurable risk and agency risk. Quantifiable risks are those that can be quantified at the firm and industry level. Transferable/insurable risks are low-frequency, high-severity risks. Agency risks are characterised by very low frequency and very high severity. These risks, according to Bhatia (2002), are not quantifiable or insurable. The irony, if we accept Bhatia's argument, is that these are the very risks that banks are told (by the Basel Committee) to quantify.

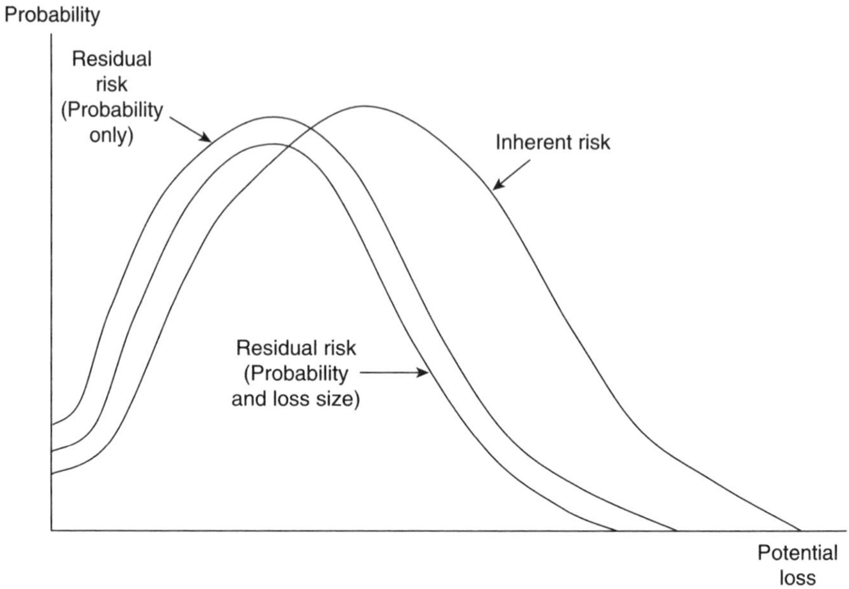

Figure 3.12 The Distributions of Inherent and Residual Risk

3.4 SURVEYS OF OPERATIONAL LOSS DATA

To get a feel of the frequency and severity of operational loss events in recent years, we examine the findings of three operational loss data surveys conducted by the BCBS (2003b), the Federal Reserve System et al (2005), and by the Japanese Financial Services Agency and the Bank of Japan (2007). The results of these surveys are discussed briefly in this section

It is noteworthy here that the empirical risk maps appearing in this section are plotted by measuring severity on the horizontal axis and frequency on the vertical axis (unlike the theoretical risk map in Figure 3.6). In addition to the absence of a clear convention on which axis is used to measure frequency and severity, this switch indicates that the plots do not represent functional relations between frequency and severity, because they are independent of each other (recall the argument that frequency and severity are determined by different factors). A risk map is a graphical representation of the classification of actual or potential loss events according to frequency and severity. This classification is not affected by which axis is used to measure which parameter.

The BCBS Loss Data Collection Exercise

In 2002 the BCBS asked participating banks to provide information on operational losses in 2001. A total of eighty-nine banks participated in the

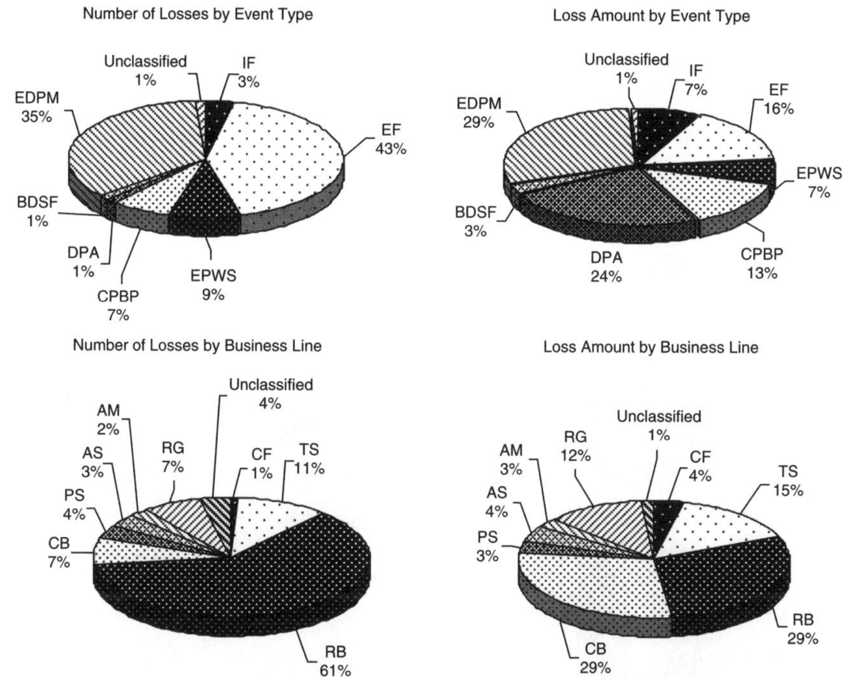

Figure 3.13 Loss Events by Type and Business Line (BCBS Data)

exercise, reporting the number of loss events and the amounts involved (in millions of Euros). The reported losses were classified by business lines and event types according to the BCBS's classification scheme, but some reported losses were unclassified. A total of 47,269 events were reported worth EUR7.8 billion.

Figure 3.13 displays the number of losses and loss amounts classified by event type and business line. The most frequent event type turned out to be external fraud (43% of the total), whereas most of the losses were incurred in retail banking (more than 60%). As far as the loss amount is concerned, 29% came under EDPM and 29% was under RB and CB. In terms of business line/event type combinations, the most frequent losses resulted from external fraud in retail banking, whereas the largest loss amounts resulted from DPA in CB.

Switching now to the concepts of frequency and severity, the frequency is the number of loss events, whereas average severity can be calculated by dividing the total loss incurred under a certain loss event type or business line by the corresponding number of losses. Figure 3.14 displays the average severity of the losses by event type and business line. It shows that the most severe losses occurred in CB, taking the form of DPA. Note, however, that these are averages that pertain to this particular sample of data. One would expect the severity of a loss incurred as a result of the activities of a rogue trader to be greater than the losses resulting from DPA unless, of course, we are

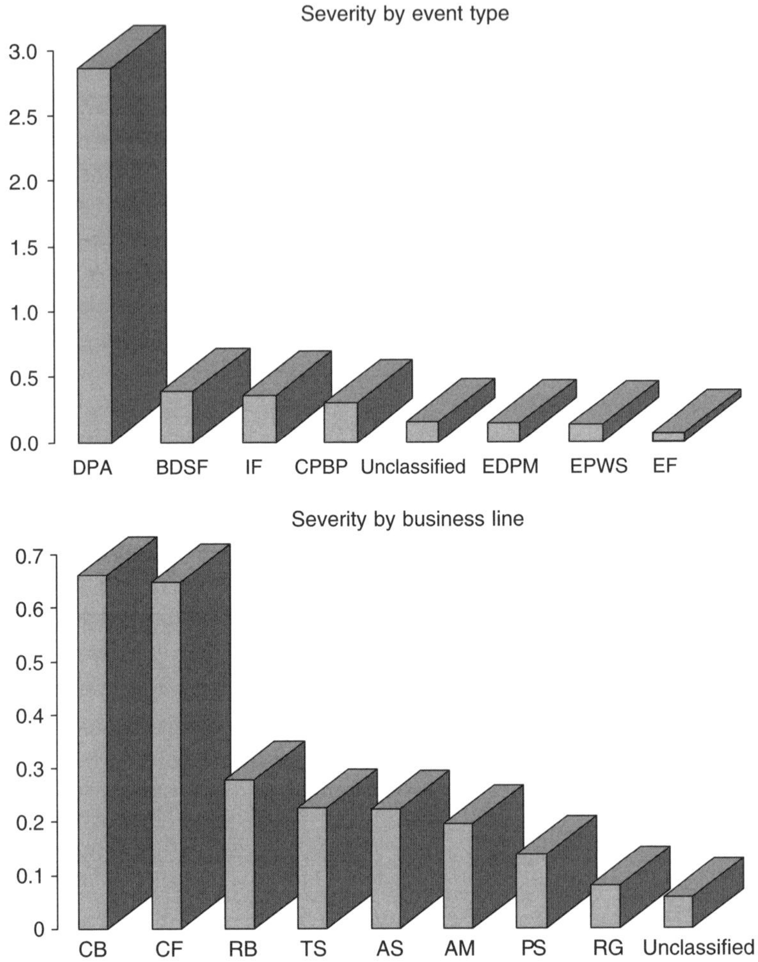

Figure 3.14 Severity by Business Line and Event Type (BCBS Data)

talking about an event involving a natural disaster or a major terrorist attack on the corporate infrastructure.

Figure 3.15 is a risk map exhibiting all combinations of business lines/ event types (each dot represents a single event type/business line combination). The risk map is drawn in such a way as to show three classes of severity and frequency (low, medium and high). As we can see, there is a concentration of points in the lower left-hand corner, implying that most of the events fall in the low-frequency, low-severity category. Only one combination appears as a high-frequency, low-severity event and three combinations represent low-frequency, high-severity events. There are also some combinations that appear in the low-frequency, medium-severity category.

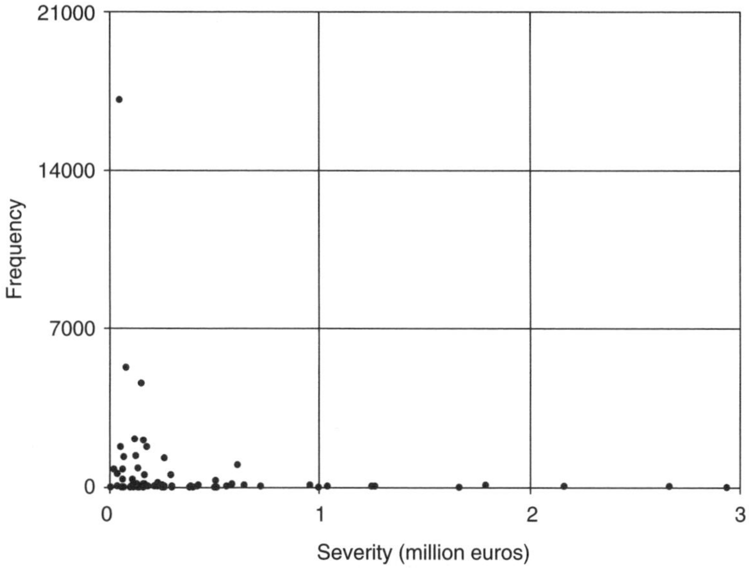

Figure 3.15 A Risk Map of the BCBS Loss Events (by Event Type/Business Line)

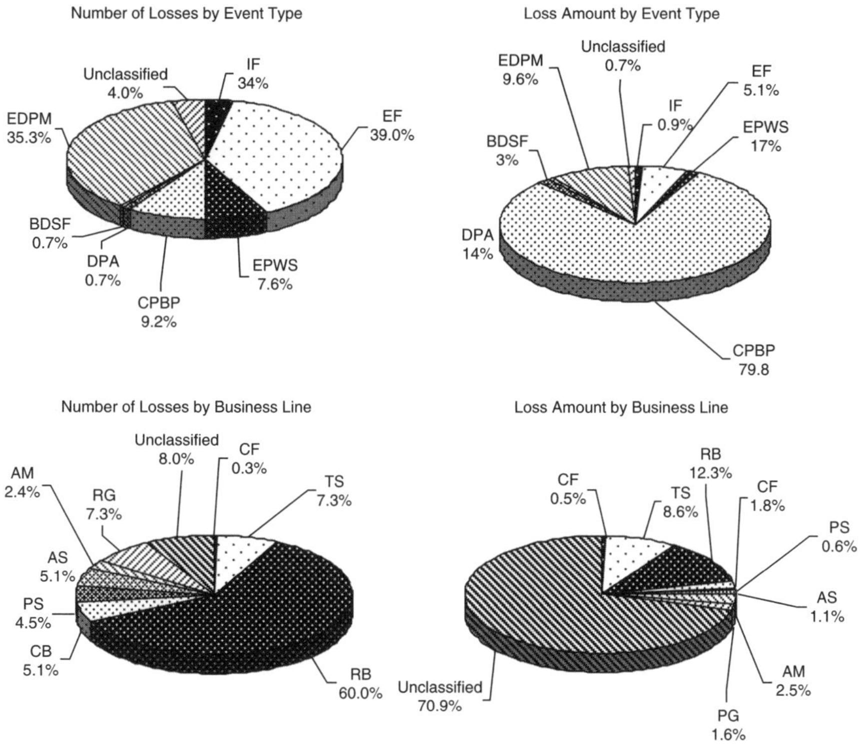

Figure 3.16 Loss Events by Type and Business Line (US LDCE Data)

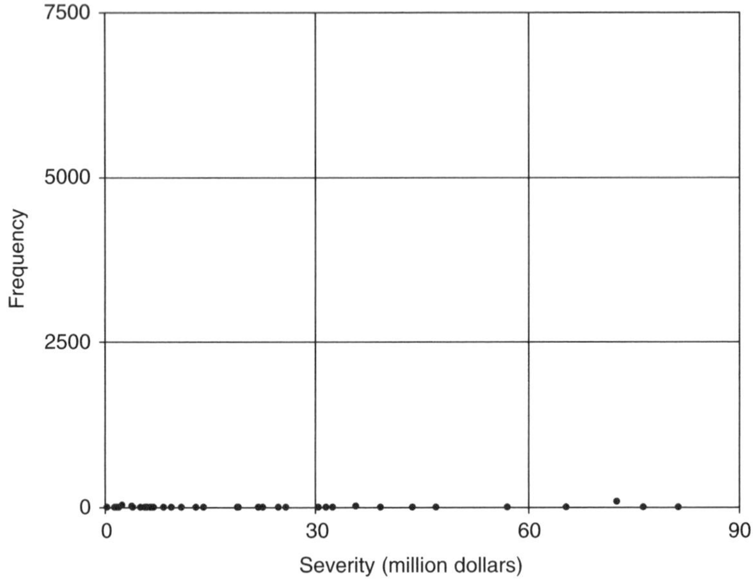

Figure 3.17 A Risk Map of the US Loss Events (by Event Type/Business Line)

The US Loss Data Collection Exercise

A similar data collection exercise was undertaken in the US in 2004 by the Federal Reserve System, Office of the Comptroller of the Currency, Office of Thrift Supervision and the Federal Deposit Insurance Corporation (FDIC). A total of twenty-seven institutions took part in the survey (for more details, see Federal Reserve System et al, 2005).

Figure 3.16 reports the classification of the 56,000 (out of a submitted total of 1.5 million loss events) losses exceeding $10,000 by event type and business line. More than half of the losses occurred in retail banking, taking mostly the form of external fraud and execution, delivery and process management. The majority of total loss amounts fall under "unclassified" with respect to business lines and under consumer, product and business practices with respect to event types. The risk map in Figure 3.17 shows that losses incurred in combinations of business lines and event types were mostly low-frequency, low-severity events, although some appear under low-frequency, medium-severity events and low-frequency, high-severity events.

The Japanese Loss Data Collection Exercise

The Japanese loss data collection exercise (LDCE) was conducted jointly by the Financial Service Agency and the Bank of Japan in 2007. A total

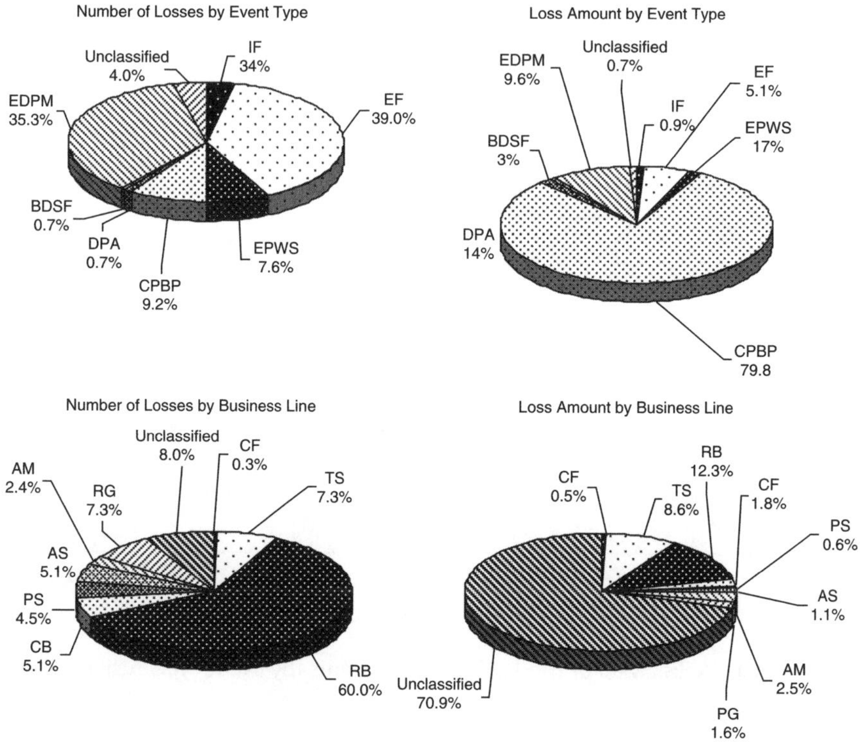

Figure 3.18 Loss Events by Type and Business Line (Japanese LDCE Data)

of fourteen banks and bank holding companies participated in the survey. Figure 3.18 shows the classification of loss events by type and business line.

More than half of the losses (in number) occurred in RB than in CB. With respect to event type, execution, delivery and process management (EDPM) and external fraud accounted for the largest number of losses. Nearly half of the total loss amount was reported in CB, followed by trading and sales. With respect to event type, EDPM and CPBP accounted for more than three quarters of the total loss amount. The risk map in Figure 3.19 shows that most events occurred in combinations of types and business lines are low-frequency, low-severity events, although there are a few high-frequency low-severity events.

Comparing the Patterns of Numbers/Amounts

Table 3.2 shows the event types and business lines where the highest and lowest numbers and amounts were recorded in the three surveys. There seems to be a regular pattern with respect to the number of events: in all of the three surveys, the highest number of events occurred in retail banking,

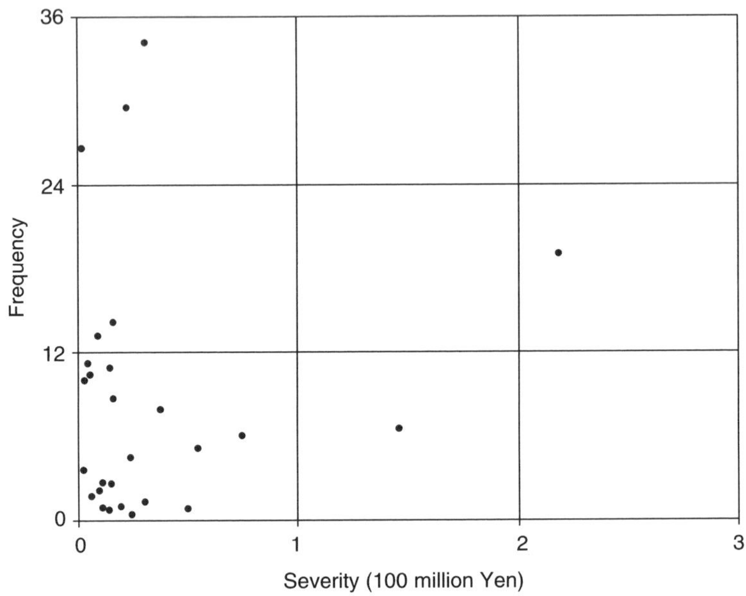

Figure 3.19 A Risk Map of the Japanese Loss Events (by Event Type/Business Line)

Table 3.2 The Patterns of Numbers/Amounts

	BCBS	*U.S.*	*Japan*
Number			
Event Type (Highest)	EF	EF	EDPM
Event Type (Lowest)	BDSF, DPA	BDSF, DPA	CPBP
Business Line (Highest)	RB	RB	RB
Business Line (Lowest)	CF	CF	CF
Amount			
Event Type (Highest)	EDPM	CPBP	EDPM
Event Type (Lowest)	BDSF	IF	IF
Business Line (Highest)	CB, RB	CB	CB
Business Line (Lowest)	AM	CF	PS

whereas the lowest number occurred in corporate finance (CF). The other regular pattern is that CB is the business line where the largest loss amounts were incurred. No other regular pattern can be observed.

3.5 EXTERNAL OPERATIONAL LOSS DATABASES

External databases may take two forms: consortium databases and public databases. These two forms of public databases are discussed in turn.

Consortium Databases

A consortium (industry-pooled) database is a contributory scheme where members contribute their own loss data in return for access to the loss data of other members. Examples of consortium databases are the database of the British Bankers' Association (BBA), (the global operational loss database (GOLD), and the Operational Riskdata eXchange (ORX). According to Samad-Khan et al (2006), a problem with GOLD is that the losses are classified by cause rather than according the Basel loss events. ORX follows specific reporting standards (available at www.orx.org). The database contains information on the loss amount, event type, business line, country and the relevant dates, as well as information on the gross income produced by each business line. A coded identifier field allows the investigator to determine which losses were incurred by the same bank, while maintaining the confidentiality of the bank's identity. The loss data comes from a heterogonous group of forty-two banks.

There are currently plans to establish consortium databases in other parts of the world. In November 2007, the Asian Banking Council (comprising banking association executives from 10 Asian countries) agreed to establish an external database for member countries. The appetite for this project has been gauged via an extensive survey of member associations and banks. The Indian Banking Association is also moving in this direction by calling for expression of interest from 16 companies, including ORX and Risk Business. Some member countries, such as Singapore, have tried to establish databases on their own, but these endeavours produced nothing. One reason for the failure to establish a database is that the number of banks in one country is too small to ensure anonymity, whereas international banks operating in the same country have other arrangements, in which case they are not interested.

A feature of consortium databases is that they do not contain descriptive information for the purpose of maintaining confidentiality. Only general statistics are provided, which makes any meaningful scaling of the data rather difficult, if not impossible. Because these databases do not allow event-by-event access to the losses, they cannot be used to construct a database combining external and internal data (Dahen and Dionne, 2007), which is a prerequisite for modelling operational risk.

Public Databases

Public databases, which record publicly released loss events, are classified into quantitative databases (such as those run by Aon, Fitch (OpVar) and SAS), and qualitative databases, such as Fitch (First). Quantitative databases contain loss information, description and supplementary data (e.g., the size of the firm). The loss events are classified according to the Basel standards.

Qualitative databases contain long write-ups and useful information obtained from multiple sources providing a comprehensive analysis of the circumstances under which the loss events occur, but no supplementary data are provided. The focus of qualitative databases is not on capturing every event that takes place but rather to capture events that are of greater relevance and interest to the subscriber. This selectivity invariably results in reporting bias, which is a serious problem associated with external data. A qualitative database typically provides the information shown in Table 3.3.

Baud et al (2002) identify two differences between public databases and industry-pooled (consortium) databases, the first of which is the threshold for the recorded losses, as the threshold is expected to be much higher in the case of public databases than in consortium databases. This is because operational loss data are collected with some threshold, in the sense that loss amounts below the threshold will not be recorded in the database. The second difference is the level of confidence one can place on the information provided by the database. For example, nothing ensures that the threshold declared by a consortium database is the actual threshold, as banks are not necessarily prepared to uncover all losses above this threshold even though they pretend to do so. Samad-Khan et al (2006) argue that the advantage of consortium databases over public ones is that the former are free from the media reporting bias. There are, however, other problems with consortium data. In some firms, internal reporting is not comprehensive and categorisation tends to be less consistent. Because consortium data represent a subset of total loss data, it may not contain sufficient information in the high risk classes.

External data, therefore, may be obtained from consortium or public databases. In both cases, operational loss data are either provided by the member firms or extracted from the media. Another source of external data is insurance brokers. Insurance data, which originate from insurance claims

Table 3.3 Elements of the Information Provided by a Qualitative Database

Item	*Description/Example*
Organisation	
■ Name	The name of the "umbrella" organisation
■ Firm	The specific firm (or subsidiary) within the umbrella organisation
■ Country	The country where the firm is located
Details	
■ Loss Amount	For example, 5 million
■ Currency	For example, US dollar
■ Original Currency Amount	For example, Hong Kong dollar
■ Status	Closed/Still Going
■ Geography	Region/Country
Dates	
■ Start	The date on which the event materialises
■ End	The date on which the event comes to an end
■ Settlement	The date on which the financial consequences of the event are settled
Description	
■ Event Detail	A more detailed account of the loss event
■ Corrective Actions and Management Response	Corrective measures taken by the firm in the aftermath of the event
■ Lessons Learned	Lessons learned by firms and regulators that may help avoid or reduce the severity of loss events in the future
Other Information	
■ Entity Type	For example, retail bank
■ Business Unit Type	For example, e-banking
■ Service/Product Type	For example, custodial services
■ Loss Detection Sources	For example, whistle blowing
■ Market Focus	For example, retail services
■ Event Cause	The source of risk (for example, technology risk)
■ BCBS Event Category	For example, internal fraud
■ BCBS Business Line	For example, retail banking

made by financial institutions, are quite reliable. However, the coverage of risk types depends on the range of policies held by institutions, which is restricted to the risk types that are insurable.

Biases in External Databases

In publicly available data, larger firms and losses are more likely to be reported in the media. Gustafsson et al (2006) suggest that reporting bias can be dealt with by asking subject matter experts (SMEs) to estimate the extent to which reporting bias appears in publicly available data. These estimates are then used to derive an under-reporting function that (when combined with publicly available data) creates an estimate of a bank's true loss profile. The problem with this suggestion is that the introduction of SMEs may lead to another kind of bias resulting from the "inherent subjectivity of the probability of elicitation process."

Control bias, which appears in all external databases, is the relevance of losses that come from institutions with different control mechanisms. To overcome this problem only a subset of the external database that is most relevant to the underlying firm's operation and structures is chosen. If a financial institution is not involved in trading, it will not be exposed to the risk of rogue trading and hence these loss events are irrelevant. Samad-Khan et al (2006) warn against selecting relevant data points on the basis of similar quality control standards unless an objective way of doing so is formulated.

Scale bias arises because the losses recorded come from institutions of different sizes. Dahen and Dionne (2007) suggest that no single factor can explain a significant proportion of the variation in loss size but rather a combination of factors such as size, location, business line and risk type. Scale bias does not only pertain to severity but also to frequency.

External Data: Relevance and Myths

Samad-Khan et al (2006) provide some guidelines as to how to deal with external data to make it more relevant to the firm under consideration. The guidelines include the following:

- Consider scaling individual data points to the size of the underlying firm. The most important point to observe is that the scale factor should be determined empirically rather than subjectively. For example, the choice between assets and revenues as a scale factor depends on which one of them is more statistically related to the magnitude of operational losses. Shih et al (2000) investigate the statistical relation between operational losses and three measures of firm size.

- Be careful about attempting to scale individual losses to the quality of the firm's internal control environment. This is because no empirical studies have been done to investigate the effect of internal controls on the frequency and severity of loss events.

- Avoid the selection of external loss events on the grounds of whether or not the loss event could occur in the underlying firm. This is because a firm engaged in a certain business is exposed to the risks associated with that business.

- Be careful of the selection of external loss events based on the similarity between the underlying firm and other firms (in terms of control quality at least). This is because there are no objective criteria to determine the similarity of control quality.

- Be careful of the selection of external loss events based on the similarity of location and business line. What is important is whether or not there is a significant difference between the inherent risk profiles of the two geographical regions or businesses.

On the other hand, Cagan (2005) presents ten myths in (what seems to be) defence of using external data. These myths are the following:

- External loss events can be translated into distinct data points. Cagan believes that viewing external data as simply "data" is "short sighted," overlooking the complexity and richness that can be gleaned from a thorough analysis of an event that has occurred to another firm.

- External events are not relevant to a particular firm because they occurred in another firm under a different control environment. This is because external events can be used to analyse thoroughly the difficulties that other firms have encountered.

- Only events that occurred to firms in a similar sector and environment to that of the underlying firm are relevant. This is because lessons can be learned from a variety of external events.

- External losses can be easily scaled according to scale factors such as revenue and total assets. Cagan shares the view that the scaling of external losses is not as simple as it may be portrayed.

- If it is impossible to scale losses by financial criteria, then it is not possible to scale losses at all. Control breakdowns have some implications for the relevance of external events.

- Analysis of external events is useful for qualitative assessment as opposed to quantitative modelling. Cagan casts doubt on the validity of this argument, arguing instead for the usefulness of external events for quantitative modelling, particularly for large and rare events.

- Since external events happened in the past, they are irrelevant to the future. If this argument is true for external loss data, it must also be true for internal loss data. It remains true, however, that history is relevant to the present and future, even in operational loss analysis.

- Scenarios can be just as effective as external loss data. The problem with scenarios is that they are subjective.

- External loss data are biased, which makes them limited in usefulness. One advantage of external loss data is that less defensiveness is involved in discussing what happened to other firms.

- The need for external data gets eroded over time as firms collect more internal data and use more industry-pooled data. Cagan argues that firms will always need external data because internal data and consortium data cover only a small subset of the total population of firms.

3.6 INTERNAL OPERATIONAL LOSS DATABASES

Cagan (2001a) argues that internal databases resemble external databases in the sense that both need to be supported by a well-defined body of data standards, but they differ with respect to the type of losses they cover. While internal databases record the high-frequency, low-severity losses that characterise daily operations, external databases tend to cover low-frequency, high-severity losses.

Motivation

Collecting internal operational loss data is motivated by two considerations: (i) regulatory requirements; and (ii) operational risk management. The Basel II Accord places significant emphasis on the construction of internal loss databases. The BCBS (2003c) stipulates that data on operational losses is a tool that can be used for validating risk estimates, being a component of risk reporting and a key input in any AMA model of operational risk. According to Basel II, regulators expect internal loss databases to be comprehensive and to include several years of data prior to formal approval for use in calculating the capital charge against operational risk. Specifically, the Accord requires a minimum of three years of data for the initial implementation and five years for the use of the AMA. Regulatory requirements provide one reason why financial institutions have been indulged in the construction of internal databases.

KPMG (2005) asserts that collecting data on operational losses is not only required for regulatory purposes, but it is important for risk management. The report puts forward the point that "the systematic collection of information about operational risk losses is an essential basis for developing quantitative methods," that "loss data are also used for validation of both the quantitative and qualitative risk assessments as well as for early-warning risk systems," and that "loss data are key to identifying risk causes, to deriving risk management measures, and to reviewing the effectiveness of such measures realized beforehand." The process is also useful for deriving decisions aiming at adjusting the risk profile. The collection of data on operational losses should be viewed as a means to an end, not as the end itself. KPMG (2005) stipulates that "the important step is to establish a regular flow of information between the operational risk management function and functions including IT, legal, insurance and purchasing department."

Problems and Related Issues

KPMG (2005) estimates three years as the time period required for the completion of a new process for loss data collection. In KPMG (2003) the same idea is expressed by saying that "the establishment of a loss data collection process takes time." Furthermore, this process, according to the KPMG (2005) report, involves setting incentives for loss data collection, establishing transparency at all organisational levels, and establishing a sanction process for cases of non-compliance. In KPMG (2003) the incentive issue is also raised as it is argued that "an internal loss data collection process should have a number of built-in incentives and controls to ensure a high degree of data coverage and quality." One important problem recognised by KPMG (2005) is that operational risk is often seen as the outcome of negative effects (such as human failure), which means that the desire to disclose such information is understandably limited. This is also a reason why data quality (with respect to completeness, accuracy and coverage) is improving rather slowly.

An important question that crops up in any endeavour to construct an operational loss database is what constitutes an operational loss event (that is, what to record and what to leave out). According to the Basel II Accord, only direct losses (which encompass categories ranging from the write-down of financial assets to the loss of physical assets) are to be recorded. The justification for this restriction is that these effects are objective and can be measured directly and consistently. Another important issue is the determination of the loss threshold, which is the amount below which the underlying loss event will not be recorded. The answer is simply that the choice of a threshold is a matter of costs and benefits, which means that it should vary across firms and activities. The implications of the choice of the threshold for modelling operational risk and the calculation of the capital charge against it are discussed by Mignola and Ugoccioni (2007).

Collecting data on direct losses only is a matter of convenience that brings with it a problem. If a capital charge that will supposedly save a firm from insolvency is calculated on the basis of direct losses only, it will be deficient because indirect losses may be huge. This is rather puzzling because on one hand, the Basel Committee preaches a 99.9% confidence level but on the other hand, the Committee chooses to ignore indirect losses as a matter of convenience. However, Haubenstock (2004) recommends the collection of data on near misses, which are events where some type of failure occurred without incurring financial loss, and indirect losses (or associated costs), which include items such as business interruption, forgone income, loss of reputation and poor quality. The importance of near misses is highlighted by Power (2005) who raises the question whether or not historical losses are more important than critical events such as near misses and potential losses. Haubenstock also recommends the inclusion of strategic or business risk events. More specifically, KPMG (2005) identifies the core information loss data as: (i) gross loss amount; (ii) insurance benefits and other recoveries; (iii) receptive risk category; (iv) business area where the loss occurred; (v) date of occurrence and date of discovery of the event; (vi) business areas primarily responsible for the management of the loss; and (vii) causes of the event.

Determining the value of the loss is a critical issue, which can be illustrated with the following example. Suppose a bank lost \$100 million because of fraud. Subsequently, \$50 million is recovered such that the cost of the recovery operation is \$2 million. Insurance claim brings back \$20 million. Further costs are incurred to finance the internal investigation and take remedial actions, a total of \$3 million. What is the loss amount to be recorded in this case? It is not clear which single figure to choose, but what is clear is that all of these figures are important for the risk management process and should be recorded on the database. However, distinction should be made between gross direct loss (\$100 million) and net loss, which is calculated as the difference between the direct loss and the recovered amount/insurance compensation plus other relevant costs.

It is not only the amount that should be recorded, as further information is required on the identification and classification of the loss event. Identification encompasses such items as the reporting location, the unit in which the loss event occurred, and the reporter of the event. As for classification, the information required includes the event category and sub-category (such as external fraud/robbery), the cause of the category (such as processing) and the cause sub-category (such as the unavailability or inadequacy of procedures). A further piece of information is the status of the event, whether it is still open or whether it has been closed after settlement. The associated dates are required and must be recorded on the database.

The problem of determining whether a loss event is actually an operational loss event brings us back to the discussion of the distinction between operational and other loss events. As we concluded from the discussion of this issue, distinction should be based on the cause of the loss. In general, an operational loss event is an event that is consequential for the firm's profit and loss account and is caused by (i) illegal or unauthorised activities and unintentional mistakes made by employees or people external to the firm; (ii) failures and shortcomings in internal processes, systems and control measures; and (iii) adverse external factors.

What is important in the construction of internal operational loss databases is the so-called "CoCoCo" principle, which stands for coverage, completeness and correctness. Coverage requires the implementation of infrastructure to capture operational losses. The infrastructure should cover technical and procedural issues. Completeness requires the implementation of procedures that allow the identification of all operational losses. Correctness requires the implementation of procedures necessary to guarantee that all data fields are entered accurately into the database.

Identifying loss events is not the only problem encountered in the construction of an internal operational loss database. Other problems include the determination of the following: (i) who is responsible for the input of the data; (ii) the "owner" of the data; (iii) the granularity of events and the cause categories; (iv) the threshold; (v) whether or not a loss event is an operational loss event; (vi) when a loss event is recorded; and (vii) the magnitude of the loss.

Reporting Losses to the Internal Database

Collecting data on operational losses is a process that requires communication between the "data collectors" in the business units (where the losses are identified) and the central database. Power (2005) argues that the data collection process has important "behavioural dimensions." For example, there are disincentives to report relevant events if they are likely to increase the capital charge assigned to a particular business unit. Furthermore, risks and losses may be reported and overestimated as part of an argument to secure more resources. Goodhart (2001) suggests that the data collection methods used to limit the adverse effects of an event may result in incentives that would increase the number of such events. The process, therefore, is not straightforward.

There are two alternative ways of reporting data to the central database. Reporting may be indirect, where there is hierarchy in the reporting process. If, for example, a department consists of several business units and a division consists of several departments, then under the indirect reporting system, the business units report loss events to the departments and the departments report those to the divisions and then the divisions report the data to the central database. Under direct reporting, losses are reported directly by the business units, departments and divisions to the central database. Direct and indirect reporting of operational loss data are represented diagrammatically in Figure 3.20.

There is also the issue of choice between local and central databases, because some business units may prefer local databases to fulfil local needs. Although this may sound an unnecessary duplication, local databases may be allowed, provided the same information is transmitted to the central database. Figure 3.21 shows that some business units choose to keep local databases but others do not, reporting instead directly to the central database.

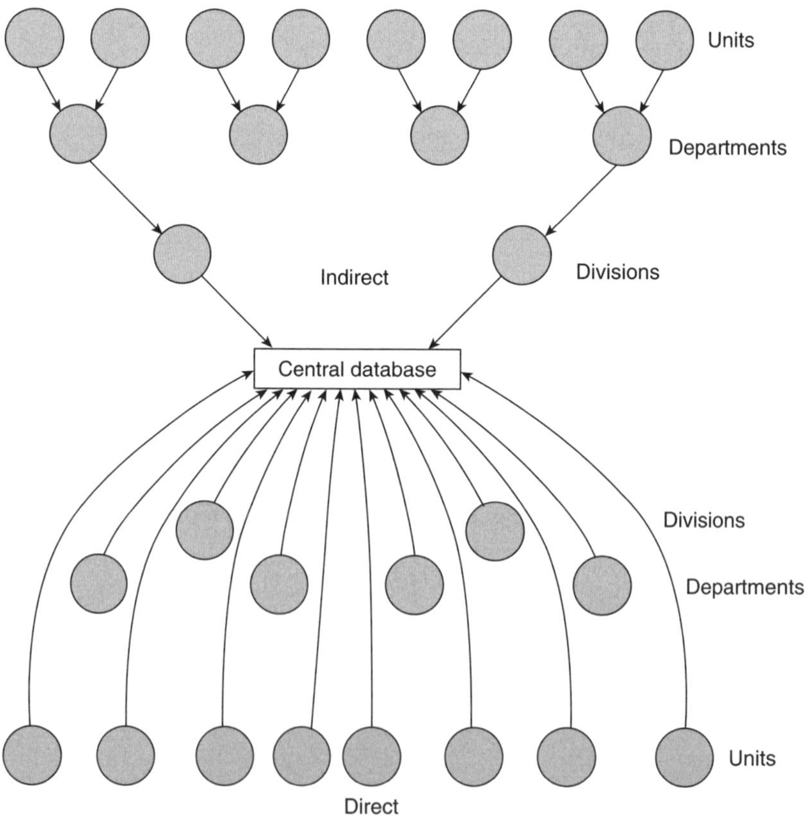

Figure 3.20 Direct and Indirect Reporting of Operational Loss Data

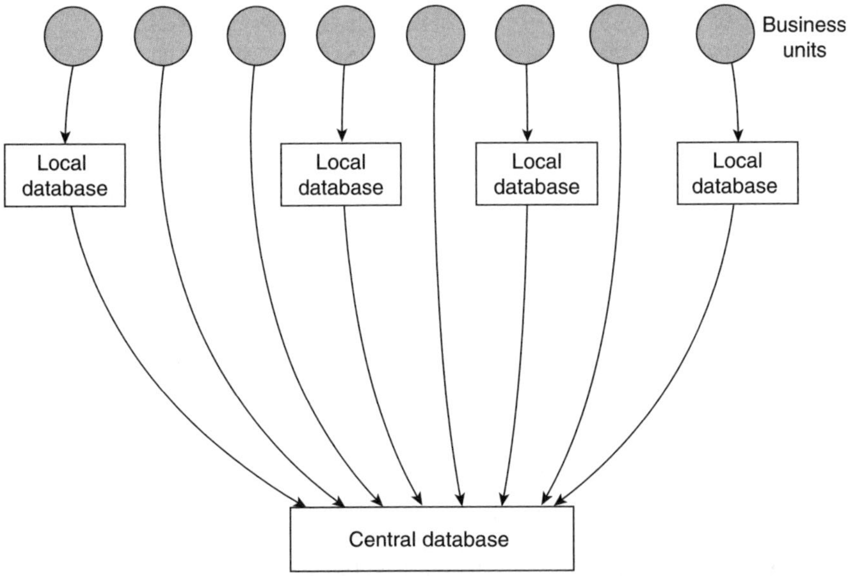

Figure 3.21 Local and Central Databases

APPENDIX 3.1: THE FOREIGN EXCHANGE COMMITTEE'S SIXTY BEST PRACTICES

The Foreign Exchange Committee (2003) suggests a collection of practices that may mitigate some of the operational risks that are specific to the foreign exchange business. These practices are classified by the seven steps involved in a foreign exchange transaction as well as those involved in the trading of options and non-deliverable forwards. The following is the list of the sixty best practices:

Step 1: Pre-Trade Preparation and Documentation

- Know your customer
- Determine documentation requirements
- Use master netting agreements
- Agree upon trading and operational practices
- Agree upon and document special arrangements

Step 2: Trade Capture

- Enter trades in a timely manner
- Use straight-through processing
- Use real time credit monitoring
- Use standing settlement instructions
- Operations should be responsible for settlement instructions
- Review amendments
- Closely monitor off-market transactions

Step 3: Confirmation

- Confirm and affirm trades in a timely manner
- Be diligent when confirming by nonsecure means
- Be diligent when confirming structured or non-standard trades
- Be diligent when confirming by telephone
- Institute controls for trades transacted through electronic trading platforms
- Verify expected settlement instructions
- Confirm all netted transactions

- Confirm all internal transactions
- Confirm all block trades and split allocations
- Review third-party advices
- Automate the confirmation matching process
- Establish exception processing and escalation procedures

Step 4: Netting

- Use online settlement netting systems
- Confirm bilateral net amounts
- Employ timely cut-offs for netting
- Establish consistency between operational practices and documentation

Step 5: Settlement

- Use real-time nostro balance projections
- Use electronic messages for expected receipts
- Use automated cancellation and amendment facilities
- Implement timely payment cut-offs
- Report payment failures to credit officers
- Understand the settlement process and settlement exposure
- Prepare your crisis situations outside your organisation

Step 6: Nostro Reconciliation

- Perform timely nostro account reconciliation
- Automate nostro reconciliation
- Identify non-receipt of payments
- Establish operational standard for nostro account users

Step 7: Accounting/Financial Control

- Conduct daily general ledger reconciliation
- Conduct daily position and P&L reconciliation
- Conduct daily position valuation
- Review trade prices for off-market rates
- Use straight-through processing of rates and prices

Step 8: Additional Best Practices

- Establish clear policies and procedures for the exercise of options
- Obtain appropriate fixings for non-standard transactions
- Closely monitor option settlements.
- Ensure segragation of duties.
- Ensure that staff understand business and operational roles
- Understand operational risks
- Identify procedures for introducing new products, new customer types, and new trading strategies.
- Ensure proper model signoff and implementation
- Control system access
- Establish strong independent audit/risk control groups.
- Use internal and external operational performance measures.
- Ensure that service outsourcing conforms to industry standards and best practices
- Implement globally consistent processing standards
- Maintain records of deal execution and confirmations
- Maintain procedures for retaining transaction records
- Develop and test contingency plans

APPENDIX 3.2 THE BCBS'S SOUND PRACTICES

- The board of directors and senior management are responsible for approving the establishment and review of a framework for managing operational risk.
- Senior management is responsible for implementing the operational risk strategy consistently throughout the entire firm.
- Information, communication and escalation flows must be established to maintain and oversee the effectiveness of the framework and management performance.
- Operational risks inherent in all current activities, processes, systems and new products should be identified.
- Processes necessary for assessing operational risk should be established.
- Systems should be implemented to monitor operational risk exposures and loss events by major business lines.
- Policies, processes, and procedures to control or mitigate operational risks should be in place, together with cost/benefit analyses of alternative risk limitation and control strategies.
- Supervisors should not require banks to have an effective system in place to identify, measure, monitor and control strategies.
- Supervisors should require banks to have an effective system in place to identify, measure, monitor and control operational risks.
- Supervisors should conduct (directly or indirectly) regular independent evaluations of these principles and ensure that effective reporting mechanisms are in place.
- Sufficient public disclosure should be made to allow market participants to assess an organisation's operational risk exposure and the quality of its operational risk management.

Source: BCBS (2002, 2003a).

APPENDIX 3.3: DESCRIPTION OF SOME HIGHLY PUBLICISED LOSS EVENTS

In this appendix a brief description of some highly publicised loss events is presented. The stories were obtained from various (media) sources, using the Google search engine. The designation of event types and business lines is based on the author's judgment. Pinpointing the start, end and settlement dates may not be easy, so the dates associated with each event are also based on the author's judgment.

Enron Corporation
Start: 1 January 1998
End: 31 December 2001
Settlement: 15 July 2005
Loss Amount: $1,595 million
Event Type: Clients, Products and Business Practices
Business Line: Trading and Sales

Description
On 15 July 2005, it was announced that Enron reached a $1,595 million settlements with authorities in California, Washington and Oregon to settle allegations that the company was involved in market manipulation and price gouging during the energy crisis on the West Coast in 2000–2001. On 17 October 2005, an energy trader working for Enron pled guilty to one count of fraud, when he admitted to manipulating California's energy market through a fraudulent scheme during the period 1998–2001.

Microsoft Corporation
Start: 1 December 1998
End: 23 November 2006
Settlement: 23 November 2006
Loss Amount: $3.9 billion
Event Type: Execution, Delivery and Process Management
Business Line: Unclassified

Description
The loss resulted from two fines imposed by the European Union (EU) in 2004 and 2006 for abusing control of the market and failure to comply with the 2004 order ($613 million and $357 million, respectively). The other part of the total loss was incurred due to settlements with some IT companies as well as the Computer and Communications Industry Association. It all started in December 1998 when Sun Microsystems complained that

Microsoft had refused to provide interface information to enable Sun to develop products that would communicate properly with Windows.

Northern Rock
Start: 9 August 2007
End: 17 September 2007
Settlement: –
Loss Amount: –
Event Type: Unclassified
Business Line: Retail Banking

Description
Northern Rock experienced a run on its deposits as it suffered from a lack of liquidity resulting from the US subprime crisis. The situation arose because of the Bank's excessive reliance on funding from the capital markets, thus creating a big funding gap (loans less deposits). By 25 October 2007, Northern Rock had borrowed some 20 billion pounds from the Bank of England. Eventually, the unthinkable had to happen: Northern Rock was nationalised by the British government.

Central Bank of Brazil
Start: 6 August 2005
End: 8 August 2005
Settlement: 8 August 2005
Loss Amount: $70 million
Event Type: External Fraud
Business Line: Commercial Banking

Description
In August 2005 a group of twenty (smart) thieves pulled off an audacious bank robbery when they dug a tunnel to access the vault of the Central Bank of Brazil in Fortaleza. The theft took place sometime over the weekend of 6–8 August. The event was reconstructed in a brilliant Discovery Channel documentary.

Yukos Oil Company
Start: 1 July 2003
End: 25 August 2004
Settlement: 20 December 2004
Loss Amount: $9.3 billion
Event Type: Internal Fraud
Business Line: Unclassified

Description
In December 2004 the Russian government seized the assets of Yukos Oil Company on the grounds of unpaid taxes. Later it was announced that the seizure was intended to correct flaws in the privatisation of the early 1990s, when public assets were squandered by Boris Yeltsine, the then Russian president. Yukos was created by the Russian government for the purpose of integrating a number of parts of the former oil industry in April 1993.

Long-Term Capital Management
Start: 17 August 1998
End: 23 September 1998
Settlement: 23 September 1998
Loss Amount: $4.4 billion
Event Type: Execution, Delivery and Process Management
Business Line: Trading and Sales

Description
The collapse of LTCM was caused by excessive exposure to leverage, sovereign, model, liquidity and volatility risks. On 17 August 1998, Russia announced that it was restructuring its debt by extending the terms of payout on short-term bonds, which was effectively a default event. It is ironic that the failure came when two Nobel Prize winners who were managing LTMC (Robert Merton and Myron Scholes) were convinced that markets would behave as predicted by their highly sophisticated models. Specifically, they were convinced that markets could only go down by a certain percentage before experiencing a correction within a specified time frame. So much for over-confident finance academics!

Allied Irish Bank
Start: 1 January 1997
End: 6 February 2002
Settlement: 24 October 2002
Loss Amount: $691.2 million
Event Type: Internal Fraud
Business Line: Trading and Sales

Description
On 2 June 2002 the Allied Irish Bank revealed that a currency trader had disappeared, having caused trading losses of $691.2 million at a US subsidiary (Allfirst Financial Inc.). John Rusnak pleaded guilty to one count of bank fraud on 24 October 2002 when he was sentenced to a prison term of 7.5 years. Rusnak was in significant violation of his trading limits, which was undetected for five years.

Bank of Credit and Commerce International (BCCI)
Start: 1 January 1980
End: 5 July 1991
Settlement: 5 July 1991
Loss Amount: $17 billion
Event Type: Clients, Products and Business Practices
Business Line: Payment and Settlement

Description
On 5 July 1991 regulators in seven countries raided and took control of branch offices of the BCCI, following a scandal that resulted in the largest experienced loss in the history of bank fraud. The bank was involved in money laundering and the financing of arms trafficking. The bank had clients who were involved in various drug and crime cartels. Following the scandal, the BCCI deservedly acquired the name "Bank for Crookes and Criminals International."

Central Bank of Iraq (CBI)
Start: 19 March 2003
End: 19 March 2003
Settlement: 19 March 2003
Loss Amount: $980 million plus EUR90 million
Event Type: External Fraud
Business Line: Commercial Banking

Description
On 19 March 2003, a hand-written letter from the former Iraqi president Saddam Hussein was delivered to the governor of the CBI demanding the delivery of $980 million and EUR90 million in cash that was kept at the vaults of the CBI. The money was loaded on three tractor-trailers and moved to an undisclosed location. At a later stage, it was reported that some American soldiers stumbled on $600 million in cash while on patrol in Baghdad. This amount was reported to have been shipped to New York for authentication. Non-one seems to know the whereabouts of the remaining balance.

Societe Generale
Start: 1 January 2005
End: 18 January 2008
Settlement: 24 January 2008
Loss Amount: $7.2 billion
Event Type: Internal Fraud
Business Line: Trading and Sales

Description
On 24 January 2008, the French bank, Soceite Generale, announced a EUR4.9 billion loss as a result of the unauthorised activities of a rogue trader on positions in stock index futures worth EUR50 billion. The rogue trader, Jerome Kerviel, managed to breach five levels of controls, having gained knowledge of how to circumvent the bank's control systems from his position in the back office. The fraud was discovered after he made a mistake in his attempt to cover up fictitious trades. Another trader alerted the bank's management of a discrepancy on the trading book of a counterparty that was contacted to confirm the trade.

Barings Bank
Start: 1 February 1995
End: 27 February 1995
Settlement: 27 February 1995
Loss Amount: $1.3 billion
Event Type: Internal Fraud
Business Line: Trading and Sales

Description
Barings Bank, a 233 years old British bank, suffered a $1.3 billion loss as a result of the unauthorised trading activity of Nick Leeson who was based in Singapore. The loss was greater than the bank's entire capital base and reserves, which created an extreme liquidity shortage. As a result, Barings declared bankruptcy and subsequently got acquired by the Dutch bank ING.

MF Global
Start: 26 February 2008
End: 26 February 2008
Settlement: 26 February 2008
Loss Amount: $141.5 million
Event Type: Internal Fraud
Business Line: Trading and Sales

Description
On 28 February 2008, and in the wake of the massive loss incurred by Societe Generale, MF Global announced that it had suffered a loss amounting to $141.5 million as a result of unauthorised trading. A rogue trader was the culprit as he exceeded his limits on wheat futures before the market turned against him. Apparently, the trader managed to exceed his limits because of the failure of a retail order entry system. The loss incurred by MF Global was equal to 6% of the company's equity capital.

CHAPTER 4

The Advanced Measurement Approach to Operational Risk

4.1 OPERATIONAL RISK MEASUREMENT, ASSESSMENT AND MODELLING

The introductory section of this chapter deals with the concepts of measurement, assessment and modelling as applied to operational risk. The concepts are subsequently related to the operational risk management process.

Measurement or Assessment?

It is often argued that, in relation to operational risk, the word "measurement" means something closer to the word "assessment." However, Knot et al (2006) distinguish between risk measurement and risk assessment by arguing that risk measurement refers to the quantification of risk, whereas risk assessment is a broader concept in the sense that it also entails the interpretation of non-quantitative pieces of information. Sometimes, risk assessment is considered an entirely qualitative process. For example, KPMG (2003) points out that "risk assessment provides banks with a qualitative approach to identify potential risks of a primarily severe nature." The proposition that risk measurement is crucial for the purpose of developing the knowledge necessary for risk management can be challenged on many grounds. For example, it is typically assumed that risk measurement is a "scientific" process that produces fairly accurate estimates of risk. Then what about the costs and benefits of "scientific" measurement of risk? It will be argued throughout this book that risk quantification is not the only road to sound risk management. The views of those who believe that the quantification of risk is a pre-requisite for risk management will be presented in this chapter.

If we accept the argument that risk measurement is necessary for risk management, it does not necessarily follow that mathematical sophistication is a conduit to more accurate measurement (or sound management) of operational risk. In January 2008 Societe Generale lost $7.2 billion as a result of unauthorised transactions conducted by a rogue trader. On this issue, The Economist (2008a) reported that the management of Societe Generale had been criticised before the announcement of the loss, not only for poor standards of disclosure but also for the lack of transparency and for "taking an overly mathematical approach to risk." Mathematical sophistication, therefore, can be a source of complacency, which could severely damage the underlying firm.

Figure 4.1 shows how risk assessment/measurement is portrayed to be an integral part of the risk management process. This process is represented by a continuous loop in which monitoring precedes identification, which is followed by assessment, then reporting and management. Risk management itself leads to monitoring, and so on. The measurement (or rather assessment) of risk is also a factor that determines the action to be taken to manage operational risk. If risk is exceptional, it would be avoided. If it is nominal, or expected, it would be assumed. And if it is ordinary or unexpected, it would be transferred or reduced. Measurement, it is postulated, tells us which category a particular risk belongs to.

Doerig (2003) places risk measurement as the third stage in a four-stage operational risk management framework, coming after identification, metrics and tracking and before integrated management. This is an elegant rationalisation of the importance of formal measurement, but then when we consider reality, it becomes evident that this is no more than rhetoric. Consider, for example, what a practicing risk manager says about the quantification and management of reputational risk. Philippa Girling, the director of operational risk at Nomura Holdings America, is cited by Pennington (2008b) as saying that "we don't necessarily need to quantify it, as reputational risk is not something you need to hold capital for, but you do want to manage it." This obviously implies that quantification is needed for regulatory compliance, not for sound risk management. What Girling says is that reputational risk can (and should) be managed, but this can be done without the need for quantification. This argument is also valid for other types of operational risk.

Bhatia (2002) argues that measurement of operational risk is not only motivated by the incentive of holding lower regulatory capital and that it is beneficial for the following reasons: (i) it enables banks to implement

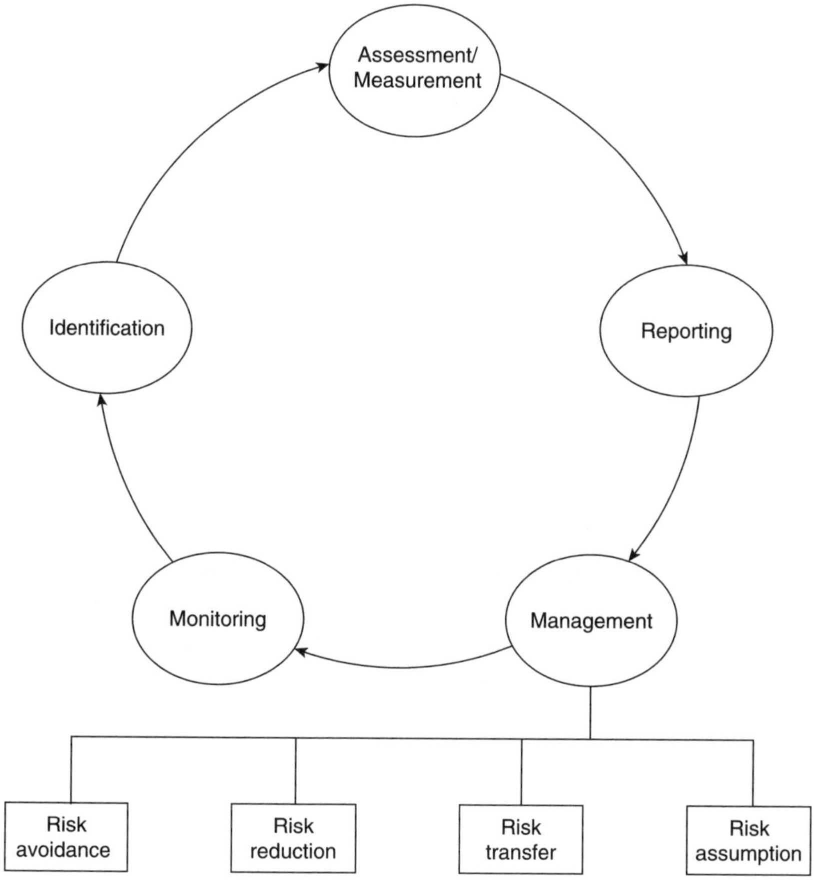

Figure 4.1 Risk Assessment/Measurement as a Component of Risk Management

risk-based audits, allowing it to become more risk-focused; (ii) it supports a risk-awareness culture; (iii) it enables identification of profitable business lines and competitive advantages; and (iv) it enables the implementation of risk diversification. Bhatia (2002) distinguishes between two approaches to operational risk identification and measurement: top-down and bottom-up. In the top-down approach, data from the financial statements are converted into a risk amount. This is the basic indicators approach (BIA) in Basel II. The problem with this approach, Bhatia argues, is that it does not lead to proper capturing of risk, nor does it work as an incentive to reduce risk. In the bottom-up approach, risks are analysed for each business line and then these are combined to get the overall risk exposure of the firm. This is the advanced measurement approach (AMA) in Basel II (also the standardised approach (STA)).

Measuring risk is problematical, and measuring operational risk is even more so. In a particular reference to operational risk, Pezier (2003a) argues that risk cannot be measured, which is contrary to popular opinion. Risk, he point out, "is not like the length of hosepipe that can be checked by anyone with a measuring tape and which can be connected to other lengths of hosepipe to reach the back of the garden." Because risk is about the future, it can be assessed only by using a model that represents future realisations. Crouchy (2001) argues that the difficulties encountered in measuring operational risk do not imply that it should be ignored. Indeed, Crouchy uses the difficulty of identifying and measuring operational risk as a reason why this kind of risk should be paid more attention. This is certainly a valid argument: operational risk is difficult to measure but it is too serious to be ignored.

Measurement with and without Modelling

The measurement of operational risk may be based on modelling or otherwise. Modelling operational risk takes many shapes and forms and follows a variety of procedures, as we are going to see later. However, the most commonly used approach to modelling operational risk for the purpose of measurement (the statistical or actuarial approach) boils down to the objective of arriving at the best-fit distribution for potential operational losses over a given period of time (normally a year). Typically, the distribution of operational losses is obtained by combining the loss frequency and loss severity distributions. The measurement of operational risk in this case amounts to arriving at a single figure (VAR) that tells us how much the underlying firm is likely to lose with a certain probability, so that a correspondingly adequate amount of capital is held for the purpose of protecting the firm from insolvency.

In the AMA, measurement is based on modelling, for example by using a given percentile of the total loss distribution. However, measurement can be based on *ad hoc* methods (and so it is measurement without modelling) as in the BIA and the STA. The link between modelling and measurement is viewed by van Lelyveld (2006) as a common pattern underlying all state-of-the art models in that they ultimately determine a number called "economic capital." Whether or not this "number" is reliable is a debatable issue.

The Importance of Modelling/Quantifying Operational Risk

Quantification is arguably a powerful tool for enhancing transparency, as long as it is credible (which is a crucial qualification). Young (1979) suggests that the sixteenth–seventeenth century scientific revolution in Europe has intensified the quest for knowledge based on the quantifiable aspects of phenomena or events (correct, but measuring risk is not the same as measuring the temperature of a fluid in a controlled laboratory experiment). Although Bocker and Kluppelberg (2005) trace operational risk modelling to the insurance risk theory of the early twentieth century, interest in this topic has grown tremendously in the last ten years or so, and not only for regulatory purposes. Indicative of the fact that financial institutions were interested in operational risk measurement prior to the advent of Basel II is that major banks have made some early attempts in this direction (see, e.g., Cruz, 2003b). Adusei-Poku (2005) makes this point by attributing the rapid development of operational risk models to an external factor (regulatory compliance) and internal factor (the desire to boost the effectiveness and efficiency of operational risk management). He also (correctly) argues that the external factor is currently stronger than the internal factor. However, critics have highlighted the limitations and less desirable consequences of blind quantification (Young, 1979).

A question may arise as to why modelling operational risk is necessary, given that banks appear to have been managing it successfully? The very survival of banks (and firms in general) would suggest that they have the skills and procedures for managing operational risk without measurement, let alone modelling. Peccia (2003) responds to the question about the need for operational risk measurement by arguing that modelling operational risk has become important because the environment in which banks operate has changed dramatically. To remain fit, he argues, banks must adapt to the new reality, given that the new environment is much more complex in terms of product offerings, delivery channels and jurisdictions. Peccia (2003) argues that a model is "simply a telescope and compass" that banks need to navigate in a rapidly shifting environment. But there is also the regulatory requirement of the Basel II Accord that an operational risk model is needed to be in a position to use the AMA, which is attractive because it results in lower regulatory capital than under the other two approaches (this is a disputable proposition, as we are going to see later). Indeed, it is arguable that one advantage of operational risk modelling is that the resulting models allow the firm to meet regulatory requirements. It will be argued repeatedly that indulging in a modelling exercise should not be motivated by the desire to achieve regulatory compliance.

Fujii (2005) points out that quantifying operational risk is a prerequisite for the formulation of an effective economic capital framework. Furthermore, Consiglio and Zenois (2003) emphasise the importance of operational risk models by attributing some widely publicised loss events to the use of inadequate models rather than anything else. For example, they wonder whether the collapse of Long-Term Capital Management (LTCM) was due to liquidity risk or the inappropriate use of models. They also wonder whether Barings' demise was due to the "tail below its value at risk exposure." Actually, Giraud (2005) attributes the collapse of LTCM in 1998 (with a total loss of $4.4 billion) in large part to "model bias in the risk management process." This argument, however, does not seem to be valid for the big loss event endured by Societe Generale in January 2008 as a result of unauthorised trading (internal fraud). It seems, after all, that modelling (no matter how sophisticated) cannot overcome the complacency or incompetence of management; neither can it prevent a rogue trader from inflicting severe damage or destruction on the institution he/she works for. The development and increased sophistication of risk measurement models seem to be inversely related to severity of losses. We have gone from $1.3 billion at Barings in 1995 to $4.4 billion at LTCM in 1998 and to $7.2 billion at Societe Generale in 2008!

Doerig (2003) questions the usefulness of operational risk modelling by raising the following questions to which his answer is "no":

- Did the models of LTCM work, with the smartest quant brains available worldwide (referring to the two Nobel Prize winners responsible for the disaster because of overconfidence in their models)?

- Would any of the present and potentially upcoming quantification approaches for operational risk (including VAR, extreme value theory (EVT), chaos theory, etc.) have been of relevant use at the time of the occurrence?

- Would such theoretical quantification *ex ante* have avoided the mishaps?

- Would any of today's quant-approaches have produced a large enough capital requirement to avoid the collapse of Bank for Credit and Commerce International (BCCI) or Barings? If so, would they have been as competitive as before the collapse?

One has to bear in mind that models are used to support (rather than replace) management judgment. This is because judgment is sometimes inadequate, particularly in the case of certain types of operational risk, and when it comes to dealing with unexpected losses. While it is relatively easy for the management to make judgment about frequent events, such as credit card fraud, it may be rather difficult to make judgment about rare events. However, it is not easy to sell the argument that "models are used to extend business judgment about expected losses to the unknown territory of unexpected losses." This sounds like what the EVT is supposed to do, which is a debatable issue that we will come back to. More acceptable propositions have been put forward by Cagan (2001b): "operational risk measurement is not the same as operational risk management" and "quantifying these op risks that lend themselves to quantification and neglecting the rest does not constitute best practices."

4.2 CLASSIFICATION OF OPERATIONAL RISK MODELS

Operational risk models are not exclusively about fitting a distribution to loss amounts. A variety of models have been suggested to accomplish various objectives. This section deals with the classification of operational risk models.

The Three Approaches

Operational risk models can be classified under three approaches, which are further classified into other (sub-) approaches as shown in Figure 4.2. In the process approach, the focus is on the individual processes that make up operational activities. The processes are decomposed into components, and each component is examined to identify the operational risk associated with it. By aggregating the operational risk inherent in the individual components, one can arrive at a measure of operational risk for the whole process. Figure 4.3 displays the decomposition of a foreign exchange transaction process into four components: (i) price discovery; (ii) decision making; (iii) settlement; and (iv) position keeping. For example, two kinds of risk are involved in the settlement of a foreign exchange transaction: Herstatt risk and liquidity risk. The position keeping component involves the risk of a rogue trader hiding losses. As we have seen, the Foreign Exchange Committee (2003) of the Federal Reserve Bank of New York stipulates seven steps in the execution of a foreign exchange transaction: (i) pre-trade preparation; (ii) trade capture; (iii) confirmation; (iv) netting; (v) settlement; (vi) nostro reconciliation; and (vii) accounting/financial control processes.

In causal networks, historical data are used to work out statistics for the behaviour of the components in the past, which makes it possible to identify the problem areas. Then it is possible to use scenario analysis or simulations to predict how the process will work in the future. The technique of statistical quality control and reliability analysis is rather similar to causal networks, used widely to evaluate manufacturing processes. The emphasis in connectivity analysis is on the connections between the components of the process. A connectivity matrix is used to estimate the potential losses arising from the process. Smithson and Song (2004) add other techniques under the same heading: Bayesian belief networks, fuzzy logic and system dynamics.

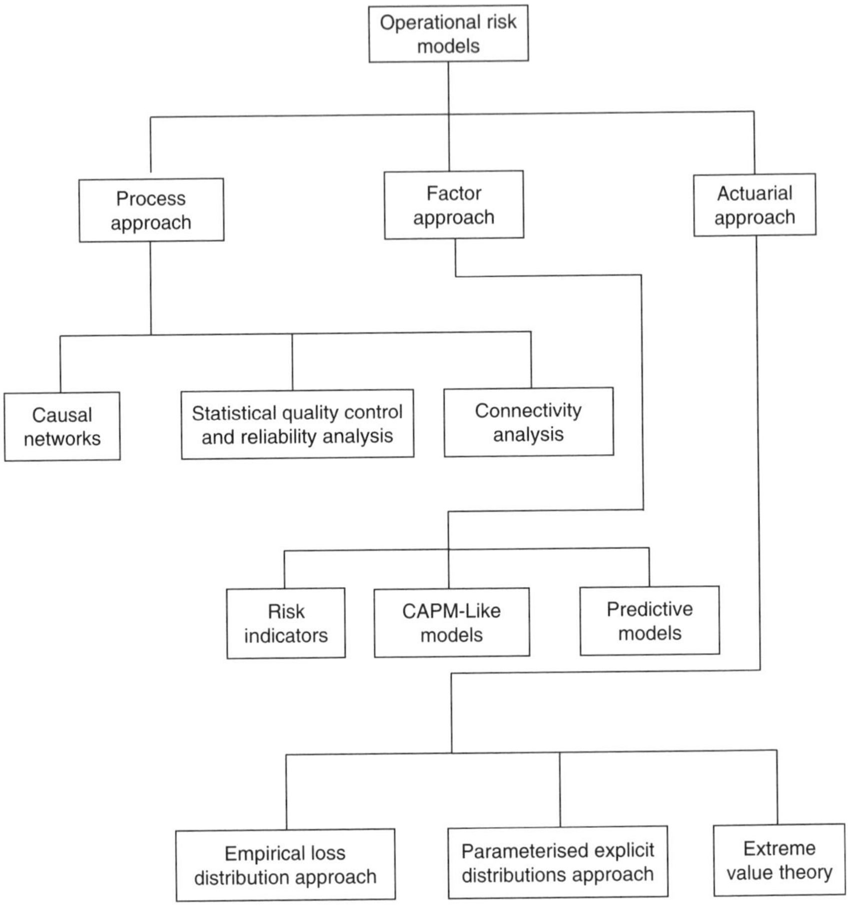

Figure 4.2 Classification of Operational Risk Models

By following the factor approach, an attempt is made to identify the significant determinants of operational risk by specifying an estimatable functional relation between operational risk and its determinants (risk factors). The risk indicators approach is a regression-based technique that is used to identify risk factors such as the volume of operations, audit ratings, employee turnover, employee training, age and quality of the systems used, and investment in new technology. Once an equation has been estimated, it can be used to calculate expected losses. CAPM-like models (also known as arbitrage pricing models or economic pricing models) are used to relate the volatility of returns (operational risk earnings) to operational risk factors. Predictive models cover discriminant analysis and similar techniques, which are used to identify the factors that lead to operational losses.

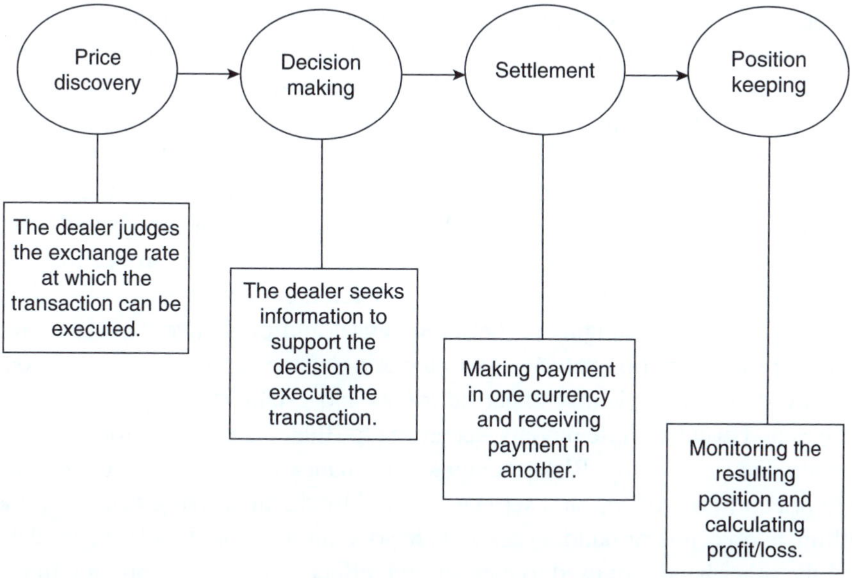

Figure 4.3 Decomposition of a Foreign Exchange Transaction Process

The actuarial approach focuses on the loss distribution associated with operational risk (e.g., Mango, 2006). The empirical loss distributions technique involves the collection of data on losses and plotting them in a histogram. Wei (2007) argues that the actuarial approach seems to be the natural choice to quantify operational risk by estimating the frequency and severity distributions separately. The problem with this technique is that even after utilising external data, it is likely that an empirical histogram will suffer from limited data points, particularly in the tail of the distribution. The solution to this problem can be found in the parameterised explicit distributions technique, which is used to smooth the distribution by choosing an explicit distributional form.

The EVT is used to describe the distribution of extreme values in repetitive processes. One proclaimed advantage of EVT is that it can be used to predict the probability of events that have never happened, which can be done by extrapolating the stochastic behaviour of past events. More will be said about the EVT and the actuarial approach in general when we undertake the task of evaluating the AMA later on in this chapter.

Other Classification Schemes

Jobst (2007a) identifies three of what he calls "major concepts of operational risk measurement." First is the volume-based approach, which utilises the assumption that exposure to operational risk is a function of the complexity of business activity. Second is the qualitative self-assessment of operational risk, which is based on subjective judgment and involves a comprehensive review of various types of errors in processes, with a view to evaluate the likelihood and severity of losses resulting from internal and external factors. Third are the quantitative techniques, which have been developed by banks for the purpose of estimating economic capital. Jobst (2007a) criticises the quantitative methods of operational risk management on the grounds that they "ignore the quality of potentially offsetting risk control procedures and qualitative criteria that elude objective measurement concepts."

Bhatia (2002) distinguishes between causal and predictive models on the basis of the distinction between expected and unexpected losses. Causal models are deigned to identify expected losses and establish a relation between losses and events. These models, according to Bhatia, are helpful for risk mitigation and risk pricing. Risk pricing is a mechanism whereby expected losses are priced into products and services offered by the underlying firm, with the ultimate objective of building reserves for operational risk. Predictive models, on the other hand, are used to measure the effect of losses and provide measurements for risk to operations that are not linked to the causes. This means that predictive models are designed to account for and predict unexpected losses.

Doerig (2003) suggests three measurement methods for operational risk: (i) expert input; (ii) data analysis; and (iii) modelling. The techniques classified under expert input include the Delphi method, relative fractiles assessment, preference among bets, log of odds assessment and the Bayesian approach. Data analysis encompasses empirical distributions, stochastic simulation and regression. The most sophisticated and complex techniques fall under "modelling," including stochastic processes, EVT, causal theories and decision/event/fault trees.

Austega (2007) classifies the methods used to measure operational risk into four categories: (i) the proxy, analogue or surrogate method; (ii) the earnings volatility method; (iii) the loss modelling method; and (iv) the direct estimation or scenario method. The first method is a top-down method that is often used by large firms comprising several divisions with independent business lines. The earnings volatility method is based on the statistical variability in the earnings of the firm. The loss modelling method is similar to the actuarial approach to estimating a loss distribution. The direct estimation method relies on the collaborative line manager judgments to estimate distributions for the risks they run.

4.3 THE ADVANCED MEASUREMENT APPROACH(ES)(AMAS)

The AMA is more than one approach as it encompasses the loss distribution approach (LDA), the internal measurement approach (IMA), the scenario-based approach (SBA), and the scorecard approach (SCA). As we are going to see later, the AMA may encompass any internally developed methodology that is deemed appropriate by the regulator, but for the time being we consider the LDA, IMA, SBA and SCA. Although there is no mention of the IMA in the recent publications of the BCBS (e.g., the 2006 Basel II document, BCBS, 2006a), it will still be considered here for its relevance to some issues discussed in this section, because it can be viewed as a variant of the LDA, and because it was the original means to ensure that the AMA produces lower capital charges through proper (but subjective) calibration.

The Loss Distribution Approach

The standard LDA model expresses the aggregate loss as the sum of individual losses, which gives

$$L = \sum_{j=1}^{n} L_j \tag{4.1}$$

where L is the aggregate loss, n is the number of losses per year (the frequency of events) and L_j is the loss amount (the severity of events). Hence, losses arise from two sources of randomness, frequency and severity, both of which have to be modelled. It is assumed that frequency and severity are independent, and that $L_1, \ldots, L_n$ are independent random variables following the same distribution.

Haubenstock and Hardin (2003) put forward a schematic representation of the LDA, using a step-by-step procedure. This presentation involves three primary steps and additional steps with their components, which are shown in Figure 4.4. We can see, however, that the additional steps boil down to the incorporation of scorecards and risk indicators, which (strictly speaking) means crossing the boundaries of the LDA to the SCA. What this means is that the allocated capital charge is adjusted to reflect the quality of internal controls and the assessment of risk drivers, which is allowed under Basel II. We will have more to say about modelling and Monte Carlo simulation in Chapter 6. Here, we want to say something about the calculation of the capital charge.

In general, the capital charge (also called regulatory capital or the regulatory capital requirement) is calculated from the total loss distribution (obtained from Monte Carlo simulation) by using the concept of VAR, which is a measure of the maximum limit on potential losses that are unlikely to be exceeded over a given holding period at a certain probability. Frachot et al (2004a) point to the ambiguity about the definition of the capital charge,

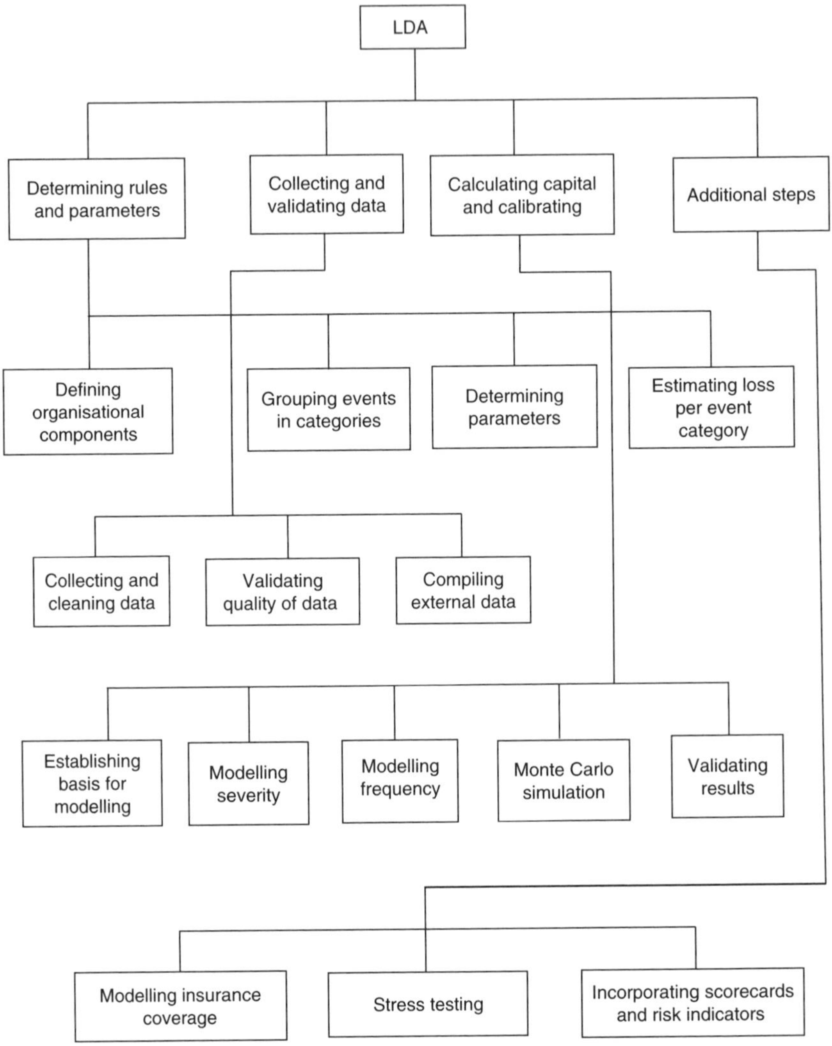

Figure 4.4 Steps Involved in the Loss Distribution Approach

hence suggesting three alternative definitions. The first definition is that it is the 99.9th percentile of the total loss distribution, which means that the probability of incurring a loss bigger than the operational VAR is 0.1 per cent. The 99.9th percentile implies a 99.9 confidence level that losses would not exceed the percentile (operational VAR). This means that, on average, only one out of 1000 similar banks experience losses that are greater than the percentile. Otherwise, it means that a particular bank would experience such a loss once in a thousand years.

The second definition pertains to the unexpected loss only, which means that the capital charge is equal to the difference between the 99.9th percentile and the mean of the distribution. The third definition considers only losses above a threshold, which means that the capital charge is the 99.9th percentile of the distribution of losses in excess of the threshold. The three definitions are represented diagrammatically in Figure 4.5.

The advantages of the LDA, according to Haubenstock and Hardin (2003) are as follows: (i) the results are based on the unique characteristics of each

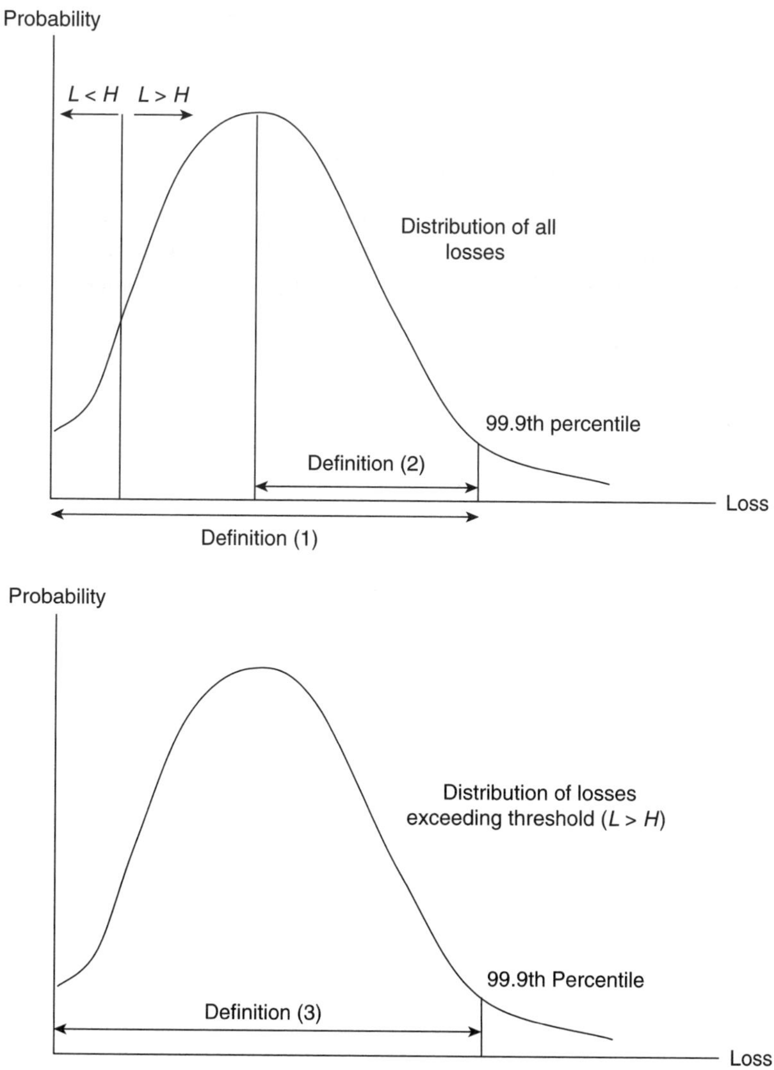

Figure 4.5 Definitions of the Capital Charge

firm instead of relying on a proxy operational risk industry averages; (ii) the results are based on mathematical principles similar to those used to estimate the capital required to cover market risk and credit risk; (iii) the effect of insurance can be modelled explicitly; (iv) the costs and benefits of the change in frequency or severity can be measured; and (v) the results evolve over time. Doerig (2003) believes that the LDA (or what he calls the "simulation method") offers four advantages: (i) strong quantitative support once validated with sufficient firm-specific data; (ii) the parameters (such as the confidence interval) are consistent with those employed for market risk and credit risk; (iii) a specification that allows the model to generate operational VAR; and (iv) a high degree of integration in the overall risk management framework, which allows the derivation of bottom-up capital allocation mechanisms for operational risk.

The Internal Measurement Approach

A variant of the LDA is the IMA. For some reason, this approach has disappeared from the BCBS publications, but we will discuss it for the reasons stated earlier. It is in fact the operational loss equivalent of the internal ratings-based approach (IRBA) used to determine capital charges for credit risk.

The difference between the LDA and the IMA is that in the former unexpected losses are estimated directly without an assumption about the ratio between expected and unexpected losses. In the LDA, simulation is used to estimate the entire loss distribution, whereas the IMA provides an analytical approximation to the unexpected loss. Under the IMA, the capital charge for cell ij (where a cell is a business line/event type combination) is calculated as

$$K = \sum_{i=1}^{8} \sum_{j=1}^{7} \gamma_{ij} E_{ij} P_{ij} L_{ij} \tag{4.2}$$

where $i = 1, 2, \ldots, 8$ are business lines and $j = 1, 2, \ldots, 7$ are event types, E is an exposure indicator, P is the probability of a loss event and L is the loss given event. Thus $E_{ij}\ P_{ij}\ L_{ij}$ is the expected loss in cell ij. The parameter γ_{ij} is used to translate expected loss into unexpected loss, such that the capital charge is equal to the unexpected loss (the maximum amount of loss per holding period within a certain confidence interval). Summation over business lines and event types indicates that no allowance is made for correlation because of the difficulty of estimating a 56×56 correlation matrix. To capture the risk profile of an individual bank (which is invariably different from that of the industry as a whole), equation (4.2) is modified to

$$K = \sum_{i=1}^{8} \sum_{j=1}^{7} \gamma_{ij} E_{ij} P_{ij} L_{ij} R_{ij} \tag{4.3}$$

where R is the risk profile index (1 for the industry). For a bank with a fat tail distribution, $R > 1$ and vice versa.

The Scenario-Based Approach

For low-frequency events, a very long observation period (greater than ten years) may be required to estimate the expected frequency, let alone other parameters such as the mean and standard deviation of the severity of operational risk. One way to fill the data gap is to create synthetic data by using scenario analysis. One reason for contemplating various scenarios is that the process sets no boundaries for thinking. In operational risk modelling, scenario analysis is a means of assuming the amount of loss that will result from, and the frequency of, operational risk incidents that may be faced by a financial institution (Bank of Japan, 2007). If a number of staff members feel that, based on their experience, a loss amounting to several million dollars may occur once in 10 years, it is possible to use this information when formulating risk scenarios. A formal definition of scenario analysis in relation to operational risk is suggested by Bilby (2008). He defines scenario analysis as a "systematic process of obtaining expert opinion from business managers and risk management experts to derive reasoned assessment of the likelihood and impact of plausible operational losses." He goes on to argue that the use of well-reasoned scaled external data is effectively a form of scenario analysis.

In the SBA, the frequency and severity distributions are guesstimated using all available quantitative and qualitative information, including the subjective judgement of business line and senior management. Once the simulated loss distribution is obtained, expected and unexpected losses should be compared against similar businesses and evaluated for reasonableness by the risk management team and business line managers. If adjustment is required for the initial guesstimates, the whole process should be repeated. The SBA consists of the steps shown in Figure 4.6.

Scenarios are constructed by teams consisting of business managers, operations managers, risk managers, chief financial officers, legal experts, internal auditors as well as specialists in compliance, technology and information security. Typically, more than one meeting is required to construct and review scenarios. And typically, scenarios are updated on an annual basis and when material changes to the business occur. The construction and review of scenarios requires the evaluation of the validity of the scenarios relative to actual experience. It is also important to incorporate an appropriate number of low-frequency, high-severity scenarios to represent tail events. Attention is paid to the following points: (i) whether or not the scenario frequency projections match internal annualised loss experience; (ii) whether or not the distribution of losses in the scenarios match the actual

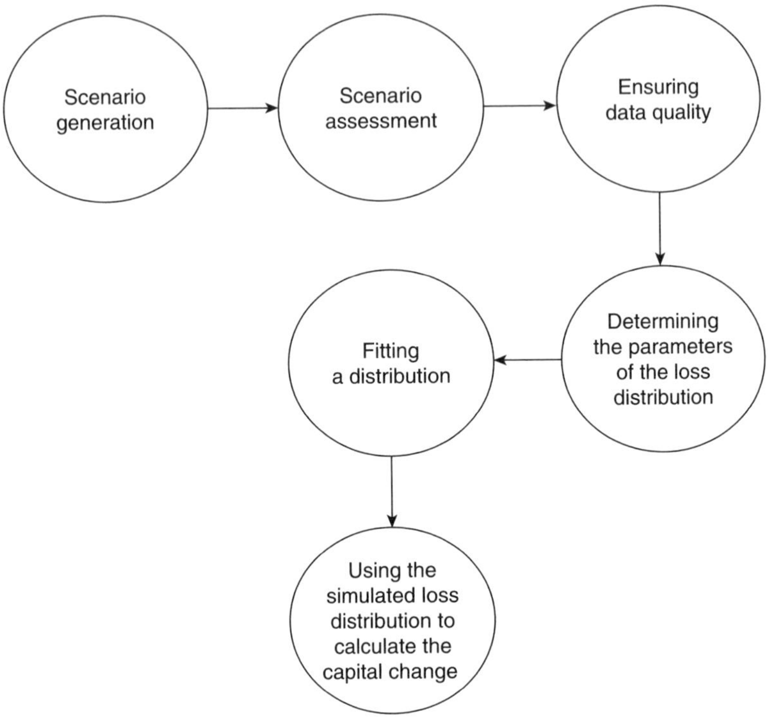

Figure 4.6 Steps Involved in the Scenario-Based Approach

loss experience; and (iii) whether or not the maximum loss data will influence scenario model inputs.

One of the perceived benefits of the SBA is that it generates data that can be used to supplement historical data, particularly at the tail of the distribution. For example, it is possible to construct an optimistic scenario, a pessimistic scenario and a catastrophic scenario for operational losses. Once these scenarios have been constructed, they can be converted into three data points that are added to the set of historical data. Otherwise, the weighted average loss resulting from the three scenarios (where the weights are the corresponding probabilities of occurrence) can be added as one data point. Another procedure is to generate the loss distribution parameters from the scenarios, and these can be combined with similar parameters derived from historical data. The advantage of supplementing historical internal data with scenario data, as opposed to external data, is that external data suffer from different kinds of bias, as we saw in Chapter 3. On the other hand, scenarios are thought to be relevant and most accurate in the absence of good-quality internal data.

In a workshop on scenario analysis held at the Bank of Japan in July 2007, an interesting question was raised: suppose Basel II was not invented, would scenario analysis have been used by financial institutions as a useful tool for bank management? One of the participants replied by saying that "in those days, when the term operational risk did not exist, I used to conduct a scenario analysis that relied on instinct to determine 'if this happens here, it will result in that'." Another respondent said "at our bank, although we did not use the word [sic] scenario analysis in 2001, I think, even without Basel II, we would probably have introduced risk control tools under the same scheme." Most of the participants agreed with the view that scenario analysis is still at an "early stage" and that it is a subject that needs further review by the industry as a whole (Bank of Japan, 2007). We will explore the problems with the SBA in the following section.

The Scorecard Approach

The name "scorecard approach" is derived from the fact that the results of the risk evaluation process are reported on scorecards, which typically show scores for operational risk. The scores are expressed in monetary terms for potential loss severities, in the number of times per year for potential loss frequencies, and in the form of ratings for operational qualities (excellent, good, poor). Blunden (2003) describes a scorecard as "simply a list of a firm's own assessment of its risks and controls, containing the risk event, risk owner, risk likelihood, risk impact, controls that mitigate the risk event, control owner, control design and control impact" (the term "risk likelihood" is a manifestation of confusion between "risk" and "loss"). Typically, the SCA is questionnaire-based.

A scorecard may specify a range of expected frequency, whereas the exact point on the range would be fixed by scenario analysis, using comparison with actual loss data, if available, or external data otherwise. Frequency may be defined in relation to the frequency classes corresponding to certain probability ranges. For example, an event that is considered to be "almost impossible" has a probability range of 0–0.0001, whereas an event that is considered to be "very likely" falls in the probability range 0.90–1.0.

The SCA depends heavily on the concept of risk classes, key risk drivers (KRDs) and key risk indicators (KRIs). KRDs are the risk characteristics that distinguish the level of operational risk in one firm or business line from others. These include complexity of the product, complexity of the delivery system, growth rate of the firm or the business line, frequency of the system downtime, capacity usage and the skill level of the staff. KRDs are obtained from performance measures and from intuition, based on deep knowledge of the business activity. KRDs are defined by the BCBS (2002) as "statistics and/or metrics, often financial, which can provide insight into a bank's risk position." KRIs are a broad category of measures used to monitor the activities and control environment. While drivers constitute an *ex ante* concept, indicators constitute an *ex post* concept. Examples of KRIs are profit and loss breaks, open confirmations, failed trades, and system reliability. Related concepts that are used less frequently are key cost indicators (KCIs) and key trouble indicators (KTIs).

Alexander (2003a) gives examples of KRDs and KRIs for various operational risk types. In the case of credit card fraud, for example, a KRD is the quality of the authentication process, whereas a KRI is the number of unauthorised credit card transactions. Another example is the risk of EPWS, where KRDs include recruitment policy with respect to discrimination, pay structure and safety measures, whereas the KRIs include the number of employee complaints, staff turnover and time off work. Sundmacher (2007a) lists, as the risk drivers in the high-profile case of the Allied Irish Bank, poor control environment, poor management, human errors, system errors and incentive structure.

A related concept is that of risk controls, which include any measure that is taken to reduce operational risk of a certain type, typically measured in monetary terms because they constitute cost to the underlying firm. For example, to eliminate the risk of rogue trading completely, a firm must abandon its trading activity and put an end to trading operations. In this case, the control is completely effective but the cost is the trading profit forgone as a result of this kind of action. In a less dramatic case, partial control of the risk of rogue trading may be achieved by putting stringent limits on traders and subjecting them to scrutiny. This will reduce the risk of rogue trading but only at the cost of forgone trading profit, albeit smaller than the cost in the previous case. Likewise, the risk of system failure and the risk of credit card fraud can be eliminated completely by switching to manual processing of transactions and abandoning the use of credit cards. These controls are measured by the cost of inconvenience to customers and inefficiency. One has to remember that while the application of controls reduces risk, that happens at a decreasing rate. Resources allocated to risk controls are determined by the point of intersection of the allocated resources curve and the (loss) event reduction curve, as shown in Figure 4.7.

Scorecards are constructed on the basis of "expert" evaluations and self-assessment exercises, the latter taking the form of well-designed questionnaires. Once the "experts" have completed the questionnaires and the corresponding scorecard reports have been produced, the need arises for the validation of data. For this purpose, each expert's evaluation needs to be approved by a different person, whereas the internal auditor reviews the evaluations. The independent oversight function ensures consistency across different questionnaires as well as the quality of the answers. Following validation, the data can be used to measure the capital charge against operational risk. For this purpose, it is necessary to assign values to the elements

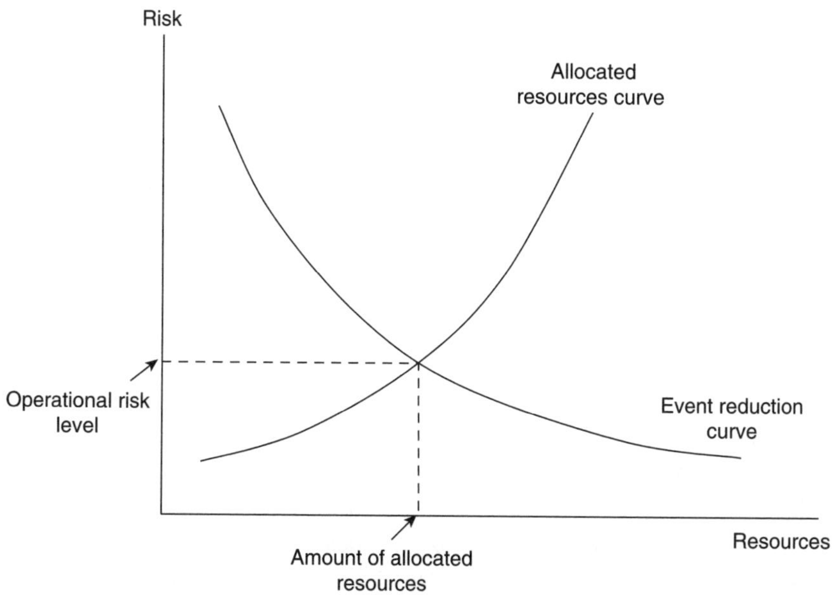

Figure 4.7 Determination of Resource Allocation to Reduce Operational Risk

of the scorecard (such as the percentage of occurrence for the risk likelihood) a monetary value for the risk impact. Historical loss data may play a role in the SCA to (i) identify risk drivers and mitigators; (ii) determine the initial level of capital; (iii) cross check the accuracy of questions in the responses and challenging the existing scorecards in terms of frequency and severity.

The main advantage of the SCA is that it is flexible, as it fits with the underlying firm's identified risks and controls. Furthermore, it does not require an external view of the risk categories faced by a firm. It also allows the firm to obtain skills and knowledge by starting operational risk capital calculation early rather than waiting to build up an internal database or using external data that may not be relevant to the firm. And, by quantifying risks and controls, a firm can perform analysis on its risk "inventory," which allows it to see (in monetary terms) the likely increase in the risk exposure resulting from the removal of a control or the likely reduction in exposure resulting from an increase in the quantity of control. Finally, the SCA, unlike the LDA, is forward-looking, which is a useful feature, particularly if we are trying to measure the operational risk associated with a new business line or activity that has no history within the firm. However, the SCA is subjective to the extent that makes these perceived advantages pale into insignificance.

4.4 A CRITIQUE OF THE AMA

This section draws heavily on Moosa (2008b) where there is a more detailed version of these arguments. The AMA can be criticised for at least three reasons: (i) the lack of consensus on what constitutes the approach; (ii) the problems of using the approach to measure regulatory capital; and (iii) the appropriateness, costs and benefits of the AMA. These problems will be discussed in turn.

What Constitutes the AMA?

An examination of the literature reveals a wide range of views on what constitutes the AMA. Alexander (2003b) and Peccia (2004) effectively consider the AMA to be the LDA. The listing of three headings, by adding to the LDA the SBA and SCA, is adopted by Anders and van der Brink (2004), Martin Davies (2005), and by Haubenstock and Hause (2006). The BCBS (2001b) lists only two headings: LDA and IMA, which is the view adopted by Bee (2006). But the BCBS (2001a) adds the SCA to the list. In BCBS (2003d), scenario analysis is added as a procedure that may "form the basis of operational risk analytical framework." Subsequently, however, the BCBS dropped the IMA, describing the AMA loosely as encompassing the use of internal data, external data, scenarios, and business environment and control (the fractured jigsaw).

Some authors, including Chernobai and Rachev (2004), Kalyvas et al (2006), Reynolds and Syer (2003) and Kuhn and Neu (2005) exclude the SBA from the listing, claiming that the AMA encompasses the LDA, IMA and SCA. Fujii (2005), on the other hand, talks about the LDA and SCA only. Finally, there is the view of "let a thousand flowers bloom," adopted by those who play it safe and argue that any internal methodology is part of the AMA, which makes one wonder about the inconsistency between the words "any" and "advanced."

One version of the "let a thousand flowers bloom" is that the AMA comprises internal data, external data, scenario analysis and the business environment and internal control factors (which is consistent with the imprecise description of the AMA that is used by the BCBS). These components are typically portrayed as forming a jigsaw. Right, but the jigsaw is fractured, looking like what is shown in Figure 4.8. Then, one problem with the "let a thousand flowers bloom" doctrine pertains to the usefulness of the "use test." Martin Sprenger, head of the operational risk team at the Swiss Federal Banking Commission, said in a regulatory panel discussion held during the OpRisk Europe 2008 conference that "the use test is not particularly important." The reason for this assertion is that while regulators are "meant to let a thousand flowers bloom," "the use test could be implemented in such a way

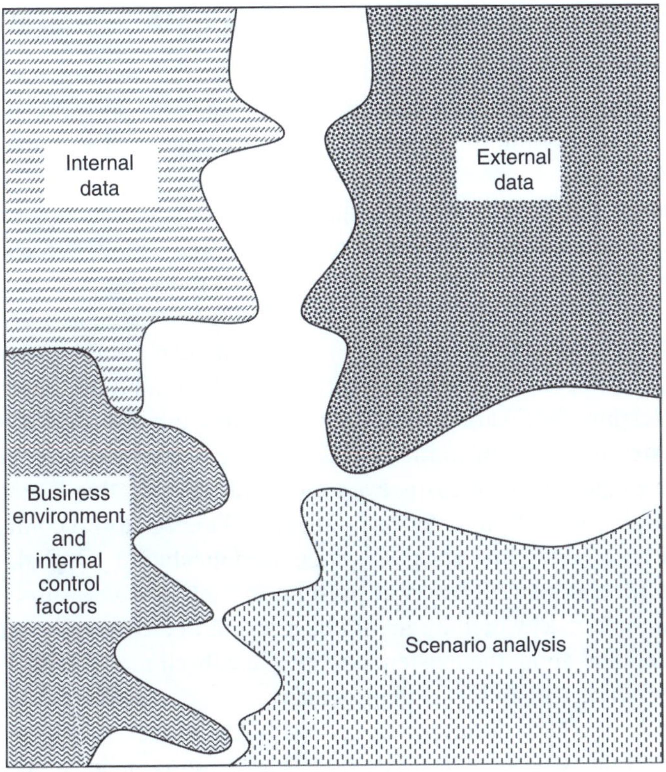

Figure 4.8 A Fractured AMA Jigsaw

to force banks into operational risk methodologies that they disagree with" (*OpRisk & Compliance*, May 2008, p. 10). Regulators cannot expect banks to use internal data, external data, scenario analysis, and scorecards equally vigorously for calculating regulatory capital and for risk management.

No-one seems to know for sure the "correct" listing of the items that constitute the AMA, and this is why Nash (2003) describes it as being "not a single approach that banks can take and adopt." "Felxibility" could be the name of the game here, but Nash (2003) correctly argues that treating the AMA as a "laboratory in which banks can test and develop approaches to operational risk quantification.... places a great burden on supervisors to verify and accept banks' approaches to operational risk." The implementation of the AMA is hard enough without this confusion about what and what does not come under its umbrella. Indeed, the Basel Committee seems to recognise this problem, warning that the wide range of practices involved in modelling and measuring operational risk is conducive to a situation where banks with similar risk profiles have different levels of operational risk capital charges (BCBS, 2006b).

The Problems of Implementing the AMA: General

Many problems are associated with the implementation of the AMA, in the sense of using it to calculate the capital charge against operational risk. We start with a discussion of the general problems involved in implementing the AMA.

In general, there are problems with the process of constructing a total loss distribution and measuring value at risk (VAR) at a certain percentile. This problem is described as "general" because it is valid irrespective of whether the loss distribution is constructed by using internal data only, in conjunction with external data or by adding scenario analysis and expert opinion. A general criticism of the AMA is directed at the notion of "internal models," as Herring (2002) argues that internal models are insufficiently reliable to replicate the approach (initially designed for market risk) to operational risk. The Economist (2008d) is even more assertive on this issue, arguing that internal models "can be seriously flawed." Doerig (2003) points out that "there is no credible and satisfying model applicable to 'OpRisk at large' available for the quantification at present, except for some sub-categories [of operational risk] which might not be relevant in the overall context." He is also sceptical about the existence of one "catch-all model with a credible outcome (hence, "more sizzle than steak").

Schachter (2008) describes a certain VAR model (published in the February 2008 issue of *Asia Risk*, p. 38) as a "straw man, more attribute to their [the authors'] intelligence and cleverness than a source of useful insight." He also criticises the reverse thinking of "if I can build a model that has some correspondence with something observed, then the model must represent the underlying truth and its predictions must be valid." He adds by saying "the fact that there may be many, many models that also fit those same facts, each with different implications somehow doesn't appear to enter into the authors' thinking." Compare this statement with what a VAR modeller says in defence of his "bread and butter." In a seminar held in Melbourne on 10 June 2008, Chris Finger (Head of Research at RiskMetrics, the inventors of VAR) labelled the critics of what he called good VAR-based models as being "irresponsible." This statement actually confirms the characterisation of VAR model enthusiasts suggested by Schachter.

Wood (2008) raises the question whether or not the industry's AMA models are any good, citing a "high-profile quant" as saying that "a lot of them are disastrous" and that "op risk modeling is currently in terribly, terribly bad shape." Wood also points out that "practitioners and regulators alike will argue that AMA models do what they say on the tin: they measure a bank's operational risk and generates an appropriate capital number," but in private "they're more willing to admit to doubt and frustration." Furthermore, Wood cites Richard Pike, product director with software vendor Ci3 in Dublin as saying that "many of the industry's operational risk managers claim to be happy with the numbers their models produce but if you ask them to guarantee that it's correct then, no- they can't." In a Ci3 survey published in the October 2007 issue of *OpRisk & Compliance*, complaints aimed at the AMA included the following: (i) they do not capture the risk of tail events; (ii) they are not forward looking; and (iii) they encourage too great a focus on measuring rather than managing risk. Pike mentions the VAR system at one bank, which is supposed to generate a number that would be the bank's maximum loss nineteen days out of twenty. In August 2007, that same bank exceeded the maximum loss sixteen times. Pike attributes the poor performance of the model to the "pure quantification approach." He puts it succinctly by saying "you make so many assumptions in the mathematics and if these assumptions are incorrect, the model is practically useless."

The VAR methodology has been criticised severely as a measure of risk in general terms and in relation to operational risk in particular (e.g., Danielsson et al, 2001; Hubner et al, 2003). The use of the concept of VAR to measure operational risk capital charges has not escaped criticism. For example, Hubner et al (2003) argue against using a "VAR-like figure" to measure operational risk, stipulating that although VAR models have been developed for operational risk, questions remain about the interpretation of the results. Another problem is that VAR figures provide an indication of the amount of risk but not of its form (e.g., legal as opposed to technology).

Moreover, some doubts have been raised about the use of the 99.9th percentile, which implies a 99.9% confidence level that losses would not exceed the percentile (operational VAR). For example, Alexander (2003b) points out that the parameters of the total loss distribution cannot be estimated precisely because the operational loss data are incomplete, unreliable and/or subjective. This makes the estimation of risk at the 99.9th percentile implausible. Alexander argues that regulators should ask themselves very seriously if it is sensible to measure the capital charge on the 99.9th percentile.

McConnell (2006) describes the use of the 99.9th percentile as an "unrealistic level of precision" that would introduce moral hazard, thus encouraging managers to claim that risk has been fully mitigated rather than address the serious issues underlying large loss events in particular. He also describes it as an "illusory search for precision" and wonders why it is that epidemiologists work within a six point scale for the primary risk of death whereas banks are required to estimate capital to cover monetary losses to a precision of 1 in 1000. He correctly concludes that this is an "unattainable task." Likewise, Jobst (2007a) points out that the 99.9th percentile makes the quantitative criteria of the AMA appear overly stringent (perhaps the word "appear" should not appear here). The level of precision is unheard of even in experimental physics, which makes one wonder why the Basel

Committee believes that operational risk can be measured more easily than the thrust of a jet engine. It is perhaps easier to estimate the age of Planet Earth than to mess around with the tail of the distribution, but again scientists do no claim that they aspire to estimate the age of the Planet to a 99.9% precision.

Yet another problem is the assumption to be made about the correlation of operational loss events. Frachot et al (2004b) cast doubt on the validity of the proposition that operational losses occur simultaneously, describing it as being "rather dubious and hardly supported by empirical evidence." However, it is difficult to assess the level of correlation between different risk types and/or business units because of the lack of historical data. A further correlation-related problem is that the assumption to be made about correlation would invite subjectivity and bias to achieve the objective of minimising regulatory capital against operational risk. The validity of this proposition will be demonstrated in Chapter 6.

It is arguable that the most fundamental question to raise when an attempt is made to measure operational risk is whether or not it shows a statistical pattern at all. The issue is not finding the best way to estimate the frequency and severity of losses but if indeed stable frequency and severity distributions do exist.

Approach-Specific Problems

In this section we discuss the problems associated specifically with the implementation of the three specific approaches that fall under the AMA: LDA, SCA and SBA.

Aue and Kalkbrener (2007) argue that the application of the LDA to the quantification of operational risk is a difficult task, listing the three problems of (i) shortage of data; (ii) the context-dependent nature of operational risk; and (iii) lack of a strongly risk-sensitive exposure measure in operational risk modelling. By far the most serious problem is that of data, which will be discussed in a separate sub-section.

The main shortcoming of the "expert opinion"-based SBA and SCA is subjectivity. "Expert opinion"-based data is invariably subjective because it is provided by employees who are under scrutiny and have little incentive to be forthcoming. Peccia (2004) points out that there is a problem here because the experts typically have little or no experience in the low-frequency, high-severity events. Furthermore, Rao and Dev (2006) describe as a "difficult task" any attempt to incorporate the effect of qualitative scores on the estimated capital or on the frequency and severity distributions in the LDA.

While Haubenstock and Hardin (2003) advocate the use of the LDA on the grounds that it has several advantages, they also argue that it has the following limitations: (i) it is data-intensive, requiring a loss history or a set of scorecard data; (ii) it is potentially backward-looking, because it is based on historical data; (iii) data are too sparse to determine frequency and severity at lower levels, and so modelling is typically performed for business units falling one or perhaps two levels below the firm-wide results; and (iv) it does not capture the impact on revenue or margin from operational causes (these risks are excluded from the Basel definition).

The problems with scenarios are that they are subjective and open to "gaming," with respect to the tendency to hold less capital. Other problems with scenario analysis are that it may not capture the impact of multi-dimensional loss events, it has a debatable statistical integrity and that it is difficult to relate to high confidence intervals (over 99%). Yet another problem is that the answers may be biased, depending on the way in which questions are asked. Some suggestions have been put forward to reduce the subjectivity of scenarios (Bank of Japan, 2007). These include the following: (i) introducing a method to solve the problem that the answers vary depending on the ways in which the questions are asked; (ii) everybody should get together to have discussions and find as many ways as possible of increasing the objectivity of risk assessment; and (iii) checking scenarios for consistency and compliance.

The SCA induces subjectivity for several reasons. The first is that the industry standards for KRIs that should be used for each risk type have not been developed, which makes the choice subjective. The approach is also subjective because frequency and severity scores are usually assigned by the "owner" of the risk. Furthermore, the scores are mapped in a subjective manner to monetary loss amounts, which is particularly the case with human risks. Finally, to use scorecard data in the AMA, the minimum requirement is to assess both expected frequency and expected severity quantitatively from scores that may be purely qualitative. Apart from subjectivity, a major shortcoming of the SCA is that it does not give any indication of the required capital, basically resulting in a relative risk comparison of the different activities. This is why Holmes (2003) casts doubt on the ability of this approach to give reliable information about risk over time or rank the relative risk of two firms.

Data-Related Problems

The data-related problems have been highlighted by Allen and Bali (2004), Cagan (2001a), Chernobai et al (2006), Danielsson et al (2001), Haas and Kaiser (2004), Muzzy (2003) and Pezier (2003a). For example, Cagan (2001a) argues that appropriate data is absent for all but a handful of banks and that industry standards for such data are still lacking. Chernobai et al (2006) believe that all statistical approaches become *ad hoc* in the presence of incomplete data, which would result in misleading estimates of expected and unexpected losses. KPMG (2003) asserts that "the loss database of a single financial institution may not contain sufficiently granual data to support statistically meaningful estimates of the capital charge against operational risk. Furthermore, unless the sample size is extremely large (which is not typically the case), a histogram of internal loss data appears disjointed because internal data come from different non-homogenous distributions. Doerig (2003) describes the rule "garbage in, garbage out" as being of "extreme importance" when quantifying operational risk, arguing that "models and quantifications are only as good as the data they build on." He further argues that "it will take some years until OpRisk data availability is such that it provides credible, transparent and relevant databases." Power (2005) concludes that "there is, almost by definition, data poverty where it is most needed for heterogeneous catastrophic events" and that "except for a range of normal errors, e.g. transaction processing, firm-specific data is generally inadequate."

One solution to the data availability problem is to augment internal data with external data on the operational losses incurred by other firms, but this solution is not straightforward. For example, Dahen and Dionne (2007) argue that using external data to supplement internal data is useful because it fills out the extreme losses missing from the tail, but certain types of risk (such as EDPM) will not be properly represented as losses of this nature are unlikely to be reported to the media.

Samad-Khan et al (2006) suggest that while internal loss data seem to be insufficient, external loss data appear to have many deficiencies. Calling external data to the rescue is a solution that is daunted by the problems of appropriateness (to account for differences in business structure) and scaling (to account for differences in size). To appreciate this problem, we need some exact specification of external data, which includes items other than external databases: (i) losses of the underlying bank with respect to other banks; (ii) losses incurred in a particular business line in India relative to those incurred in the same business line in Belgium; (iii) losses of a recently acquired bank; (iv) losses incurred in 2006 relative to those incurred in 2007; and (v) losses incurred in retail brokerage operations before and after the introduction of the straight through processing (STP) system. Because of the diversity of external data, it is likely that they would be different from a statistical point of view in the following senses: (i) they may come from the same distribution but they are selected with different criteria (e.g., different thresholds); (ii) they may come from a distribution with definite relations with the internal data distribution (e.g., scaling); and (iii) they may come from completely different distributions. This is why KPMG (2003) urges caution in dealing with external data through careful screening and adjustment to "enable a close resemblance to the bank's specific environment of processes, systems and people."

External loss data are also affected by reporting biases and idiosyncratic factors, such as size, controls, culture, legal environment and geographical location. Reporting bias is typically associated with publically available loss data, which are drawn from newspaper reports, regulatory filings, legal judgments, etc. Reporting bias arises because smaller losses are less likely to be reported than larger losses, particularly because there is a reporting threshold (losses below the threshold, which may be rather high, are not captured). Because of the bias, it is not possible to extrapolate frequency or severity parameters directly from the data. In other words, reporting bias distorts the loss frequency and severity distribution parameters, producing misleadingly high operational VAR estimates.

A particular data problem is the limited data points at the tail of the loss distribution, which makes the estimation of VAR at the 99.9th percentile (as required by Basel II) impossible. Wei (2007) makes this point explicit, stating that "while many banks have adequate data for modelling the body of the distribution, few have sufficient internal data to estimate the tail distribution." Power (2005) puts forward a similar view by arguing that "data for operational risk management is most needed where it is both thin and conceptually problematic, i.e. for rare high impact possibilities." Mignola (2008) points out that the implication of using the 99.9th percentile is that the measurement of the capital charge requires the observation of 1000 annual losses, which means an observation period of at least 1000 years or the presence of 1000 banks that are similar in terms of the operational risk profile and operating environment. It follows then that for the calculation of the 99.9th percentile we must look for "banks that have been collecting loss data since 1007." This is why Mignola suggests that "banks and regulators should rethink their approach, relaxing some of the most critical requirements, especially the 99.9% annual loss confidence level." He also suggests the alternative of finding "a new, maybe less theoretically attractive but more practical, approach to the operational risk regulatory capital requirement."

The EVT has been suggested to deal with this problem as it can arguably be used to predict the probability of events that have never happened, which can be done by extrapolating the stochastic behaviour of past events. EVT, however, has been criticised severely. In Embrechts et al (1997), it is stated very clearly that EVT is not "a magical tool that could produce estimates out of thin air." Hubner et al (2003) describe as a "myth" the ability of EVT to make an important contribution to the assessment of exceptional operational risk, arguing that any attempt to apply the theory to a small set of unrelated operational losses in different firms around the globe is "another triumph of wishful thinking over reason." Pezier (2003a) describes what he calls "extreme value simulation" as a "blind approach." Chavez-Demoulin et al (2005) point out that the application of EVT to operational loss data raises difficult issues which are not due to a technical justification of EVT but "more to the nature of the data." Wood (2008) cites Leonard Matz, director of liquidity risk consulting with SunGard BancWare in New York, as casting doubt on the usefulness of EVT, arguing that "for operational risk, in almost all banks, there is no distribution of outcomes from risk events that would include a Nick Leeson or Jerome Kerviel." It is ironic then that the victim of Kerveil's unauthorised trading, Societe Generale, is one of the French banks that have been permitted to use the AMA.

Wood (2008) also cites Anna Chernobai, an operational risk academic, saying that "we can't apply it [EVT] to historic events in order to predict future losses." Chernobai further argues that "even if there have been one or two extreme events in the past history of the banks, presumably the bank knows what the issues were, knows the sources of risk, and has taken steps to prevent a repeat." In his keynote speech at the OpRisk US 2008 conference, Nassim Taleb makes the interesting observation that a turkey has a good life until (all of a sudden) it becomes someone's Christmas lunch. This is an extreme event for the turkey because "nothing in its experience prepared it for, or led it to expect, the trip to the slaughter house" (*Op Risk & Compliance*, March 2008, p. 28).

A related problem is raised by McConnell (2006) who argues that extreme loss events may not be generated by the loss distribution but they are rather outliers. According to Chernobai and Rachev (2006) outliers are observations that are very different from the rest of the data, which makes them worthy of special consideration. They can occur as a result of data collection/recording errors, problems of group or correlation or because they violate model assumptions. The problem that arises here is that given a sample of losses, do we remove extreme losses as in conventional statistical analysis? Chernobai and Rachev (2006) suggest the use of robust statistics to determine whether extreme losses are indeed outliers that should be moved or that they should be retained because they belong to the same distribution. On the other hand, "modeling outliers is pointless if the outliers themselves are of no consequence," according to Nassim Taleb who made this observation in a keynote speech at the OpRisk USA 2008 conference (*OpRisk & Compliance*, March 2008, p. 28).

The Costs and Benefits of the AMA

The implementation of the AMA, if at all possible, is rather difficult and expensive, particularly because there is more than one reason to believe that the quality of the output (the estimated capital charge) would be questionable. Presumably referring to the capital charge, Doreig (2003) argues that "a simple number can be so intriguing, but do not ever forget the 'garbage in-garbage-out' effects." He also argues that "understanding and managing OpRisk is more important than putting a regulatory value on it." de Fontnouvelle et al (2005b) point out that developing the data and models necessary to quantify credit and operational risk requires a sizable fixed cost investment. And even if these models have been developed, it is likely to be the case that the regulators do not have the expertise to evaluate (or validate) them, as it is getting more and more difficult to recruit risk management talents.

The question that arises is the following: is the AMA viable in terms of costs and benefits? This question is typically overlooked particularly by the engineers of Basel II. Doerig (2003), for example, argues that "financial institutions and regulators/supervisors should be aware of the cost/benefit relationship of setting in place the quantification of OpRisk involving data gathering, models, procedures, systems and staff." Likewise, Sundmacher (2007a) points out that "the development and maintenance of systems that allow financial institutions to collect, pool and analyse relevant operational risk data is costly," because "financial institutions would have to employ additional, specialized personnel or would have to train existing staff for the proper use of these systems."

The anticipated benefits of the AMA are as follows: (i) it would reduce or eliminate incentives for regulatory arbitrage; (ii) it would provide banks with an incentive to improve their risk management processes; and (iii) compliance cost would be reduced to the extent that the business is regulated in the same way that it is managed. These perceived benefits of the AMA rest on the following propositions: (i) aligning regulatory capital with economic capital is a good idea; (ii) internal models are relevant and conducive to sound risk management; and (iii) an incentive to use the AMA is that it produces a lower capital charge than the BIA and STA.

It can be demonstrated that these propositions are questionable and even flawed. To start with, it is not a good idea to align regulatory capital with economic capital and to regulate banks in the same way as they are managed. Rebonato (2007) argues against the first proposition on the grounds of differences between regulators and risk managers. Linking the development of internal models to improved risk management is a dubious proposition. Pzeier (2003a) casts doubt on the proposition that the AMA is conducive to better operational risk management. Rebonato (2007) argues that "although the quantitative approach remains the high route to risk management, a lot of very effective risk management can be done with a much simpler approach."

The proposition that the use of the AMA leads to a lower capital charge is sometimes taken for granted to the extent that a diagram like that in Figure 4.9 is used to depict the inverses relation between the capital charge and the complexity of the approach used to it (e.g., Tinca, 2007). But we have already seen that the BIA and STA produce very close capital charges,

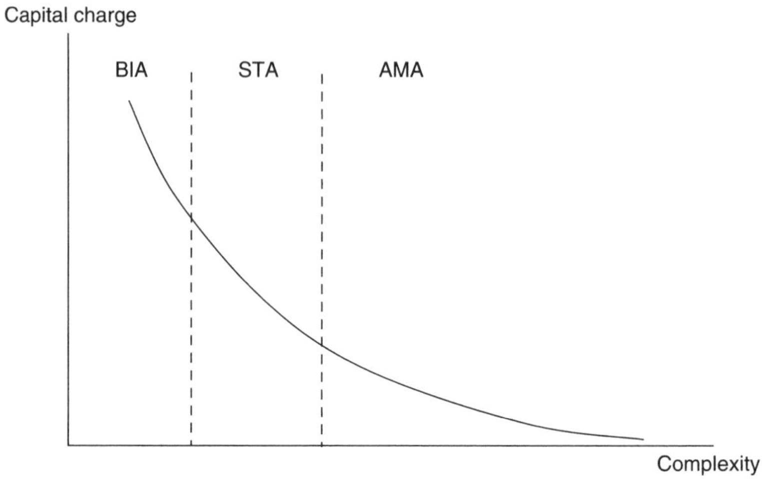

Figure 4.9 Capital Charge versus Complexity of the Approach (?)

in which case the argument that remains is that the AMA is conducive to lower capital charges than the BIA and STA. If this is true, then it would indeed represent a problematical feature of Basel II because only large, internationally active banks will be allowed to use the AMA. This means that the perception that the AMA produces lower capital charges leads to the belief that Basel II will boost the competitive advantage of big banks relative to that of small banks.

Moosa (2008b) presents strong arguments to invalidate the explanations for why the AMA would produce a lower capital charge than the BIA and STA. These explanations include the following: (i) relaxing the assumption of perfect correlation among business lines and event types will reduce the capital charge; (ii) the AMA takes into account risk mitigation such as insurance; (iii) the AMA would produce a lower capital charge because the latter is calculated on the basis of the unexpected loss only; and (iv) a lower capital charge would result under the IMA (which has gone, anyway) if the gamma factors (relating unexpected to expected loss) are calibrated in such a way as to "ensure that there is a systematic reduction in capital required by the IMA compared to the Standardised Approach" (BCBS, 2001b). This is probably why de Fontnouvelle et al (2005b) note that "the intent of the Basel Committee is for the simpler approaches to yield higher operational risk capital than the AMA." It is not clear whether the reduction in capital charges under the AMA would result from mathematical sophistication or it is what the Basel Committee wants. According to Jobst (2007b), the Basel Committee specifies two main causes of lower capital charges, the diversification benefits and the effect of insurance.

It seems, however, that the AMA would produce a lower capital charge only because any internal model can be manipulated in a large number of ways to produce the lowest possible capital charge. It is subjectivity, rather than anything else, that may produce lower capital charges. Banks adopting the AMA will strive to construct an internal model that produces the lowest possible capital charge by letting "one thousand flowers bloom" and by experimenting extensively in the "laboratory" of the AMA. This view is held by Kabir Dutta, a Boston-based principal with consultancy firm CRA International, who asserts that "the alternatives I see in the research are susceptible to manipulation to calculate the amount of capital you would like to hold." Dutta actually uses the term "capital-massaging models" to describe the *status quo*. Likewise, Dutta and Perry (2007) conclude, on the basis of their results, that "using different models for the same institution can result in materially different capital estimates."

Let us, for the sake of argument, accept the proposition that the AMA produces lower capital charges than the simple approaches, irrespective of the reason why this would be the case. This will create a problem, given the difference between implementation in Europe and in the US. In the US, the AMA will be the only option for quantifying operational risk exposure for those banks opting in for Basel II. In the EU, where all financial institutions will be required to be Basel II compliant, simpler methods are allowed for less sophisticated institutions. This means that an American bank and a European bank, both of which are Basel II compliant and both have the same risk profile, will have different capital charges, which means that the European bank will hold capital that is at least equal to what is held by the US bank. This is not exactly a "level playing field." Even if there are net benefits of capital reduction for banks using the AMA, these benefits are described by de Fontnouvelle et al (2005b) as "variable." This is why they argue that smaller US financial institutions, which do not have to be on Basel II, will choose at least initially to forego both costs and benefits by remaining under Basel I.

There is indeed some survey evidence on the benefits of the AMA as perceived by the banks that have already implemented the approach and those that have not. A survey sponsored by the London-based consulting firm Chase Cooper (the results of which were published in the March 2008 issue of *OpRisk & Compliance*) showed that 66.7% of the participants who have adopted the AMA said that it provided "significant benefit," while 33.3% said it provided "small benefit." Surprise, surprise! Well, a bank manager who spends huge sums of money on the implementation of the AMA is not going to say that that the money has been spent for nothing. As a matter of fact, what is truly surprising is that is that 33.3% (a significant proportion) said that the AMA provided small benefit, probably implying that it is not viable in terms of costs and benefits. One has to admire the honesty of these people and salute them for not being too economical with the truth. Naturally, we cannot expect anyone who has implemented the AMA to say that it is totally useless, unless one is talking to them in a party at 2.35 am.

What matters more are the views of those who are planning to use the AMA. Only 37.5% said that the AMA would provide significant benefit, while 47.9% said it would offer some benefit. Another 12.5% said it would offer small benefit, and 2.1% said that it would provide no benefit whatsoever. Among the respondents who will not use the AMA, 28.6% said that it would not provide any benefit, another 26.6% said that it would not even give them capital reduction and 11.9% said it was "too complex." John Kiddy, the CEO at Chase Cooper, admits that firms believe that the AMA is rather complicated and very expensive and requires amounts of loss data that do not exist. Being a beneficiary of the AMA, the Chase Cooper boss claims that "the business benefits flowing from an AMA are initially unclear – except to get a lower capital charge [!]." He also believes that institutions have the wrong view of the AMA because "there has been so much written from an academic perspective" (blame it on the poor academics). Mr Kiddy claims that the AMA was not just for lower capital charge but also because "it was to have a risk-based charge for capital with all the benefits it brings."

But what are these alleged benefits? Mr Kiddy makes a list of the alleged benefits on page 40 of the same issue of *OpRisk & Compliance*, including the following: (i) more comprehensive event capture; (ii) more effective and focused event analysis; (iii) greater clarity in defining and using risk appetite; (vi) greater focus and analysis of external losses; and (v) higher standards for the Risk and controls self assessment (RCSA) process. He goes on by claiming that "the AMA process is thus a catalyst for extra focus on components of op risk management that results in better risk management and significant impact profiles and loss reduction," etc ... Sounds like rhetoric, doesn't it? It remains for me to say that page 40 on which Mr Kiddy praises the AMA unreservedly was devoted to a sponsored statement, an "ad" by Chase Cooper. I should not forget to say that Chase Cooper is a risk and compliance management solutions provider that carries out AMA model reviews. No wonder.

In the OpRisk Asia conference held in Singapore in June 2008, regulators and risk managers raised question marks about the AMA, although some of them reiterated Mr Kiddy's rhetoric. Him Chuan Lim, the head of group risk at the DBS Group, described as a "challenge" the connection to reality of operational risk quantification, arguing that "no framework/tools can replace commonsense and right mindset." He described as "strange numbers" the output of their LDA at DBS (Lim, 2008). Adrenne Haden, of the Federal Reserve Board, raised the question why "the 1 in 1000 or 1 in 10,000 events," as predicted by operational risk models, "occur more frequently" (Haden, 2008). And while Patricia Jalleh, of the United Overseas

Bank Group, had a few good things to say about the quantitative approach to operational risk, she defended the qualitative approach and argued for "management before measurement" (Jalleh, 2008). This statement is plausible simply because the 99.9th percentile of a loss distribution that does not reflect reality has nothing to do with risk management.

4.5 CONCLUDING REMARKS

Whether or not operational risk should be regulated, as required by the Basel II Accord and otherwise, is a controversial issue, as there is significant scepticism about the role of regulation as a means of achieving financial stability. But given the special importance of banks, some sort of regulation may be warranted, and holding capital against operational risk is a proposition that has some merits.

What is not a good idea is the use of the AMA for this purpose, the idea of requiring banks to develop internal models to align regulatory capital with economic capital. This is a bad idea: not only that the implementation of the AMA is problematical, but also because regulating banks in the same way as they are managed is not right because regulators and managers have different objectives. The AMA has already brought complaints from small banks, but this does not mean that large banks are happy about it either, despite the (alleged) carrot of lower capital charges. There are reports that large (particularly US) banks are not happy about the AMA because it is too complex and expensive. Then as Phlippa Girling puts it, "people could expend a lot of energy becoming AMA compliant, and not have addressed the material other risks under Pillar II" (Pennington, 2008b). It is doubtful if the AMA, which is a great intellectual exercise, is feasible in terms of costs and benefits.

CHAPTER 5

Theoretical and Empirical Studies of Operational Risk

5.1 INTRODUCTION

The academic and professional literature on operational risk has been mushrooming as a result of growing interest in what was once an unrecognised (at least explicitly) kind of risk and because of the advent of Basel II and its compliance requirements. In this chapter, a brief and selected survey of a subset of the literature is presented, the subset that deals with the main theme of this book: modelling and quantifying operational risk. This is probably the area of research (in finance and related fields) that gets most contributions from professionals to academic journals, because the topic is of practical significance. Indicative of the tendency of practitioners to contribute significantly to this research is that the editor of the *Journal of Operational Risk* and seven out of thirteen associate editors are practitioners.

The studies examined in this chapter can be classified under three headings: methodological studies; (ii) empirical studies; and (iii) studies of the effects of operational losses. There is significant overlap between these studies. For example, the theoretical methods and models used for quantifying operational risk are applied to actual data, which makes these studies both methodological and empirical. This is why it may be felt that a particular study appears in the wrong section of this chapter or that another study may appear in two different sections. Studies of the effect of operational losses are also empirical, but they invariably employ the technique of event studies, which puts them in a special category. The empirical studies discussed in this chapter deal not only with the quantification of operational risk per se, but also with related issues such as the relation between operational risk and firm size. The three kinds of operational risk studies (which may have significant overlap) will be discussed in turn in the following three sections.

5.2 METHODOLOGICAL STUDIES

Methodological studies deal with the development of methods and models to quantify operational risk and the associated regulatory and economic capital, which is not an enviable task. Several (mathematically and statistically) innovative methods have been proposed for modelling operational risk and measuring capital charges. Alexander (2003a), Cruz (2003a), and Giudici and Bilotta (2004) suggest the use of Bayesian networks, which are graphical models. Bee (2005) and Embrechts et al (2003) suggest the use of copula-based multivariate models for this purpose. According to Wei (2007), these models have several drawbacks because Bayesian networks introduce significant subjectivity, whereas the copula-based method requires large amounts of data. This is why he advocates the actuarial loss approach, which he considers to be the "natural choice" to quantify operational risk by separately estimating the frequency and severity distributions.

Concepts and Tools

In methodological studies, we invariably come across concepts and tools, including (among others) extreme value theory (EVT), peaks over threshold (POT), correlation (dependence) and copulas, which are used to describe dependence. While we have come across at least some of these concepts before, a brief revisit would be useful.

During the development of Basel II, much work was done on identifying statistical methods for estimating the 99.9th percentile of the loss distribution. EVT is described by Dutta and Perry (2007) as a "branch of statistics concerned with the study of extreme phenomena or rare events that lie in the tail of the probability distribution." Applying EVT requires the division of a loss distribution into two sectors: the body and the tail, such that the losses below a certain threshold are taken to represent the body whereas those above the threshold represent the tail. A consensus has emerged that the EVT can be used to satisfy the quantitative standards set by the Basel Committee.

EVT is appealing because it can be used, given certain assumptions about the underlying data, to derive a closed-form equation for the 99.9th percentile. But while EVT may be used successfully across the industry, its application to a single institution can prove to be problematical because of the lack of data, which is inevitable in the case of operational risk. Even proponents of EVT, such as Embrechts et al (1997), point out that EVT is designed to estimate external events under very precise conditions and that if these conditions are not satisfied, the theory can lead to incorrect estimates of the likelihood of extreme events. The reason why EVT is popular in the insurance sector (justifiably so) is that while extreme events are very rare, a large number of insurance losses resulting from extreme events can be used to construct a loss distribution. It is not entirely clear what may justify the use of EVT to quantify operational risk. As we have seen, EVT does not constitute a magical solution to the problems encountered in modelling operational risk.

The POT method is typically used in conjunction with EVT. It is designed to estimate losses over and above a high threshold. The Pickands-Balkema-De Haan theorem (Embrechts et al, 1997) stipulates that if the threshold is sufficiently high, then for a certain class of distributions, excesses over a threshold follow a GPD distribution. Embrechts et al (1997) present a more in-depth discussion of the POT method used to model losses over a high threshold. Wei (2007) is not sure that the POT method works better than the conventional actuarial models. This is a typical fancy procedure with a high degree of mathematical elegance that produces nothing much in terms of practical significance.

Modelling dependence is described as being crucial for the measurement of operational risk, not only because it makes a lot of intuitive sense but also because it is perceived to be one way of reducing the firm-wide capital charge (compared to that resulting from summing up the capital charges assigned to each business line). Some aspects of dependence may be caused by the simultaneous impact of macroeconomic conditions on many risk types. Other kinds of dependence are not specifically related to macroeconomic causes. Statistical dependence is typically (but not always correctly) represented by a single number, the correlation coefficient, which is often used as a synonym for dependence. However, dependence can be too complex to be described by a single number. This is far more than a technical distinction, as it can affect the quantification of operational risk significantly (perhaps conveniently). Dependence is most obvious in extreme events (called tail dependence). For example, a large earthquake causes simultaneous large losses in business lines that do not exhibit any dependence under normal conditions.

Copulas provide a mathematical tool for expressing different forms of dependence. There are different types of copulas, and the choice of the copula is critical for determining how well the model describes the likely impact of an extreme event. Each business line is typically modelled with its own parameters, but eventually the distribution of the sum of the lines (and/or event types) is needed to calculate the firm-wide capital charge. To get the distribution of the sum, dependence among the business lines must be taken into account. The multivariate distribution of individual lines is used to obtain the distribution of the sum. Copulas provide a convenient way to combine individual distributions into a single multivariate distribution, a rather ingenious device.

By selecting from among the many available copulas, a good deal of control can be exercised over where correlation takes place (e.g., in the tail). Examples of bivariate copulas are the Frank copula, Gumbel copula, normal copula and the heavy right-tail copula. But only the t-copula and the normal copula are used for multivariate distributions, both of which take the correlation matrix as an input. Copulas are generally fit by maximum likelihood, but in complicated cases the sum of squared errors between empirical and fitted copulas can be useful. Kerps (1998) has pioneered a methodology to combine independent and correlated scenarios to model how much of the correlation occurs in the right tail. The "beauty" of these copulas (without denying the extraordinary brain power of those who invented them) is that they provide a means to manipulate internal models in such a way as to produce a lower capital charge than that obtained under the BIA and STA (recall the discussion in Chapter 4). Reshetar (2008) suggested mixed models as an alternative to the copulas for the purpose of modelling dependence. These are often used for modelling credit risk as described by Duffie and Singelton (1999), Frey and McNeil (2003) and Lando (1998).

The Loss Distribution Approach and Related Issues

The LDA consists of several steps, starting with the calibration of frequency and severity of loss distributions, which may involve the use of EVT and POT. Monte Carlo simulations follow, using the calibrated distributions as we are going to see in Chapter 6. The capital charge is then calculated as operational VAR (or that minus the expected loss). This kind of work may also involve the modelling of dependence (to obtain the firm-wide capital charge) and accounting for insurance, controls and risk mitigation measures. Several studies addressing these issues of modelling have been carried out, but as the standard LDA originates from the actuarial techniques used in the insurance industry, a lot of information on the subject can be found in the works of Klugman et al (1998), Panjer (1981), Panjer and Willmot (1986), Robertson (1992), Tripp et al (2004), Venter (1983) and Willmot and Lin (2000).

Aue and Kalkbrener (2007) present a detailed description of the LDA model developed at Deutsche Bank, which is a rather "rare event," since banks do not like to publish their models or reveal their operational losses. They start by pointing out (correctly) that the application of the LDA to the quantification of operational risk is a difficult task, which they attribute not only to the "ambitious soundness standards for risk capital" but also to problems related to operational risk data and the definition of operational risk. Specifically, they mention the problems of (i) shortage of relevant operational risk data; (ii) the context dependence nature of operational risk data; and (iii) the current lack of a strongly risk-sensitive exposure measure in operational risk modelling. They consider a variety of data sets, including internal loss data, consortium data, data from commercial loss databases, and scenario-based data. Internal loss data is then used to model frequency and severity distributions and to analyse the dependence structure of the model. They also show how external loss data and data derived from scenario analysis are incorporated. They point out that for modelling severity tails, empirical distributions are not sufficient, and this is why they combine empirical distributions with parametric distributions for the purpose of quantifying the loss potential beyond the highest experienced losses. For the purpose of specifying the parametric distribution they use what they call the algorithmic version of EVT, which is the POT method.

Peters et al (2007) consider two alternative approaches to standard Monte Carlo simulation, suggesting two procedures for the simulation of the annual loss distribution. The two Monte Carlo simulation procedures make use of the Panjer recursion (Panjer, 2006), importance sampling (Doucet and Tadic, 2007) and transdimensional Markov Chain Monte Carlo (Green, 2003). They focus on a setting in which the severity and frequency distributions take a parametric form that admits explicit density representation. They also use the Volterra integral equation of the second kind to reformulate the problem of evaluating the density of a random sum as the calculation of an expectation. It is demonstrated how the use of sampling and transdimensional Markov Chain Monte Carlo algorithms can be used to evaluate this expectation with an application to the calculation of value at risk (VAR) and expected shortfall.

Ergashev (2008) points out that the estimation of capital charges is affected not only by the choice of the frequency and severity distributions but also by the estimation method. He presents an evaluation of the maximum likelihood method against three alternatives, which are based on minimising different types of statistics that measure the distance between empirical and fitting loss distributions. The alternative methods are as follows: (i) the Cramer-von-Mises statistic; (ii) the Anderson–Darling (A–D) statistics; and (iii) the quantile distance method, which is based on the measurement of the distance between the quantiles of empirical and fitting distributions. He also suggests the use of an advanced optimisation technique called simulated annealing (the word "annealing" comes from metallurgy, a technique involving heating and controlled cooling of a material to increase the size of its crystals and reduce their defects). Ergashev points out that this technique is superior to the standard classical techniques "because it is capable of finding the global optimum of an objective function... in situations when there exist several local optima." The results of this study reveal that the quantile distance method is superior to the other estimation methods when loss data sets are relatively small and/or the fitting model is possibly misspecified. The superiority of this method to the Maximum Liklihood Estimator (MLE) method is that the focus in the latter is on matching accurately the bodies of the empirical and fitting distributions (where the likelihood mass is concentrated), which means that it fails to fit the right tail of the loss distribution accurately. He concludes that the quantile distance method produces more accurate estimates of capital charges.

Bazzarello et al (2006) and Frachot et al (2004b) deal with the modelling of insurance and the correlation structure, respectively. Bazzarello et al suggest a model that takes insurance into account by examining the residual risk inherent in insurance contracts such as payment uncertainty and the default risk of the counterparty (insurance company). They demonstrate that insurance contracts can be included in the operational loss distribution model, suggesting that insurance coverage can be modelled in an LDA framework. Frachot et al (2004b) argue that the perfect correlation assumption across risk types or business lines leads to higher capital charge than under the STA, which would be a disincentive for the use of the AMA. They suggest that there are strong arguments for low levels of correlation between aggregate losses and that capital charge summation is "exaggeratedly conservative," subsequently showing how to incorporate correlation in the standard LDA model. They also provide empirical simulations, partly based on Credit Lyonnaise historical data, and point out that correlation between aggregate losses may result from correlation between frequencies, severities or both. Their results indicate that the correlation between two aggregate losses is typically below 0.05, concluding that this opens a wide scope for large diversification effects, much larger than those the Basel Committee seems to have in mind. They also suggest a formula for calculating the capital charge that takes correlation into account.

Also dealing with correlation are Kuhn and Neu (2005) who propose a VAR-based model to compute the equity capital necessary to cover potential losses due to operational risk. They explore the analogy to a lattice gas model from physics to model correlations between sequential failures by, as functionally defined, heterogeneous couplings between mutually supportive processes. It is demonstrated that in contrast to the traditional risk models for market and credit risk, where correlations are described by the covariance of a Gaussian process, the dynamics of the model shows collective phenomena such as bursts and avalanches of the process failures.

Reshetar (2008) address the issue of how to account for the dependence of loss events in the calculation of operational VAR, assuming that dependence of losses can be attributed to dependence of frequencies and severities. The results produced by this study show that the operational VARs obtained by applying the LDA are different from (higher than) those obtained by applying the alternative methodology he suggests. The results also show that the closer loss dependence between risk classes approaches one, the smaller the difference between the operational VARs calculated under the two approaches. It is also shown that using the expected shortfall instead of VAR produces higher capital charges than VAR. It is argued that the use of expected shortfall is better than VAR in reflecting exposure to extreme losses, which makes it more reliable.

Temnov and Warnung (2008) distinguish among three methods that can be used to aggregate operational risk: (i) Monte Carlo simulations; (ii) the FFT approach, which is based on the Fourier transformation; and (iii) the CreditRisk+ methodology, which is a recursion approach. They argue that the estimates of VAR obtained from Monte Carlo simulations tend to have high variances, whereas the other two methods produce more reliable results. The FFT approach is based on a consideration of the characteristic function of the aggregate loss, which can be used to determine its probability distribution. Once this has been obtained, it can be inverted numerically, using the discrete Fourier transformation. The CreditRisk+ methodology was developed by Credit Suisse First Boston (1997) for large credit portfolios (a detailed description of various extensions can be found in Gundlach and Lehrbass, 2004). In this approach, calculation of the loss distribution is performed by the expansion of the probability generation function of the loss.

Chapelle et al (2004) propose a methodology for analysing the implications of the AMA for the assessment of operational risk. Their methodology relies on an integrated procedure for the construction of the aggregate loss distribution using internal and external data. For a major European bank, they found that when the dependence structure between losses and the nonlinear adjustment of external data are explicitly taken into account, the capital charge turns out to be substantially lower than what is produced under the BIA and STA. They also estimate the effects of operational risk management actions on bank profitability by using a measure of RAROC that is adapted to operational risk. The results suggest that substantial savings can be achieved through active management techniques, but they admit that the estimated effect of a reduction of the number, frequency or severity of operational losses depends crucially on the calibration of the aggregate loss distribution (hence, subjectivity and model manipulation to produce low capital charges).

Further applications of EVT and POT to the quantification of operational risk are demonstrated by de Fontnouvelle et al (2005a) and Moscadelli (2005). de Fontonouvelle et al (2005a) used two external databases and utilised POT to estimate the severity distribution of operational losses, with the ultimate objective of calculating capital charges. They found consistent results based on the two databases and that the capital charge against operational risk often exceeds that for market risk. de Fontnouvelle et al (2004) applied both actuarial models and POT to the BCBS data for six large, internationally active banks and found that both lognormal and generalised Pareto distributions from POT seemed to provide a reasonable fit. Moscadelli (2005) used the BCBS data and pooled the individual banks' losses according to the business line classification. He obtained results indicating poor performance of conventional severity models in describing the overall data characteristics. He demonstrated that the EVT explains the behaviour of losses in the tail area rather adequately. These studies in general concluded that banks have significant exposure to operational risk. One major difference between these two studies is that while Moscadelli (2005) aggregated data across all banks, de Fontnouvelle et al (2004) used data at the individual bank level. Furthermore, de Fontnouvelle et al used the technique of Huisman et al (2001) to correct for potential bias in the tail parameter estimate. They also explored several models of the loss frequency distribution, which makes it possible to obtain indicative estimates of economic capital for operational risk.

The use of the 99.9th percentile as required by the AMA is a rather controversial issue as we saw in the previous chapter. This is an issue that Jobst (2007a) addresses by using EVT, together with the g-and-h distribution within a full data approach to derive point estimates of unexpected operational losses at the 99.9th percentile. He suggests that a marginally lower percentile of 99.7% would "entail an outsized reduction of the optimal loss threshold and unexpected loss at disproportionately smaller estimation uncertainty." The results provide estimates of the impact of unexpected operational losses on the financial performance of selected US commercial banks. It is demonstrated that the impact of operational risk on fundamental performance seems minimal at the 99.9th percentile.

Studies of Tail Data

One of the aspects of the data problem encountered in studies of operational risk is the lack of data in the tail of the loss distribution (a typical histogram of operational loss data is shown in Figure 5.1). The problem is that tail events are the ones that could wipe out a firm, and so they should be considered seriously. This is why a large number of methodological studies have been conducted to sort out this problem. Wei (2007) argues that it is difficult but very important to obtain an accurate estimation for the right tail of the distribution for two reasons: (i) the tail of the distribution contributes most to the capital charge against operational loss; and (ii) for the purpose of pricing operational risk insurance, banks are more likely to transfer some layers of the tail risk to the insurance company. The concepts of EVT and POT crop up in these studies.

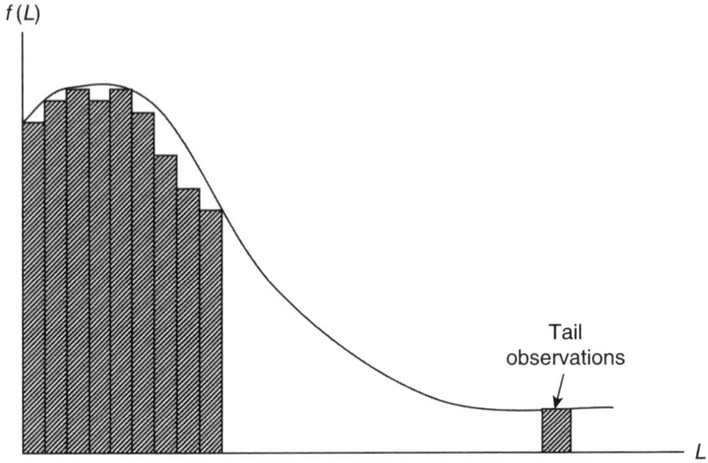

Figure 5.1 A Typical Histogram of Operational Loss Data

Wei (2007) estimates the aggregate tail operational risk by deriving the frequency and severity distributions separately. A Bayesian approach is used to estimate the frequency distribution and a covariate is introduced to estimate the severity distribution. This framework allows the use of both external data and firm-specific information to quantify operational risk so that firm-specific calculations can be performed. The contributions of Wei's paper are as follows: (i) it provides a framework that can be used to quantify firm-specific exposure of operational risk; and (ii) it compares the POT method with the traditional actuarial models.

Bayesian-based models (what they call a "new class of models adopting a Bayesian approach to inference") are suggested by Carvalho et al (2008), who compare the results obtained by using these models with the results of traditional VAR-based models. They argue that the traditional VAR models suffer from shortcomings, including the following: (i) the assumption that severity and frequency are independent and identically distributed through time, which is not verified frequently (although it makes a lot of sense theoretically); and (ii) the possibility of underestimating the VAR because of uncertainty about the parameters associated with the probability distribution function. They argue that "an understated VAR, or capital charge, can be dangerous for an institution's management regarding its decision-making process and appropriate risk management." By contrast, they argue, the suggested Bayesian models permit the fitting of the frequency and severity distributions simultaneously and that under this approach it is straightforward to carry out sampling from the posterior. However, they do not reach a definitive conclusion about the comparison between the traditional and Bayesian approaches. This paper, however, shows once more that the resulting capital charge is highly sensitive to the model used to estimate it, which means that capital charge reduction under the AMA can be achieved by trying out various models.

Also addressing the issue of parameter uncertainty and how to deal with it by using a Bayesian framework is Shevchenko (2008) who argues that "Bayesian inference is a statistical technique well suited to model parameter uncertainty." The method he suggests also allows for expert opinion or external data to be incorporated in the analysis by specifying prior distributions for model parameters. He finds that the capital charge estimated under this framework is larger than the point estimator of the 0.999 quantile of the annual loss distribution calculated using maximum likelihood, which means that extra capital is required to cover for parameter uncertainty. This is yet again the same story: model selection can be used to reduce the capital charge. What is not clear here is that both Shevchenko and Carvalho et al seem to think that holding a low capital charge is a bad thing. So much, then, for the alleged advantage of the AMA that it produces low capital charges.

Neslehova et al (2006) present some issues underlying the modelling of operational risk by using the LDA in the presence of heavy-tailed loss data, warning against "too naïve optimism concerning the calculation of an operational risk, AMA based capital charge." The paper aims at clarifying some of the issues underlying what they call "one huge loss causes havoc paradigm." While they point out that many problems are associated with the EVT, they argue that it offers a "perfect tool for pointing at data which are about to enter this paradigm." They present some models that make it possible to describe data contamination as a core issue that is in need of further research. They also suggest other related research areas, including risk measures and risk measurement procedures to be used in the presence of very heavy-tailed data.

Dutta and Perry (2007) model the severity distribution by using three techniques: parametric distribution fitting, EVT and nonparametric empirical sampling (also called historical simulation). For parametric distribution fitting they assume that the data follow a specific parametric model, choosing the parameters that allow the model to fit the underlying distribution of the data in an optimal way. For this purpose they consider the following distributions: exponential, gamma, generalised Pareto, loglogistic, truncated lognormal and Weibull. They also used the generalised beta distribution of the second kind (GB2) and the g-and-h distribution, which have the property that many different distributions can be generated from them for specific values of their parameters. The results revealed that the g-and-h distribution produces a meaningful operational risk measure in that it fits the data, providing "consistently reasonable" estimates of capital charges. While it is typically the case that it is not possible to find a single distribution that fits both the body and the tail of the data, they found that the g-and-h distribution could do the job, thus avoiding the need for data truncation. They also found that applying different models to the same firm yielded "vastly different capital estimates." This conclusion is supportive of one of the criticisms raised against the AMA in Chapter 4 that subjectivity and model manipulation lead to lower capital charges. This assertion has been repeated frequently for its importance.

Chernobai and Rachev (2006) deal with the issue of outliers in operational loss data, which create a paradox because outliers represent the low-frequency, high-severity events that can inflict destruction on the firm; hence they cannot be ignored. The problem is that classical statistical methods cannot deal adequately with the outliers found in operational risk data. For example, classical estimators that assign equal importance to all available observations are highly sensitive to outliers and (in the presence of just few extreme losses) can produce arbitrarily large estimates of the mean, variance and other vital statistics of operational losses. A high mean can be caused by one large loss. They suggest the use of robust methods that take into account the underlying structure of the data and separate the majority of data points from outliers, thus avoiding upward bias.

Gustafsson et al (2006) consider non-parametric smoothing techniques along with a parametric base with a particular view to comparison with EVT. While the parametric approach to operational risk involves the use of probability distributions, the non-parametric approach is to draw information directly from observed data. Given the lack of data, they present an approach whereby a parametric structure is adopted and modified using observed data. Following the application of non-parametric kernel smoothing, they apply continuous credibility theory to density estimation, facilitating the appropriate weighting of pooled losses as compared to data from individual business lines. They present a step-by-step guide to the smoothed estimator and the final credibility estimator as follows: (i) knowing the data; (ii) estimating the start distribution; (iii) transformation of data; (iv) correcting with non-parametric smoothing technique; and (v) obtaining a credibility estimator.

In an application to an unidentified Australian bank, Evans et al (2007) report the results of estimating operational risk and derive a model to represent the distribution of losses. They show that the use of conventional methods to model severity is inadequate because the data exhibits kurtosis and right skewness. They argue that conventional models place emphasis on fitting the central body of the data, thus neglecting the extreme percentiles. And while they suggest the use of EVT for this purpose, they point out that the lack of data inhibits capturing the generalised Pareto nature of excess distributions without sacrificing the majority of the data set. They conclude that it may take years before banks can convincingly justify the use of any sophisticated dependence structure between various risk cells, thus reaping the benefits of diversification. It is not clear, however, why it would take years to do that, given that the name of the game (under the AMA) is to use "sophisticated" models to reduce the capital charge. One tends to think that this is already happening with the blessing of the regulators.

Other Data Problems: Thresholds and Mixing

Some methodological studies deal with other data problems, specifically the problem of data collection threshold and the procedures used to mix internal data with external data. Mignola and Ugoccioni (2007) investigate the effect of lower data collection threshold on risk measures (VAR, expected loss and unexpected loss) in what they call a "realistic laboratory setup." Their results show that the risk measures are largely insensitive to the presence of a collection threshold, which is true up to fairly high thresholds, at least to the fiftieth percentile of the severity distribution. Moreover, the reconstruction of the severity and frequency distributions below the threshold introduces the assumption that the same dynamics drive both small and intermediate/large losses. They, therefore, advocate an approach consisting of describing correctly only the data above the threshold. Luo et al (2008) examine the impact of ignoring data truncation on the estimation of operational risk under the "shifted" and "naïve" models, which represent two cases of ignoring data truncation, when loss frequency and severity are modelled with the Poisson and lognormal distributions, respectively. Their results show that the shifted model underestimates frequency and overestimates severity, whereas the naïve model underestimates frequency and the high percentile of severity.

Lambrigger et al (2007) present an illustration of the LDA and the quantification of operational risk by using Bayesian inference methods to combine internal data, external data and expert opinion. The method allows for structural modelling of different sources of information. It is based on specifying prior distributions for the parameters of frequency and severity using industry data. The prior distributions are weighted by the actual observations and expert opinion from the bank to estimate the posterior distributions of the model parameters. They argue that estimation of low-frequency risks using their method has several appealing features such as stable estimators, simple calculations and the ability to take expert opinion and industry data into account. It also allows for the calculation of VAR with parameter uncertainty taken into account. Shevchenko and Wuthrich (2006) describe the use of the Bayesian inference approach (in the context of operational risk) for the estimation of frequency/severity distributions in a risk cell where expert opinion or external data is used to estimate prior distributions. Paolo Giudici of the University of Pavia is cited by Wood (2008) as advocating the use of Bayesian modelling to solve the problem that the AMA models fail to take into account qualitative information. Giudici proposes a model that is not designed to produce a capital number but to produce an ordinal ranking of risks (a risk "hit list") that can be used to focus management attention on areas of concern.

Instead of using the concepts of external data and internal data, Alexander (2003b) distinguishes between hard data (recent and relevant internal data) and subjective soft data (data from an external consortium or from risk scores based on the opinions of industry experts or the "owner" of the risk). Soft data can also be past internal data collected following a merger, acquisition or the sale of assets. Alexander argues that when a bank's operations undergo a significant change in size, it may not be sufficient simply to scale the capital charge by the size of its current operations because the internal systems processes and people are likely to have changed considerably.

Bayesian estimation of the mean and standard deviation of a loss severity distribution works as follows. Suppose that we have n observations of hard data, $L_1^h, L_2^h, \ldots, L_n^h$, and m observations on soft data, $L_1^s, L_2^s, \ldots, L_m^s$. Alexander (2003b) shows that the Bayesian estimates of the mean and variance of total loss severity, L, are calculated as

$$\bar{L} = \frac{w^h \bar{L}^h + w^s \bar{L}^s}{w^h + w^s} \tag{5.1}$$

where w^h and w^s are the weights assigned to hard data and soft data, respectively. If the weights are taken to be the reciprocals of the variances, then

$$\bar{L} = \frac{[1/\sigma^2(L^h)]\bar{L}^h + [1/\sigma^2(L^s)]\bar{L}^s}{[1/\sigma^2(L^h)] + [1/\sigma^2(L^s)]} \tag{5.2}$$

The combined variance is calculated as

$$\sigma^2(L) = \frac{1}{1/\sigma^2(L^h) + 1/\sigma^2(L^s)} \tag{5.3}$$

The maximum likelihood estimates of the mean and variance that are based on the combined sample are

$$\bar{L} = \frac{1}{n+m}\left[\sum_{j=1}^{n} L_j^h + \sum_{j=1}^{m} L_j^s\right] \tag{5.4}$$

$$\sigma^2(L) = \frac{1}{n+m-1}\left[\sum_{j=1}^{n}(L_j^h - \bar{L})^2 + \sum_{j=1}^{m}(L_j^s - \bar{L})^2\right] \tag{5.5}$$

One should expect the soft data to be more volatile, and perhaps to have a higher mean value, than the hard data. If this is the case, then the Bayesian mean and variance should be lower than the maximum likelihood estimates.

Figini et al (2008) also address the optimal way to mix internal and external data with respect to frequency and severity, proposing a rigorous way to tackle this issue through a statistically optimised methodology, which they develop to ensure that merging internal data with external data leads to unbiased estimates of the loss distribution, thus pooling data in an optimal way. Baud et al (2002) point out that loss data (particularly consortium and public data) may be severely biased towards high losses, resulting in overestimation of the capital charge. They suggest the use of internal data for calibrating the main body of the severity distribution and external data for the tail of the distribution. They argue that the main source of heterogeneity is different thresholds, which underlie data generating processes. As a consequence, they point out, thresholds should be taken into account explicitly in the calibration process in the form of additional parameters that have to be estimated along with other parameters of the loss distribution. Provided the thresholds are managed carefully, they further argue that internal and external data are made comparable and that most of the heterogeneity is then eliminated. The methodology they suggest relies on maximum likelihood principles, which can be shown to be statistically sound and produce unbiased capital charges.

Bayesian Networks

The use of Bayesian networks has been suggested as a viable alternative to the use of actuarial models of operational risk. Adusei-Poku et al (2007) define a Bayesian network (in a particular application) as a probabilistic graphical model that can be used to represent the components of the settlement process, the associated risks, their causal factors and their probabilistic dependencies. Neil et al (2005) show how Bayesian networks are used to model statistical loss distributions in financial operational loss scenarios. The focus is on modelling the long tail events using mixtures of appropriate loss frequency and severity distributions, where these mixtures are conditioned on causal variables that represent the capability or effectiveness of the underlying controls process.

The usefulness of Bayesian networks is advocated by Adusei-Poku et al (2007), who argue that a Bayesian network makes it possible to circumvent the difficulty of managing operational risk at the business level, which is hampered by the unavailability of historical data. They argue that a Bayesian network can be used to model the causal relation between risk factors, key risk indicators (KRIs) and a desired operational risk attribute for a specific process. They outline the steps involved in the construction of a model to manage operational risk within the foreign exchange settlement process of a bank. Available historical data are then used to check the model, which reveals that the loss distribution generated by the model has a slightly larger mean and fatter tail than they observed. It is suggested that the model can be used to estimate VAR for the process and also to perform scenario and sensitivity analysis.

Likewise, Cowell et al (2007) construct a Bayesian network that models various factors and their combination into an overall loss distribution. By using this model, they show that the methodology can be applied to the following: (i) form posterior marginal distributions of variables based on evidence; (ii) simulate scenarios; (iii) update the parameters of the model using data; and (iv) quantify how well the model predictions compare with actual data. They also suggest a specific example of Bayesian networks application to operational risk in an insurance setting.

Sahay et al (2007) suggest an alternative to the statistical modelling of rare events via EVT and Bayesian networks. They identify problems with these two approaches: the data problem is one, while the second is that the statistical approach does not provide any business insight as to how different factors relating to people, systems and processes can be modified to control and manage operational risk. While they argue that causal models, such as Bayesian networks, may be useful for assessing and predicting the effect of various causal factors on operational risk, the differencing problem in Bayesian networks is computationally hard. A more fundamental limitation is that there is no systematic method to construct these networks based on the business processes. An alternative method is proposed, as they construct a probabilistic network for a financial institution based on the physical and logical infrastructure of the business process. The advantage of this approach is that it allows financial institutions to assess and quantify operational risk, based on the capability of mapping and modelling the business process, which is usually an existing part of their management system. The model underlying the suggested approach is based on the premise that a business process can be defined using combinations of constructs such as processes, sub-processes and tasks (activities).

5.3 EMPIRICAL STUDIES

The empirical studies described in this section deal with various issues. To start with, an alternative to the estimation of operational risk as a percentile of the total loss distribution is to measure it as the residual of an econometric model that accounts explicitly for market risk and credit risk. This is what Allen and Bali (2004) do. Another alternative is to use the factor approach, which is what Chernobai et al (2007) wanted to do to identify the determinants of operational losses. Other empirical issues include the choice of the scaling variable applied to external data to supplement internal data. One particular question arises on whether or not "size does matter" in the sense that large firms incur large losses, and vice versa. This question leads to a consideration of the appropriateness of the BIA and STA, which are based on a scale factor, gross income. When this issue is taken further, it leads to a consideration of measures of operational risk based on accounting ratios. Then, of course, there is the critical question of whether or not the AMA leads to lower capital charges than the BIA and STA. Studies dealing with these issues are discussed in turn in this section.

To deal with the data problem, Allen and Bali (2004) estimate an operational risk measure for individual financial institutions using a monthly time series of stock returns over the period 1973–2003. The model is represented by an ordinary least squares (OLS) regression of the monthly rate of return on a large number of explanatory variables, which include the first difference of twenty-two variables representing credit risk, interest rate risk, exchange rate risk and market risk. The three Fama–French (1993) factors are also used as explanatory variables: overall excess return on the market, a measure of the performance of small stocks relative to large stocks and a measure of the monthly stock returns on a portfolio of value stocks relative to growth stocks. A momentum factor is used, measured as the average return on the two highest prior return portfolios minus the average return on the two lowest prior portfolios. Finally, three alternative industry factors are employed, measured as the average monthly return for each industry sector: depository institutions, insurance companies and securities firms. The results obtained by Allen and Bali led them to the following conclusions:

- The capital charge for operational risk often exceeds the charge for market risk. They produce figures of the same order of magnitude as those reported by Hirtle (2003) for market risk capital requirement of top US banks.

- Reporting bias in external data is significant. Accounting for bias reduces significantly the estimated operational risk capital charge.

- The distribution of observed losses varies significantly by business line. It is not clear, however, whether this is driven by cross-business line variation in operational risk or by variation in the sample selection process.

- Supplementing internal data with external data on extremely large events could improve models of operational risk significantly.

Chernobai et al (2007) examine the microeconomic and macroeconomic determinants of potential losses in financial institutions. On the basis of twenty-four years of US public operational loss data covering the period 1980–2003, they demonstrate that the firm-specific characteristics (such as size, leverage, volatility, profitability and the number of employees) turned out to be highly significant in their models. They also found that the overall macroeconomic environment is less important, although operational losses tend to be more frequent and more severe during economic downturns. The evidence they obtained indicates that contrary to the traditional view that operational risk is unsystematic, operational loss events cluster at the industry level in excess of what is predicted by the stochastic frequency estimates. This investigation is based on the assumption that the arrival of operational loss events is a point process whose intensity is driven by firm-specific and macroeconomic covariates.

The use of external data to supplement internal data is advocated by Cope and Wills (2008) who report the results of a study conducted in May 2007 by the Operational Riskdata eXchange Association (ORX) to examine the usefulness of external data for the purpose of evaluating the operational risk of a particular firm. In particular, the objective of the study is to address the key question of whether or not internal and external loss data can be realistically integrated for the purpose of modelling operational risk. The study assessed the similarities that could be observed among the loss categories, focusing on event type, business line and business line/event type combinations. The methods of analysis included the traditional statistical tests of distributional equality as well as newer techniques including regional frequency analysis. The study also assessed the similarity of loss distributions according to improvement in predictive accuracy that would result by using pooled data. For that purpose, the concept of error improvement ratio was used to predict the error associated with certain quantiles of the loss distribution that would result if a randomly selected bank were to pool its internal loss data with scaled consortium data. The study found that for many loss categories a 20–30% reduction in predictive error was possible by combining internal and external data.

The use of external data requires a procedure for scaling. Na et al (2005) describe a way to circumvent the problem of data availability by proposing a scaling mechanism that enables a firm to put together data originating from several business units, each having its specific characteristics like size and exposure to operational risk. The same scaling mechanism can be used to enable a firm to include the external data originating from other firms.

Another study of the scale factor is that of Shih et al (2000) who examined the relation between losses and firm size, where size is proxied by revenue, assets and the number of employees. Specifically, they used a logarithmic specification of the form

$$\log(L) = a + b\log(S) + \varepsilon \tag{5.6}$$

where L is the loss incurred by a particular firm and S is its size. By estimating this model using OpVaR data of 4700 loss events, they reached a number of conclusions, including the following:

- The magnitude of loss is related to the size of the firm but the relation is nonlinear (hence, the logarithmic equation).
- Size accounts for a very small portion of the variability in loss severity.
- Revenue is more correlated with loss size than either assets or the number of employees.

They conclude that the weak relation between size and loss magnitude can be attributed to factors such as inherent differences in risk (based on the type of business), management competence and the quality of the internal control environment. This sentiment is shared by Aue and Kalkbrener (2007) who refer to evidence based on a regression analysis of Opvantage data performed at Deutsche Bank, which produced "no significant relationship between the size of a bank and the severity of its losses." However, Wei (2007) argues that there is indeed some connection between size and the severity of losses, pointing out that "a bank with $1 trillion assets is probably more likely to have more and larger losses than a bank with $100 million assets." He produces cross-sectional regression results showing a positive and statistically significant relation between the logarithm of losses and the logarithm of assets.

Bonson et al (2007) conducted an empirical study to judge the desirability of measuring operational risk by using the income-based BIA and STA versus what they call the "information-based method," which is effectively a version of the AMA. They tested the following hypotheses:

- There is a positive linear relation between operational losses and gross income in the published accounts of the firm.
- A ratio of losses to gross income in the range 12–18% is adequate.
- The ratio is constant over time.

- The ratio is independent of other characterising variables, such as size and juridical nature (that is, these characteristics do not affect the indicator selected for measuring operational risk).

To test these hypotheses, they employ the following two models:

$$L = a + bY + \varepsilon \tag{5.7}$$

$$L/Y = \alpha_0 + \alpha_1 S + \sum_{j=1}^{3} \phi_i D_i + \varepsilon \tag{5.8}$$

where L is the operational loss, Y is gross income, S is size and D_i is a dummy variable for the underlying firm (D_1=1 when the firm is a bank and zero otherwise, D_2=1 when the firm is a savings bank and zero otherwise, and D_3=1 when the firm is a foreign institution and zero otherwise). By estimating the models using pooled data, they obtained results showing that the ratio between operational losses and gross income is not stable with respect to entity and time and that it is not in the range 12–18%. Although some evidence is presented for the presence of a significantly positive relation between operational losses and gross income, they find the coefficient to be lower than 15% as specified by the BCBS.

On the basis of their results, Bonson et al conclude that the income statement-based methods "represent a blind instrument of protection and may handicap the competitive capacity of entities by generating excessively high capital requirements in the majority of them." They also suggest that the AMA is the preferred approach "because it is based on principles of management accounting and internal control, rather than being based on variables published in the accounts of these entities." However, they cast doubt on the variability of purely statistical methods, which in effect means that they prefer the SCA to the LDA. They also admit that the feasibility of implementing this approach "remains as a challenge to those entities that do not find in the income statement-based methods an adequate response to the pressing need for active management of operational risk."

The view put forward by Bonson et al is not shared by Tripe (2000) who sees some benefit in using ratios derived from financial statements to determine capital requirements for a number of New Zealand banks based on the volatility of non-interest expenses. After outlining the difficulties encountered in implementing the statistical approach, he considers two ratios: the ratio of operating expenses to total assets and the ratio of operating expenses to income. The figures suggest that bank capital levels should embody a significant element of operational risk. This issue can be taken further by attempting to find out if the econometric and actuarial measures of operational risk are correlated with the accounting measures.

Ford and Sundmacher (2007) advocate the use of the cost to income ratio as a leading indicator of operational risk. The underlying argument is that while a reduction of this ratio, which is essentially a measure of efficiency, is favourable because it implies lower cost per dollar of income, there is some critical threshold at which the relation between cost and income cannot be sustained without an escalation in exposure to operational risk. The volatility of this ratio is also a leading indicator because it results from factors associated with operational risk such as asset write-downs, unstable or unpredictable cost structures and volatile income sources. They also suggest non-financial indicators of operational risk, including the ratio of back office to front office staff, the number of daily trades per individual trader, expenditure on training per staff member and the proportion of incentive-based remuneration. They suggest that incentive-based remuneration was a common cause of the operational losses endured by Barings Bank, the Allied Irish Bank, and the National Bank of Australia. They also introduce some psychological explanations for the occurrence of operational losses, including regret theory (Tvede, 1999), group think (Pennington, 2002), and consensus-provision moral hazard (Boot et al, 1998).

Finally, we come to the question of whether or not the AMA produces lower capital charges than the BIA and STA. Kerr (2007) investigates this issue for the four largest Australian banks (Commonwealth, National Australia Bank (NAB), Australia New Zealand Bank (ANZ) and Westpac), using the LDA version of the AMA. His results show that the AMA produces a lower capital charge than that produced under the alternative approaches offered by the Basel II Accord and the Australian Prudential Regulatory Authority (APRA) (which uses some sort of a modified STA). However, he also demonstrates the problematic nature of the AMA, arguing that banks adopting this approach will strive to construct models in search of the one that produces the lowest possible capital charge. Kerr's results are similar to those obtained by Kalyvas and Sfetsos (2006) who point out that similar practice is involved in measuring market risk. They find that EVT produces lower capital charges than alternative VAR frameworks. In light of this conclusion, Kerr argues, "the quest of the Basel Committee to improve the risk management practices appear flawed, as banks seem to be motivated by the desire to hold less capital." He further argues that "no longer is the purpose of bank regulation to manage risk effectively, but to find ways to hold the least possible capital."

5.4 STUDIES OF THE EFFECTS OF OPERATIONAL RISK

Studies have been conducted to estimate the effect of operational risk by quantifying the decline in the market value of a firm following the announcement of operational losses. These studies invariably employ the technique of event studies. Therefore, it is perhaps useful to start this section with a description of this technique.

The Technique: A Description of Event Studies

The technique of event studies is described in detail by MacKinlay (1997), who stipulates that an event study can be used to measure the impact of a specific event on the value of a firm. The starting assumption is that stock markets are efficient in that public information is incorporated into market prices within a short period of time. MacKinlay argues that the usefulness of event studies comes from the fact that, given rationality in the market, the effect of an event will be reflected immediately in stock prices, which means that "a measure of the event's economic impact can be constructed using security prices observed over a relatively short period of time."

To account for the possibility of information leakage (before the actual announcement), it may be advisable to choose event windows that include days prior to the announcement. The time setup includes three windows: in addition to the event window extending between t_0 and t_1, an estimation window extending between $t_0 - k$ and t_0, and a post-event window extending between t_1 and $t_1 + m$. This setup is illustrated in Figure 5.2.

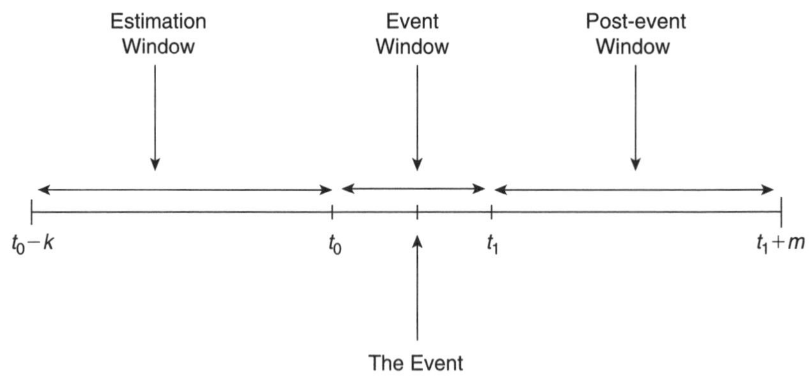

Figure 5.2 The Time Setup for Event Studies

Typically, a market model is used to estimate the normal return associated with event *i* as follows:

$$r_{it} = a_i + b_i r_{mt} + \varepsilon_t \tag{5.9}$$

where r_{it} is the rate of return on the firm's stock and r_{mt} is the rate of return on a market index. For each event, equation (5.9) is estimated over a period that ends a number of days prior to the announcement of the loss event. An event window is then defined extending between t_0 days before the announcement and t_1 days after the announcement, hence having a length of $t_1 - t_0$. However, equation (5.9) is not the only model that can be used to calculate the normal return on a particular security. MacKinlay (1997) classifies the models used for this purpose into two categories: statistical and economic. Statistical models are based on the statistical assumptions pertaining to asset returns, and do not have any economic foundations. Conversely, economic models are based on hypotheses pertaining to investor's behaviour. An example of a statistical model is the constant mean return model, which can be written as

$$r_{it} = \mu_i + \varepsilon_{it} \tag{5.10}$$

where $E(\varepsilon_{\text{it}}) = 0$ and $\text{Var}(\varepsilon_{\text{it}}) = \sigma_\varepsilon^2$. Although this is a rather simple model, Brown and Warner (1980; 1985) argue that it often yields similar results to those obtained from more sophisticated models. The market model represented by equation (5.10) is another statistical model. Examples of economic models are the capital asset pricing model (CAPM) of Sharpe (1964) and Linter (1965) and the arbitrage pricing theory (APT) of Ross (1976). MacKinlay (1997) points out that the use of CAPM for this purpose has almost ceased because of the invalid restrictions imposed on the market model. He also argues that the gains from using the APT relative to the market model are insignificant because the most important factor behaves like a market factor.

Hence, the market model represented by equation (5.9) is typically used to calculate normal return. Having done that, abnormal returns are calculated for each day in the event window as follows:

$$AR_{it} = \varepsilon_t \tag{5.11}$$

To quantify the impact of an announcement over the event window, it is important to aggregate abnormal returns by calculating the cumulative abnormal return (*CAR*) over the window interval as follows:

$$CAR_{i[t_0,t_1]} = \sum_{t_0}^{t_1} AR_{it} \tag{5.12}$$

For *N* events, the sample aggregated abnormal returns can be calculated as follows:

$$\overline{AR_t} = \frac{1}{N}\sum_{i=1}^{N} AR_{it} \tag{5.13}$$

which means

$$\overline{CAR_{[t_0,t_1]}} = \frac{1}{N}\sum_{i=1}^{N} CAR_{i[t_0,t_1]} \tag{5.14}$$

MacKinlay shows that the null hypothesis that the abnormal returns are zero can be tested by using the asymptotic distributional result

$$\frac{\overline{CAR_{[t_0,t_1]}}}{\text{var}(\overline{CAR_{[t_0,t_1]}})^{1/2}} \sim N(0,1) \tag{5.15}$$

To estimate the impact of operational loss announcements on the market value of a firm, the following regression equation is used

$$-CAR_{i[t_0,t_1]} = \alpha + \beta L_i + \xi_i \tag{5.16}$$

where L_i is the announced loss. The null hypothesis that the loss announcement has no effect on the market value of the firm, H_0: $\beta = 0$, is tested against the alternative H_1: $\beta \neq 0$.

Event Studies of Operational Risk

Perry and de Fontnouvelle (2005) measure reputational losses by examining a firm's price reaction to the announcement of a major loss event, by assuming that if the firm's market value declines by more than the announced loss amount, this is interpreted as a reputational loss. They found that market values fall one-for-one with losses caused by external events but fall by over twice the loss percentage in cases involving internal fraud. The results are consistent with the hypothesis that there is a reputational impact for losses due to internal fraud while externally caused losses have no reputational impact. The results are based on data covering 115 loss events and firms worldwide between 1974 and 2004.

Cummins et al (2006) assess the market value impact of operational loss announcements by US banks and insurance companies. Their results reveal that market values respond negatively to operational loss announcements, with insurance stocks having a larger reaction than bank stocks. They also found a positive relation between losses and Tobin's Q, suggesting that operational loss announcements have a larger market impact for firms with better growth prospects. The results revealed that market value losses are more severe than the announced losses, which indicates reputational losses.

Palmrose et al (2004) assess market reaction to earnings restatement announcements, where the restatements result from operational losses. By collecting data from the Lexis-Nexis and SEC filings, they found that in a two-day window surrounding the announcement average abnormal returns are approximately -9%. They also found market reaction to be more negative for restatements involving fraud.

Karpoff and Lott (1993) analyse the reputational losses that firms experience when they face criminal fraud charges. By using events of this sort over the period 1978–1987, they find that alleged or actual corporate fraud announcements produce statistically significant losses in the underlying firm's market value. Very little of this loss (about 5.5%) can be attributed to the firm's legal fees and penalties. It is possible to compute larger portions of the loss that could reflect higher expected penalties for future fraud and the lost value of the firm's profits resulting from the committed fraud. The remaining portion represents lost reputation.

Murphy et al (2004) examine the market impact on firms alleged to have committed acts of misconduct such as antitrust violations, bribery, fraud and copyright infringement. Out of these types of misconduct, fraud is found to have the most significant adverse effect on stock prices. They also found that firm size is negatively related to the percentage loss in the market value and that allegations of misconduct are accompanied by increased variability of stock returns. The influence of firm size on market losses is attributed to both an economy-of-scale effect and a reputational effect.

Wei (2003) conducted an empirical study of operational risk in the insurance industry to test the following hypotheses:

- Operational loss events do not lead to significant changes in the stock prices of insurance companies.
- No relation exists between operational losses and changes in stock prices.

- Operational losses resulting from market conduct problems and those resulting from other types of events have the same effects on stock prices.

- The insurance industry is not affected by the operational loss events of a few insurers.

- Operational loss events due to firm-specific problems and events due to common problems within the industry have the same effect on the industry as a whole.

- Non-announcing insurers are affected in a similar manner, regardless of differences in firm characteristics, by operational loss events.

In general, these hypotheses fall under either the information effect hypothesis or the contagion effect hypothesis. By using data from the OpVar operational loss database, he found results indicating that operational loss events have a significant negative effect on the market value of the affected insurers and that the effect of operational losses goes beyond the firm that incurs them. The conclusion derived from this study is that "the significant damage of market values of both the insurers and the insurance industry caused by operational losses should provide an incentive for operational risk management in the U.S. insurance industry."

In another study, Wei (2006) examined the impact of operational loss events on the market value of announcing and non-announcing US financial institutions using data from the OpVar database. The results reveal significantly negative impact of the announcement of operational losses on stock prices. He also found that the decline in market value significantly exceeds the operational losses causing them, which supports the conjecture put forward by Cummins et al (2006) that there is a significant contagion effect. By using data from the same source, Cummins et al (2006) conduct an event study of the impact of operational loss events on the market values of US banks and insurance companies, obtaining similar results to those obtained by Wei (2006). They found losses to be proportionately larger for institutions with higher Tobin's Q ratios.

5.5 A FINAL THOUGHT

In this chapter we reviewed a selection of studies dealing with the modelling and measurement of operational risk as well as some studies of the effect of the materialisation of operational losses (including those resulting from the loss of reputation, although reputational risk is not part of operational risk under Basel II). We did not review any study dealing with operational risk management in this chapter, not at all because the management of operational risk is not important. On the contrary, the main objective of this book is to convey the message that the mathematical and statistical sophistication employed in the studies surveyed in this chapter is not necessarily conducive to better risk management, which should be the ultimate objective of endeavours to unravel the mysteries of operational risk. It is unfortunately the case that coming up with sophisticated models of operational risk has become an end by itself, rather than a means to an end. That end should be operational risk management. As mathematically elegant as they are, it is not that obvious how the studies surveyed in this chapter are useful for operational risk management.

On the other hand, studies conducted to measure the effect of operational losses on the enduring firm are important. They convey the message that operational risk is a serious threat to the well-being of the underlying firm, which means that it should be managed carefully. The management of operational risk should be preventive in nature, aiming to avoid losses rather than dealing with them through an amount of capital calculated a priori by using fancy mathematical and statistical tools. After all, risk management and loss management are two different creatures. The problem, as Richard Pike puts it, is that "too much of the industry's time and resources have been gobbled up by the attempt to ever-more-finely measure risk, when they should really be worrying about how to manage it" (Wood, 2008). If any of the techniques described or mentioned in this chapter is useful for operational risk management, it is more likely to be Bayesian networks than any other. After all, this technique can be used in forensic science (Sanford, 2008).

CHAPTER 6

Monte Carlo Simulation: Description and Examples

6.1 INTRODUCTION

The objective of this chapter is to demonstrate how to use Monte Carlo simulation to estimate the capital charge against operational risk, following the LDA. A simplified exposition of the procedure will be presented using hypothetical data (which, in reality, is not available for the banks required to go through the same exercise). The results are then used to support the proposition presented in Chapter 4, that only subjective manipulation of the underlying model can reduce the capital charge.

Monte Carlo methods involve the use of random numbers to solve problems, constituting a computational algorithm that relies on repeated random sampling to produce results and derive inference. Dupire (2006) points out that the first documented account of Monte Carlo methods dates back to 1768 when a simulation technique involving the use of needles and striped floor was used to calculate the value of pie (π). He also argues that many people had used Monte Carlo simulation (without knowing that the procedure would be known as "Monte Carlo simulation") for many purposes, including the estimation of the probability of the face of a biased die by rolling it hundreds of times. The term "Monte Carlo" was coined by Metropolis and Ulam (1949) in reference to a famous casino in Monaco where Ulam's uncle used to borrow money to gamble (Hubbard, 2007). The resemblance between the computational procedure and gambling is attributed to the use of randomness and the repetitive nature of the process, which is just like the activity of a gambler in a casino.

Monte Carlo simulation has been traditionally used in physics, particularly since the 1940s when (the) von Neumann laid the foundations for pseudo-random generators and inverse cumulative distribution functions. It has also been used in other fields of pure and applied science, including biology, astronomy and engineering. In finance, Monte Carlo methods are used for asset pricing and investment valuation by simulating the various sources of uncertainty affecting the underlying variables (see, e.g., Dupire, 2006). The introduction of Monte Carlo methods in finance was pioneered by Hertz (1964), who discussed the technique in relation to corporate finance. Boyle (1977) introduced the use of the technique in the valuation of derivatives.

We came across the concept of Monte Carlo simulation in Chapter 1, but in this chapter we examine the procedure in relation to operational risk, and more specifically how it is used to implement the loss distribution approach (LDA). We start with a description of the basic principles of the computational technique.

6.2 THE BASIC IDEA

Anders (2003) describes Monte Carlo simulation as being "a big dice-rolling exercise where the dice are shaped so that their different sides fall with different likelihoods." Instead of dice, however, probability distributions are used for this purpose. If, following the LDA, the frequency and severity distributions are modelled separately (assuming that they are independent) the total loss distribution is obtained by conducting Monte Carlo simulations as follows:

- A random draw is taken from the frequency distribution to produce the simulated number of loss events per year. The random numbers representing the frequency of events have to be whole numbers, which means that they must be drawn from a discrete distribution.

- A number of random draws that is equal to the simulated number of loss events is taken from the severity distribution. If, for example, the number drawn from the frequency distribution is five, then five numbers should be drawn from the severity distribution representing five loss amounts. Sine loss amounts do not have to be whole numbers, severity must be represented by a continuous distribution.

- The annual loss amount is obtained by summing the simulated losses obtained in step 2. If, on the other hand, each draw from the severity distribution is considered to be average severity for a particular year, total loss is calculated as the product of frequency and average severity.

- Steps 1, 2 and 3 are repeated a large number of times to obtain a large number of values (amounts) of the annual loss, which are used to plot a histogram representing the distribution of the total annual loss.

- A capital charge is calculated as the operational VAR at the 99.9th percentile or the difference between the percentile and the mean of the distribution, depending on which definition of the capital charge we wish to use. This depends on whether the capital charge is intended to protect the firm against both expected and unexpected losses or against unexpected losses only.

- The process is repeated for each event type and business line to arrive eventually at the firm-wide capital charge.

The description of Monte Carlo simulations can be represented diagrammatically as in Figure 6.1, which shows a simulation exercise that consists of n iterations. Starting with iteration 1, the draw from the frequency distribution gives an annual loss frequency f_1. The severity distribution is then used to generate f_1 losses per year, $L_{1,j}$, where the subscript 1, j refers to the iteration number and the number of draws $j = 1, 2, \ldots, f_1$. The total annual loss derived from iteration 1 (L_1) is the sum of $L_{1,1}$, $L_{1,2}$, ……, $L_{1,j}$. The process is repeated in iteration 2 to obtain another figure for the annual loss, L_2, and so on until we obtain L_n from iteration n. The observations L_1, L_2, ……, L_n are then used to plot a histogram that represents the distribution of the annual loss. Further details on the calculation of VAR by using Monte Carlo simulations can be found in Owen and Tavella (2006), Picoult (2006), Quinlan (2006) and Shaw (2006).

6.3 SPECIFICATION OF FREQUENCY AND SEVERITY DISTRIBUTIONS

For a given type of operational risk in a given business line, a discrete probability density $b(n)$ is chosen to represent the number of loss events n in one year, while loss severity is represented by a continuous conditional probability density, $g(L|n)$. The annual loss has the combined density

$$f(L) = \sum_{n=0}^{\infty} b(n) g(L \mid n) \tag{6.1}$$

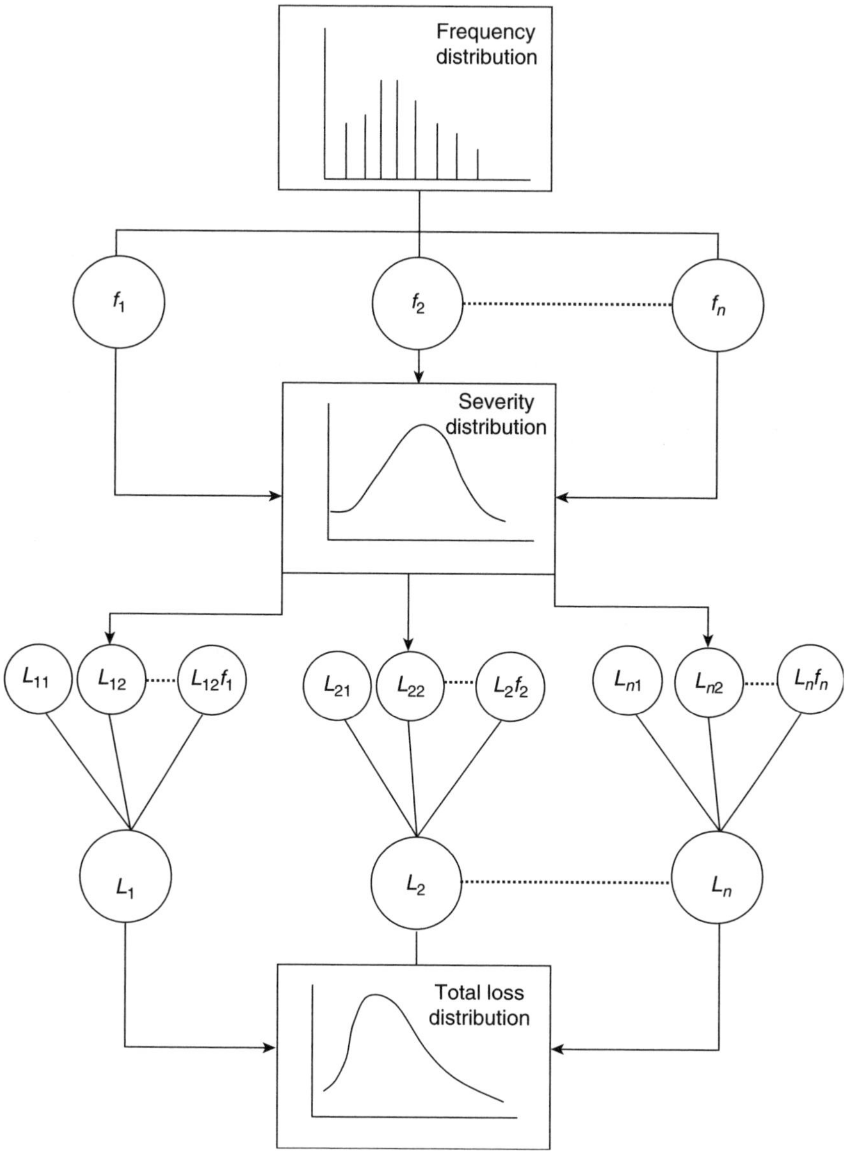

Figure 6.1 Monte Carlo Simulations of Frequency and Severity

The question that arises here is about the functional form to be assigned to the frequency and severity distributions. Loss frequency can be represented by a binomial distribution $B(N,p)$ where N is the total number of events that are susceptible to operational loss and p is the probability of a loss event. If events are assumed to be independent, the density function of the frequency distribution is

$$b(n) = \left(\frac{N}{n}\right) p^n (1-p)^{N-n} \tag{6.2}$$

where $n = 0,1,\ldots, N$. The problem with the binomial density function is the need to specify the total number of events, N. When p is small, the binomial distribution can be approximated by the Poisson distribution, which has a single parameter, the expected frequency of loss events, $\lambda = Np$ (because the mean and variance are equal). The Poisson distribution density function is specified as

$$b(n) = \frac{\lambda^n e^{-\lambda}}{n!} \tag{6.3}$$

where $n = 0,1,\ldots$.

Alexander (2003b) suggests that a better representation of the loss frequency is the negative binomial distribution, which allows for variances that are greater than the mean. The negative binomial distribution has the density function

$$b(n) = \left(\frac{\alpha + n - 1}{n}\right)\left(\frac{1}{1+\beta}\right)^{\alpha}\left(\frac{\beta}{1+\beta}\right)^{n} \tag{6.4}$$

The functional form for the severity distribution may be different across different risk types. High-frequency risks may have a lognormal severity distribution of the form:

$$g(L) = \frac{1}{\sqrt{2\pi}\sigma L}\exp\left[-\frac{1}{2}\left(\frac{\log(L) - \mu}{\sigma}\right)^2\right] \tag{6.5}$$

for $L > 0$. Anders (2003) suggests that the results of research conducted at Dresdner Bank support the proposition that the lognormal distribution works very well with internal historic operational loss data. However, Alexander (2003b) suggests that some severity distributions may have substantial leptokurtosis and skewness, in which case a better fit would be a two-parameter density such as the gamma density, which is given by

$$g(L) = \frac{x^{\alpha-1} \exp(-L/\beta)}{\beta^{\alpha}\Gamma(\alpha)} \tag{6.6}$$

where $\alpha\beta$ is the mean of the gamma distribution and $\Gamma(.)$ is the gamma function. The alternative is the two-parameter hyperbolic density function, which is given by

$$g(L) = \frac{\exp(-\alpha\sqrt{\beta^2 + L^2})}{2\beta B(\alpha\beta)} \tag{6.7}$$

where $B(.)$ denotes the Bessel function.

Other possibilities include, among others, the extreme value distribution. The suitability of these distributions for the representation of loss severity is due to the fact that they are (unlike the normal distribution) fat-tailed and asymmetrical. A fat tail means that high-severity losses occur with a much higher likelihood than a normal distribution would suggest (the tail is fatter or heavier), while asymmetry means that low-frequency, high-severity losses are not symmetrical to the high-frequency, low-severity losses. Dutta and Perry (2007) consider the exponential, Weibull, gamma, lognormal, logistic and generalised Pareto distributions. Ergashev (2008) suggests the use of the log-t distribution (whereby the logarithm of losses has a t distribution) because "it is flexible enough to fit the tail distribution." However, he points out that "the hunt for more appealing severity and frequency distributions is not over yet." It is hoped, however, that this hunt is not motivated by the desire to produce a lower capital charge as opposed to the desire to seek the "truth."

Having chosen the distributions, they must be parameterised by assigning numerical values to the mean, variance and other parameters if necessary. Reshetar (2008) describes the process of calibrating frequency and severity distributions, which is an integral step of the application of the LDA, as "the most demanding task because of the poor quality and small sample size of available operational loss data."

Appendices 6.1 and 6.2 describe some common discrete and continuous probability distributions that can be used to model frequency and severity, respectively. The parameters needed to define each one of these distributions are stated explicitly. The normal distribution, for example, is defined precisely by two parameters, the mean and standard deviation. Other distributions require three or four parameters. For example, the beta distribution is defined by four parameters: maximum, minimum, alpha and beta, the last two of which determine the shape of the distribution within the minimum and maximum values. Therefore, we have the following possibilities: (i) if $\alpha = \beta$, the distribution is symmetric; (ii) if $\alpha = 1$ and $\beta > 1$ or $\alpha > 1$and $\beta = 1$, the distribution is J-shaped; (iii) if $\alpha < \beta$, the distribution is positively skewed; and (iv) if $\alpha > \beta$, the distribution is negatively skewed. As another example, the t distribution is defined by three parameters: midpoint, scale and degrees of freedom. The midpoint is the central location of the distribution, which is equal to the mode. The degrees of freedom determine the shape of the distribution, such that smaller values produce thicker tails. The scale parameter affects the width of the distribution.

6.4 FITTING SEVERITY DISTRIBUTIONS

Instead of specifying the severity distribution and its parameters by using theoretical reasoning or expert opinion, this can be done by fitting distributions to historical data, naturally only if the data are available. If we do not have any apriori idea about the most appropriate distribution, we fit a range of distributions (such as those listed in Appendix 6.2), then we employ statistical testing to pick the distribution with the best fit. Figure 6.2 shows two distributions (A and B) fitted to a histogram of historical data. It is clear that the skewed distribution A fits better than the more symmetric distribution B because the data has a thick right tail. This procedure can also be used with the total loss data, as opposed to severity, if we do not wish to model frequency and severity separately. Graphical methods and formal tests can be used to judge the appropriateness of a fitted distribution. The graphical methods and three formal tests are discussed in turn.

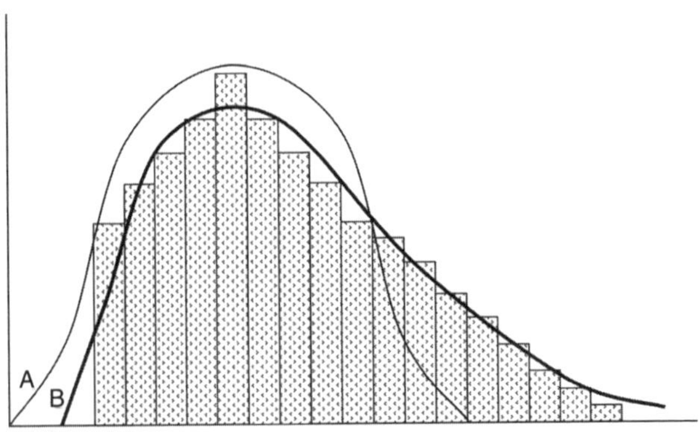

Figure 6.2 Fitting Distributions to a Histogram of Historical Data

The Graphical Methods

The graphical methods, which do not constitute formal testing of the goodness of fit, include the Quantile-Quantile (Q-Q) plot and the normalised probability-probability (P-P) plot, the first of which is more widely used. The plots reveal whether or not a fit is poor but cannot be used to tell whether or not the fit is good in a statistical sense. One advantage of the graphical methods is that they can be used to compare the fit of more than one distribution at the same time.

The Q-Q plot involves a comparison between the observed values and those estimated from the fitted distribution. A perfect fit would be represented by a Q-Q plot in which all of the points fall on the 45 degrees line. The Q-Q plot may be shown separately for the body and the tail of the distribution, as in Figure 6.3. In this case, the tail of the distribution is taken to be in the range above the 97th percentile (which is not a rule). We can see from the diagram that the distribution fits better for the body than for the tail of the distribution. It is typically the case that the observed loss quantiles are measured on the horizontal axis, whereas the expected loss quantiles are measured on the vertical axis. If the sample sizes of actual and predicted levels are the same, the Q-Q plot is essentially a plot of sorted data sets against one another. If the sample sizes are different, the quantiles are selected to correspond to the sorted values from the smaller data sets; then the quantiles for the larger data set are calculated. The Q-Q plot is useful for detecting shifts in location, shifts in scale, changes in symmetry and the presence of outliers. For example, if the Q-Q plot shows a straight line that is parallel to the 45 degrees line, the two distributions are similar except for the difference in location.

A variant of the Q-Q plot is known as the probability-probability (P-P) plot. Let $F(x)$ be the cumulative density function, such that $g[F(x)]=x$. It follows that $E(x_i)=G[(i-0.5)/n$, where $i = 1, 2, \ldots, n$ (n is the number of observations in the sample). While the Q-Q plot is a plot of x_i against $E(x_i)$, the P-P plot is a plot of $F(x_i)$ against $(i-0.5)/n$. The stabilised probability (SP) plot is a plot of the rescaled probabilities so that the variances of the plotted points are approximately equal over the range of probability values.

The Chi-Square Test

Although the chi-square test is flexible, it has low power relative to other goodness of fit tests. The test is based on the division of the null distribution into cells. Then a comparison is made between the observed cell counts and the expected cell counts under the null. The test statistic is calculated from the deviations of the fitted values from the actual values. Cohen and Sackrowitz (1975) and Mann and Wald (1942) have shown that the chi-square

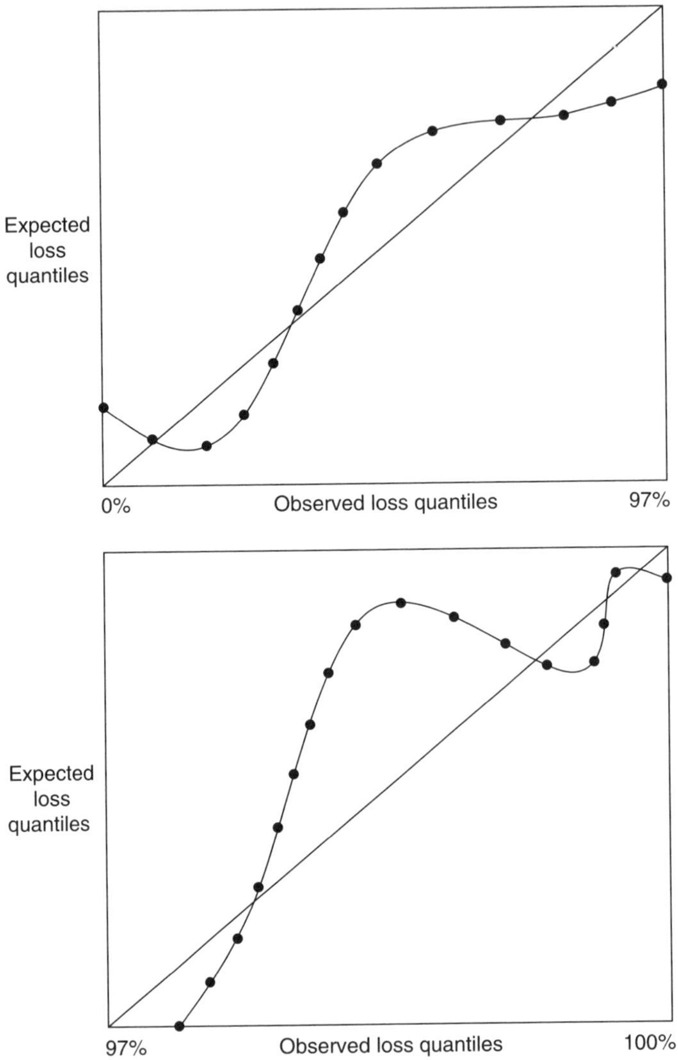

Figure 6.3 Q-Q Plots for the Body and Tail of the Distribution

test statistic is unbiased when the cells are chosen to have equal probabilities under the null. The test has the following shortcomings: (i) the division of distributions into cells results in the loss of information about continuous distributions, which reduces the power of the test; (ii) the test results are sensitive with respect to the number and size of cells; and (iii) the sample size should be large enough so that the expected cell frequency in each cell exceeds four.

The Kolmogorov–Smirnov (K–S) Test

The K–S test is a non-parametric supremum test based on the empirical cumulative distribution function. The test statistic is calculated as:

$$D = \sup[|H_n(x) - H(x)|] \tag{6.8}$$

where $H_n(x)$ and $H(x)$ are the empirical and expected cumulative probability distributions (CDFs), respectively. While the test statistic is easy to calculate, the test has some shortcomings: (i) it is low in power; (ii) it is more sensitive to deviations in the centre of the distribution than in the tail; and (iii) if the null distribution contains shape parameters, the critical values of the test statistic must be simulated. The second shortcoming is particularly troubling in the case of operational risk because the calculation of operational VAR (and the capital charge) is based on the tail distribution.

The Anderson–Darling (A–D) Test

Unlike the K-S test, the A-D test puts more weight on the tail of the distribution. The test statistic is calculated as

$$A^2 = \int_{-\infty}^{\infty} \frac{[H_n(x) - H(x)]^2}{H(x)[1 - H(x)]} dH(x) \tag{6.9}$$

The main disadvantage of this test is that different critical values must be used for each null distribution. Because of its sensitivity to the null distribution, the A-D test is more powerful than the K-S test.

6.5 MODELLING RISK DEPENDENCE TO CALCULATE THE FIRM-WIDE CAPITAL CHARGE

To calculate the firm-wide capital charge, assumptions must be made about correlation among the losses arising in various business lines, losses of different types and combinations thereof. If the assumption of perfect correlation is made (that is, losses occur at the same time), the capital charge for the whole firm is calculated by adding up the individual capital charges for each risk type/business line combination. This is shown in Figure 6.4 for two business lines, A and B. The capital charge in this diagram is taken to be the difference between the percentile and the mean of the distribution.

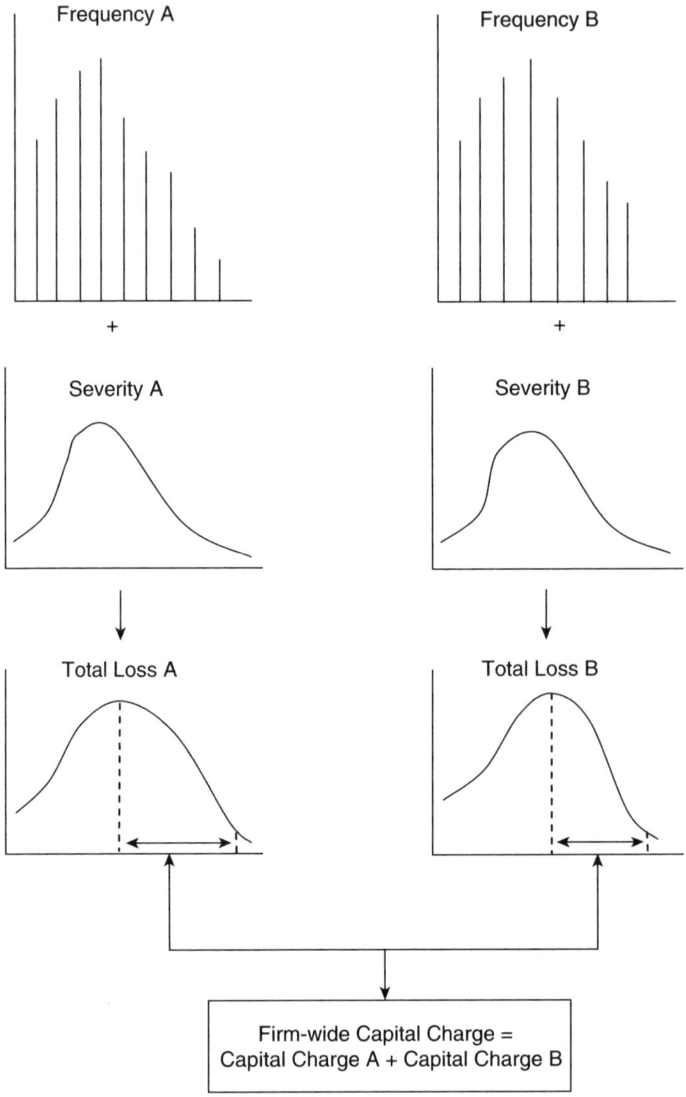

Figure 6.4 The Firm-wide Capital Charge (Perfect Correlation)

At the other extreme, the assumption of zero correlation among risk categories (that is, they are independent of each other), the firm-wide capital charge is calculated by compounding all distribution pairs into a single loss distribution for the firm. This is done by calculating the total loss produced by each iteration of the Monte Carlo simulation. Figure 6.5 shows the calculation of the firm-wide capital charge in this case. If L_{Ai} and L_{Bi} are the loss observations obtained by combining observations from the frequency and severity of business lines A and B, respectively, then the observations from the total loss distribution are $L_{Ai} + L_{Bi}$.

In between the two extremes of assuming perfect correlation and zero correlation, it is possible to specify a certain value for the correlation coefficient, either on the basis of historical data, if available, or on the basis of "expert opinion." However, some (particularly the hardcore quants) would argue that correlation, which is a simple form of the first moment of the joint density of two random variables, does not capture all forms of dependence between the two variables (it is a measure of linear association between the

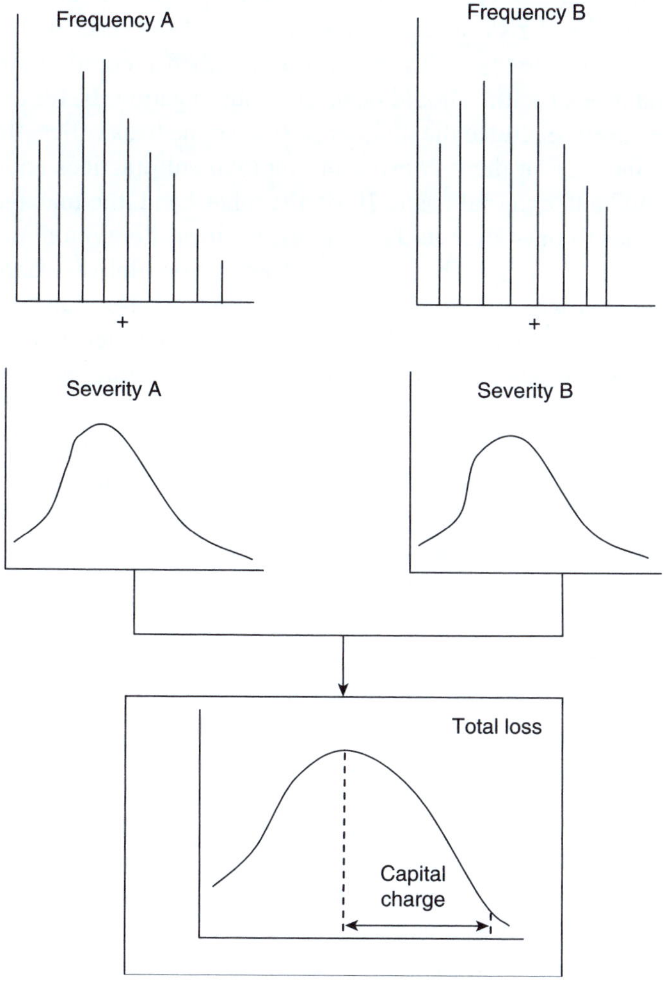

Figure 6.5 The Firm-wide Capital Charge (Zero Correlation)

two variables). Everts and Liersch (2006) argue that the crucial assumption behind the use of correlation for this purpose is that of multivariate normal distribution, which means that if this assumption is violated (which is invariably the case with the total loss distribution), then correlation is not an appropriate measure of dependence. Another problem with correlation is that it varies over time. This is why, the argument goes, it is more appropriate to use the copula for this purpose (a copula is an expression of a bivariate or multivariate distribution in terms of the marginal distributions). Copulas are used to combine two or more distributions to obtain a joint distribution with a prespecified form of dependence.

What procedure is used to select the appropriate copula? This is done by looking at the sources of risk (the so-called risk drivers). For example, if two operational risk types are believed to be positively related, because a set of operational risk sources tends to boost these risks while another set of risk sources tends to bring them down, then a copula with a positive dependence structure should be used for aggregation. If, for example, a decision is taken to reduce the number of staff in the back office, this would lead to an increase in the risk event of employment practices and those of internal fraud and external fraud. If, on the other hand, the management of a firm decides to outsource its IT systems, business disruption and system failures become less risky but the risk of execution, delivery and process management, as well as the risk of employment practices and workplace safety (EPWS), will increase. This seems to be a more sensible procedure than attempting to specify a correlation matrix involving each and every combination of loss event and business line.

Following Saita (2004), Everts and Liersch (2006) identify the advantages and disadvantages of using correlation and copulas for the purpose of aggregation. Starting with correlation, it is simple, intuitive and easy to explain to people without formal training in statistics. It is also simple with respect to parameter estimation while allowing the calculation of regulatory capital analytically. The disadvantages of correlation are the problems arising from the assumption of normality, its changing pattern (over time) and that it can be underestimated if too short data series are used. The advantages of copulas, on the other hand, are that they do not require the assumption of a particular joint distribution and, if the right copula is used, dependence can be captured accurately while maintaining the original distribution. Copulas, however, are difficult to explain to people without formal training in statistics, and the calculated capital charge will be sensitive to the copula used for the purpose of aggregation. Furthermore, choosing the right copula may require a time series of considerable length.

All of this makes a lot of sense. However, no-one would argue that a capital charge calculated by using copulas puts a firm in a better position against possible operational risk-driven insolvency than another capital charge calculated by using simple correlation. For all we know, there is no reason to believe that a firm that switches from correlation to copula will be "better off," whatever that means. Copulas provide another example of a magnificent intellectual exercise that produces zero value added in certain applications.

6.6 EXAMPLES USING HYPOTHETICAL DATA

In this section, Monte Carlo simulations are illustrated by using hypothetical data on the frequency and severity of losses in two business lines of a particular firm (assuming that the firm consists of two business lines only). The data are collected over a period of twenty years, consisting of 198 events in business line A and 167 events in business line B. Figure 6.6 exhibits the individual losses year by year (1 to 20). Table 6.1 reports the means and standard deviations of frequency and severity.

Calculating Separate Capital Charges for Business Lines A and B

To calculate separate capital charges for the two business lines, the choice falls on Poisson and binomial distributions to represent the frequency of losses in business lines A and B, respectively. The Q-Q plots for the frequency distributions are shown in Figure 6.7, which obviously shows that a Poisson distribution fits better for A than a binomial distribution for B. For

Table 6.1 Frequency and Severity of Hypothetical Loss Events

	Business Line A	*Business Line B*
Number of Events	198	167
Frequency (mean)	9.9	8.4
Frequency (standard deviation)	4.2	5.7
Severity (mean)	73.4	126.6
Severity (standard deviation)	34.8	51.1
Total Loss (mean)	726.3	1054.0
Total Loss (standard deviation)	264.3	754.6

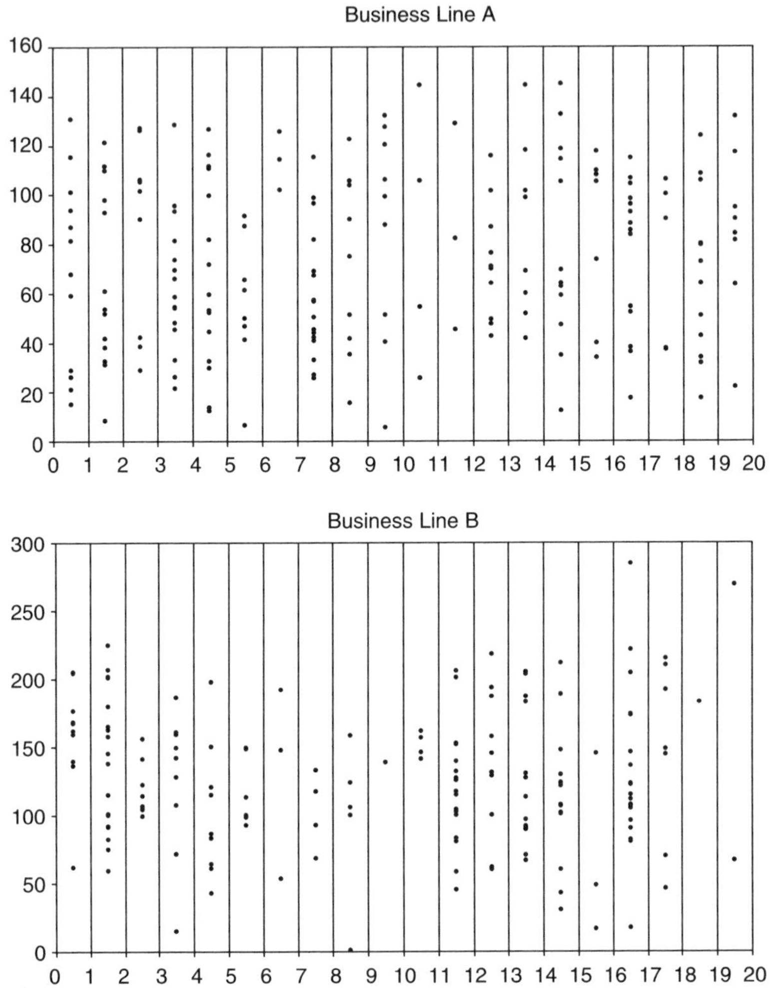

Figure 6.6 Hypothetical Loss Data

severity, a total of thirteen distributions were tried, then ranked by the A-D test. The results of fitting the distributions are shown in Table 6.2. Judged by the A-D test statistic, the best fit for the severity of losses in business line A is a Weibull distribution with the following parameters: location (−2.3), scale (85.4) and shape (2.31). For business line B, the best fit distribution is a gamma distribution with the following parameters: location (−289.5), scale (6.3) and shape (66.42). The Q-Q plots for the severity distributions are shown in Figure 6.8: the two distributions seem to fit well.

Having fitted and calibrated the frequency and severity distributions, Monte Carlo simulations can be used to generate total loss distributions. By

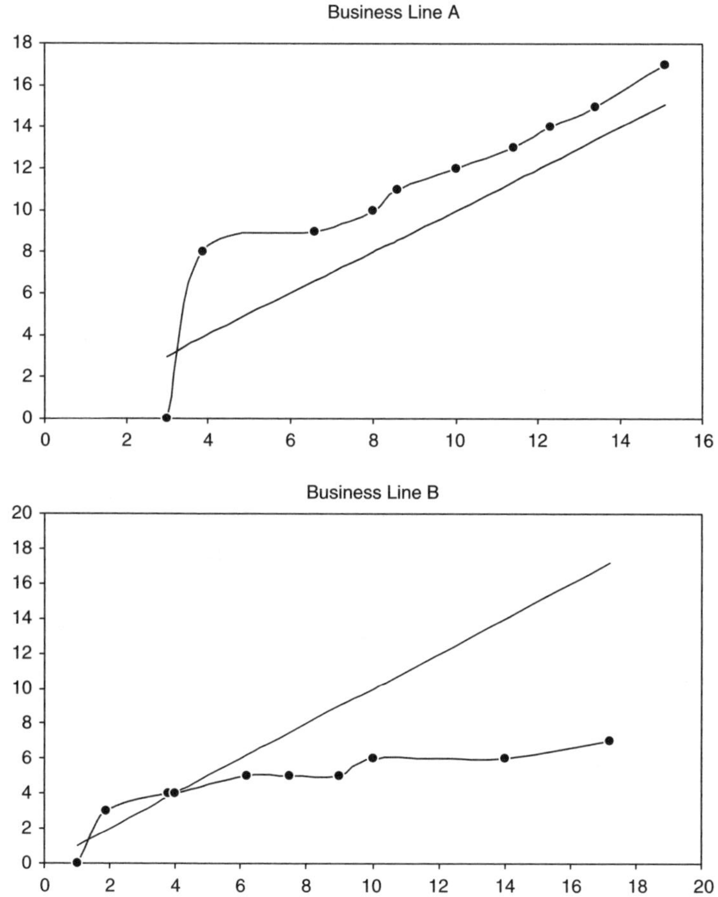

Figure 6.7 Q-Q Plots of the Frequency Distributions

using *Crystal Ball*, a Monte Carlo simulation software, the total loss distributions for business lines A and B were constructed after 100,000 iterations each. In both cases, the best fit for the total loss distribution turned out to be beta, as shown in Figures 6.9 and 6.10 respectively. Figure 6.11 shows the Q-Q plots for the total loss distributions. It is obvious that the beta distribution fits rather well for business line A with the exception of the tails. Conversely, it is a rather bad fit (although it is the best) for business line B. No significant difference can be seen between the goodness of fit for the body of the distribution and that for the tail.

Following the simulation of the total loss distributions, we are in a position to calculate the capital charges against operational risk in business lines A and B. The 99.9th percentile (99.9% operational VAR) turned out to be

Table 6.2 Severity Distributions (in order of goodness of fit)

Distribution	*A-D*	*Chi-Square*	*K-S*
Business Line A			
Weibull	1.75	28.81	0.084
Gamma	2.11	26.24	0.087
Normal	2.16	21.54	0.085
Student's t	2.19	27.60	0.088
Max Extreme	2.35	40.48	0.096
Logistic	2.51	38.21	0.085
Min Extreme	2.91	49.87	0.103
Beta	3.14	9.57	0.040
Uniform	3.75	34.42	0.097
Triangular	3.81	25.18	0.125
Lognormal	4.31	52.45	0.115
Exponential	21.86	157.75	0.239
Pareto	52.20	631.09	0.406
Business Line B			
Gamma	0.28	10.47	0.036
Beta	0.29	11.14	0.037
Normal	0.40	15.00	0.049
Logistic	0.45	21.37	0.053
Weibull	0.48	12.65	0.046
Student's t	1.31	28.74	0.065
Max Extreme	1.39	28.41	0.078
Min Extreme	3.15	37.13	0.096
Triangular	3.58	28.91	0.106
Lognormal	7.50	68.82	0.161
Uniform	16.63	112.41	0.229
Exponential	26.24	160.70	0.306
Pareto	63.27	864.05	0.531

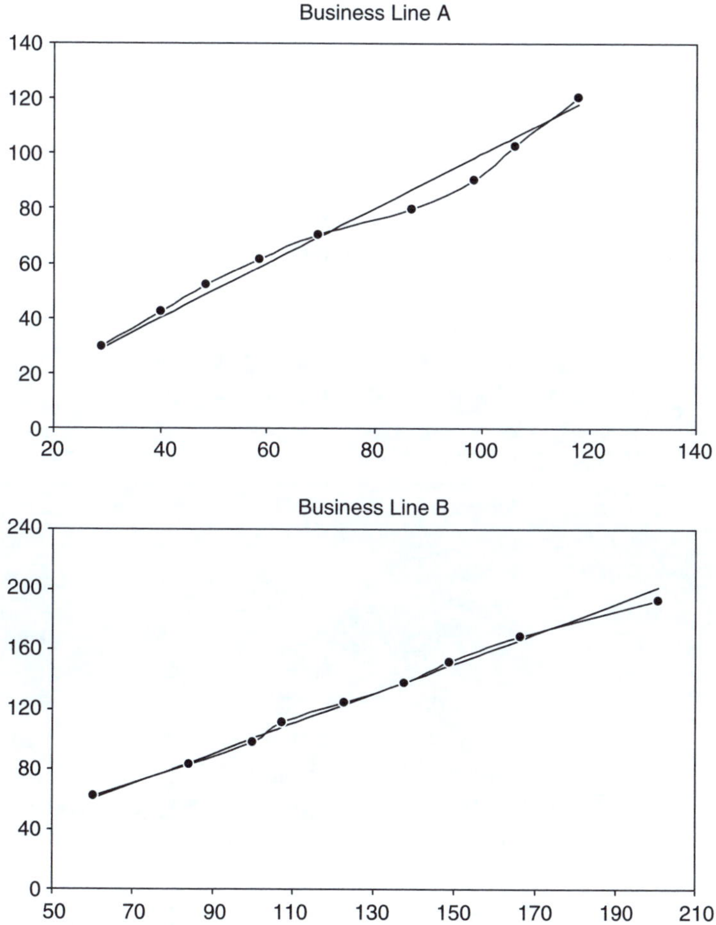

Figure 6.8 Q-Q Plots of the Severity Distributions

3193.25 in business line A and 4459.63 in business line B. If the capital charge is to cover unexpected losses only, it is calculated as the difference between the 99.9th percentile and the mean of the distribution, which is 907.14 (A) and 2080.26 (B). The capital charges should then be 2286.11 and 2379.37. Under the assumption of perfect correlation, the firm-wide capital charge should be 4665.48. Great, but the only problem is that in practice banks do not have high-quality operational loss data as the hypothetical data used in this exercise. And there is more than that: even if the data were available, any change in the procedure or the underlying assumption produces significantly different capital charges, as we are going to see.

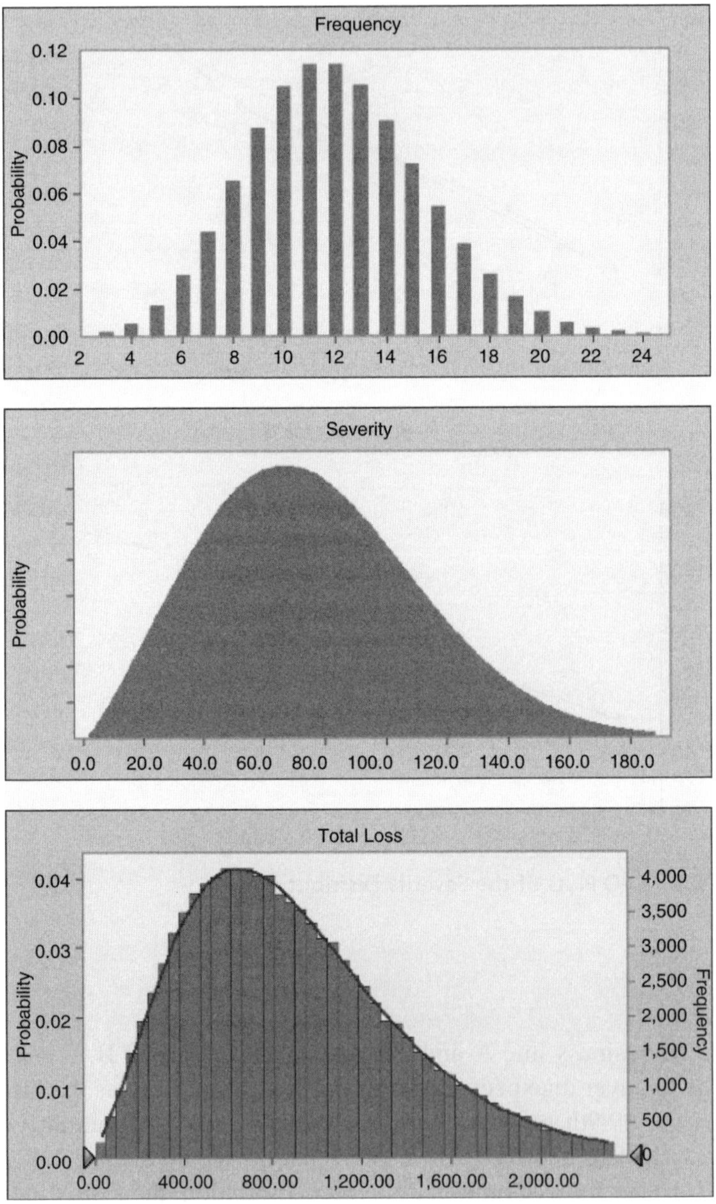

Figure 6.9 Frequency, Severity and Total Loss Distributions (Business Line A)

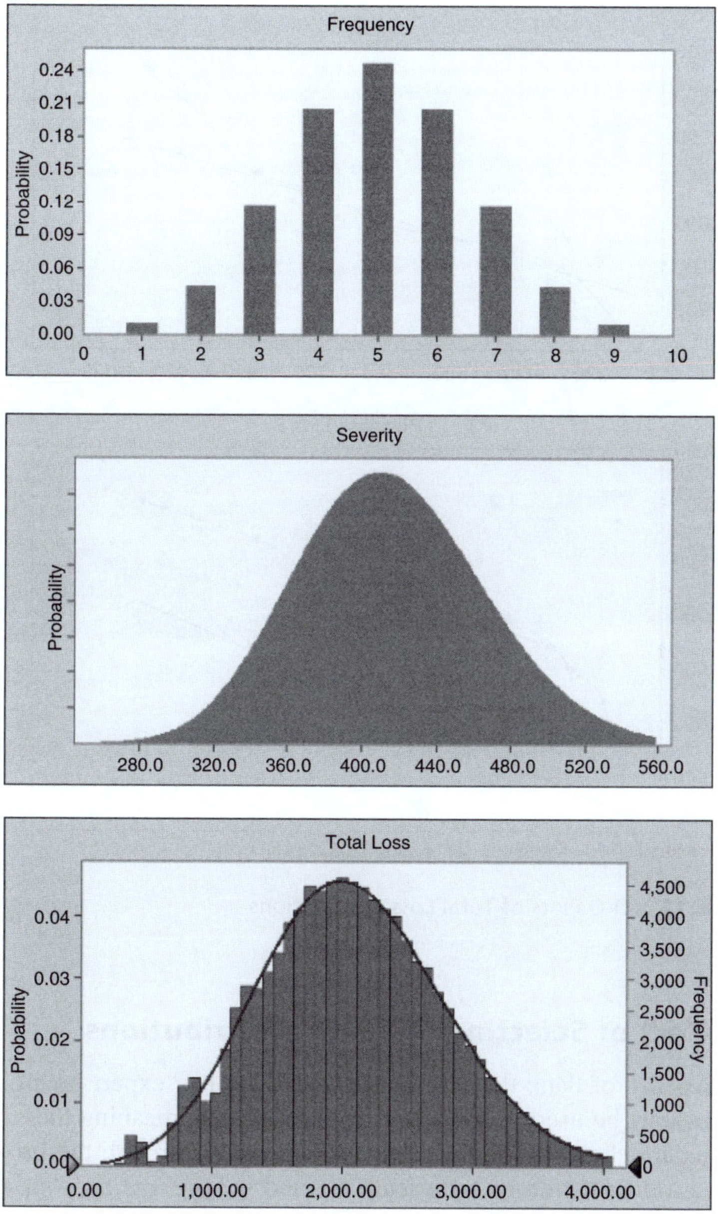

Figure 6.10 Frequency, Severity and Total Loss Distributions (Business Line B)

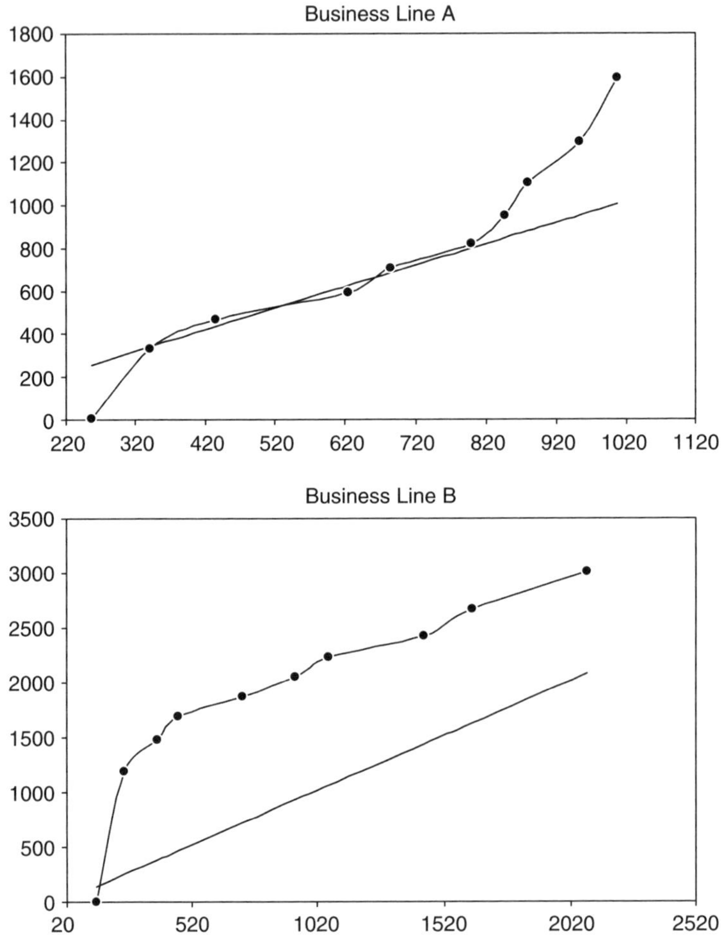

Figure 6.11 Q-Q Plots of Total Loss Distributions

The Effect of Selecting Different Distributions

In the absence of data, the information provided by "expert opinion" and scenarios may be used to calibrate the distributions, meaning that the distributions are chosen and calibrated without going through the procedure of fitting a distribution to historical data and judging the appropriateness of this distribution on the basis of statistical testing. To illustrate this point, six different distributions are used to represent the total loss distribution in business line A: minimum extreme, Weibull, logistic, gamma, beta and normal. Figure 6.12 shows the six fitted distributions.

Table 6.3 reports the estimated 99.9% operational VARs, the means and capital charges for each one of these distributions. We can readily make two

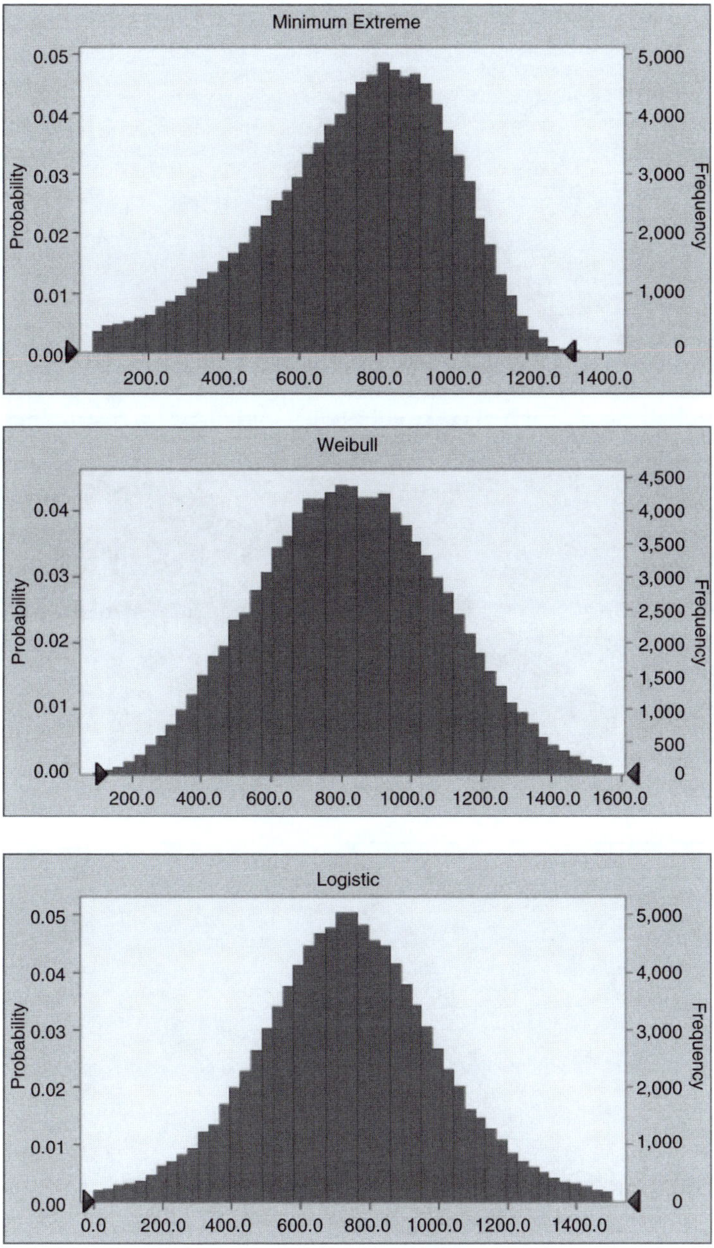

Figure 6.12 The Effect of Changing the Loss Distributions (Business Line A)

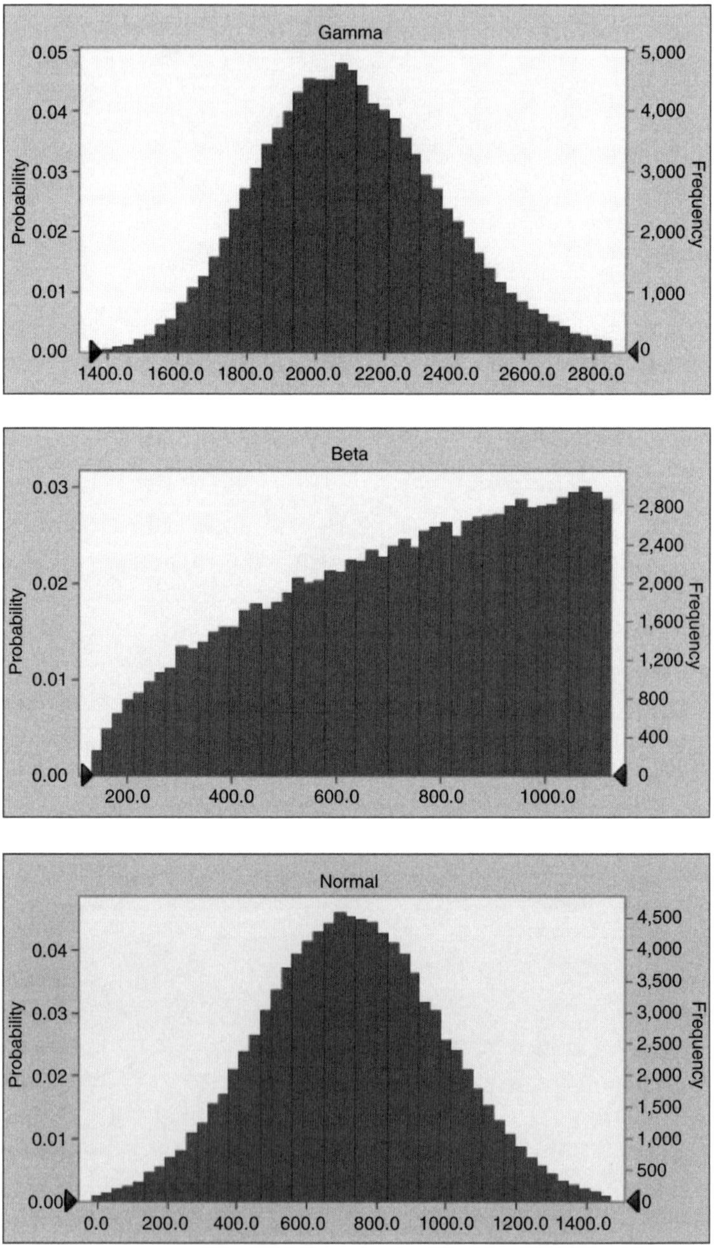

Figure 6.12 Continued

Table 6.3 Capital Charges under Various Total Loss Distributions (A)

Distribution	*Parameters**	*VAR*	*Mean*	*Capital Charge*
Min Extreme	850.1, 220.7	1293.2	743.0	550.2
Weibull	-52.3, 868.8, 3.2	1687.5	830.1	857.4
Logistic	738.8, 155.5	1904.6	746.9	1157.7
Gamma	-688.6, 50.3, 28.1	3129.5	2102.7	1026.8
Beta	130.7, 1125.5, 1.5, 1.0	1125.4	728.3	397.1
Normal	726.3, 264.3	1582.4	726.3	856.1

* The parameters are as follows: min extreme (likeliest, scale); Weibull (location, scale, shape); logistic (mean, scale); gamma (location, scale shape); beta (minimum, maximum, alpha, beta); normal (mean, standard deviation).

interesting observations. The first is that sampling from the total loss distribution directly produces significantly lower capital charges than when the severity and frequency distributions are modelled separately. The second observation is that the choice of the distribution produces widely diverse results as the capital charge falls between a minimum of 397.1 for a beta distribution and 1157.7 for a gamma distribution. The point to be made here is that if a bank wishes to minimise its capital charge for a business line like A, it will choose to sample from a beta total loss distribution, claiming that this is the most sound representation according to "expert opinion."

The Effect of Correlation

Here we sample from the total loss distributions for business lines A and B. The fit produces a minimum extreme for A and a Weibull for B, and capital charges of 550.5 for A and 3783.8 for B. Under the assumption of perfect correlation, the firm-wide capital charge is 550.5+3783.8 = 4334.3. Under the assumption of zero correlation, however, the capital charge is calculated by sampling from the total loss distribution for the whole firm (that is, the distribution of A+B). In this case, the capital charge turns out to be 3900, which is (as expected) lower than under the assumption of perfect correlation.

To examine the effect of correlation in more detail, we calculate the firm-wide capital charge while varying the correlation coefficient between the total losses of business line A and those of business line B from +1 to −1 in a step of 0.2. Figure 6.13 shows the total loss distribution for the whole firm under various correlation assumptions. To start with, the correlation assumption changes the total loss distribution for the firm: for high positive

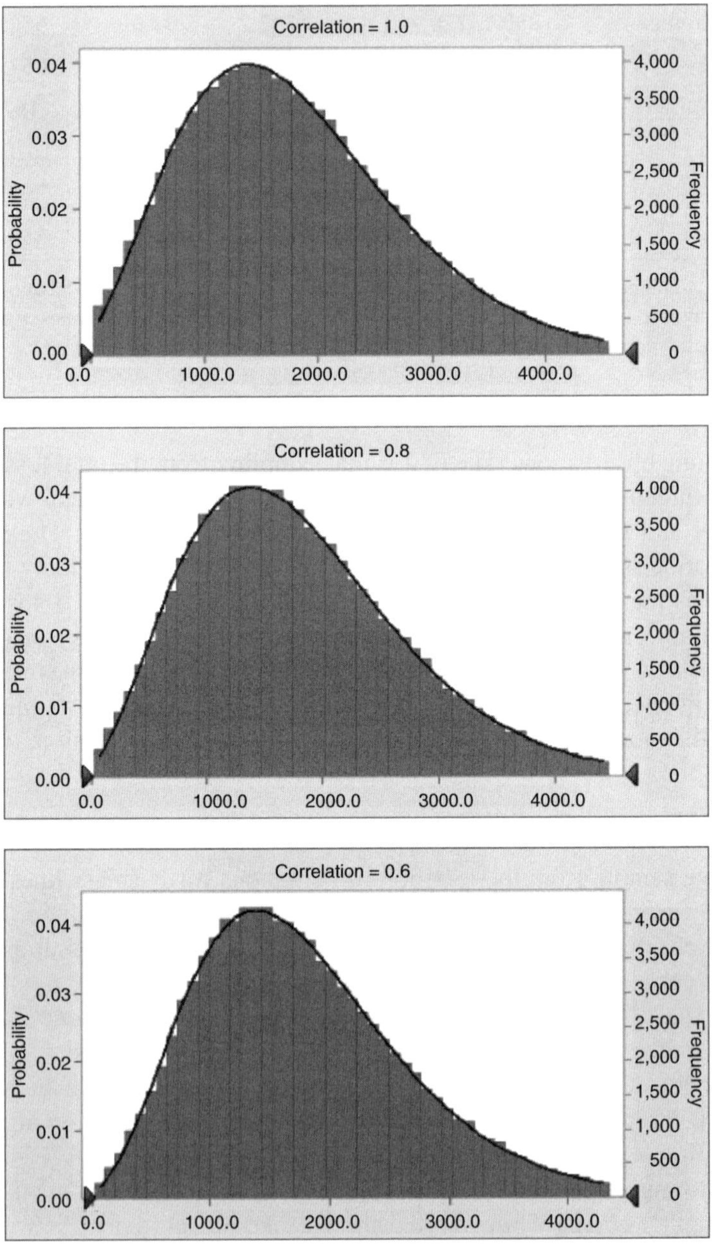

Figure 6.13 The Effect of Correlation on the Firm-wide Capital Charge

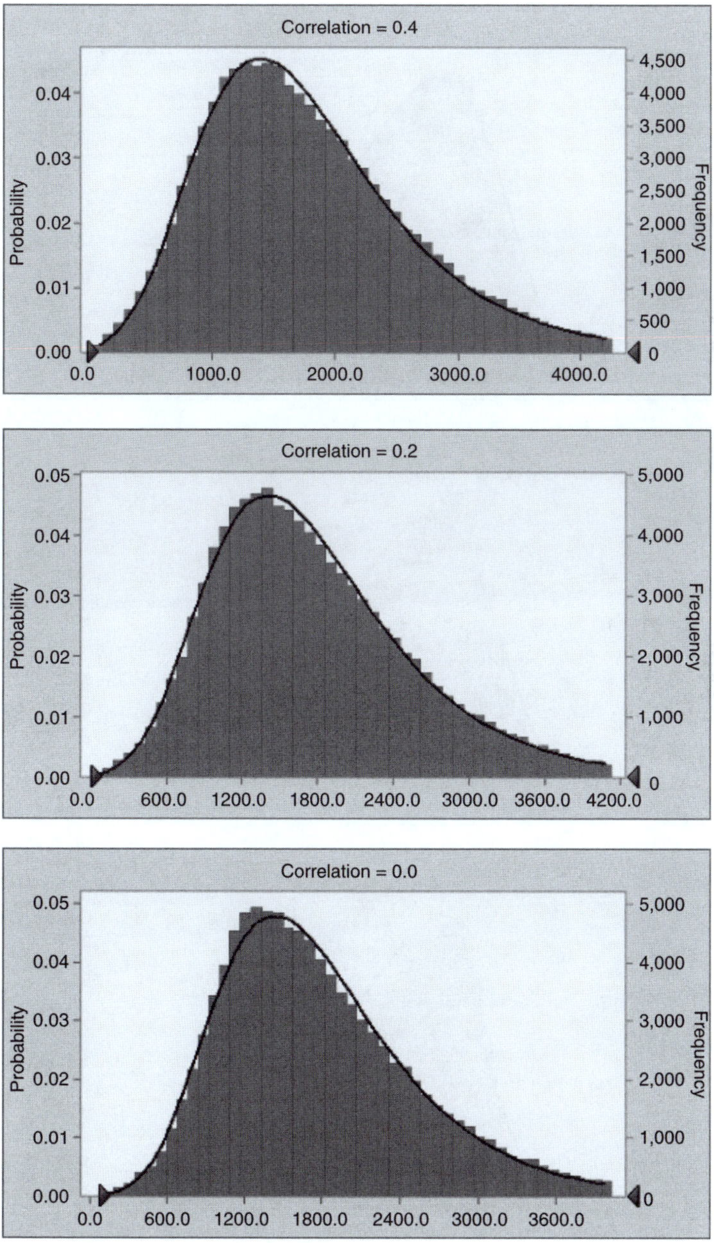

Figure 6.13 Continued

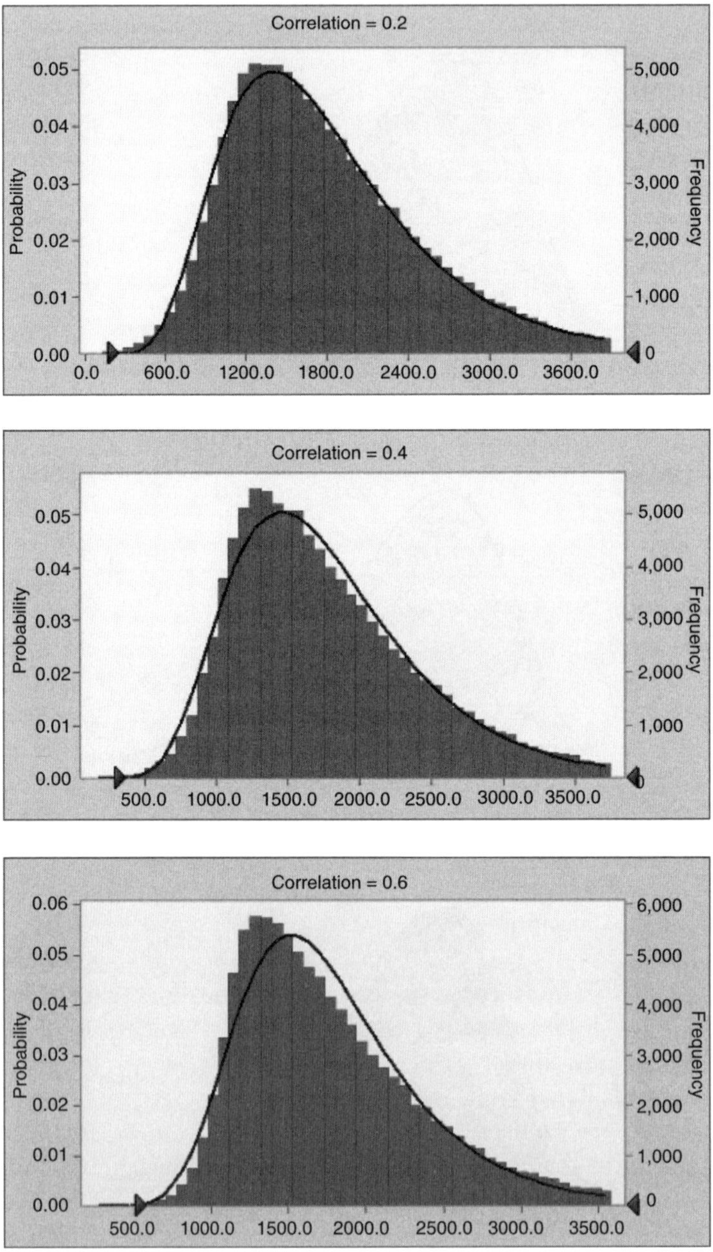

Figure 6.13 Continued

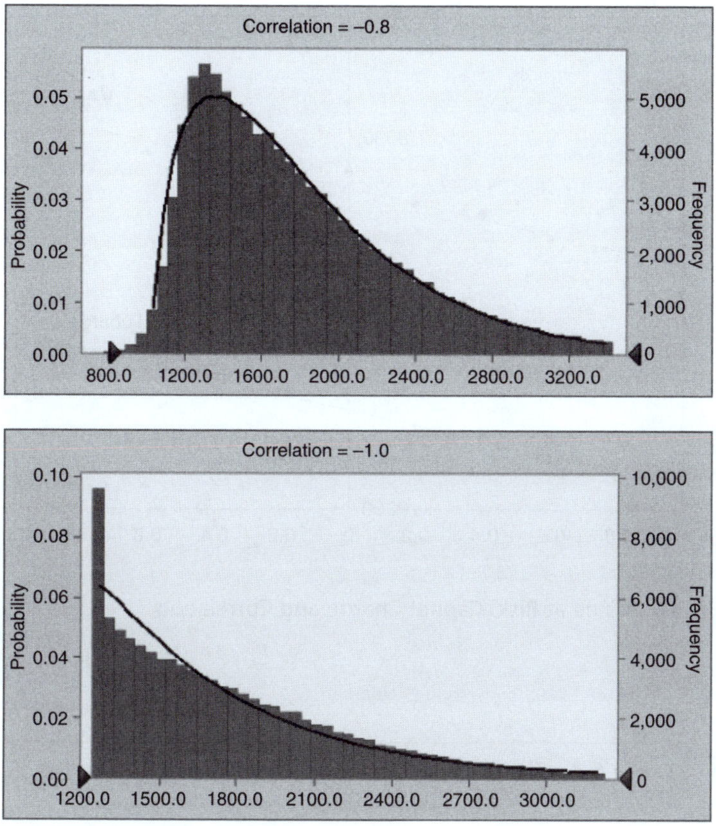

Figure 6.13 Continued

and negative correlations, the distribution is beta or gamma; for medium to low positive correlations, it is maximum extreme; and for medium negative correlations, it is lognormal. We can also see that the capital charge ranges between 4406.2 under perfect positive correlation and 3145.3 under perfect negative correlation. The last column shows the reduction in the capital charge (relative to the case of perfect positive correlation) as the correlation coefficient assumes lower values. Figure 6.14 shows remarkable linear fit between the calculated VAR and capital charge, on one hand, and the correlation coefficient, on the other.

It is noteworthy that the capital charges under perfect positive correlation and zero correlation reported in Table 6.4 are different from what was stated previously, because the results are based on different Monte Carlo simulation exercises. What is important is that the results show that the objective of reducing the capital charge can be achieved by making an "appropriate" choice of correlation between the losses incurred in different business lines. In the absence of good quality historical data, this choice will be subjective.

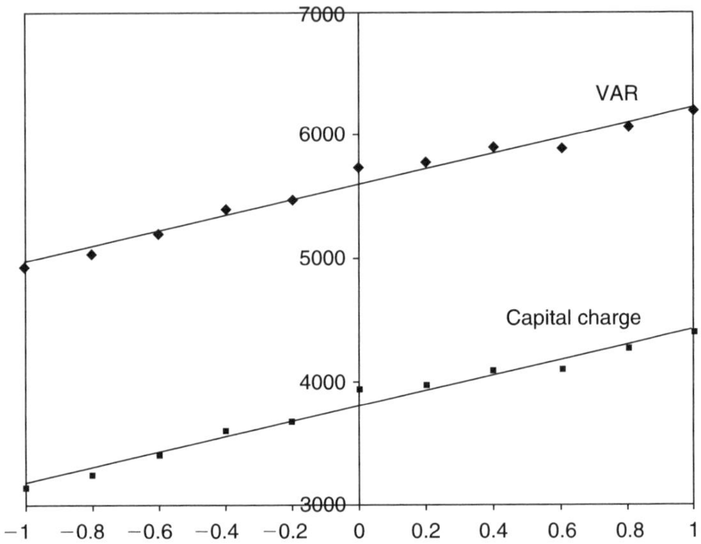

Figure 6.14 Value at Risk, Capital Charge and Correlation

Table 6.4 The Effect of the Correlation Assumption on the Firm-wide Capital Charge

Correlation	*Distribution*	*VAR*	*Mean*	*Capital Charge*	*Reduction* (%)*
1.0	Beta	6198.9	1792.7	4406.2	
0.8	Beta	6081.3	1802.0	4279.3	2.9
0.6	Gamma	5896.6	1794.4	4102.2	6.9
0.4	Max Extreme	5882.6	1796.3	4086.3	7.3
0.2	Max Extreme	5775.3	1793.6	3981.7	9.6
0.0	Max Extreme	5731.1	1790.1	3941.0	10.6
-0.2	Lognormal	5482.2	1800.8	3681.4	16.5
-0.4	Lognormal	5393.9	1797.1	3596.8	18.4
-0.6	Max Extreme	5202.1	1784.4	3417.7	22.4
-0.8	Beta	5044.0	1799.9	3244.1	26.4
-1.0	Gamma	4940.2	1794.9	3145.3	28.6

* Relative to the case of perfect positive correlation.

6.7 CONCLUSION

In Chapter 4, the proposition that the AMA would produce lower capital charges as compared with the STA and BIA was disputed, as it was argued that only subjective model manipulation would produce lower capital charges. The results presented in this chapter show clearly that taking account of correlation between the losses incurred in different business lines has the effect of reducing the firm-wide capital charge. However, this does not remove subjectivity, particularly in the absence of reliable historical loss data. This is because banks will find it appropriate to assume (depending on "expert opinion") that correlation is low, perhaps negative.

Subjectivity, however, is not only triggered by the sensitivity of the results with respect to correlation. We have seen how the estimates of the capital charge are affected by the choice of the frequency, severity and total loss distributions. We have seen the effect of the choice of sampling from the frequency and severity distributions separately as opposed to sampling from the total loss distribution. We have also seen estimates of the capital charge for individual business lines and for the firm as a whole falling within a wide range. The temptation of picking the model that gives the lowest capital charge is irresistible. And then there is no reason to believe that any of these figures will be lower, or more reliable, than those produced by the BIA and STA.

Finally, a word about the technique of Monte Carlo simulation. This is a great intellectual exercise that can be extremely useful when experimental data are available. It is extremely useful for the study of the aerodynamics of planes in a wind tunnel, as the experiments can be repeated to collect data. It is quite useful in other areas of research in physics, as long as controlled experiments can be conducted repeatedly. It is also useful in the insurance business because of the availability of a large amount of high-quality data on insurance claims. It is even useful in the area of option pricing. But the application of this technique to the estimation of the capital charge against operational risk is not such a good idea, and the exercise is not worthwhile in terms of costs and benefits. Actually, it invariably leads to misleading results. The use of EVT, copulas, POT, etc. provides no salvation for the LDA and will not change this conclusion. In this respect, the quants cannot pull rabbits out of hats, so to speak.

APPENDIX 6.1: DISCRETE FREQUENCY DISTRIBUTIONS

<table>
<tr><th>Distribution</th><th>Description</th><th>Shape</th></tr>
<tr><td>Binomial</td><td>The distribution (defined by probability and trial) is used to describe the number of times an event occurs in a fixed number of trials.</td><td>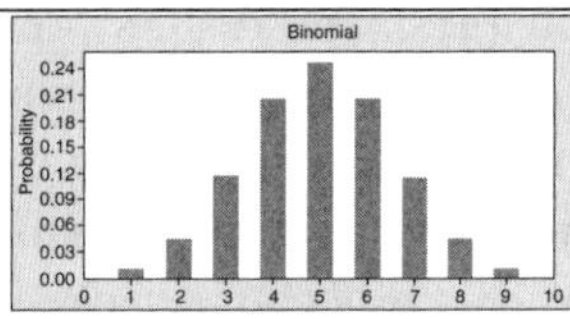
</td></tr>
<tr><td>Discrete Uniform</td><td>Used to generate integer values between a minimum and maximum that are equally likely to occur.</td><td>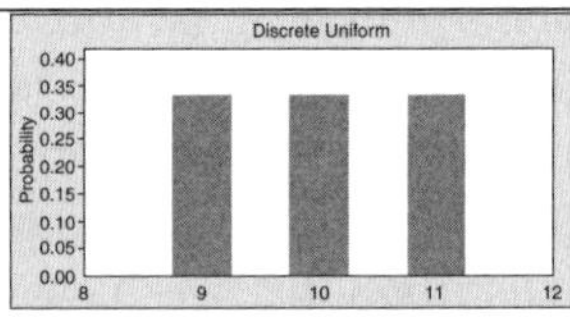
</td></tr>
<tr><td>Geometric</td><td>The distribution is used to describe the number of trials until the first successful occurrence. The probability of success is fixed.</td><td>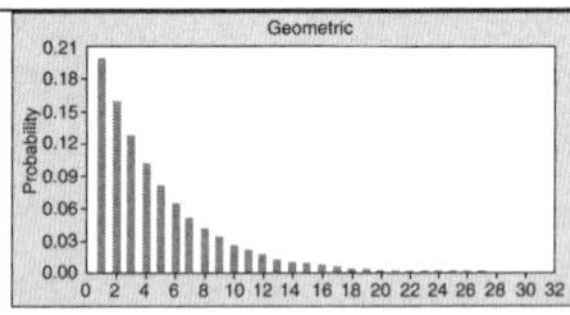
</td></tr>
<tr><td>Hypergeometric</td><td>Similar to the binomial distribution, except that trials are not independent. It is defined by success, trails and population.</td><td>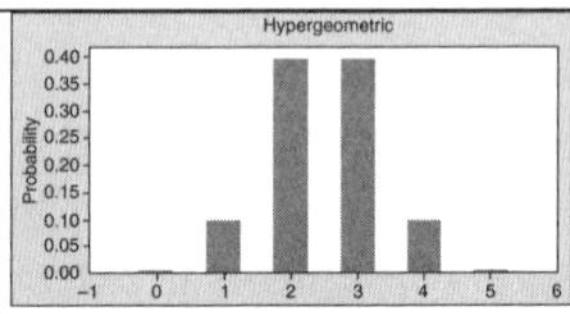
</td></tr>
<tr><td>Negative Binomial</td><td>The distribution of the number of trials until the nth successful occurring. It is defined by probability and shape.</td><td>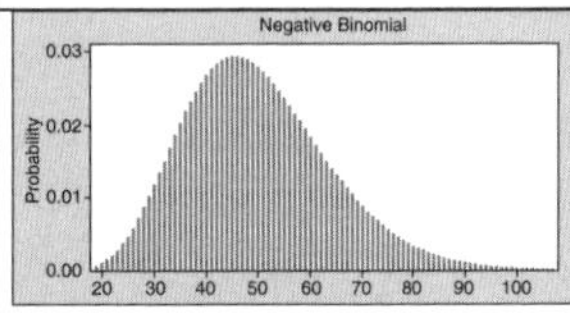
</td></tr>
<tr><td>Poisson</td><td>The distribution is defined by one parameter: rate. It describes the number of times an event occurs in a given time period.</td><td>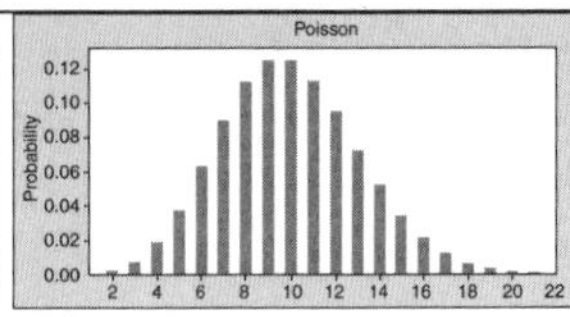
</td></tr>
</table>

APPENDIX 6.2: CONTINUOUS SEVERITY DISTRIBUTIONS

Distribution	Description	Shape
Beta	The random variable falls between a minimum and maximum values. The distribution is defined by four parameters: minimum, maximum, alpha and beta.	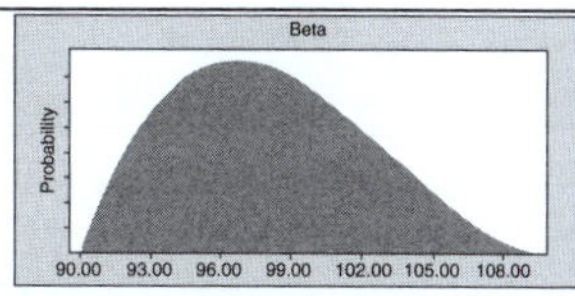
Exponential	The distribution is defined by one parameter: rate. It is primarily used to describe events recurring at random points in time	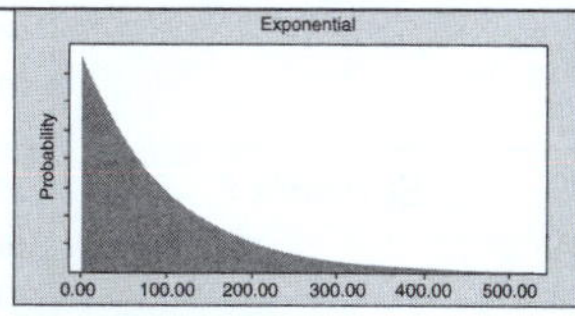
Gamma	The distribution is defined by three parameters: location, scale and shape. By adjusting the parameters, Erlang and chi-square distributions can be obtained.	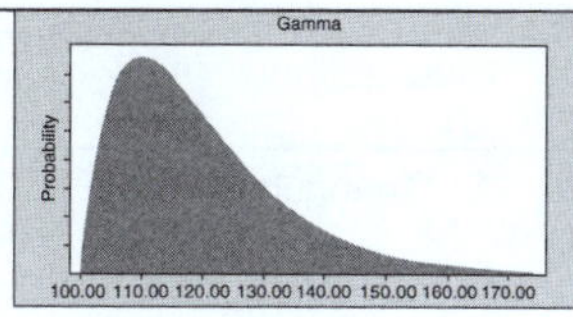
Logistic	The distribution is defined by two parameters: mean and scale. The scale is related to the variance.	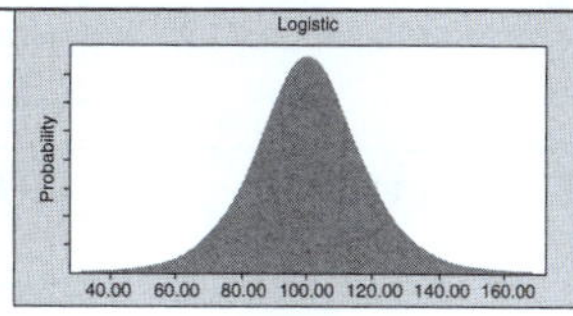
Lognormal	It is used to represent a random variable that can increase without limit but cannot fall below zero. It is defined by the mean and standard deviation.	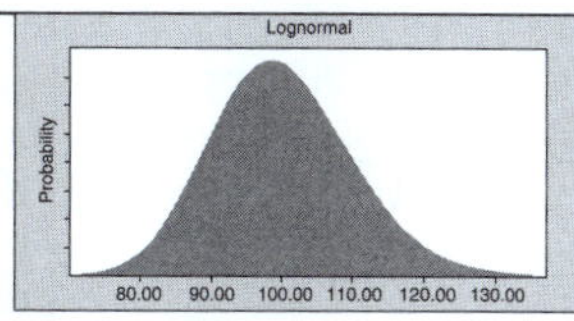
Maximum Extreme	The distribution is defined by two parameters: likeliest and scale. The likeliest is the highest point on the distribution. The scale is related to the variance.	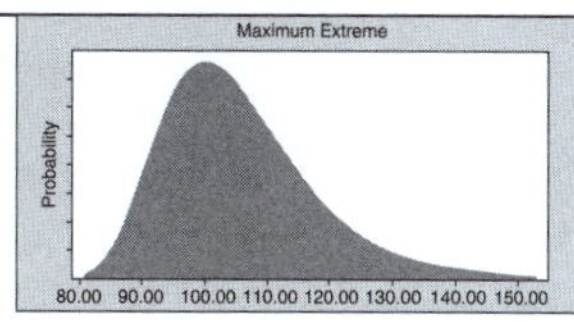
Minimum Extreme	Similar to the maximum extreme distribution, except that it is used to describe the smallest value of a response over a period of time.	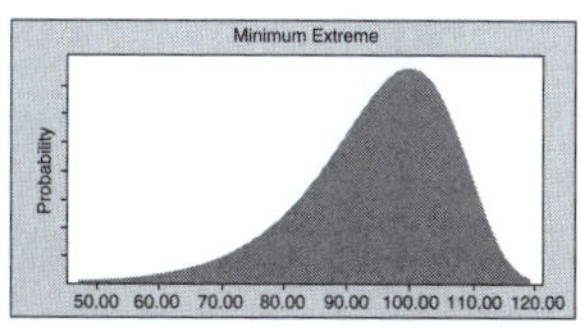

Distribution	Description	Shape
Normal	The normal distribution is symmetrical around the mean, which is the most likely value. It is defined precisely by the mean and standard deviation.	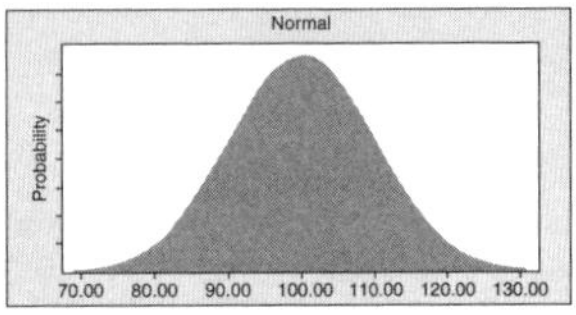
Pareto	The distribution is defined by two parameters: location (lower bound) and shape, which is related to the mean and location.	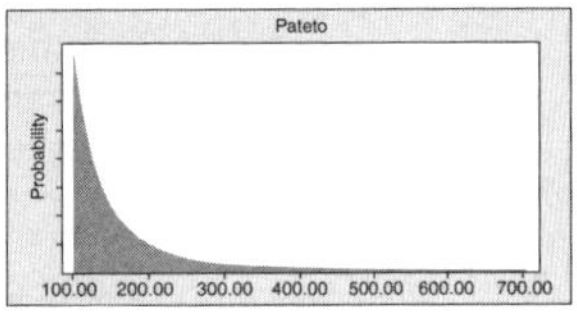
Student's t	A symmetrical distribution defined by the midpoint, scale (width) and degrees of freedom (shape).	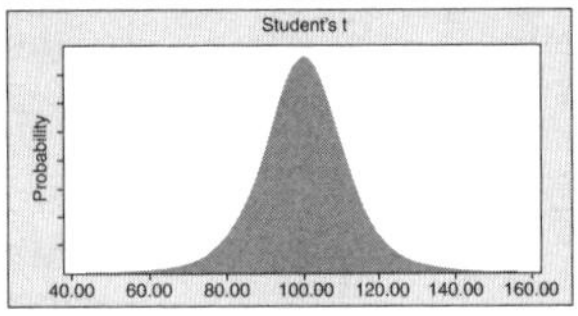
Triangular	Three parameters define the distribution: minimum, likeliest and maximum. The minimum and maximum values are fixed.	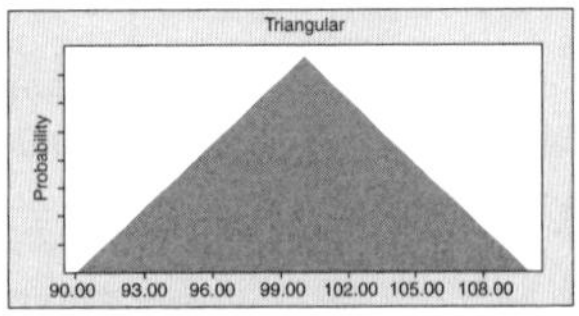
Uniform	Minimum and maximum values are fixed. All values between the minimum and maximum occur with equal likelihood.	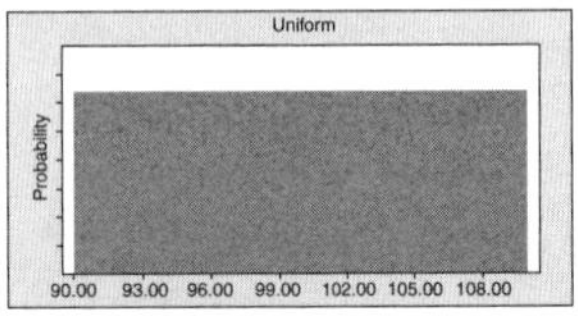
Weibull	A family of distributions that can assume other distributions such as the Rayleigh distribution. It is defined by location, scale and shape.	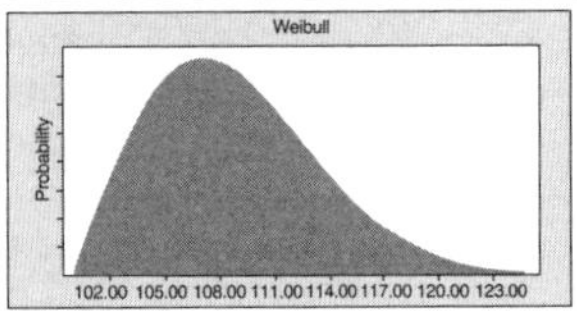

CHAPTER 7

Operational Risk: Where Do we Stand?

7.1 RECAPITULATION

In the previous six chapters of this book we dealt with issues of controversial nature using both expository (positive) and critical (normative) approaches. The discussion has led to the emergence of highly plausible propositions, at least as far as the present author is concerned. To start with, it seems that there is no universal agreement on how to measure risk in general: some risks are either unquantifiable or difficult to quantify, particularly some types of operational risk. Furthermore, many propositions have been put forward implying the near-impossibility of measuring the risks arising from infrequent events. This is the basis of distinguishing between financial and non-financial risk. Of particular importance to the measurement of operational risk is that measurement in terms of frequency and severity is inadequate for the purpose of assessing the continuity of business operations. While capital may protect a firm from insolvency, it is no guarantee that the firm will recover and resume normal operations following the onslaught of a major loss event.

There is also no agreement on the classification of risk. Of particular importance in this respect is the issue of whether or not reputational risk and business risk can be classified as operational risks. The official Basel definition of operational risk implies that they are not, which means that the capital charge against operational risk (designed to protect the firm from insolvency in the face of operational loss events) does not cover reputational and business risks. This does not make sense. In the PricewaterhouseCoopers and Economic Intelligence Unit (2004) survey, most respondents declared that reputational risk was the greatest potential threat to the market value of the firm. Furthermore, operational losses produce reputational losses (the difference between the fall in the market value of a firm and the operational loss can be taken to be the reputational loss). If we firmly believe that holding capital protects a firm from insolvency, then the capital requirements should cover reputational and business risks.

Several reasons can be suggested to justify the proposition that banks are special, but this does not mean that only banks are exposed to operational risk, or that only bank failure can bring down the financial system (recall the impact of the failure of LTCM in 1998 and, more recently, the collapse of Bear Stearns, which is not a bank in the traditional sense). Because banks are special, some sort of regulation is required, but there is no agreement on that either. There is no agreement on how banks should be regulated and how much regulation should be put in place. The view put forward by this author is that some sort of regulation is required but regulation should be directed at the conduct of business, to protect customers from unfair practices. And while it is often claimed (justifiably) that deposit insurance creates moral hazard and adverse selection, it is argued here that regulatory capital is similar in this respect. Banks will always operate under conditions that are conducive to moral hazard and adverse selection (even without deposit insurance and regulatory capital) because they use other people's money in ventures offering positive risk-return trade-off.

What is not clear is the reason for/benefit of imposing regulatory capital requirements in the presence of a deposit insurance scheme. One problem with the regulation of risk in particular is that regulators do not take into account the fact that risk creates value. Corporate survival is not about compliance with regulatory capital requirements but about sustainable profitability. It is also strange that while it is argued that a capital cushion is required to protect a bank from insolvency, little attention is paid to liquidity risk (Basel II has no provisions to deal with liquidity risk such as the imposition of upper limits on the funding gap). There is no point of having a capital cushion if a bank cannot resume business as usual after enduring a loss event.

It is not clear to this author why the holding of capital has become a regulatory issue. It is a sound practice for banks to hold adequate and well-structured capital, but this is not a matter for the regulators to preach. After all, capital is (and should be) endogenous. Banks and other firms have been dealing with the issue of determining the level and structure of capital for ages, yet we have had more corporate financial mishaps since the introduction of capital regulation in Basel I. What regulators could do is to let banks determine the level and structure of capital, then monitor their leverage ratios and funding gaps. Recall that research has revealed substantial evidence for a negative relation between leverage ratios and bank insolvency, but not between risk-based capital ratios and bank insolvency. Then banks should be left to determine their risk management practices, monitoring crucial metrics (KRDs, KRIs, KCIs, KTIs, etc.), and imposing the necessary controls.

In Chapter 2, several problems with the Basel Committee and its Accords were identified. The Committee has a biased and unrepresentative composition (in terms of member countries), its accountability is unclear, and it is far away from being viable in terms of costs and benefits. Basel I arguably lacked sensitivity towards risk, creating incentives for regulatory capital arbitrage and failed to consider risk mitigation and risk correlation. More important, however, is the fact that it ignored the risk management process. Basel I was a crude prescription for credit loss (not risk) management. But wait a minute, Basel II is no where close to being a great leap forward compared to Basel I.

Basel II has been subjected to more scrutiny than its predecessor (and justifiably so). While it is argued by the Basel II enthusiasts that the Accord has led banks to invest in risk management, the sceptics would argue that this is no good if it is done for the purpose of compliance and that banks strive to improve their risk management systems with and without the Basel Committee. The objectives of Basel II have been identified as follows: (i) promoting safety and soundness of the financial system; (ii) enhancing competitive equality; (iii) establishing a more comprehensive approach to risk; and (iv) equating economic capital with regulatory capital. But all of these objectives are questionable because of the following: (i) risk-based capital regulation seems to lead to more risk-taking; (ii) competitive equality will be eroded by allowing big banks to hold proportionately lower capital charges by manipulating their internal models; (iii) it is not entirely clear what "a comprehensive approach" means, but it probably refers to the consideration of operational risk that was overlooked by Basel I; and (iv) equating regulatory capital with economic capital is not such a good idea.

Basel II can be criticised for several reasons, including the following:

- Reliance on rating agencies, which sounds ludicrous following the role played by these agencies in the subprime crisis.
- Too much standardisation (e.g., the classification of business lines and the application of the same rules in developed and developing countries).
- Regulators typically do not have the expertise to evaluate internal models. High-flying quants would rather work for banks as model developers than for regulatory bodies as model evaluators (the private sector–public sector salary differential is one reason for that).
- Evaluating and approving models amounts to regulatory capture, as regulators are pushed to believe that they would be responsible for bank failure if it materialises. Involvement of the regulators in bank management is not a good idea.

- It is up to the local regulator (not to the BCBS) how the Accord is implemented, hence different standards will be implemented and observed in different countries (Where is the level playing field, then?).
- It intensifies the procyclicality of banking, thus exacerbating the business cycle.
- It ignores non-bank financial intermediaries, hence making banks less competitive in this era of universal banking (so much for the objective of enhancing competitive equality).
- Capital regulation involving "sophisticated" approaches to risk modelling creates a sense of complacency (the attitude of "we know the risk and we are ready for it because we have a powerful model").
- It brings with it the risk of non-compliance, which is one more thing to worry about, let alone the unnecessary diversion of resources for this purpose.
- It is unnecessarily complex, perhaps just to give the impression that it is a great leap forward from Basel I. Documentation of the rules go into hundreds of pages, the reading of which (let alone understanding and implementation) takes a fair bit of time that can be spent doing better things.
- There is a problem of interface between the Basel rules and domestic legislation. It is still not clear whether or not the Basel rules require domestic parliamentary approval.
- Pillars 1 and 2 are at odds with each other. Pillar 2 gives the impression that capital adequacy standards as prescribed by Pillar 1 are deficient.
- The Accord is not viable in terms of costs and benefits, carries the seeds of its own destruction and it is a superficial change on Basel I.
- The BIA does not necessarily produce a higher capital charge than the STA. So, what is the incentive for moving from the BIA to the STA?

In Chapter 3, we examined the definition and classification of operational risk. While there is no common practical definition, this should not hinder attempts to manage it. What is more important than finding a precise definition is pinpointing the risk categories that fall under operational risk, which could be specific to each firm. The problem with the Basel definition is that it excludes reputational risk and business risk, as well as indirect losses. This means that the capital charge will not cover these items, but it is exactly these items that can wipe out a firm. Losses are losses whether they are direct or indirect. A definition (which may be arbitrary) should not be the basis for dictating what to include and what to exclude from a "package" designed to protect a firm from insolvency.

In Chapter 3 we also considered the distinguishing features of operational risk, including its diversity and the difficulty of measuring, managing and regulating it. There are other distinguishing features of operational risk, including the difficulty of defining a suitable unit of risk: it is not limited to operations (which casts doubt on the validity of the BCBS's classification of business lines); the concept of exposure is not clear; and operational risk pertains mainly to tail (rare) events. But there seems to be a number of misconceptions about operational risk, which are more of a source of concern than the actual definition. One misconception is that there is no risk-return trade-off when operational risk is encountered, which begs the question why financial institutions do not eliminate the risk of unauthorised trading by firing all of the traders, just in case a *gini* like Nick Leeson or Jerome Kerviel jumps out of a bottle. The other misconception is that operational risk is idiosyncratic, which begs the question why the Basel Committee was established in the first place following the collapse of Bankhaus Herstatt and why operational risk should be regulated. Another myth about operational risk is that it is transferable via insurance. Taking insurance does not eliminate exposure to operational risk, as it merely provides financial compensation should a loss event materialises. Therefore, insurance represents risk financing, not risk transfer.

Chapter 4 dealt with the measurement of operational risk, concluding that mathematical sophistication is not necessarily a conduit to better risk management and that it could be a source of complacency. Measurement and management are two different things, and the argument that (accurate) measurement is a prerequisite for (sound) management is not at all convincing. Strong arguments were presented to explain why the AMA is a futile exercise. First of all, no-one seems to know what constitutes the AMA: is it the LDA or "let a thousand flowers bloom"? Nothing seems to be advanced about the SCA and SBA, which are rather subjective. The "let a thousand flowers bloom" doctrine puts a lot of burden on the regulators, a burden that they cannot bear, which the BCBS admits in its observed range of practices paper (BCBS, 2006b). Then there are the problems of implementing the AMA. The models can be flawed, even disastrous by the admission of some quants who are making a living out of it. VAR is problematical and the 99.9th percentile is a delusional and unrealistic level of precision that may lead to complacency. There is also the correlation problem and the data problem that cannot be solved by resorting to external data. The AMA is simply not viable in terms of costs and benefits. The conclusion derived from Chapter 4 was that the only way the AMA produces lower capital charges (which is discriminatory against small and "unsophisticated" banks) is subjective model manipulation. Furthermore, the exercise is so expensive that banks are bound to pass the cost on to their customers, which is a blatant transfer of income (in a reverse Robin Hood way) from customers to the consultants advising banks on the AMA (recall the millennium bug fiasco).

Chapters 5 and 6 provided support for the proposition that subjective model manipulation can and will be used to obtain lower capital charges. The survey of theoretical and empirical studies of operational risk presented in Chapter 5 showed that estimated capital charges are rather sensitive to the methodology and the underlying assumptions. In Chapter 6, Monte Carlo simulation was applied to a set of hypothetical data covering two business lines of a hypothetical firm. It was shown that the estimated capital charge for the whole firm varies considerably, falling within a very wide range. The estimates depend on the following: (i) the assumptions made with respect to the choice of frequency and severity distributions; (ii) whether sampling is carried out from separate distributions (for frequency and severity) or directly from the total loss distribution; and (iii) the assumptions made about correlation between losses in the two business lines. All in all, it seems that the *sataus quo* is very unsatisfactory indeed.

7.2 THE SUBPRIME CRISIS AS AN OPERATIONAL LOSS EVENT

In this section, we examine the subprime crisis as it provides good lessons for banks, bank customers and regulators. The main argument put forward in this section is that the subprime crisis represents a series of operational (as opposed to credit and/or market) loss events.

Origin of the Crisis

The subprime crisis started to surface in June 2007 to become a household name. It is the product of default on mortgage loans extended by US financial institutions to borrowers with questionable creditworthiness and the consequent decline in the prices of mortgage-backed securities (MBS) as they were downgraded by the rating agencies. The contagious effect of the crisis has hit financial institutions in Europe and Australasia, damaging the health of a significant number of those institutions and reducing the ability of others to run their business properly. Some institutions were so severely affected that they filed for bankruptcy.

The crisis is typically viewed as a credit crisis, implying that the losses incurred by financial institutions are credit-related losses, which means that the crisis represents a credit loss event (or a series of events, to be more precise). This sounds plausible, as the crisis started with the default of a large number of mortgage borrowers, which is a credit loss event resulting from exposure to credit risk. There are, however, several examples of loss events that are mistaken for one another, particularly those involving simultaneous exposure to market risk, credit risk and operational risk, which are the three kinds of risk covered by the Basel II Accord. Mistaking an operational loss event for a market or credit loss event, or vice versa, is invariably the result of failure to distinguish between the cause of the event and the factor driving the severity of the loss. It is sometimes suggested that loss events resulting from exposure to more than one kind of risk may be viewed as "hybrid" loss events. However, whether a loss event is to be classified as an operational loss event or otherwise is (or should be) determined by the causes rather than the consequences of the event.

The Barings case may be portrayed as a market loss event in the sense that the market moved against the positions taken by Nick Leeson, which caused the losses. However, what Barings Bank experienced in 1995 was an operational loss event because the causes were rogue trading (which is a form of internal fraud) and management incompetence. Both these factors are classified under the heading "failure of people," which results from incompetence (weak management at Barings) and malice (rogue trading and hiding losses by Nick Leeson). The Barings case is a classic operational loss event in which the severity of the loss was driven by adverse market movements. On the other hand, the subprime crisis provides the perfect example for how an operational loss event may be viewed as a credit loss event. Default on a loan given to a customer who is not worthy of a loan (for incompetence or sinister motives on the part of the loan officer approving the loan) is an operational loss event caused by the failure of people and processes. It is not a credit loss event.

Causes and Consequences

The subprime crisis can be attributed to several factors, including lax monetary policy (hence, low interest rates) for a long time, lacking or improper regulation, reckless lending by US financial institutions to dodgy borrowers, and excessive securitisation that has resulted in the emergence of unnecessarily complex debt securities. Globalisation contributed to the contagious effect of the crisis as it spread across the Atlantic and Pacific. The very diversity of the factors giving rise to the subprime crisis is tantamount to the crisis being an operational loss event.

Subprime loans, as opposed to prime loans, are also called B loans and second-chance loans. They are granted to borrowers who do not qualify for loans at the market interest rate because they have poor credit records. Since subprime loans are risky, the borrowers are typically charged an interest rate of two percentage points higher than what is paid by regular (prime) borrowers. The high interest rate charged to subprime borrowers boosts the probability of default, hence the process constitutes a vicious circle. On the other hand, the subprime market was seen by subprime lenders as a niche market. During the period 2004–2006, 21% of mortgage applications were from subprime borrowers compared to 9% during the period 1996–2004. By March 2007 the value of subprime mortgages was estimated at $1.3 trillion, which is bigger than the gross domestic product (GDP) of most countries. The spectacular growth of subprime lending in recent times could not have happened without the fact that financial institutions have become increasingly complacent about the credit risk of subprime borrowers. This complacency can be attributed to two factors: the moral hazard created by government intervention on previous occasions and the change in the nature of the mortgage granting process, particularly the introduction of risk transfer through securitisation.

Moral hazard on the part of the subprime lenders and other financial institutions is typically instigated by government intervention to rescue troubled financial institutions even though the trouble was due to incompetence and greed on the part of those institutions. In the 1980s, the US government instituted a taxpayer-funded bailout related to mortgages during the savings and loans crisis. And in 1998, the Federal Reserve Bank of New York was heavily involved in the rescue of the ill-fated Long-Term Capital Management (LTCM), on the grounds that the failure of LTCM could have caused systemic failure. The problem with government intervention to rescue failed institutions is that it signals the government's willingness to come to the rescue whenever financial institutions are in trouble.

It is this "big brother" factor that has given the impression of attractive risk-return trade-off in subprime lending. The problem is that even in the aftermath of the crisis, the Bank of England and the Federal Reserve System were involved actively in the salvage operations of Northern Rock and Bear Stearns, respectively. The action of the two central banks has been justified on the grounds that the alternative could have been a systemic failure, but not everyone is convinced of this argument. Spring (2008) argues that the British government committed billions of taxpayers' pounds to rescue what he calls "Northern Wreck" because "the workforce, borrowers and individual investors [of the Rock] are concentrated in the [labour] party's Northeast England heartland."

Complacency has also resulted from changes in the mortgage granting process. At one time, financial institutions were very careful whom they would lend to because they would keep the loans on their books until maturity (at that time, finance was essentially based on the principle of "originate and hold"). Under that process, banks and other mortgage originators would do their own homework to assess home valuation and check the borrower's income and creditworthiness. Securitisation has since been used to transform mortgages, credit card receivables and similar income streams to rather complex marketable securities, including the structured products created by pooling loans through credit scoring. Structured products were created typically by adding subprime and similar high-risk credits to investment packages consisting mainly of low-risk assets, such as the bonds of semi-government agencies, to enhance their yield. This is what Spring (2008) correctly describes as "injecting deadly viruses into otherwise-healthy bodies."

The process involves other players, including mortgage brokers, home appraisers and rating agencies. Financial institutions used this process to manage their balance sheets and boost profitability because selling securitised loans frees up capital for new business. Covering exposure to the risk of default through securitisation made these institutions more willing to indulge in reckless lending. The problem is that most of these institutions held mortgage-backed securities through structured investment vehicles (SIVs) or lent money to investors trading these securities. By eliminating or reducing exposure to credit risk, they got exposed to the market risk of falling security prices.

The subprime crisis was triggered by the decline in house prices, as the housing bubble (which was supported by low interest rates) burst. A vicious circle ensued as the drop in house prices led to increasing mortgage defaults and further drops in house prices. Because of the intricate link between home loans and the mortgage-based securities market, the prices of securities started to decline, particularly as the rating agencies downgraded these securities, having granted them undeservedly high ratings initially. In 2007 many banks, mortgage lenders, real estate investment trusts and hedge funds started to declare losses. By the end of 2007, subprime losses were estimated to be in excess of $80 billion. Between April and November 2007, a number of financial institutions applied for bankruptcy, including New Century Financial Corporation, Ameriquest (both subprime lenders) as well as Sentinel Management Group (investment fund) and Terra Securities. A large number of institutions suffered losses from asset write-downs, including Merrill Lynch and Citigroup whose CEOs were forced to resign their positions. Things went from bad to worse in 2008 when the Federal Reserve System (using taxpayers money) helped JP Morgan acquire Bear Stearns, one of the earliest victims of the crisis (see, e.g., The Economist, 2008b). Losses from asset write-downs kept on piling, forcing major financial institutions to indulge in massive redundancy plans.

In general, the crisis has hit individual home owners who have lost their homes (hundreds of thousands of them), as well as financial institutions that incurred losses either directly from default or indirectly through asset write-downs and liquidity shortage. Another source of loss has been (and will be for some time) lawsuits, which constitute operational losses resulting from exposure to legal risk. Investors are suing not only mortgage lenders and institutions that promoted mortgage-backed securities, but also insurance companies, bond funds, rating agencies and home builders. The Economist (2007) suggests that the cost of the subprime crisis in terms of settlement, awards and legal fees "will climb well above the billions stemming from the internet bubble."

The Failure of People

The failure of people, as a causing factor of the subprime crisis, encompasses borrowers and those running financial institutions, subprime lenders and otherwise, who seem to have been under the influence of group think. Encouraged by the belief that house prices will keep on rising, subprime borrowers took on mortgage deals without realising the type of risk involved in those deals. The naivety of borrowers, coupled with external factors, led to the loss of their homes. It is arguable that borrowers were subject to external fraud as unscrupulous brokers convinced them that little risk was involved in the deals they were offered.

There are many facets to the failure of people in financial institutions. It is ironic that most of those institutions believed that securitisation would shelter them from credit risk at a time when they were exposing themselves to the risk of falling prices of mortgage-backed securities. Subprime lending itself was motivated by greed and supported by the moral hazard created by government intervention on previous occasions. An element of operational risk was the provision of inappropriate mortgage incentives, such as the interest-only adjustable rate mortgage. This can be classified under the Basel Committee's loss event of client, products and business practices.

The tendency for excessive exposure to mortgage-backed securities involved an error of judgment. Take, for example, Stanley O'Neal, the very person who took Merrill Lynch to the structured products market. When he was the boss, he encouraged the acquisition of the so-called "super senior" collateralised debt obligations (CDOs). But when it turned out that there was nothing "super" or "senior" about CDOs, he sacked a senior executive who was going to be a whistle blower. It is very likely that O'Neal himself did not fully understand the risk embodied in these securities. This makes sense because not everyone can claim to understand and comprehend the principles of "financial engineering." Bhusnurmath (2007) argues that sophisticated hedge funds and investment banks may not know better than the average buyer when it comes to the risk of complex securities. He cites the CEO of American Express who in 2001 admitted that his company did not comprehend the risk when it lost $826 million on CDOs. This case shows elements of people risk (disclosure-related issues) as well as losses and potential losses that can be classified under clients, products and business practices (CPBP).

The failure of people can also be seen in the case of Northern Rock, a British bank that was doing extremely well up to September 2007. On 13 September, Northern Rock asked the Bank of England (as a lender of last resort that did not know anything about what was going on inside the Rock) for emergency funds due to problems in raising funds in the money market as a result of the subprime crisis. The bank was neither a subprime lender nor insolvent, yet it suffered a run by its depositors. Reliance on other banks and capital markets for three quarters of its funding created too wide a gap between loans and deposits. This extreme financing model was not adopted by other banks, and this is why they did not have to face the horror of a bank run. The Northern Rock case exhibits several elements of operational risk factors, including not only liquidity risk, but also the absence of adequate risk management systems for the funding strategy and model bias in the risk management process. Similar risk factors had previously led to the demise of several hedge funds, including LTCM.

The Failure of Processes

Securitisation started in the late 1970s as the tendency to raise capital via marketable securities rather than bank loans. The process has produced several benefits, starting with lower borrowing costs. The securitisation of loans made them subject to market valuation, which encouraged the efficient use of capital. Also, the broad distribution of credit risk brought about by securitisation reduces the risk of any one holder going bust. This common view is debatable because spreading risk means that it may be taken by parties that are least able to comprehend it or withstand losses, should they materialise. Finally, securitisation has made the system safer because risk ends up with those who want to be exposed to it.

Consider now the problems that securitisation has brought with it. The first of these problems is the unnecessary complexity of products, which makes their valuation rather difficult and induces investor confusion about the underlying risk. The complexity of financial assets is typically considered a reason for increased exposure to operational risk and the actual realisation of operational losses. Second is the problem of fragmentation of responsibility. Securitisation has spread risk across the system to the extent that it has become impossible to track, making it difficult for investors to tell who has what exposure. Although securitisation is hailed as a conduit to disintermediation, it effectively replaces one middleman with several, which creates the so-called "principle agent problem." One consequence of this state of affairs is that the loan originator has little incentive to vet borrowers carefully because risk will be off its books.

It is undeniable that securitisation has been a revolution that brought up significant gains for borrowers, lenders and the economy at large, but it has also brought with it costs that are only now becoming clear, perhaps because it has been taken too far (securitising anything under the sun). This is not to say that securitisation should be uninvented, but that its costs and benefits must be balanced more carefully. The process failed because this balance was overlooked or, as Bhusnurmath (2007) puts it, "on paper, a brilliant piece of financial engineering – securitisation – in reality, a failure to realise its limits."

The Role of External Factors

External sources of operational risk lie in the actions of external parties (external to those exposed to risk), including the behaviour of competitors, external fraud and regulatory changes, as well as macroeconomic and socio-economic changes. Several external factors have contributed to the emergence of the crisis, including the fall in house prices, excessive globalisation and the roles played by policy makers, regulators, brokers, appraisers and rating agencies.

The crisis was triggered by the fall of US house prices (which represents a change in the economic environment). One reason for the housing bubble was the Fed's policy of cheap money that was in place for a long time, resulting in low interest rates. A common, but inappropriate, practice for central banks is to worry about growth and commodity price inflation but not about asset price inflation. The cheap money policy provided an incentive for financial institutions to indulge in subprime lending and for borrowers to seek funds excessively.

Excessive globalisation was the reason why the crisis became global so quickly. Bhusnurmath (2007) argues that what saved the Indian economy from the East Asian crisis and the subprime crisis was respectively "our lack of openness" and the fact that "our banking system is less integrated with the global financial system." This does not mean that globalisation should be undone, but rather that it should be handled with care. It seems that we have not learned from the Asian crisis that rushing into capital account convertibility without preparing for it is a hazardous course of action.

Furthermore, there has been lacking or inappropriate regulation, motivated by the rigid market ideology that regulation of the financial system is bad. Some legislation, such as the US Community Reinvestment Act, forces banks to lend to otherwise uncreditworthy consumers. One example of inappropriate regulation is dependence on capital adequacy to regulate banks as required by the Basel Accords, because capital adequacy on its own is not an adequate indicator of bank resilience. While capital adequacy rules are designed to protect banks from insolvency, the main problem in the subprime crisis was illiquidity. It has now become apparent that the UK's Financial Services Authority (FSA) should have done something about Northern Rock's risky funding strategy. Furthermore, the run on Northern Rock has cast doubt on the viability of separating the lender of last resort function (which is the responsibility of the Bank of England) from other supervisory roles (undertaken by the FSA and Treasury).

The role played by the rating agencies can be justifiably described as external fraud, or at best as a conflict of interest. Mortgage-based securities and CDOs were marketed successfully because they offered high yields and also because they were initially rated highly (as a good debt with little risk of default) by the rating agencies such as Standard & Poor's and Moody's. This is certainly a fiasco, because the rating agencies are paid for their services by the issuers (not the buyers) of the securities, which means that it is in their interest and the interest of their clients (the issuers) to rate the assets highly. It is ironic, therefore, that the Basel II Accord has provisions for depending extensively on the ratings provided by the rating agencies, which comprise an oligopolistic unregulated industry.

The role of appraisers and mortgage brokers was equally scandalous. Appraisers used inflated figures to value houses, thus allowing borrowers to obtain much bigger mortgages than what they could afford to repay (biting off more than what they could chew). Mortgage brokers do not lend their money but rather earn commissions, which gives them financial incentives to sell as many big and risky loans as possible. Barr (2007) argues that "hidden fees and other dubious practices have contributed to the surge in delinquencies" and that "problems and abuses are happening because brokers see it as their right to make as much money as they can." On 19 June 2008, it was announced that more than 400 people (including real estate agents) were arrested by the FBI and charged with fraud, including lending fraud, foreclosure rescue scams and mortgage related bankruptcy schemes.

Positive Consequences

Looking at the bright side of the crisis, it has resulted in some changes and initiatives, unfortunately nothing related to Basel II. In the aftermath of the crisis, there has been a tendency to rethink financial regulation and reconsider the role played by the rating agencies.

On 31 March 2008, US Treasury Secretary, Henry Paulson, announced an "ambitious plan" to overhaul the US financial system with the objective of promoting "stable and resilient markets" and "a more competitive financial services industry." Those regulatory changes were designed to enhance the Federal Reserve's supervisory powers over the entire financial industry, including investment banks. Under the plan, the Fed would be empowered to gather appropriate information, disclose information, collaborate with other regulators on rule writing and take corrective actions when necessary to ensure financial market stability. As The Economist (2008c) puts it, "the role, which the Fed rehearsed with its rescue of Bear Stearns, would allow it to hunt anywhere for systemic risk, including among the entangled roots of hedge funds and investment banks." While these proposals may not be implemented because another Treasury Secretary will be in office starting January 2009, they seem to be based on the view that regulatory functions should not be segregated, a point that was discussed in Chapter 1. The handling of the Northern Rock crisis by the FSA and the Bank of England seems to have led to a reconsideration of the segregation of regulatory function. When segregation is taken too far, one regulator will not know what the other regulator does as they compete for "glory." The Economist (2008e) expresses this view by commenting on the effect of the Northern Rock fiasco on the British Prime Minister, Gordon Brown. When he was the Chancellor of the Exchequer, The Economist argues in an editorial, he put in place a "badly designed regulation system, with the result that nobody was really in charge of overseeing the banks when the credit crunch hit."

As far as the rating agencies are concerned, calls have emerged for the need to regulate these agencies, which have been acting as an unregulated oligopolistic industry. In June 2008, The Economist reported that "at least six government or global industry bodies have been examining the rating agencies' role in the crisis" (The Economist, 2008k). It was also reported that the big three (Standard and Poor's, Moody's and Fitch) were on the verge of striking an agreement with the State of New York Attorney General that would prevent them from indulging in "ratings shopping" whereby new issuers play off the agencies against each other to elicit the "most generous" ratings. The agreement would also force the rating agencies to disclose the collateral of the instruments they rate.

The rating agencies have been put under pressure to reinvent themselves. Fitch Ratings started to review the rating methodology it uses on CDOs with the intention of making its standards for rating synthetic CDOs more reflective of the real nature of these products. Kearney (2008) reports some of the changes that Fitch intends on introducing, including the following: (i) re-examining default probabilities and recovery rates; (ii) updating historical default rates; (iii) introducing a simplified and intuitive correlation framework; and (iv) using mechanisms to identify and provide additional protection against poorly selected names and portfolios. Standard & Poor's has also been reported to be "reforming" its credit rating process (*OpRisk & Compliance*, March 2008, p. 7). Moody's divided its business into separate analytics and ratings divisions at the end of 2007 to "reinforce its ratings' independence." All this is fine, but what is more important is that the rating agencies should not be paid for their services by the issuers of the securities, which represents a blatant conflict of interest on their part.

7.3 SOCIETE GENERALE ET AL.

Nick Leeson, John Rusnack and Jerome Kerviel are (notorious) names that appear quite frequently in the literature on operational risk. They are the names of rogue traders who cost the institutions they worked for massive losses that could have been avoided. Motivated by greed, and encouraged by a remuneration scheme that awards bonuses on the basis of profit, these traders indulged in risky trading to maximise their bonuses. In the process they surpassed their trading limits and concealed losses by circumventing inadequate controls. No Basel II provision could have prevented those losses, although the best practices recommended by the Basel Committee could have helped. The problem with those best practices is that they are standardised, when in fact best practices should be specific to each institution.

At Societe Generale, Kerviel used fake hedges and false documents to trigger the biggest trading loss in banking history. He took unauthorised positions on futures linked to European stock markets and stole computer passwords that allowed him to enter his fictitious deals into various trading systems. He managed to circumvent the (not-good-enough) controls through five years of back office work. The fraud was discovered on 19 January 2008, and the positions were quickly unwound, following suspicion of a confirmation e-mail supposedly sent by one of his trading partners on 18 January. Steven Toll, a securities lawyer at Cohen Milstein, is cited by Larson (2008) as saying that "Societe Generale did in fact authorize a culture of risk to flourish," for example, by failure to follow up on seventy-five warnings about Kerviel's trades. According to The Economist (2008a), two big blind spots saved Kerviel from detection, the first of which was the bank's focus on traders' net exposure. By creating a fictitious portfolio of trades that appeared to be balanced, his net exposure stayed within the limit. The second was that margin data from Eurex showed only consolidated positions, which is why the margin calls on Kerveil's positions did not trigger alarms (margins on the consolidated positions looked acceptable for a bank the size of Societe Generale).

Green (2008) argues that cutting-edge technologies might have plugged some loopholes that Kerviel exploited. To deflect a supervisor's question about whether he might be hedging his own trades, Kerviel crafted e-mails detailing order requests from ghost clients. Green believes that Societe Generale did not use the most advanced trading fraud detection technology. The standard risk management technology used by most banks monitors traders' e-mails, searching for keywords that might point to unauthorised activity. Some banks also use software to alert them to changes an employee might make to an e-mail that is then forwarded to others. But advanced software can profile the different actions a trader takes over time, rather than simply flagging breaches of certain restrictions such as trade limits or moving money to certain countries. Such a system might have established when and how often Kerviel was logging in with co-worker's accounts.

Green also argues that even less sophisticated measures might have prevented Kerviel from inflicting such a big loss on Societe Generale. Trading systems would have been changed in such a way as to set restrictions on the types, size and volume of trades that specific traders are supposed to be engaging in. It is ironic therefore that Societe Generale's 2006 annual report devotes twenty-six reassuring pages to its risk management practices (The Economist, 2008a). What is more ironic, ludicrous and preposterous is that after the fiasco, Societe Generale was granted permission to use the AMA, presumably to calculate a capital charge that will in the future protect the bank from another rogue trader who may be Kerveil's incarnation. It is doubtful if the capital charge will be of any use. Societe Generale will be better off allocating the resources to tighten their controls and reduce incentives for unauthorised trading than to indulge in a highly intellectual exercise that will most likely be of little practical significance.

What happened at Barings, the Allied Irish Bank, and other financial institutions that have experienced the horror of rogue trading (such as the National Australia Bank (NAB)) was not dissimilar. In each case the losses were incurred as a result of the behaviour of one or more traders, triggered by a profit-based remuneration scheme and facilitated by management incompetence and the absence or inadequacy of controls. Ford and Sundmacher (2007) identify a further contributory factor, which is a "corporate culture that discouraged critical examination of traders engaging in allegedly profitable transactions." They characterise the culture in these three institutions as a "superstar culture" leading to "arrogance in dealing with warning signs." They conclude that it is "highly unlikely that these losses would have been recognised and consequently prevented under the revised capital standards for financial institutions currently promulgated by the Basel Committee."

7.4 OPERATIONAL RISK MANAGEMENT: THE RIGHTS AND WRONGS

Rebonato (2007) argues that "although the quantitative approach remains the high route to risk management, a lot of very effective risk management can be done with a much simpler approach," describing the latter as being "a measurable and meaningful approximation to the quantitatively correct answer." In particular, Rebonato is sceptical about the ability of risk managers to move from the probabilistic assessment of risk to decisions. He also argues that regulators should not force banks to devote resources to the development of internal models to calculate "numbers of dubious meaning" for regulatory purposes. The recommendation is as follows: keep it simple or let banks decide whether or not they want to develop internal models.

The problem is that obsession with sophisticated models that misrepresent reality obscure the true picture and distract risk managers away from the task of risk management. For example, while a "sophisticated" model could not have prevented what happened at Societe Generale et al, a simple measure could have: auditing the structure of payment systems to detect potential sources of operational losses and implementing risk-adjusted incentive systems that discourage traders from taking on excessive risk (Ford and Sundmacher, 2007). Similar arguments are raised in a special report on international banking in the 17 May issue of The Economist. In The Econmomist (2008g), it is argued that "VAR leads to the illusion that you can quantify all risks and therefore regulate them." Then in The Economist (2008h), it is argued that banks, executives and traders receive rewards that "are not properly aligned with the risks that are being taken." This system of compensation, the argument goes, "gives them an incentive to take excessive risks because the long-term upside is far greater than the long-term downside." The suggested solutions to this problem are "to pay a greater proportion of compensation in shares" and "to stagger bonus payments over a period of years, providing employees with an incentive to think about the institution's long-term performance."

The use of appropriate controls is a preventive measure that should be considered seriously. Controls cover a wide area, including the following (see the March 2008 issue of *OpRisk & Compliance*, pp 20–27):

- Information technology (IT), such as the establishment of user profiles for traders and monitoring user access to detect unusual activity.
- Tools for execution, including tool limitations for executing and processing trades.
- Limit setting, monitoring and management.
- Operational controls, such as the trade confirmation process.
- Reporting, including reliability and effectiveness of book management.
- Risk culture and governance, including the clarity of risk policies.

In the same round table discussion reported in the March 2008 issue of *OpRisk & Compliance*, Edward Doyle of Norkom advised operational risk and compliance executives to follow seven steps to prevent a Societe Generale type fiasco: (i) moving towards enterprise-wide risk management; (ii) monitoring the monitoring system; (iii) maintaining clear division between front-, middle- and back office operations; (iv) reviewing the classification of product risk; (v) introducing multi-factor authentication to prevent compromises of information; (vi) testing operational risk, information and corporate security functions; and (iv) tightening internal audits to expose fictitious trades. Davidson (2008) adds another factor, which is the backlogs in equity derivatives confirmations, arguing that this is a factor that "could have slowed the uncovering of the false trades at Societe Generale."

Obsession with financial measures of risk is also wrong. Sundmacher (2007b) suggests a number of useful indicators for the detection of increased operational risk taking. These indicators include the following:

- Ratio of back office to front office staff. A low ratio may be indicative of increased likelihood of errors in back office processes.

- Number of daily trades per individual trader. This indicator can be used to detect changes in trading behaviour.

- Expenditure on training per staff member. If the back office staff is not well-trained, a rogue trader can take advantage of that. In general, poor training means lower probability of detecting errors.

- Proportion of incentive-based remuneration. The higher the portion of remuneration in the form of profit-related bonuses, the higher will be the tendency to take risk.

Identifying risk drivers and taking necessary measures does not need a high-calibre quantification model. The classification of extreme events (suggested by McConnell, 2006) into perfect storm, ethical meltdown, infrastructure disasters and learning curve provides suitable background and a starting point for any effort to take precautionary measures. Understanding these processes makes it possible to design and implement controls that would reduce the frequency and severity of loss events.

The category of ethical meltdown involves the use of psychology to explain why people behave in certain ways under particular circumstances. Economists have already found out that introducing psychology into economic analysis has done a lot of good to neoclassical economics that depended predominantly on rigorous optimisation models. This is clearly indicated by the popularity of Behavioural Economics and Behavioural Finance. Doing the same thing in the field of operational risk would also prove to be useful. For example, Ford and Sundmacher (2007) distinguish two stages in the activities of a rogue trader: (i) taking excessive risk; and (ii) engaging in fraudulent trading to cover losses. They explain these two aspects of behaviour by introducing some principles of psychology. Drummond (2002) and Stein (2000) have attempted to come up with psychological explanations for what happened at Barings. Ford and Sundancher suggest that the concepts of regret theory, group think and consensus-provision moral hazard can be useful for studying operational risk.

While most of the discussion in this section pertains to internal fraud, non-quantitative approaches can be used to study any kind of operational risk. The principle is simple: identify risk drivers and introduce the necessary controls. Doerig (2003) identifies what he calls "basic checks" for "areas of future concern" in a financial institution. These include business continuity planning, customer complains, IT migration, IT security, outsourcing, money laundering, fraud, settlement and communication. For example, some of the basic checks he suggests for customer complaints are the following: (i) whether or not staff is properly trained to counsel customers; (ii) how they handle a situation involving a customer making a mistake; and (iii) whether or not recurring complaints lead to action?

To conclude, the argument put forward in this section is that quantitative risk modelling is not necessarily the right approach to sound operational risk management. The quantitative approach, at least as it is enshrined in the AMA, is remedial, not preventive: hold so much capital, just in case (and it may or may not work). The right thing to do would be to identify the sources of risk and implement the necessary controls. High-calibre models are not needed in this approach.

7.5 THE GOOD, BAD AND UGLY

We have thus reached a stage where we should specify explicitly the good, bad and ugly aspects of the issues dealt with in this book. Naturally, we start with the good things. First of all, it is good to recognise the importance and seriousness of operational risk, no matter how it is defined. It is also good to indulge in sound operational risk management practices, but these should be firm-specific, not standardised by a regulator (although the best practices specified by the Basel Committee can serve as a starting point). Preventing operational losses is always better than clearing the mess in the aftermath of a loss event. This is just like saying that it is better to prevent car accidents from happening than arranging for insurance to pay for the damage. After all, operational risk is not transferable by insurance in the sense that taking insurance against fire does not mean that the premises of the insured will not catch fire. The other good thing is for banks to hold the amount of capital that ensures business continuity and maximisation of market value. While this is not an easy task, the underlying message is that bank capital should not be regulated.

Now the bad things. It is bad not to have any regulation whatsoever. It is this author's view that free banking is not a viable proposition, because banks are too important to be left to market forces. What is bad is too much regulation (the kind that results in regulatory capture when regulators become involved in the day-to-day management of banks). What is also bad is the wrong kind of regulation, particularly the risk-based capital regulation embodied in the Basel Accords. Numerous studies have shown that this kind of regulation may boost risk (by encouraging banks to seek out more risky activities) and reduce profitability. In any case, the international harmonisation of capital standards is a bad idea because countries have different rescue policies in times of financial crises.

Regulation based on capital adequacy is inadequate because capital adequacy is not the same as bank resilience. Regulation of the conduct of business and preventing malpractices would always be good. As pointed out earlier, regulators should let banks determine the size and structure of capital and design their risk management system. Regulators should monitor the banks' leverage ratios, funding gaps and maturity mismatches. The importance of the leverage ratios (which seem to be better indicators than the risk-adjusted capital ratios) was highlighted by the fate of Bear Stearns. In 2005, Bear Stearns' leverage ratio (measured as the ratio of total assets to equity) was 26, but it rose to 32.8 in 2007 (The Economist, 2008f). The Economist (2008j) correctly argues that "regulators clearly need more than wait for disasters to strike," suggesting that regulators should "take a view on a bank's optimal funding profile" and that they "have to be more vigilant about maturity mismatches between banks' assets and liabilities." Leverage ratios, funding gaps and maturity mismatches are easier to calculate and monitor than regulatory risk-adjusted capital. They are also more effective.

Also bad is obsession with the desire to find an exact definition of operational risk and believing that a precise definition is needed for sound risk measurement and that "accurate" measurement is a prerequisite for sound risk management. It is also bad to believe that regulatory capital is needed to protect a firm from operational-loss triggered insolvency, but at the same time exclude reputational risk, business risk, and indirect losses (according to the BCBS's definition of operational risk) from the capital cover. What is also bad is to think that mathematical and statistical sophistication leads to better estimates of the capital charge and hence better risk management (recall the mathematical sophistication of Societe Generale).

On the proposition that risk models are a necessary condition for sound risk management, Greenspan (2008) argues that no matter how complex risk models (and economic models) are they are still too simple to capture the full array of governing variables that drive reality. A model, he notes, is an abstraction from the full detail of the real world. One reason why risk management based on the state-of-the-art statistical models can perform so poorly is that "the underlying data used to estimate a model's structure are drawn generally from periods of euphoria and periods of fear." It seems, to this author at least, that out of the dozens of "sophisticated" methods and models that have been suggested in the literature, only the technique of Bayesian networks has some merit in operational risk management.

Now the ugly. What is truly ugly is the advanced measurement approach (AMA), particularly the imposition by the regulators of the requirements that banks calculate a capital charge to a confidence level of 99.9%. If banks want to do that, it is fine but that should not be imposed on them. The imposition of the AMA may distract banks from the crucial business of managing operational risk and avoiding huge operational losses. It is also an added cost that will be passed on to the customers.

It is ugly to tell "unsophisticated" banks that only "sophisticated" banks can use the AMA and that the AMA leads to lower capital charges (which is not true anyway, except when banks indulge in subjective manipulation of their internal models for this purpose). Where does that put banks from emerging and developing countries? It is ugly to regulate banks in the same why as they are managed (by attempting to equate economic capital and regulatory capital). This is because while regulators are concerned about systemic risk, managers are concerned about the risk-return trade-off in daily operations. Regulators do not seem to understand that risk can create opportunities, in which case risk cannot be regulated. Actually, it is ugly to proceed with Basel II as it is (even better, forget about it).

7.6 A CONCLUDING NOTE

We have gone from $1.3 billion loss at Barings, to $4.4 billion at LTCM, to $7.2 billion at Societe Generale. Just a few weeks after the Societe Generale fiasco, MF Global got struck by a rogue trader. Why is it that financial institutions are not learning?

It could be that financial institutions are more preoccupied with regulatory compliance than with actual risk management, believing that the management of risk depends on sophisticated risk models. They seem to forget the fact that truly effective operational risk management will continue to remain primarily underpinned by qualitatively stronger elements such as solid corporate governance, healthy risk culture throughout the firm, tight procedures and controls, performing technology and (most importantly) well-qualified and honest people. They do not seem to know the rights and wrongs of how to deal with operational risk, perhaps because the regulators are distracting them. Let us hope that this unsatisfactory state of affairs will change.

References

Acharya, V.V. (2000) Is the International Convergence of Capital Adequacy Regulation Desirable? Mimeo, Stern School of Business, New York University.

Adusei-Poku, K. (2005) Operational Risk Management: Implementing a Bayesian Network for Foreign Exchange and Money Market Settlement, Unpublished PhD Thesis, University of Gottingen.

Adusei-Poku, K., van den Brink, G.J. and Zucchini, W. (2007) Implementing a Bayesian Network for Foreign Exchange and Money Market Settlement: A Case Study of Operational Risk Management, *Journal of Operational Risk*, 2 (Summer), 101–107.

Alexander, C. (2003a) Managing Operational Risks with Bayesian Networks, in Alexander, C. (ed.) *Operational Risk: Regulation, Analysis and Management*, London: Prentice Hall-Financial Times.

Alexander, C. (2003b) Statistical Models of Operational Loss, in Alexander, C. (ed.) *Operational Risk: Regulation, Analysis and Management*, London: Prentice Hall-Financial Times.

Allen, B. (2008) The Liquidity Link, *Asia Risk*, March, 44–46.

Allen, L. (2004) The Basel Capital Accords and International Mortgage Markets: A Survey of the Literature, *Financial Markets, Institutions and Instruments*, 13, 41–108.

Allen, L. and Bali, T.G. (2004) Cyclicality in Catastrophic and Operational Risk Measurements, Working Paper, City University of New York, September.

Allen, L. and Jagtiani, J. (1997) Risk and Market Segmentation in Financial Intermediaries' Returns, *Journal of Financial Services Research*, 12, 159–173.

Allen, L., Jagtiani, J. and Landskroner (1996) Interest Rate Risk Subsidization in International Capital Standards, *Journal of Economics and Business*, 48, 251–267.

Altman, E.I. and Saunders, A. (2001) An Analysis and Critique of BIS Proposal on Capital Adequacy and Ratings, *Journal of Banking and Finance*, 25, 25–46.

Anders, U. (2003) The Path to Operational Risk Economic Capital, in Alexander, C. (ed.) *Operational Risk: Regulation, Analysis and Management*, London: Prentice Hall-Financial Times.

Anders, U. and van den Brink, G.J. (2004) Implementing a Basel II Scenario-Based AMA for Operational Risk, in Ong, K. (ed.) *The Basel Handbook*, London: Risk Books.

Aue, F. and Kalkbrener, M. (2007) LDA at Work: Deutsche Bank's Approach to Quantifying Operational Risk, *Journal of Operational Risk*, 1 (Winter), 49–93.

Austega (2007) Which Measurement Method? Available at http://austega.com/risk/ meas/opriskmeth.htm.

Avery, R.B. and Berger, R.B. (1991) Risk-Based Capital and Deposit Insurance Reform, *Journal of Banking and Finance*, 15, 847–874.

Bank of Japan (2007) Summary Record of the Operational Risk Scenario Analysis Workshop. Available at www.boj.jp.

Barr, A. (2007) Subprime Crisis Shines Light on Mortgage Brokers. Available at http://www.marketwatch.com/news/story.

Barth, J.R., Brunsbauch, R.D. and Wilcox, J.A. (2000) The Repeal of Glass-Steagall and the Advent of Broad Banking, Economic and Policy Analysis Working Papers, No 2000–5.

Baud, N., Frachot, A. and Roncalli, T. (2002) How to Avoid Over-estimating Capital Charge for Operational Risk? Working Paper, Credit Lyonnais.

Bawa, V.S. (1975) Optimal Rules for Ordering Uncertain Prospects, *Journal of Financial Economics*, 2, 95–121.

Bazzarello, D., Crielaard, B., Piacenza, F. and Soprano, A. (2006) Modeling Insurance Mitigation on Operational Risk Capital, *Journal of Operational Risk*, 1 (Spring), 57–65.

BCBS (1998) *Operational Risk Management,* Basel: Bank for International Settlements, September.

BCBS (1999) *Update on Work on a New Capital Adequacy Framework,* Basel: Bank for International Settlements, November.

BCBS (2001a) *Basel II: The New Basel Capital Accord-Second Consultative Paper,* Basel: Bank for International Settlements, January.

BCBS (2001b) *Operational Risk: Supporting Document to the New Basel Capital Accord*, Basel: Bank for International Settlements, January.

BCBS (2002) *Sound Practices for the Management and Supervision of Operational Risk,* Basel: Bank for International Settlements, July.

BCBS (2003a) *Sound Practices for the Management and Supervision of Operational Risk*, Basel: Bank for International Settlements, February.

BCBS (2003b) *The 2002 Data Collection Exercise for Operational Risk: Summary of the Data Collected*, Basel: Bank for International Settlements, March.

BCBS (2003c) *Basel II: The New Basel Capital Accord – Third Consultative Paper*, Basel: Bank for International Settlements, April.

BCBS (2003d) *Supervisory Guidance on Operational Risk: Advanced Measurement Approaches for Regulatory Capital*, Basel: Bank for International Settlements, July.

BCBS (2004) *Basel II: International Convergence of Capital Measurement and Capital Standards: A Revised Framework*, Basel: Bank for International Settlements, June.

BCBS (2005) *Basel II: International Convergence of Capital Measurement and Capital Standards: A Revised Framework*, Basel: Bank for International Settlements, November.

BCBS (2006a) *Basel II: International Convergence of Capital Measurement and Capital Standards: A Revised Framework – Comprehensive Version*, Basel: Bank for International Settlements, June.

BCBS (2006b) *Observed Range of Practice in Key Elements of Advanced Measurement Approaches (AMA)*, Basel: Bank for International Settlements, October.

BCBS (2006c) *The IRB Use Test: Background and Implementation*, Basel: Bank for International Settlements, September.

BCBS (2007a) *Consultative Document: Principles for Home-Host Supervisory Co-operation and Allocation Mechanisms in the Context of Advanced Measurement Approach (AMA)*, Basel: Bank for International Settlements, February.

BCBS (2007b) *Principles for Home-Host Supervisory Co-operation and Allocation Mechanisms in the Context of Advanced Measurement Approach (AMA)*, Basel: Bank for International Settlements, November.

BCBS (2007c) *Progress on Basel II Implementation: New Work Streams and Outreach*, Basel Committee Newsletter, No 11, Basel: Bank for International Settlements, November.

BCBS (2008) *Liquidity Risk: Management and Supervisory Challenges*, Basel: Bank for International Settlements, February.

Bee, M. (2005) Copula-Based Multivariate Models with Applications to Risk Management and Insurance, Social Science Research Network, Working Paper Series.

Bee, M. (2006) Estimating the Parameters in the Loss Distribution Approach: How Can we Deal with Truncated Data?, in Davis, E. (ed.) *The Advanced Measurement Approach to Operational Risk*, London: Risk Books.

Benink, H. and Wihlborg, C. (2002) The New Basel Capital Accord: Making it Effective with Stronger Market Discipline, *European Financial Management*, 8, 103–115.

Benink, H., Danielsson, J. and Jonsson, A. (2008) On the Role of Regulatory Banking Capital, *Financial Markets, Institutions and Instruments*, 17, 85–96.

Benston, G.J. and Kaufman, G.G. (1996) The Appropriate Role of Bank Regulation, *Economic Journal*, 106, 688–697.

Berger, A.N., Herring, R.J. and Szego, G.P. (1995) The Role of Capital in Financial Institutions, *Journal of Banking and Finance*, 19, 393–430.

Bernanke, B. (2007) Central Banking and Bank Supervision in the United States, Remarks before the Allied Social Sciences Association Annual Meeting, Chicago, 5 January.

Bhatia, M. (2002) New Basel Accord: Operational Risk Management – Emerging Frontiers for the Profession, *Information Systems and Control Journal*, 1, Available at www.isaca.org.

Bhusnurmath, M. (2007) Myth, Reality and Subprime Crisis, *Economic Times*, 20 August. Available at www.economictimes.indiatimes.com.

Bikker, J.A. and Hu, H. (2002) Cyclical Patterns in Profits, Provisioning and Lending of Banks and Procyclicality of the New Basel Capital Requirements, *BNL Quarterly Review*, 221, 143–175.

Bilby, R. (2008) Using Scenario Analysis to Achieve Sound Operational Risk Management, Paper Presented at the OpRisk Asia Conference, Singapore 2–4 June.

Blochwitz, S. (2008) Validation of Banks' Internal Rating System: A Challenging Task? *Journal of Risk Model Validation*, 1 (Winter) 3–16.

Blum, J. (1999) Do Capital Adequacy Requirements Reduce Risks in Banking? *Journal of Banking and Finance*, 23, 755–771.

Blunden, T. (2003) Scoreboard Approaches, in Alexander, C. (ed.) *Operational Risk: Regulation, Analysis and Management*, London: Prentice Hall-Financial Times.

Bocker, K. and Kluppelberg, C. (2005) Operational VAR: A Closed-Form Approximation, *Risk*, December, 90–93.

Bonafede, C.E., Cerchiello, P. and Giudici, P. (2007) Statistical Models for Business Continuity Management, *Journal of Operational Risk*, 2 (winter), 79–96.

Bonson, E., Escobar, T. and Flores, F. (2007) Sub-Optimality of Income Statement Methods for Measuring Operational Risk Under Basel II: Empirical Evidence from Spanish Banks, *Financial Markets, Institutions and Instruments*, 16, 201–220.

Boot, A.W, Milbourn, T.T. and Thakor, A.V. (1998) Killing the Bearer of its Tidings: A Theory of Consensus-Provision Moral Hazard, Tinbergen Institute Discussion Papers, No 98–061/2.

Boyle, P.P. (1977) Options: A Monte Carlo Approach, *Journal of Financial Economics*, 4, 323–338.

Briault, C. (2002) Revisiting the Rationale for a Single National Financial Services Regulator, London School of Economics, Special Paper 135.

British Bankers' Association, ISDA, RMA and PriceWaterhouseCoopers (1999) *Operational Risk: The Next Frontier*, Philadelphia: RMA.

Brown, S. and Warner, J.B. (1980) Measuring Security Price Performance, *Journal of Financial Economics*, 8, 205–258.

Brown, S. and Warner, J.B. (1985) Using Daily Stock Returns: The Case of Event Studies, *Journal of Financial Economics*, 14, 3–31.

Buchelt, R. and Unteregger, S. (2004) Cultural Risk and Risk Culture: Operational Risk after Basel II, Financial Stability Report No 6. Available at www.oenb.at/en/img/fsr_06_cultural_risk_tcm16–9495.pdf.

Bugie, S., Azarchs, T., Burger, T.Y. and Quinn, S. (2003) Basel II: No Turning Back for the Banking Industry, *Standard and Poor's Research Report*, August.

Burnside, C., Eichenbaum, M., Kleshcelski, I. and Rebelo, S. (2006) The Returns to Currency Speculation, NBER Working Papers, No 12489.

Cagan, P. (2001a) Seizing the Tail of the Dragon, *FOW/Operational Risk*, July, 18–23.

Cagan, P. (2001b) Standard Operating Procedures, *Erisk.com*, March.

Cagan, P. (2005) External Data: Reaching for the Truth, Available at www.operationalriskonline.com.

Calem, P.S. and Rob, R. (1996) The Impact of Capital-Based Regulation on Bank Risk-Taking: A Dynamic Model, Board of Governors of the Federal Reserve System, Finance and Economics Discussion Series, 96, 12.

Calomiris, C. and Herring, R. (2002) The Regulation of Operational Risk in Investment Management Companies, *Perspective*, 8, 1–19.

Caprio, G. and Klingebiel, D. (1996) Bank Insolvency: Bad Luck, Bad Policy or Bad Thinking, Annual World Bank Conference on Development Economics.

Carpenter, S.B., Whitesell, W. and Zakrajsek, E. (2001) Capital Requirements, Business Loans and Business Cycles: An Empirical Analysis of the Standardized Approach in the New Basel Capital Accord, Unpublished Paper, Board of Governors of the Federal Reserve System.

Caruana, J. (2005) Implementation of Basel II, *Financial Markets, Institutions and Instruments*, 14, 253–265.

Carvalho, R., Migon, H.S. and Paez, M.S. (2008) Dynamic Bayesian Models as an Alternative to the Estimation of Operational Risk Measures, *Journal of Operational Risk*, 3 (Spring), 25–49.

Cech, R. (2007) Event Horizon. Available at www.opriskandcompliance.com.

Centre for the Study of Financial Innovation (2002) *Banana Skins*, London: CSFI.

Chapelle, A., Crama, Y., Hunber, G. and Peters, J.P. (2004) Basel II and Operational Risk: Implications for Risk Measurement and Management in the Financial Sector, Working Paper, National Bank of Belgium.

Chavez-Demoulin, V., Embrechts, P. and Neslehova, J. (2005) Quantitative Models for Operational Risk: Extremes, Dependence and Aggregation, Swiss Federal Institute of Technology, Zurich. Available at www.gloriamundi.org.

Chernobai, A. and Rachev, S. (2004) Stable Modelling of Operational Risk, in Cruz, M. (ed.) *Operational Risk Modelling and Analysis*, London: Risk Books.

Chernobai, A. and Rachev, S. (2006) Applying Robust Methods to Operational Risk Modeling, *Journal of Operational Risk*, 1 (Spring) 27–41.

Chernobai, A., Jorion, P. and Yu, F. (2007) the Determinants of Operational Losses, Unpublished Working Paper.

Chernobai, A., Menn, C., Rachev, S., Truck, S. and Moscadelli, M. (2006) Treatment of Incomplete Data in the Field of Operational Risk: The Effects on Parameter Estimates, EL and UL Figures, in Davis, E. (ed.) *The Advanced Measurement Approach to Operational Risk*, London: Risk Books.

Cohen, A. and Sackrowitz, H.B. (1975) Unbiasedness of the Chi-Square, Likelihood Ratio and other Goodness of Fit Tests for Equal Cell Case, *Annals of Statistics*, 4, 959–964.

Consiglio, A. and Zenios, S.A. (2003) Model Error in Enterprise-wide Risk Management: Insurance Policies with Guarantees, in Mestchian, P. (ed.) *Advances in Operational Risk: Firm-wide Issues for Financial Institutions* (second edition), London: Risk Books.

Cope, E. and Wills, S. (2008) External Loss Data Helps: Evidence from the ORX Database, *OpRisk & Compliance*, March 48–49.

Cowell, R.G., Verrall, R.J. and Yoon, Y.K. (2007) Modelling Operational Risk with Bayesian Networks, *Journal of Risk and Insurance*, 74, 795–827.

Credit Suisse First Boston (1997) CreditRisk+: A Credit Risk Management Framework. Available at www.csfb.com/creditrisk.

Crouchy, M. (2001) *Risk Management*, New York: McGraw Hill.

Cruz, M. (2003a) *Modeling, Measurung and Hedging Operational Risk,* New York: Wiley.

Cruz, M. (2003b) Operational Risk: Past, Present and Future, in Field, P. (ed.) *Modern Risk Management: A History*, London: Risk Books.

Cummins, J.D., Lewis, C.M. and Wei, R. (2006) The Market Value Impact of Operational Loss Events for US Banks and Insurers, *Journal of Banking and Finance*, 30, 2605–2634.

Currie, C.V. (2006) A Test of the Strategic Effect of Basel II Operational Risk Requirements on Banks, *ICFAI Journal of Monetary Economics*, 4, 6–28.

Dahen, H. and Dionne, G. (2007) Scaling Methods for Severity and Frequency of External Loss Data, Working Paper 70–01, Canada Research Chair in Finance, January.

Danielsson, J., Jorgensen, B.N. and Sarma, M. (2005) Comparing Downside Risk Measures for Heavy Tailed Distributions, Working Paper, London School of Economics. Available at www.riskresearch.org.

Danielsson, J., Embrechts, P., Goodhart, C., Keating, C., Muennich, F., Renault, O. and Shin, H.S. (2001) An Academic Response to Basel II, LSE Financial Markets Group, Special Paper No 130.

Davidson, R. (2008) Looking to Beat the Backlog, *Asia Risk*, April, E9–E11.

Davies, H. (2005) A Review of the Review, *Financial Markets, Institutions and Instruments*, 14, 247–252.

Davies, M. (2005) The Risk Indicator Framework as a Tool for AMA Exposure Analysis, in Davis, E. (ed.) *Operational Risk: Practical Approaches to Implementation*, London: Risk Books.

Davis, E. (2008a) Now it's Op Risk's Turn to Take Centre Stage, *OpRisk & Compliance*, February, 4.

Davis, E. (2008b) Beyond the Blueprint, *Asia Risk*, March, 47–49.

de Fontnouvelle, P., Rosengren, E. and Jordan, J. (2004) Implications of Alternative Operational Risk Modeling Techniques, Working Paper, Federal Reserve Bank of Boston, June.

de Fontnouvelle, P., DeJesus-Rueff, V., Jordan, J. and Rosengren, E. (2005a) Capital and Risk: New Evidence on Implications of Large Operational Losses, *Journal of Money, Credit and Banking*, 38, 1819–1846.

de Fontnouvelle, P., Garrity, V., Chu, S. and Rosengren, E. (2005b) The Potential Impact of Explicit Basel II Operational Risk Capital Charges on the Competitive Environment of Processing Banks in the United States, Unpublished Paper, Federal Reserve Bank of Boston, January.

De la Pena, V.H. and Rivera, R. (2008) Dynamic Backtesting of Value-at-Risk Models under Regime Change, *Journal of Risk Model Validation*, 1 (Winter), 95–110.

Dewatripont, M. and Tirole, J. (1993) Efficient Governance Structure: Implications for Banking Regulation, in Mayer, C. and Vives, X. (eds) *Capital Markets and Financial Intermediation*, Cambridge: Cambridge University Press.

Dewatripont, M. and Tirole, J. (1994) *The Prudential Regulation of Banks*, Cambridge, MA: MIT Press.

Dhane, J., Goovaerts, M.J. and Kaas, R. (2003) Economic Capital Allocation Derived from Risk Measures, *North American Actuarial Journal*, 7, 44–56.

Diamond, D.W. and Dybvig, P.H. (1983) Bank Runs, Deposit Insurance and Liquidity, *Journal of Political Economy*, 91, 401–419.

Dietsch, M. and Petey, J. (2002) The Credit Risk in SME Loans Portfolios: Modeling Issues, Pricing and Capital Requirements, *Journal of Banking and Finance*, 26, 303–322.

Doerig, H.U. (2003) Operational Risks in Financial Services: An Old Challenge in a New Environment, Working Paper, Credit Suisse Group.

Doucet, A. and Tadic, V. (2007) On Solving Integral Equations Using Markov Chain Monte Carlo, Technical Report CUED-F-INFENG, No 444, Cambridge University.

Dowd, K. (1993) *Laissez-Faire Banking*, London: Routledge.

Dowd, K. (1996a) *Competition and Finance: A New Interpretation of Financial and Monetary Economics*, London: Macmillan.

Dowd, K. (1996b) The Case for Financial Laizes-Faire, *Economic Journal*, 106, 697–687.

Drummond, H. (2002) Living in a Fool's Paradise: The Collapse of Barings, *Management Decision*, 40, 232–238.

Duebel, H.J. (2002) Mortgage Credit Risk, Regulatory Standards and the Basel II Banking Supervision Reforms, *Housing Finance International*, 17, 3–11.

Duffie, D. and Singleton, K. (1999) Modeling Term Structure of Defaultable Bonds, *Review of Financial Studies*, 12, 687–720.

Dupire, B. (2006) (ed.) *Monte Carlo Methodologies and Applications for Pricing and Risk Management*, London: Risk Books.

Dutta, K. and Perry, J. (2007) The Tale of Tails: An Empirical Analysis of Loss Distribution Models for Estimating Operational Risk Capital, Mimeo.

Embrechts, P., Kluppelberg, C. and Mikosch, T. (1997) *Modelling Extreme Events for Insurance and Finance*, Berlin: Springer-Verlag.

Embrechts, P., Lindskog, F. and McNeil, A. (2003) Modelling Dependence with Copulas and Applications to Risk Management, in Rachev, S. (ed.) *Handbook of Heavy Tailed Distributions in Finance*, Amsterdam: Elsevier.

Ergashev, B. (2008) Should Risk Managers Rely on Maximum Likelihood Estimation while Quantifying Operational Risk? Working Paper, Federal Reserve Bank of Richmond.

European Shadow Financial Regulatory Committee (2003) Bank Supervisors Business: Supervision or Risk Management, Statement No 16, Basel/Zurich.

Evanoff, D.D. and Wall, L.D. (2001) SND Yield Spreads as Bank Risk Measures, *Journal of Financial Services Research*, October, 121–146.

Evans, J., Womersley, R. and Wong, D. (2007) Operational Risks in Banks: An Analysis of Empirical Data from an Australian Bank, Paper Presented at the Biennial Convention of the Institute of Actuaries of Australia, Christchurch, 23–26 September.

Everts, H. and Liersch, H. (2006) Diversification and Aggregation of Risks in Financial Conglomerates, in van Lelyveld, I. (ed.) *Economic Capital Modelling: Concepts, Measurement and Implementation*, London: Risk Books.

Fama, E.F. and French, K. (1993) Common Risk Factors in the Returns on Stocks and Bonds, *Journal of Financial Economics*, 33, 5–56.

Federal Reserve System (2004) *Commercial Bank Examination Manual*, Division of Banking Supervision and Regulation, November.

Federal Reserve System, Office of the Comptroller of the Currency, Office of Thrift Supervision, and Federal Deposit Insurance Corporation (2005) Results of the Loss Data Collection Exercise for Operational Risk. Available at www.bos.frb.org/bankinfo/qua/papers.

Figini, S., Giudici, P., Uberti, P. and Sanyal, P. (2008) A Statistical Method to Optimize the Combination of Internal and External Data in Operational Risk Measurement, *Journal of Operational Risk*, 4 (Winter), 69–78.

Financial Services Agency and Bank of Japan (2007) Results of the 2007 Operational Risk Data Collection Exercise. Available at www.boj.jp.

Financial Services Authority (2005) The "Use Test." Available at www.fsa.gov.uk.

Fischer, S. (2002) Basel II: Risk Management and Implications for Banking in Emerging Market Countries, The William Taylor Memorial Lecture at the International Conference of Banking Supervisors, Cape Town, 19 September.

Fishburn, P.C. (1977) Mean-Risk Analysis with Risk Associated with Below Target Returns, *American Economic Review*, 67, 116–126.

Flannery, M. (1989) Capital Regulation and Insured Banks' Choice of Individual Loan Default Risks, *Journal of Monetary Economics*, 24, 235–258.

Ford, G. and Sundmacher, M. (2007) Leading Indicators for Operational Risk. Available at http://ssrn.com/abstract=963235.

Foreign Exchange Committee (2003) *Management of Operational Risk in Foreign Exchange*, New York: Federal Reserve Bank of New York.

Frachot, A., Moudoulaud, O. and Roncalli, T. (2004a) Loss Distribution Approach in Practice, in Ong, K. (ed.) *The Basel Handbook*, London: Risk Books.

Frachot, A., Roncalli, T., and Salmon, E. (2004b) The Correlation Problem in Operational Risk, Working Paper, Credit Lyonnais.

Frerichs, H. and Wahrenberg, M. (2003) Evaluating Internal Credit Rating Systems Depending on Bank Size, Unpublished Paper, University of Frankfurt.

Frey, R. and McNeil, A. (2003) Dependent Defaults in Models for Portfolio Credit Risk, Working Paper, Department of Mathematics, University of Leipzig.

Friedman, M. (1960) *A Program for Monetary Stability*, New York: Fordham University Press.

Fujii, K. (2005) Building Scenarios, in Davis, E. (ed.) *Operational Risk: Practical Approaches to Implementation*, London: Risk Books.

Furlong, F.T. and Keeley, M.C. (1989) Capital Regulation and Bank Risk-Taking: A Note, *Journal of Banking and Finance*, 13, 883–891.

Gatali, G., Heath, A. and McGuire, P. (2007) Evidence of Carry Trade Activity, *BIS Quarterly Review*, September, 27–41.

Gennotte, G. and Pyle, D. (1991) Capital Controls and Bank Risk, *Journal of Banking and Finance*, 13, 883–891.

Giraud, J-R. (2005) Managing Hedge Funds' Exposure to Operational Risks, in Davis, E. (ed.) *Operational Risk: Practical Approaches to Implementation*, London: Risk Books.

Giudici, P. and Bilotta, A. (2004) Modeling Operational Losses: A Bayesian Approach, *Quality and Reliability Engineering International*, 20, 407–417.

Glasner, D. (1989) *Free Banking and Monetary Reform*, Cambridge: Cambridge University Press.

Goodhart, C. (2000) The Organisational Structure of Banking Supervision, FSI Occasional Papers, No 1.

Goodhart, C. (2001) Operational Risk, Special Paper 131, Financial Markets Group, London School of Economics.

Goodhart, C. and Shoemaker, D. (1995) Should the Functions of Monetary Policy and Banking Supervision be Separated? *Oxford Economic Papers*, 47, 539–560.

Green, H. (2008) The Lesson of Societe Generale, *Business Week*, 30 January. Available at www.businessweek.com.

Green, P. (2003) *Trans-Dimensional Markov Chain Monte Carlo: Highly Structured Stochastic Systems*, Oxford: Oxford University Press.

Greenspan, A. (1998) Wanted: Bank Regulators who Act More Like the Market, *Secondary Mortgage Markets*, 15, 6–10.

Greenspan, A. (2008) We Will Never Have a Perfect Model of Risk, *Financial Times*, 16 March. Available at www.ft.com.

Group of Ten (2001) *Report on Consolidation in the Financial Sector*, Washington DC: Group of Ten.

Group of Thirty (1993) *Derivatives: Practices and Principles*, Washington DC: Group of Thirty.

Gundlach, M. and Lehrbass, F. (eds) (2004) *CreditRisk+ in the Banking Industry*, Berlin: Springer.

Gustafsson, J., Nielsen, J.P., Pritchard, P. and Roberts, D. (2006) Quantifying Operational Risk Guided by Kernel Smoothing and Continuous Credibility: A Practitioner's View, *Journal of Operational Risk*, 1 (Spring), 43–57.

Gynelberg, J. and Remolona, E.M. (2007) Risk in Carry Trades: A Look at Target Currencies in Asia and the Pacific, *BIS Quarterly Review*, December, 73–82.

Haas, M. and Kaiser, T. (2004) Tackling the Inefficiency of Loss Data for the Quantification of Operational Loss, in Cruz, M. (ed.) *Operational Risk Modelling and Analysis: Theory and Practice*, London: Risk Books, 13–24.

Haden, A. (2008) Federal Reserve Bank Perspective: Regulatory Directions in the US and Their Implications to the Future Operational Risk Landscape in Asia, Paper Presented at the OpRisk Asia Conference, Singapore 2–4 June.

Hadjiemmanuil, C. (2003) Legal Risk and Fraud: Capital Charges, Control and Insurance, in Alexander, C. (ed.) *Operational Risk: Regulation, Analysis and Management*, London: Prentice Hall-Financial Times.

Halperin, K. (2001) Balancing Act, *Bank Systems and Technology*, 38, 22–25.

Haubenstock, M. (2004) Constructing an Operational Event Database, in Ong, K. (ed.) *The Basel Handbook*, London: Risk Books.

Haubenstock, M. and Hardin, L. (2003) The Loss Distribution Approach, in Alexander, C. (ed.) *Operational Risk: Regulation, Analysis and Management*, London: Prentice Hall-Financial Times.

Haubenstock, M. and Hause, J. (2006) Practical Decisions to Successfully Model Operational Risk, in Davis, E. (ed.) *The Advanced Measurement Approach to Operational Risk*, London: Risk Books.

Hayek, F.A. (1976) Choice in Currency: A Way to Stop Inflation, Occasional Paper No 48, London: Institute of Economic Affairs.

Herring, R.J. (2002) The Basel 2 Approach to Bank Operational Risk: Regulation on the Wrong Track, Paper Presented at the 38th Annual Conference on Bank Structure and Competition, Federal Reserve Bank of Chicago, 9 May.

Herring, R.J. (2005) Implementing Basel II: Is the Game Worth the Candle? *Financial Markets, Institutions and Instruments*, 14, 267–287.

Herring, R.J. and Carmassi, J. (2008) The Structure of Cross-Sector Financial Supervision, *Financial Markets, Institutions and Instruments*, 17, 51–76.

Hertz, D.B. (1964) Risk Analysis in Capital Investment, *Harvard Business Review*, 42, 95–106.

Hirtle, B. (2003) What Market Risk Capital Reporting Tells us about Bank Risk, *Federal Reserve Bank of New York Economic Policy Review*, September, 37–54.

Holmes, M. (2003) Measuring Operational Risk: A Reality Check, 16, 84–87.

Horwitz, S. (1992) *Monetary Evolution, Free Banking and Economic Order*, Boulder, CO: Westview.

Hottori, M. and Shin, H.S. (2007) The Broad Yen Carry Trade, Bank of Japan, Institute for Monetary and Economic Studies, Discussion Paper No 2007-E-19.

Hovakimian, A. and Kane, E.J. (2000) Effectiveness of Capital Regulation at US Commercial Banks, 1985 to 1994, *Journal of Finance*, 55, 451–468.

Hubbard, D. (2007) *How to Measure Anything: Finding the Value of Intangibles in Business*, New York: Wiley.

Hubner, R., Laycock, M. and Peemoller, F. (2003) Managing Operational Risk, in Mestchian, P. (ed.) *Advances in Operational Risk: Firm-wide Issues for Financial Institutions*, London: Risk Books.

Huisman, R., Koedijk, K. Kool, C. and Palm, F. (2001) Tail-Index Estimates in Small Samples, *Journal of Business and Economic Statistics*, 19, 208–216.

Imeson, M. (2006) Basel II: Capital Accord or Capital Discord? *The Banker*, 1 March, 1.

Institute of International Finance (2007) Principles of Liquidity Risk Management, March. Available at: www.afgap.org/documents/Divers/LiquidityPaper.pdf.

Jackson, P. Furfine, C., Groenveld, H., Hancock, D., Jones, D., Perraudin, W., Radecki, L. and Yoneyama, M. (1999) Capital Requirements and Bank Behavior: the Impact of the Basel Accord, BCBS Working Papers, No 1.

Jalleh, P. (2008) Developing the Winning Op Risk Framework, Paper Presented at the OpRisk Asia Conference, Singapore 2–4 June.

Jameson, R. (1998) Playing the Name Game, *Risk*, 11, 38–42.

Jameson, R. (2001) Between RAROC and a Hard Place, *Erisk.com*, February.

Jobst, A.A. (2007a) Operational Risk: The Sting is Still in the Tail but the Poison Depends on the Dose, *Journal of Operational Risk*, 2 (Summer), 3–59.

Jobst, A.A. (2007b) The Treatment of Operational Risk under the New Basel Framework: Critical Issues, *Journal of Banking Regulation*, 8, 316–352.

Jones, D. (2000) Emerging Problems with the Basel Accord: Regulatory Capital Arbitrage and Related Issues, *Journal of Banking and Finance*, 24, 35–58.

Jordan, J., Peek, J. and Rosengren, E. (2002) Credit Risk Modeling and the Cyclicality of Capital, Unpublished Paper.

Jorion, P. (2000) *Value at Risk*, New York: McGraw-Hill.

Kalyvas, L. and Sfetsos, A. (2006) Does the Application of Innovative Internal Models Diminish Regulatory Capital? *International Journal of Theoretical and Applied Finance*, 9, 217–226.

Kalyvas, L., Akkizidis, I., Zourka, I. and Bouchereau, V. (2006) *Integrating Market, Credit and Operational Risk: A Complete Guide for Bankers and Risk Professionals*, London: Risk Books.

Karpoff, J. and Lott, J.R. (1993) The Reputational Penalty Firms Bear for Committing Criminal Fraud, *Journal of Law and Economics*, 36, 757–802.

Kashyap, A.K. and Stein, J.C. (2004) Cyclical Implications of the Basel II Capital Standards, *Economic Perspectives*, First Quarter, 18–30.

Kaufman, G.G. (2003) Basel II: the Roar that Moused, Mimeo, Federal Reserve Bank of Chicago, October.

Kaufman, G.G. (2005) Basel II vs. Prompt Corrective Action: Which is Best for Public Policy? *Financial Markets, Institutions and Instruments*, 14, 349–357.

Kaufman, G.G. and Scott, K. (2000) Does Bank Regulation Retard or Contribute to Systemic Risk? Mimeo, Loyola University Chicago and Stanford Law School.

Kearney, K. (2008) Default Lines, *Asia Risk*, March, 18–20.

Keeley, M.C. (1980) Deposit Insurance, Risk and Market Power in Banking, *American Economic Review*, 80, 183–200.

Keeley, M.C. and Furlong, F.T. (1990) A Reexamination of Mean-Variance Analysis of Bank Capital Regulation, *Journal of Banking and Finance*, 14, 69–84.

Keeton, W.R. (1989) The New Risk-based Capital Plan for Commercial Banks, *Federal Reserve Bank of Kansas City Economic Review*, 74, 40–60.

Kerps, R. (1998) Continuous Distributions, Instart Working Papers, Guy Carpenter & Co. Inc.

Kerr, M.R. (2007) Quantifying Regulatory Capital against Operational Risk under Basel II, Unpublished Honours Thesis, Monash University, October.

Khoo, G.S. (2008) Best Practices for Op Risk Models Validation: A Personal Perspective, Paper Presented at the OpRisk Asia Conference, Singapore 2–4 June.

Kilavuka, M.I. (2008) Managing Operational Risk Capital in Financial Institutions, *Journal of Operational Risk*, 3 (Spring), 67–83.

Klopfer, E. (2002) A Mortgage Insurer's Look at Basel II and Residential Mortgage Credit Risk, *Housing Finance International*, 17, 22–32.

Klugman, S., Panjer, H. and Willmot, G. (1998) *Loss Models: From Data to Decisions*, New York: Wiley.

Knight, F. (1921) *Risk, Uncertainty and Profit*, Boston, MA: Houghton Mifflin Co.

Knot, K., Bikker, J., van Broekhoven, H., Everts, H., Horsmeier, H., Klassen, P., van Lelyveld, I., Monnik, R., Ruijgt, F., Siegelaer, G. and Wanders, H. (2006) Risk Measurement within Financial Conglomerates: Best Practices by Risk Type, in van Lelyveld, I. (ed.) *Economic Capital Modelling: Concepts, Measurement and Implementation*, London: Risk Books.

Koehn, M. and Santomero, A.M. (1980) Regulation of Bank Capital and Portfolio Risk, *Journal of Finance*, 35, 1235–1244.

KPMG (2003) Basel II: A Closer Look, KPMG Financial Services.

KPMG (2005) Managing Operational Risk Beyond Basel II, KPMG Financial Services.

Krall, M. (2008) Understanding Basel II Operational and Strategic Implications, *Financial Markets, Institutions and Instruments*, 17, 97–108.

Kuhn, R. and Neu, P. (2005) Functional Correlation Approach to Operational Risk in Banking Organizations, Working Paper, Dresdner Bank AG, September.

Kupiec, P.H. (2001) The New Basel Capital Accord: The Devil is in the (Calibration) Details, Unpublished Paper, International Monetary Fund.

Laker, J. (2008) Basel II – Observations from Down Under, *Financial Markets, Institutions and Instruments*, 17, 31–42.

Lam, J. (2003) A Unified Management and Capital Framework for Operational Risk, *RMA Journal*, 58, 26.

Lambrigger, D.D., Shevchenko, P.V. and Wuthrich, M. (2007) The Quantification of Operational Risk Using Internal data, Relevant External Data and Expert Opinion, *Journal of Operational Risk*, 2 (Fall), 3–27.

Lando, D. (1998) Cox Processes and Credit Risky Securities, *Review of Derivatives Research*, 2, 99–120.

Larson, E. (2008) Societe Generale Sued in U.S. Over Trading Losses. Available at www.Bloomberg.com.

Le Pan, N. (2008) Remarks on Basel II, *Financial Markets, Institutions and Instruments*, 17, 19–29.

Leyshon, A. (1994) Under Pressure: Finance, Geo-economic Competition and the Rise and Fall of Japan's Postwar Growth Economy, in Corbridge, S., Martin, R. and Thrift, N. (eds) *Money, Power and Space*, Oxford: Blackwell.

Lim, H.C. (2008) Articulating the Value of Op Risk to Senior Management and the Board, Paper Presented at the OpRisk Asia Conference, Singapore 2–4 June.

Linter, J. (1965) The Valuation of Risky Assets and the Selection of Risky Investments in Stock Portfolios and Capital Budget, *Review of Economics and Statistics*, 47, 13–37.

Lopez, J.A. (2002) What is Operational Risk? *Federal Reserve Bank of San Francisco Economic Letter*, January.

Lopez, J.A. (2003) Disclosure as a Supervisory Tool: Pillar 3 of Basel II, *Federal Reserve Bank of San Francisco Economic Letter*, August.

Lucchetti, A. (2008) MF Global Shares Fall Again, Wall Street Journal, 1 March. Available at http://online.wsj.com/article/SB120434089408505041.html

Luo, X., Shevchenko, P.V. and Donnelly, J.B. (2008) Addressing the Impact of Data Truncation and Parameter Uncertainty on Operational Risk Estimates, *Journal of Operational Risk*, 2 (Winter), 3–26.

MacKinlay, A.C. (1997) Event Studies in Economics and Finance, *Journal of Economic Literature*, 35, 13–39.

Mainelli, M. (2004) Towards a Prime Metric: Operational Risk Measurement and Activity-Based Costing. Available at http://oprisk.austega.com.

Mango, D.F. (2006) Applying Actuarial techniques in Operational Risk Modelling. Available at www.casact.org.

Mango, D.F. and Venter, G.G. (2007) Operational Risk, in Brehm, P.J., Perry, G.R., Venter, G.G. and Witcraft, S.E. (eds) *Enterprise Risk Analysis for Property and Liability Insurance Companies*, New York: Gut Carpenter & Company.

Mann, H.B. and Wald, A. (1942) On the Choice of the Number of Class Intervals in the Application of the Chi-Square Test, *Annals of Mathematical Statistics*, 13, 306–317.

Masciandaro, D. (2004) Unification in Financial Sector Supervision: The Trade off between Central Bank and Single Authority, *Journal of Financial Regulation and Compliance*, 12, 151–169

Masciandaro, D. (2005) Central Banks and Single Financial Authorities: Economics, Politics and Law, in Masciandaro, D. (ed.) *Handbook of Central Banking and Financial Authorities in Europe: New Architectures in the Supervision of Financial Markets*, Cheltenham: Edward Elgar.

Masciandaro, D. (2006) Reforms of Financial Supervision Regimes and Central Banks: Exploring the Nexus, Paper Presented at the IMF Macroprudential Supervision Conference: Challenges for Financial Supervisors, Seoul, November.

McConnell, P. (2003) The Use of Reliability Theory in Measuring Operational Risk, in Mestchian, P. (ed.) *Advances in Operational Risk: Firm-wide Issues for Financial Institutions* (second edition), London: Risk Books.

McConnell, P. (2006) A Perfect Storm – Why are Some Operational Losses Larger than Others? Unpublished Paper, July.

McConnell, P. (2008) Operational Risk Capital under Basel II – Dead on Arrival? Available at www.riskmagazine.com.au.

McCuaig, B. (2005) The Case for Operational Risk Management, Paisley Consulting White Papers.

Medova, E.A. and Kyriacou, M.N. (2001) Extremes in Operational Risk Management, Working Paper, Centre for Financial Research, University of Cambridge.

Mestchian, P. (2003) Operational Risk Management: The Solution is in the Problem, in *Advances in Operational Risk: Firm-wide Issues for Financial Institutions*, London: Risk Books.

Metcalfe, R. (2003) Operational Risk: The Empiricists Strike Back, in Field, P. (ed.) *Modern Risk Management: A History*, London: Risk Books.

Metropolis, N. and Ulam, S. (1949) Monte Carlo Methods, *Journal of the American Statistical Association*, 44, 335–341.

Meulen, H. (1934) *Free Banking: An Outline of a Policy Individualism*, London: Macmillan.

Mignola, G. (2008) Uphill Struggle, *OpRisk & Compliance*, 9 (February), 36–37.

Mignola, G. and Ugoccioni, R. (2007) Effect of Data Threshold in the Loss Distribution Approach, *Journal of Operational Risk*, 1 (Winter), 35–47.

Miller, K. (1992) A Framework for Integrated Risk Management in International Business, *Journal of International Business Studies*, 23, 311–331.

Monfort, B. and Mulder, C. (2000) Using Credit Ratings for Capital Requirements on Lending to Emerging Market Economies, Unpublished Paper, International Monetary Fund.

Moosa, I.A. (2007a) Misconceptions about Operational Risk, *Journal of Operational Risk*, 1 (Winter), 97–104.

Moosa, I.A. (2007b) *Operational Risk Management*, London: Palgrave.

Moosa, I.A. (2007c) The Rise and Rise of Operational Risk, *Management Online Review*, November, 1–11.

Moosa, I.A., (2008a) Shelter from the Subprime Financial Crisis, *Monash Business Review*, 4, 31–33.

Moosa, I.A., (2008b) A Critique of the Advanced Measurement Approach to Regulatory Capital against Operational Risk, *Journal of Banking Regulation*, 9, 151–164.

Moscadelli, M. (2005) The Modelling of Operational Risk: Experience with the Analysis of the Data Collected by the Basel Committee, in Davis, E. (ed.) *Operational Risk: Practical Approaches to Implementation*, London: Risk Books.

Murphy, D.L., Shrieves, R.E. and Tibbs, S. (2004) Determinants of the Stock Price Reaction to Allegations of Corporate Misconduct: Earnings, Risk, and Firm Size Effects, Working Paper, Corporate Goverance Center, Unviresity of Tennessee.

Muzzy, L. (2003) The Pitfalls of Gathering Operational Risk Data, *RMA Journal*, 85, 58.

Na, H., Miranda, L., van den Berg, J. and Leipoldt, M. (2005) Data Scaling for Operational Risk Modelling, ERS-2005–092-LIS-Erasmus Research Institute of Management, Report in Research Management.

Nash, R.A. (2003) The Three Pillars of Operational Risk, in Alexander, C. (ed.) *Operational Risk: Regulation, Analysis and Management*, London: Prentice Hall-Financial Times.

Navarrete, E. (2006) Practical Calculation of Expected and Unexpected Losses in Operational Risk by Simulation Methods, Banca & Finanzas, Documento de Trabajo No 1, October.

Neil, M., Fenton, N. and Tailor, M. (2005) Using Bayesian Networks to Model Expected and Unexpected Operational Losses, *Risk Analysis*, 25, 963–972.

Neslehova, J., Emrechts, P. and Chavez-Demoulin, V. (2006) Infinite-Mean Models and the LDA for Operational Risk, *Journal of Operational Risk*, 1 (Winter), 3–25.

Ong, M. (2002) The Alpha, Beta and Gamma of Operational Risk, *RMA Journal*, 85, 34.

OpRisk Analytics (2002) How to Categorize Operational Losses? Applying Principles as Opposed to Rules. Available at www.opriskadvisory.com

Owen, A. and Tavella, D. (2006) Scrambled Nets for Value-at-Risk Calculations, in Dupire, B. (ed.) *Monte Carlo: Methodologies and Applications for Pricing and Risk Management*, London: Risk Books.

Padoa-Schioppa, T. (2003) Financial Supervision: Inside or Outside Central Banks? in Kremers, J., Shoemaker, D. and Wierts, P. (eds) *Financial Supervision in Europe*, Cheltenham: Edward Elgar.

Palia, D. and Porter, R. (2003) Contemporary Issues in Regulatory Risk Management of Commercial Banks, *Financial Markets, Institutions and Instruments*, 12, 223–256.

Palmrose, Z., Richardson, R.E. and Scholz, S. (2004) Determinants of Market Reactions to Restatement Announcements, *Journal of Accounting and Economics*, 37, 59–89.

Panjer, H. (1981) Recursive Evaluation of a Family of Compound Distributions, *ASTIN Bulletin*, 12, 22–26.

Panjer, H. (2006) *Operational Risk: Modeling Analytics*, New York: Wiley.

Panjer, H. and Willmot, G. (1986) Computational Aspects of Recursive Evaluation of Compound Distributions, *Insurance: Mathematics and Economics*, 5, 113–116.

Peccia, A. (2003) Using Operational Risk Models to Manage Operational Risk, in Alexander, C. (ed.) *Operational Risk: Regulation, Analysis and Management*, London: Prentice Hall-Financial Times.

Peccia, A. (2004) An Operational Risk Ratings Model Approach to Better Measurement and Management of Operational Risk, in Ong, K. (ed.) *The Basel Handbook*, London: Risk Books.

Pennington, D.C. (2002) *The Social Psychology of Behaviour in Small Groups*, London: Psychology Press.

Pennington, V. (2008a) Absolute Beginners, *OpRisk & Compliance*, February, 26–29.

Pennington, V. (2008b) Talking about an Evolution, *OpRisk & Compliance,* March, 26–29.

Perry, J. and de Fontnouvelle, P. (2005) Measuring Reputational Risk: The Market Reaction to Operational Loss Announcements, Unpublished Paper, November.

Peters, G., Johansen, A.M. and Doucet, A. (2007) Simulation of the Annual Loss Distribution in Operational Risk via Panjer Recursions and Volterra Integral Equations for Value-at-Risk and Expected Shortfall Estimation, *Journal of Operational Risk*, 2 (Fall), 29–58.

Pezier, J. (2003a) A Constructive Review of the Basel Proposals on Operational Risk, in Alexander, C. (ed.) *Operational Risk: Regulation, Analysis and Management*, London: Prentice Hall-Financial Times.

Pezier, J. (2003b) Operational Risk Management, in Alexander, C. (ed.) *Operational Risk: Regulation, Analysis and Management*, London: Prentice Hall-Financial Times.

Pickworth, J. (2008) The Regulatory Minefield, *OpRisk & Compliance*, March 44–46.

Picoult, E. (2006) Calculating Value-at-Risk with Monte Carlo Simulation, in Dupire, B. (ed.) *Monte Carlo: Methodologies and Applications for Pricing and Risk Management*, London: Risk Books.

Power, M. (2005) The Invention of Operational Risk, *Review of International Political Economy*, 12, 557–599.

PriceWaterhouseCoopers and Economist Intelligence Unit (2004) Uncertainty Tamed? The Evolution of Risk Management in the Financial Services Industry.

Purhonen, M. (2002) New Evidence of IRB Volatility, *Risk*, S21–S25.

Quinlan, G.D. (2006) Using Non-Normal Monte Carlo Simulation to Compute Value-at-Risk, in Dupire, B. (ed.) *Monte Carlo: Methodologies and Applications for Pricing and Risk Management*, London: Risk Books.

Rao, V. and Dev, A. (2006) Operational Risk: Some Issues in Basel II AMA Implementation in US Financial Institutions, in Davis, E. (ed.) *The Advanced Measurement Approach to Operational Risk*, London: Risk Books.

Rebonato, R. (2007) *The Plight of the Fortune Tellers: Why We Need to Manage Financial Risk Differently*, Princeton, NJ: Princeton University Press.

Reshetar, G. (2008) Dependence of Operational Losses and the Capital at Risk, Unpublished Paper, Swiss Banking Institute.

Reynolds, D. and Syer, D. (2003) A General Simulation Framework for Operational Loss Distributions, in Alexander, C. (ed.) *Operational Risk: Regulation, Analysis and Management*, London: Prentice Hall-Financial Times.

Rime, B. (2000) Capital Requirements and Bank Behavior: Empirical Evidence for Switzerland, *Journal of Banking and Finance*, 25, 789–805.

Robert Morris Associates, British Bankers' Association and International Swaps and Derivatives Association (1999) *Operational Risk: The Next Frontier*, Philadelphia, PA: RMA.

Robertson, J. (1992) The Computation of Aggregate Loss Distributions, *PCAS*, 74, 57–133.

Rochet, J.C. (1992) Capital Requirements and the Behavior of Commercial Banks, *European Economic Review*, 36, 1137–1178.

Rockoff, H. (1975) *The Free Banking Era: A Re-examination*, New York: Arno.
Ross, S. (1976) The Arbitrage Theory of Capital Asset Pricing, *Journal of Economic Theory*, 13, 341–360.
Roy, A.D. (1952) Safety First and the Holding of Assets, *Econometrica*, 20, 431–449.
Sahay, A., Wan, Z. and Keller, B. (2007) Operational Risk Capital: Asymptotic in the Case of Heavy-Tailed Severity, *Journal of Operational Risk*, 2 (Summer), 61–72.
Saita, F. (2004) Risk Capital Aggregation: The Risk Manager's Perspective, NEWFIN Working Papers.
Samad-Khan, A., Moncelet, B. and Pinch, T. (2006) Uses and Misuses of Loss Data. Available at www.opriskadvisory.com.
Sanford, A. (2008) Qualitative Research Using Bayesian Network Models, Paper Presented at the Department of Accounting and Finance, Monash University, 11 June.
Sanghera, S. (2005) How to Avoid Kicking up a Stink over an Offensive Odour, *Financial Times*, 14 October, 9.
Santos, J.A.C. (2001) Bank Capital Regulation in Contemporary Banking Theory: A Review of the Literature, *Financial Markets, Institutions and Instruments*, 10, 41–84.
Schachter, B. (2008) Kooky Science for Value-at-Risk, *Asia Risk*, March, 8.
Searing, J. (2008) Understanding and Applying Operational Risk Appetite, Paper Presented at the OpRisk Asia Conference, Singapore 2–4 June.
Sechrest, L.J. (1993) *Free Banking: Theory, History and a Laissez-Faire Model*, Westport, CT: Quorom Books.
Servaes, H. and Tufano, P. (2006) Ranking Risk and Finance According to a Survey of Chief Financial Officers at Non-Financial Companies, *Financial Times*, 9 June, 4.
Sharpe, W.F. (1964) Capital Asset Prices: A Theory of Market Equilibrium under Conditions of Risk, *Journal of Finance*, 19, 425–442.
Shaw, J. (2006) Beyond VAR and Stress Testing, in Dupire, B. (ed.) *Monte Carlo: Methodologies and Applications for Pricing and Risk Management*, London: Risk Books.
Sheedy, E. (1999) Applying an Agency Framework to Operational Risk Management, Applied Finance Centre, Macquarie University, Working Paper 22.
Shepheard-Walwyn, T. and Litterman, R. (1998) Building a Coherent Risk Measurement and Capital Optmization Model for Financial Firms, *Federal Reserve Bank of New York Economic Policy Review*, October, 171–182.
Shevchenko, P.V. (2008) Estimation of Operational Risk Capital Charge under Parameter Uncertainty, *Journal of Operational Risk*, 3 (Spring) 51–63.
Shevchenko, P.V. and Wuthrich, M.V. (2006) The Structural Modelling of Operational Risk via Bayesian Inference: Combining Loss Data with Expert Opinions, *Journal of Operational Risk*, 1 (Fall) 3–26.
Shih, J., Samad-Khan, A. and Medapa, P. (2000) Is the Size of an Operational Loss Related to Firm Size? *Operational Risk*, January, 1.
Smithson, C. and Song , P. (2004) Quantifying Operational Risk, *Risk*, July, 50–52.
Spring, M. (2008) On Target: Is This Really a Bull Trap? *Martin Spring's Private Newsletter on Global Strategy*, No 95, 5 April.
Stein, M. (2000) The Risk Taker as a Shadow: A Psychological View of the Collapse of Barings Bank, *Journal of Management Studies*, 37, 1215–1229.
Sundmacher, M. (2007a) Operational Risk Capital Charges for Banks: Consideration and Consequences. Available at http://ssrn.com/abstratct=988227.
Sundmacher, M. (2007b) Operational Risk Measurement in Banks: Arbitrage, Adjustment and Alternatives. Available at http://ssrn.com/abstratct=963231.
Sundmacher, M. (2007c) The Basic Indicators Approach and the Standardised Approach to Operational Risk: An Example and Case Study-Based Analysis. Available at http://ssrn.com/abstratct=988282.
Sundmacher, M. and Ford, G. (2007) Operational Risk Disclosures in Financial Institutions. Available at http://ssrn.com/abstratct=963244.
Temnov, G. and Warnung, R. (2008) A Comparison of Loss Aggregation Methods for Operational Risk, *Journal of Operational Risk*, 3 (Spring) 3–23.
Thakor, A.V. (1996) Capital Requirements, Monetary Policy and Aggregate Bank Lending: Theory and Empirical Evidence, *Journal of Finance*, 51, 279–324.
The Economist (2003) Deep Impact, 8 May.

The Economist (2006) A Battle over Basel 2, 26 May, 61–63.
The Economist (2007) The Fingers of Suspicion, 2 December, 111–112.
The Economist (2008a) No Defence, 2 February, 75–76.
The Economist (2008b) The $2 Bail-out, 22 March, 77–78.
The Economist (2008c) Will it Fly?, 5 April, 79–81.
The Economist (2008d) Joseph and the Amazing Technicalities, 26 April, 16–18.
The Economist (2008e) The Agony of Gordon Brown, 10 May, 13.
The Economist (2008f) Paradise Lost, 17 May (Special Report on International Banking), 3–6.
The Economist (2008g) Professionally Gloomy, 17 May (Special report on International Banking), 11–13.
The Economist (2008h) Make Them Pay, 17 May (Special Report on International Banking), 16–17.
The Economist (2008i) Tightrope Artists, 17 May (Special Report on International Banking), 17–19.
The Economist (2008j) Cycle Clips, 17 May (Special Report on International Banking), 19–23.
The Economist (2008k) Status Cuomo, 7 June, 75–76.
Theodore, S. (2002) Bank Operational Risk Management, Moody's, June.
Thomas, H. and Wang, Z. (2005) Interpreting the Internal Ratings-Based Capital Requirements in Basel II, *Journal of Banking Regulation*, 6, 274–289.
Tinca, A. (2007) The Operational Risk in the Outlook of the Basel II Accord Implementation, *Theoretical and Applied Economics*, 5, 31–34.
Tripe, D. (2000) Pricing Operational Risk, Paper Presented at the 13th Australasian Finance and Banking Conference, Sydney, December.
Tripp, M., Bradley, H. and Devitt, R. (2004) Quantifying Operational Risk in General Insurance Companies, Working Paper, Institute of Actuaries and Faculty of Actuaries.
Turing, D. (2003) The Legal and Regulatory View of Operational Risk, in *Advances in Operational Risk: Firm-wide Issues for Financial Institutions* (second edition), London: Risk Books.
Tvede, L. (1999) *The Psychology of Finance*, New York: Wiley.
Underhill, G. (1991) Markets Beyond Politics? The State and Internationalisation of Financial Markets, *European Journal of Political Research*, 19, 197–225.
Valle, L.D., Fantazzini, D. and Giudici, P. (2007) Copulae and Operational Risks, Mimeo, University of Pavia.
van Lelyveld, I. (2006) A Supervisory View on Economic Capital Models, in van Lelyveld, I. (ed.) *Economic Capital Modelling: Concepts, Measurement and Implementation*, London: Risk Books.
Venter, G. (1983) Transformed Beta and Gamma Distributions and Aggregate Losses, *Proceedings of the Casualty Actuarial Society*, 70, 156–193.
Wall, L.D. and Peterson, D. R. (1995) Bank Holding Company Capital Targets in the Early 1990s: The Regulators versus the Market, *Journal of Banking and Finance*, 19, 563–574.
Wei, R. (2003) Operational Risk in the Insurance Industry, Working Paper, Wharton School.
Wei, R. (2006) An Empirical Investigation of Operational Risk in the United States Financial Sectors, Wharton School.
Wei, R. (2007) Quantification of Operational Losses Using Firm-Specific Information and External Databases, *Journal of Operational Risk*, 1 (Winter), 3–34.
White, L. (2004) Market Discipline and Appropriate Disclosure in Basel II, in Ong, K. (ed.) *The Basel Handbook*, London: Risk Books.
Wihlborg, C. (2005) Basel II and the Need for Bank Distress Resolution Procedures, *Financial Markets, Institutions and Instruments*, 14, 359–369.
Willmot, G. and Lin, X. (2000) Lundberg Approximations for Compound Distributions with Insurance Applications, *Lecture Notes in Statistics*, New York: Springer-Verlag.
Wilson, S. (2007) A Review of Correction Techniques for the Inherent Biases in External Operational Loss Data, APRA Working Paper, November.
Wood, D. (2008) A Model Model? *OpRisk & Compliance*, March, 35–37.
Young, R.M. (1979) Why are Figures so Significant? The Role and the Critique of Quantification, in I. Miles et al (eds) *Demystifying Social Statistics*, London: Pluto Press.
Zhiling, H. (2008) CCB's Pursuit of Risk Management Excellence, *Asia Risk*, May, 48–49.

Index